I have seen the future and it is (gulp) Interactive Barney. Read this book and find out why computerized plush animals introduce a whole new range of usability problems. And why the next generation of user interfaces will finally stop cloning the Macintosh. This book is both visionary and practical: future consumer electronics, toys, and games need great usability, or customers will abandon them.

Jakob Nielsen, Usability Guru, Nielsen Norman Group

An important book. The range of subjects and perspectives it covers had me alternately nodding at good work I envied and reaching for a pen to think about things I would have done differently. Anyone involved in either inter- action design or the development of information appliances will find food for thought, and everyone in the industry should read Rob Haitani's obser- vations about designing the PalmPilot.

Alan Cooper, Cooper Interaction Design

The Morgan Kaufmann Series in Interactive Technologies

Series Editors

- Stuart Card, Xerox PARC
- Jonathan Grudin, Microsoft
- Jakob Nielsen, Nielsen Norman Group
- Tim Skelly, Design Happy

Information Appliances and Beyond: Interaction Design for Consumer Products, edited by Eric Bergman

Information Visualization: Perception for Design, by Colin Ware

Readings in Information Visualization: Using Vision to Think, written and edited by Stuart Card, Jock D. Mackinlay, and Ben Shneiderman

The Design of Children's Technology, edited by Allison Druin

The Usability Engineering Lifecycle: A Practitioner's Handbook for User Interface Design, by Deborah J. Mayhew

Contextual Design: Defining Customer-Centered Systems, by Hugh Beyer and Karen Holztblatt

Human Computer Interface Design: Success Cases, Emerging Methods and Real-World Context, edited by Marianne Rudisill, Clayton Lewis, Peter Polson, and Tim McKay

Information Appliances and Beyond

Interaction Design for Consumer Products

Edited by
Eric Bergman

MORGAN KAUFMANN PUBLISHERS

AN IMPRINT OF ACADEMIC PRESS
A Harcourt Science and Technology Company
SAN FRANCISCO   SAN DIEGO   NEW YORK   BOSTON
LONDON   SYDNEY   TOKYO

Senior Editor	Diane D. Cerra
Director of Production and Manufacturing	Yonie Overton
Senior Production Editor	Elisabeth Beller
Cover Design	Ross Carron
Cover Images	image copyright © 2000 Photodisc, Inc.
Text Design	Rebecca Evans
Copyeditor	Ken Della Penta
Proofreader	Beth Berkelhammer
Composition	Susan Riley, Mark Ong Side by Side Studios
Indexer	Steve Rath
Printer	Courier Corporation

Most art supplied by contributing authors.

Designations used by companies to distinguish their products are often claimed as trademarks or registered trademarks. In all instances where Morgan Kaufmann Publishers is aware of a claim, the product names appear in initial or all capital letters. Readers, however, should contact the appropriate companies for more complete information regarding trademarks and registration.

ACADEMIC PRESS
A Harcourt Science and Technology Company
525 B Street, Suite 1900, San Diego, CA 92101-4495, USA
http://www.academicpress.com

Academic Press
Harcourt Place, 32 Jamestown Road, London NW1 7BY, United Kingdom
http://www.hbuk.co.uk/ap/

Morgan Kaufmann Publishers
340 Pine Street, Sixth Floor, San Francisco, CA 94104-3205, USA
http://www.mkp.com

Library of Congress Cataloging-in-Publication data is available for this book.

ISBN 1-55860-600-9

This book is printed on acid-free paper.

Foreword

Donald A. Norman

Hurrah: a book of practice rather than of theory, a book that breaks away from the dominance of the personal computer and moves forward in time toward the personal information appliance, toward consumer products that require new modes of interaction, and toward new forms of enjoyment and social interaction.

I really like this book. Historically, it has been very difficult to get real practitioners to talk about their work. Usually they are too busy within the schedule-driven life of the product cycle to have the opportunity to sit back and reflect. As a result, it is rare to hear many solid stories of product design. But Eric Bergman has been tenacious in his pursuit of the lore of real products. I know how ferocious he was with me: he tracked me down and refused to let go despite my protests that I was too involved in my product-driven world to have time to write. Won't write? Then take time for an interview—and rewrite that. He refused to let go until I had yielded.

He must have been equally tenacious with the other authors: look at the collection of real product stories in this book. These stories alone provide a powerful collection of ideas. But Eric didn't stop there; he also moved to related domains—to games, to toys, to social interaction. The total package is powerful indeed. Thank you Eric; your efforts have paid off.

As this book illustrates, information technology is finally reaching maturity. The customer is no longer someone who craves neat technologies for the sake of technology but rather the everyday person who wants something that provides a real, substantive benefit. As for the device, well, it should simply work. When everyday consumers dominate the market, their needs and activities must be catered to: human-centered design moves from luxury and speculation to necessity.

As we make this transition, those of us who advocate human-centered design face new challenges. We have to break away from the tried-and-true methods of the computer and face up to design under new constraints, different environments, and restricted technology. The new world of interactive consumer-centered products poses interesting usage requirements. No longer can we assume a single user: the user may be a group. No longer can we assume undivided attention: the user may be driving an auto, walking down the street, or engaged in other activities. No longer can we assume a keyboard, a large screen, and a pointing device. Each product category poses novel challenges. Thus, games have different requirements than navigational systems, which differ in requirements from communication devices, from personal assistants, and, basically, from all that has come before.

This book looks forward to the new sets of devices, toys, games, and forms of interaction that are just starting to emerge. It offers stories of successful products, it provides valuable guiding principles, and it emphasizes the need for multidisciplinary design teams who work in an iterative spiral of behavioral data, design, rapid prototype, test, and redesign. It amplifies the new demands upon designers as the restrictions of screen size, use patterns, and special consumer needs dominate. It offers us a new era of devices that not only fit the needs of the user but have the capability of becoming attached to their users socially and emotionally.

The design domain covered by this volume spans an enormous range. It starts with traditional information appliances, small hand-held devices, and telephones. It moves on to cover vehicle navigation systems, toys, games, and social interaction. Several chapters emphasize the point that our technologies are not just about efficient delivery of information but about enjoyment, fun, and emotions. The social dimension of interaction takes on a new dimension when we have toys and game characters interacting with us. Devices that move beyond information toward persuasion raise all sorts of important questions, from design to psychology to ethics. These issues revolve around the way that our devices respond to our behavior, so it is fitting that the book closes with a chapter on persuasive computing: the new world of devices will be both persuasive and pervasive.

Above all, this is a book of practice not theory, of the near future not the recent past, of novel devices and interactions not of the traditional computer. And this is what gives the book its strength, its interest, and its importance.

Thank you Eric. Thank you fellow authors.

Donald A. Norman
Lake Forest, IL
December 1999

Contents

Introduction

ERIC BERGMAN

Sun Microsystems, Inc.

The design requirements for special-purpose interactive products are inherently different from computer "desktop" software design requirements. Creating the user experience for information appliances and related products requires the same interaction design *processes* as computer software, but the design trade-offs and issues change. Some differences are evident with little consideration. Certainly the intended users typically have even less interest in the underlying technologies than many PC users. Interaction designers and usability specialists must carefully consider and craft the relationship between hardware and software. Output and input methods are often different than in a desktop computer. Output might come via audio, phone-size screens, televisions, and other means not often seen on typical PCs. Input devices may include TV remote controls, touch screens, telephone keypads, or even furry feet on a child's plush toy!

These are only a few examples of input and output drawn from a much larger set. This range of possibilities suggests that differences among information appliances can be as great or greater than the differences between any given information appliance and a PC. This diversity should be no surprise. After all, an information appliance is called an "appliance" for the same reason as a dishwasher or washing machine. These are devices designed to accomplish a narrow set of tasks. The washing machine washes, but it is ill-suited for washing dishes. The washing task shared by these appliances becomes irrelevant because agitation is required to clean clothes, but that same agitation will shatter dishes. On the other hand, some appliances are far more interchangeable—a toaster and toaster oven, or a floor vacuum and a hand vacuum, for example.

So it is with information appliances. Each product has different requirements, resulting in different designs. Returning to the contrast between interaction design for PCs and for information appliances, it is the freedom of design choice that is the most striking. In design for desktop environments, there are style conventions, guidelines, as well as written and unwritten usage precedents that dictate the overall approach to interaction design and visual design. A designer in the information appliance realm is presented with something closer to a blank slate. This freedom suggests exciting new possibilities, but it also poses the obvious question: what belongs on that slate? Although the conventions of desktop PC design no longer apply, new and unfamiliar constraints of focused tasks, small screen size, memory limitations, different navigation models, different conceptual models, and other factors come into play. This is new territory, and interaction designers, usability specialists, engineers, marketers, and others involved in the definition, design, and evaluation of interactive products cannot rely solely on what they have learned about designing desktop computer software for guidance.

There are already many fine books on interaction design and product usability. In late 1998, however, as I worked on interaction design and usability of software beyond the desktop computer, there was little information available outside of that desktop domain. At that time there were few products on the market that could be viewed as information appliances, but it was becoming obvious that information appliances were coming soon. I saw the need to gather a group of interaction designers who had explored this domain, and to have them share their experiences with a wider audience of interaction designers, usability specialists, engineers, marketing professionals, and interested others. This book is the result.

The title, *Information Appliances and Beyond,* reflects the observation that not every technology discussed in this volume fits into a tidy categorization of an "information appliance." Most readers will agree that an interactive plush toy or an interactive game may not be an information appliance. Most readers will agree that an interactive phone or a special-purpose email device probably is an information appliance. On the other hand, readers may disagree as to whether the 3Com Palm or a device based on Microsoft Windows CE or EPOC constitutes an information appliance. The focus of this book is design outside of the desktop PC environment—a user interface realm not much discussed in books currently available. Thus, every chapter has something to say about designing in the information appliance domain—even in cases where the product discussed might arguably not constitute a pure information appliance.

I have been occasionally frustrated by authors who elaborate on a topic, page after page, using catchy phrases that they never bother to define. To avoid that fate, I will not proceed further without defining what I mean by "information appliance." In his 1998 book on information appliances, *The Invisible Computer,* Don Norman attributes the term "information appliance" to Jef Raskin. Raskin, who was at Apple Computer at the time, may have coined the term as early as 1978. Norman's definition of information appliances in *The Invisible Computer* is roughly the one I will use here. That definition is loosely based on a dictionary definition of a household appliance, as follows (p. 53):

appliance *n.*
A device or instrument designed to perform a specific function, especially an electrical device, such as a toaster, for household use.
synonyms: tool, instrument, implement, utensil

　　　—*American Heritage Dictionary,* third edition (Electronic Version)

information appliance *n.*
An appliance specializing in information: knowledge, facts, graphics, images, video, or sound. An information appliance is designed to perform a specific

activity, such as music, photography, or writing. A distinguishing feature of information appliances is the ability to share information among themselves.

My only amendment to the above definition is that I believe interactive products can be considered information appliances even if they do not have "the ability to share information among themselves." Of course, they are much less useful in that case!

Occasionally, I have been asked if a PC isn't just another name for a particular *sort* of information appliance. Using Norman's definition, it becomes clear that a PC doesn't meet the criteria for an information appliance. The PC is a general-purpose device, capable of supporting as many tasks as add-in software and hardware may permit, and provides little tuning for the requirements of specific tasks. It is the phrase "designed to perform a specific activity" that captures the essence of the information appliance, and that is what sets the focus of this book apart from current books on the topic of interaction design.

Like any definition, this one has fuzzy borders. As mentioned earlier, some would argue that the popular Palm, Microsoft Windows CE, and Psion series of personal digital assistant devices are not information appliances because they provide general-purpose capabilities. While there are interesting philosophical issues in that discussion, I am not going to spend significant time exploring them here, except to say that this question came up in my conversation with Don Norman, and you may wish to read Chapter 1 to see where the discussion leads. Whatever the fuzzy boundaries defining information appliances may be, it is clear that as computer technology becomes integrated into products that users do not perceive as being computers, the need arises for better terminology to describe those products. The increasingly popular phrase "information appliance" is the term I have chosen to use.

Like most books, this volume was planned significantly in advance of publication. Technology moves ever more rapidly, and as the book has come together, a wide variety of new products have come onto the market, or are poised to come out, many of which fall under the rubric of information appliance. These products include email appliances, digital cameras, screen phones, wireless personal digital assistants, electronic books, various flavors of TV set-top boxes, and much more. I anticipate that further exciting announcements will be made by the time this book is widely available. Fortunately, the specific products discussed here are much less important than the high-level issues raised by their designers. For that reason, the issues discussed in these pages apply not only to the products they cover, but also to the impending wave of new products, and in many cases, to those beyond . . . .

A question that I posed to each author was: What is different about designing software in this domain than designing software for a desktop computer? As you would expect, the answer to this question ultimately rests in the differences in target audience for these products, how the products are used, and the expectations their users have for the usability of everyday technology.

Each chapter of this book addresses these points from a particular perspective about interaction design beyond the confines of the PC desktop. While you should feel free to read chapters in any order you please, I recommend starting from the beginning. In particular, be sure to read Chapter 1, "A Conversation with Don Norman," and the following chapter, "Design Considerations for Information Appliances," by Michael Mohageg and Annette Wagner. These first two chapters provide complementary high-level introductions to usability and interaction design issues surrounding information appliances.

Chapter 3, "Designing Internet Appliances at Netpliance," is a case study about the design of a countertop information appliance for email and Web browsing. Authors Scott Isensee, Ken Kalinoski, and Karl Vochatzer explain the philosophy and design approach taken by the Netpliance team. The authors give attention to describing the rationale underlying their approach, and the process by which the Netpliance designs were realized.

In Chapter 4, "Designing the PalmPilot: A Conversation with Rob Haitani," the lead designer for the original PalmPilot personal digital assistant provides fascinating background on the development of what is arguably the most successful product of its kind. Rob talks at length about his philosophy of design and how this approach led directly to the success of the original PalmPilot. One point that stands out in this discussion is the fact that this design succeeded where so many others had failed. The key to the success of the design was the early adoption of user-centered design principles and processes, although ironically, most of the team members would not have used those terms to describe them.

For a different approach to personal digital assistants, see Chapter 5, "The Interaction Design of Microsoft Windows CE," by Sarah Zuberec, and Chapter 6, "The EPOC User Interface in the Psion Series 5," by Nick Healey. In the case of Microsoft Windows CE, designers were faced with the challenge of how to create an environment suitable for small devices that at the outset was intended to inherit many characteristics of the Microsoft Windows desktop environment. Healey's chapter focuses on how the EPOC user interface is used in palmtop devices that he describes as being "like a miniature PC." Despite this analogy, the EPOC team did not feel constrained to adhere to PC design principles and made decisions across a variety of dimensions aimed at improving product usability.

Nonetheless, the influence that PC user interface considerations had on the design of both Microsoft Windows CE and EPOC suggests that these teams took a different approach than that described by Rob Haitani in our Chapter 4 conversation about designing the PalmPilot. Indeed, I would argue that the products discussed in Chapters 5 and 6 embody a different *overall* design philosophy than that advocated in the first four chapters of this book. At the same time, the design target for these products was a tightly integrated PC companion for users already familiar with PC environments. In the case of the Microsoft team, it was a goal from the outset to leverage Microsoft Windows knowledge that PC users already had. I will leave it to the reader to evaluate the efficacy of these different design approaches.

Kaisa Väänänen-Vainio-Mattila and Satu Ruuska explore mobile users in Chapter 7, "Designing Mobile Phones and Communicators for Consumers' Needs at Nokia." The authors begin with a broad overview of how Nokia goes about designing products, and then go on to discuss the social/cultural issues that are part of their design considerations. Perhaps the most interesting aspect of this chapter is the overall discussion of interaction design issues that are particular to mobile phones and communicators, although certainly just as fascinating is the glimpse into Nokia's vision of future devices.

In Chapter 8, "User Interface Design for a Vehicle Navigation System," Aaron Marcus provides a case study of the development of an automobile-based user interface. Although the work was done some years ago, it is striking how many of the lessons learned still apply to current systems. The examples of design decisions driven by the particular requirements of an automobile environment suggest considerations for anyone developing systems for users on the move—particularly those in a moving vehicle.

We may not think of interactive toys and games as information appliances, but they present many of the same challenges to designers. These products are usually focused on a relatively narrow set of tasks, often require a high degree of coordination between hardware and software design, and provide a remarkable array of means for input and output. They also present a twist that truly differentiates their design from that of most PC software—the primary goal is not productivity or efficiency, it is fun. Designers should understand what makes interaction compelling and fun, and toys and games succeed or fail on just that measure. The tight fit between hardware and software becomes that much more important. Mice, keyboards, or screens may not always mediate interactions—or if there is a mouse, it might have ears!

As Erik Strommen explains in Chapter 9, "Interactive Toy Characters as Interfaces for Children," if users are young children (who happen to interact with a product via hands, feet, voice, and other means), then the rules of social interaction implicitly understood by those children become critical to the interaction design. Usability testing becomes even more significant, and the lessons learned seem to loom larger. It seems that in this domain, as in so many other aspects of life, we can learn much from children. I hope that readers will consider how these lessons can be applied to children in other contexts, as well as to users who are not children.

Although the interactive *toy* is a relatively new domain, interactive *games* have existed since the time of the first computers. Chuck Clanton points out in Chapter 10, "Lessons from Game Design," that for the most part, interactive games have been designed in the absence of formal user interface expertise. At the same time, in the game domain a body of practical experience gained from continual play testing and observation of what works and does not work suggests a different view of what constitutes a successful design. This chapter is the only one that talks much about software on a PC, but I think you will see that the world it explores is so far removed from a PC desktop that it was appropriate to include it here.

In Chapter 11, "Persuasive Technologies and Netsmart Devices," B. J. Fogg takes a more theoretical tack in his compelling discussion of the potential social effects of embedding computer technology into everyday devices and life. He suggests that as devices become "smart" and networked together (what he calls "netsmart"), they will alter people's attitudes, behavior, and the ways in which they interact with each other. He suggests that designers have an opportunity to shape not only the behavior of individuals, but the overall nature of society as well. This chapter makes for a suitable close to the book in implying that designers in this domain must consider the cumulative impact of their choices not only on individuals, but also on society as a whole.

Acknowledgments

I hope you enjoy reading this book as I have enjoyed putting it together. I cannot close without thanking the chapter authors for their long hours of effort that made the book possible. The names of the contributors are listed with each chapter, but a name you will not see there is that of Marney Beard, whom I thank for providing independent feedback to me and to the authors. Marney's insightful review of much of the book was a great sanity check for all of us. Kate Ehrlich also pitched in to review some material included here. I would like to acknowledge Mike Mohageg for introducing me to information appliance design and teaching me more about it than anybody. Past and present members of the Consumer and Embedded User Experience Group at Sun Microsystems have also contributed much to my understanding of this domain, and I thank them as well.

I would also like to thank Morgan Kaufmann, with special thanks to Diane Cerra for encouraging my initial proposal and for guiding the development of this book. Many thanks go to Belinda Breyer and Sheri Dean for their editorial and marketing efforts. I appreciate the long hours put in by the production editor, Elisabeth Beller, whose high standard of quality is reflected in the final product. Thanks also to the numerous others whose fine copyediting, composition, graphics, and much more is evident on every page of this book.

Lastly, I would like to thank Jackie, who also made this book possible.

CHAPTER One

Making Technology Invisible: A Conversation with Don Norman

ERIC BERGMAN
Sun Microsystems, Inc.

DONALD A. NORMAN
Unext.com

FIGURE **1.1**

Donald A. Norman

BERGMAN: *Why is the personal computer so difficult to use?*

NORMAN: The use of digital technology is still in its infancy. The digital computer has indeed been with us 50 years, but it's only in the last decade that the personal computer has reached the desktop of so many people in industries, in business, and in so many homes. The PC as a result has evolved by historical accident, and as it has evolved, it brings that historical legacy—it drags a heavy weight behind it. The PC as a result has become incredibly complex, as well as unstable, and I believe that to a large extent, the complexity is unavoidable.

The PC attempts to do all things for all people. It is one device: the same design for both hardware and software made to fit everybody in the entire world. You have the same machine then to do all the tasks and activities that you wish to do. As a result, there is no focus. You cannot design for a specific user's needs. You cannot design for a specific set of applications, but rather you must design for everyone. This means there must be something for everyone, which leads to an ever-increasing number of features, an ever-increasing number of specific applications, and as a result, an ever-increasing complexity.

Palm, Palm III, Palm IIIx, Palm V, and Palm VII are trademarks of 3Com Corporation or its subsidiaries.

It's not helped by the fact that as more and more people use computers, the more you have to take any new software and make sure that they can still run their old software, and this legacy really constrains what you can do. Anyway, I think the computer is too complex. We spend far too much time learning how to use it, learning shortcuts, maintaining it, upgrading it. So I think it's time to start over again.

BERGMAN: *What would it mean to start over again?*

NORMAN: If you look at a lot of industries, they often start off at the beginning with a direction that is not sustained, and at some point people begin to understand what the new product is about and get to start over again and give you the benefits of the product without the early false starts.

My favorite example of this is the electric motor. The electric motor at first was meant to replace the steam engine. [Just as we] had one steam engine that would power an entire factory with belts running the whole length of the factory to transmit the power from the steam engine, the electric motor also was a single device installed at a central location in the factory with belts running to the remote areas of the factory. As the technology improved, we reached the point where you didn't need to have a single motor with belts. You could just build the motor into each device. What this did was dramatically change the nature of the factory, since you no longer had to place the instruments where the belts could reach. Now you could place the instruments wherever it made sense to put them, and the motor became an invisible part of the instrument. In fact, in manufacturing today you don't even notice the electric motors. They're just a fundamental part of the device.

BERGMAN: *Using your analogy, how does "hiding the motor" relate to the transition from computers to information appliances?*

NORMAN: In the early 1900s you could buy a home electric motor—one motor for the entire home with a wide variety of attachments you could put on it. So you could do your sewing, attach a fan blade, attach a mixer hoop, a grinder. Notice—it was one machine with all these attachments, and so you had to do the work where the machine was located.

Today the electric motor is distributed throughout the house. You might easily have 50 motors in your home, most of which you're unaware of. Moreover, the devices that it powers are named not by the technology that's inside them, but they're named by what they do. We have an eggbeater or a coffee grinder, and if you look inside the two, you see they're almost the same. They're an electric motor that rotates a little blade with a hook on it, or a sharp pointed edge, which grinds the coffee.

I believe the same kind of transition will happen with computers, that instead of one massive device that occupies considerable space on our desktop, we will have a wide range of devices that are designed to fit the tasks that we wish to do. And that inside of them there will be computers and a communication structure, but we'll be unaware of it. It will simply empower us to do our tasks. We won't think of using the computer. We won't go to use a computer, just like today we don't go to use our electric motor. We will go to write someone a letter. Or you'll go to check on the news or check on the weather. Or we'll say, "Let's see what's playing in nearby movie theaters." Or in a strange city you might ask, "Where are the good restaurants within walking distance of where I am right this minute?"

So, I see a change occurring from the one massive, centrally located infrastructure, the personal computer, to a set of rather small, widely distributed devices that we won't even think of as computers, we won't think of as telecommunication devices even though that's what they will be. We'll just think of them as a natural part of our daily activities and the tools that we use.

BERGMAN: *Won't there be too many of these kinds of devices? What will stop us from experiencing overload from the number of appliances we have in our lives?*

[At this point in the conversation, Don Norman pulls a tiny flashlight out of his pocket to which an extremely small Swiss army knife is attached.]

NORMAN: This is a single AAA cell flashlight, just slightly bigger than the Swiss army knife, and it's a very small Swiss army knife, and the answer to your question is this . . .

We're sitting now in my living room. How many different devices do we have in the living room? There are more than 20. First of all, there're some pictures on the walls, and there's a mirror on the wall. Let's just call that one: wall hangings. There's artwork. Call that two: artwork—even though there are a number of different pieces. There's a couch that you're sitting on, and one I'm sitting on. We'll just call that one for furniture, for sitting furniture. But there's also the table in front of us. One, two, three, four—the table has a glass, five; a plate, six; a napkin, seven; a bowl, eight; with fruit in it, nine; with another fancy container, 10; with candy in it, that's 11; with my Palm on the table, 12; my notebook, 13; my pen, 14; the Swiss army knife and flashlight, call that one thing, 15; pillows, 16; lights, 17; piano, 18; and a fire detector, 19. We're up to 20 and I hadn't even decided to talk about your briefcase, the fact that I'm wearing shoes and pants and socks and a belt and a variety of clothes, which have different types of fasteners, and a wristwatch.

But somehow I don't go around and say, well, look, I have 50 different items in this room. They just seem natural. Each one of them seems to play its role and sits in its own place and does its particular thing. And that's how I think it's going to evolve. If we do this right, we just won't even question it.

BERGMAN: *Many of the things you mentioned seem to be passive recipients of our actions. They are tools we use, but they don't seem to provide much interaction themselves. You gave the example of shoes—it seems to me that you put your feet in them and walk around, but the shoes don't do much. Or your example of a banana—you might eat it, but how much does it interact with you?*

NORMAN: I can't imagine more interaction than the banana going inside my body.

BERGMAN: *Some of these devices we're discussing seem to talk back to us. Isn't that fundamentally different?*

NORMAN: I don't think it is. There is my radio set, which talks back to me in some ways; my Palm [organizer], which is interactive in the sense that I ask it questions and it provides me with answers. But I don't see any real distinction. I have my pen and pencil, which are interactive to me. I have a flashlight, which is interactive to me. I have the Palm. I don't see that one is necessarily a big break from the other.

Those of us in the computer industry like to think there's something really powerful and special about the computers. I don't think so, not when done properly. When something is done properly, it just feels like a natural part of our lives. The telephone feels like a simple device. The fact that it actually uses part of a worldwide network that allows me to talk effortlessly to anybody throughout the world is invisible to me. Our interactive devices will let us feel that's the way it ought to be. What's special about it? Things are special when they're new and novel. We only call things technology when they're new and novel. We don't call my watch technology, even though it really is very high technology.

BERGMAN: *So what are the qualities that make technology invisible? Why are some pieces of technology so visible to us, while others are not?*

NORMAN: There are two kinds of invisibility. One of them is true invisibility; the way most infrastructure in a house is invisible. So, my house could not function without the sewer, the sewage pipes and system; without the delivery of hot water and cold water throughout the house; without the electric infrastructure. But it's primarily invisible. You're only aware of it when something goes wrong with it.

That's one kind of invisibility that I expect to see more and more of. It's the same kind of invisibility of most of the electric motors in the house that we're really truly unaware of. I'm glancing around the room to see if I think there are any electric motors here, and the answer is . . . I don't know . . . Oh yes, there's one electric motor in each of the tape recorders, and therefore I have a CD player and a tape player which have motors in them. But I don't think of them as electric motors. So one kind of invisibility is that the stuff is embedded within products and I can be unaware of their presence, or they can be hidden beneath the surface, like the sewage pipes in my house and like the Internet connection to my house.

The other kind of invisibility is of a different sort. It's when the device fits the need so perfectly that I forget that it's a complex technical device. And I think that's true of my coffee grinder and maybe my eggbeater, that I think of as an eggbeater or a coffee grinder. It's hard for me to imagine it being in any other form, and it's perfectly natural to grind my coffee beans that way. So that even in thought—it really is this device that I physically use and physically move about, but it's invisible in the sense of not occupying any psychological space. My pencil is the same way—it feels like a natural part of my body at this point even though I have to physically find, use, and carry it around with me, and even though it took me a few years to learn how to use it well.

So I foresee that a lot of information technology will be that way, and maybe the epitome of it is . . . I was going to say the telephone, but I just realized I could name a number—the telephone, the wristwatch, the thermostatic control of temperature in my house. These are technologies that I take for granted, which is what I call a kind of invisibility.

BERGMAN: *Returning to the question of whether we will have too many devices—even in a world with technologies having the kind of invisibility you describe, isn't it possible we will be overwhelmed by the number of devices we will need to use?*

NORMAN: Well, it depends what the device is. I'm not in favor of single-purpose devices. I'm in favor of single-activity devices, things that bring together into one container, one unit, activities or tasks that naturally go together. What I recommend is that we observe what activities people do and what people's needs are, and try to discover the interactions among them. Then we design and build devices where there are heavy interactions, and we use separate devices where there are very few interactions. This also means that the correct set of devices will vary with the person. Our best example is the Day Timer, the type of paper scheduling books that people carry around with them. If you go to the store to buy one, you discover there isn't just one, but rather it's a system. You can choose what size notebook you want; you can choose what kind of paper you want; you can choose what format you prefer your calendar to be; and you can choose what goes together. Do you want a calendar alone, or do you want just an address book, or do you want both? Do you want a "to do" list? Do you want notes? You can assemble whatever combination best fits the way that you work. And I foresee that's how our appliances will be developed.

BERGMAN: *Are there cases of this level of choice in existing technologies?*

NORMAN: Look at the Palm. This is ideal for many business people, but it doesn't work well for, say, someone in the average household. It's perfect for me because it contains addresses, calendar, and simple notes. I find that I must use that combination frequently. But not everybody has to carry their addresses around with them all the time, and very few people have to carry a detailed calendar. Most people's lives are simple enough that they don't write down their appointments. They just remember them. It's only someone whose time is scheduled carefully at half-hour blocks throughout the day who needs a calendar like this. So for me and for many business people, it's a perfect fit. So I have one device that does three things.

If you also look at my activities, you see I use a cell phone frequently, and when I use a cell phone, what do I do? Well, I've got to look up a number, so most cell phones have an address book built into them, but now I have two address books, one in my Palm and one in my cell phone. And often the conversation on the telephone is about when can we get together and meet, so I do need a calendar. And often I want to write down notes from the conversation, so it actually makes sense that the telephone and the Palm or similar devices be merged into one.

So here is one device that will do what I consider natural activities—phone calls, names of people and their phone numbers, scheduling, and simple notes. It won't work for everybody, but it's one device that does what might have taken four devices. And if you actually look now at the total number of activities that I do, for which I want technical assistance, there's not going to be that many. There might be three or four, so I might need three or four devices. Does that mean that when I travel I should remember to take these three or four separate things and no matter what four I take, whenever I get to this faraway city I'll discover I needed a fifth? My answer to that is that I might carry very different things when I travel. That's why I have this Swiss army knife and flashlight. This is my travel kit. It's always with me in my travel bag, and I don't use it unless I'm traveling. And I often use the scissors that's part of the knife, and the knife blades, and the screwdriver, and I very often use the flashlight, if only to read menus in dimly lit restaurants.

But when I'm home, why would I use a tiny little knife or the little scissors that come with the Swiss army knife? When I'm home I'll use the dedicated appliance, so not only do I have a real knife at home, but I have about 10 of them, each of them somewhat specialized and somewhat different. And I have a number of scissors, some of which are identical, but I simply put them where I'm going to use them, so there's scissors in the kitchen, and my wife has scissors in her study. I have scissors in my desk. They're all the same, but what's nice about the appliance is you can put the tool where you want to do the work as opposed to bringing the work to the tool. At home I use a more powerful, larger flashlight, although I don't need a flashlight very often because we have electric lights. So, this is very valuable for traveling, but I use a different set at home, and I could imagine the same thing happening with our appliances.

BERGMAN: *So what will people take with them when traveling, and how will they synchronize information with any home appliances they might have?*

NORMAN: We might travel with something not unlike today's portable computer that lumps everything together, but when I get home, I'd rather use the real thing. This will only work if we have an effortless way of transferring information. If I make changes while on a trip, it should automatically update all the devices I have at home. That technology has not existed up to now, and it's just starting to appear. The underpinnings are a kind of infrastructure that the Internet has provided, coupled with software and protocol standards such as Jini that automatically let devices communicate with each other and find out their capabilities. Hewlett Packard has JetSend that allows the handshaking that says: "I have a picture, what kind of picture do you accept? Would you like JPEG? etc." In addition perhaps a radio frequency system like Bluetooth, which means that whenever my Palm comes within five feet of my home address book, they will just silently detect one another through Bluetooth and Jini and synchronize themselves. That's what's needed. All the pieces exist today, but they have not been put together yet.

BERGMAN: *Your call for merging the functions of multiple devices seems to highlight potential conflicts with how people use such devices. So while one might use both an electronic organizer and cell phone at the same time, by merging them, it becomes more difficult to access the organizer when you need to find information during a call, because the display and controls are pressed against your face. How do you reconcile such conflicts?*

NORMAN: Right. That's a really good point. I think my logical analysis of the fact that these go together is correct. However, if you really put it into one little device, if I hold it to my ear in order to talk, I can no longer read it. There are several solutions, and I believe all solutions require essentially two pieces. The two pieces are, obviously, a speaker and receiver which is near your head and a display device that you can read and write on at the same time you're speaking and listening. You can do this in several ways.

One way is what Qualcomm and Palm have done—Qualcomm now makes a cell phone that's merged with the Palm, and they assume that you will use earphones and a portable microphone. So you plug the earphone in and hold the Palm in your hand. Nokia in its earlier device had a combination cell phone, fax, email, address book, etc., and you could hold it up to your ear and then you couldn't read it, of course. But if you put it down, it opened it up to expose the display and the keyboard, and it automatically became a speakerphone. So that's how they solved the problem, the speakerphone being very convenient in its usage, except it would not work in a noisy environment and it doesn't allow much privacy.

The other method is to have a separate telephone and a separate address book, say, a telephone and the Palm. The problem is, I want to have the advantage that the two talk to each other, and in principle there's no reason why they couldn't. In fact, my Nokia cell phone and my Palm both have infrared. There's no reason I couldn't look up the address on the Palm and beam it to the Nokia phone; or even do the same thing during a phone call. Someone says, "Can you give me Tom's phone number?" I could look up Tom's address and beam it into the phone, which sends it to the other person. In fact, the infrared protocols don't talk to each other and there was evidently no thought in bringing these together. But that would be yet another solution.

BERGMAN: *You were talking about the communication among devices . . . the transfer of information. What about the individual user's ability to communicate with the different devices? Won't there be too many different ways of interacting with things, forcing us to spend a lot of time simply learning how to use each device?*

NORMAN: No, I think exactly the opposite—just the opposite. I perceive these as personal devices—that I will have this device for many years, decades maybe. In fact, even if I outgrow it or if a new version comes out, I will buy it, but it would essentially be the same kind of device. So, I will be an expert at its use and so expert—as expert as I am with a pencil—so expert that I don't even realize that I'm doing anything special. Moreover, each of these interactive devices could also learn my preferences and could change itself to work best with me. As long as I only have to use my devices, then everything's fine. And that's how it is in my kitchen. I have many specialized kitchen appliances and utensils and cooking devices, each of which I have learned. And even though there are a large number of them, each one was easy to learn, until I learned the entire ensemble over a period of time.

When I go to someone else's kitchen, I have great trouble. I can't work it. I don't know how to find their things. I don't know how to work a number of their things. When I use someone else's wristwatch, I may have trouble knowing how to control it. So, what I think will happen is we'll end up with a large number of specialized devices that are ours, our personal ones. So for any individual, there won't be any problem. It is true that I might not be able to work somebody else's without asking for instructions, but then how often would I need to?

BERGMAN: *What about the effect that we see in the PC industry where year after year after year there is a new wave of technology, with computers getting faster, having more memory, and more functionality for the same or less cost. Even with the simple devices we have been discussing, presumably each year they will get better and faster and be able to do new things. How do we as users cope with that technology curve in a world of information appliances?*

NORMAN: Hah! So now we come to the world of high technologists and their craving for newness and better and faster and bigger and more powerful, versus the rest of us who don't want to be bothered, thank you very much. That's the playground for boys with their toys. Let them have their toys, but the number of people who wish to do this is very limited—it is not the consumer market; this is what the 10 to 15% of the population who are early adopters pick.

The rest of the population, the vast majority of people (perhaps 75 to 80%), doesn't want that. They don't want to change their systems every six months, not even every year. They want stability. They want a very slow evolution toward improved devices, slow enough that they can grow with them, learn them, and feel comfortable with them. They want slow, steady evolution, not these big gigantic changes every six months.

The business model that you're talking about is fundamentally wrong. The problem is it's a dominant model in high technology today. But I believe that high technology today is doomed to fail for just this reason. It is technology for the sake of technologists. It's made by technologists for the sake of technologists.

People want convenience and value, they just want to get on with their life, and their life is their family, entertainment, education, and their work. But not this endless pursuit of the latest hot new gadgets, which complicates their life. So, the goal of the information appliance actually is that these are meant to be activity-specific devices that fit the way we work and that after we buy them, we're apt to keep them for a very long time.

BERGMAN: *How will selling to this larger and different population of users impact what, after all, has been a highly successful business model for technology companies?*

NORMAN: One reason that the technology business is the way it is . . . is because of the way you make money. You only make money by selling people new computers or new software, and because the goal is that everybody should have a computer, they just need one computer. So once you've bought a computer and your software, horrors if you are happy with it. How does the company make money from then on? The goal is to make you unhappy with what you've bought so that you upgrade it and buy more. That's not the only possible business model.

Take a look at the model of the consumer electronics companies. To a large extent, what you do there is you sell people multiple copies of the device, so how many tape recorders do you own? I've discovered, to my great surprise, I own about six tape recorders. And it doesn't bother me that I do, because what happens is that each tape recorder is located where I might need a tape recorder. There's one tape recorder in this room that plays tapes. There's a tape recorder built into each of my automobiles. I have a special tape recorder I use when I go running. My wife has one. Etc. So a different business model is that we have great longevity in our products, but that over time we accumulate a number of them and put them in places where it's most convenient.

BERGMAN: *Scott McNealy, CEO of Sun Microsystems, was recently quoted in a business magazine as saying something to the effect of "You already have zero privacy. Get over it." What do you think of that statement?*

NORMAN: I am willing to take half that statement. You already have surprisingly little privacy. But I think that's a bad thing. I disagree rather fundamentally with anyone who says, "Get over it." I don't have an answer. It's an extremely complex question.

There are at minimum three different factors that trade off against each other. One is your right to privacy. The second is society's right to mitigate harm to others and damage to itself, to society itself. In other words, there are criminals and bad guys among us, and we have to have some way of enforcing civility and enforcing adherence to our system of laws. And that requires the good guys to be able to find out what the bad guys are doing. And at the same time, you don't want to break the privacy of the innocent average citizen, and that creates a real tension and I don't know how to solve it. Nobody knows how to solve it, and that's what the American Constitution and the U.S. system of government are all about, trying to reach some harmonious balance. Then a third point, which has only recently been discussed, is that as we have ever more distributed connected computational systems so that our computers can talk to any other computer at any place in the world, there has to be some way of distinguishing the messages sent by one from the messages sent by another—distinguishing one device from another. Just like every telephone has a unique identification number, every computer and every message must have a unique identification number, for technical reasons. But as soon as you have that coupled with computational powers, suddenly you can now trace to any individual every single message ever sent. And once again, I don't know what the solution to this problem is because it seems like a necessity to make our communication networks work.

In addition, in our society there are government agencies that would like to know more and more about what you're doing. There are political parties that would like to know how you vote, or what causes you to vote one way or another. There are commercial firms and advertising agencies that feel they could provide a better job or give better service or make more money if only they knew much more about your personal life. Some of these collect this information surreptitiously, some openly, and some even pay you to provide them with the information. But all of this is also causing some conflict. But these other issues strike me as somewhat different from the more fundamental ones I mentioned before: first, the personal need for privacy; second, the need for society to overcome the privacy at times for the benefit of peace-keeping and law-keeping; and third, the technical requirements of devices to know from whom and where the information is coming.

BERGMAN: *You've mentioned a number of social issues regarding the potential impact of these technologies. How will having information appliances everywhere change the way individuals live on a daily basis? And how will it change our society?*

NORMAN: Not much. A lot. So, if we do this properly, the information appliances will probably have no immediate impact on your life, except, I hope, to simplify it. You won't notice them. That's the point. Over time, they may actually simplify your life and make a lot of things you do much easier and nicer and friendlier, and you may even be relatively unaware of that fact because it has come about so naturally. So, one of the minor things I imagine is that my wife and I can keep in touch with one another more easily. Sometimes we get separated, we've agreed to meet, and now we can't find one another. We had a horrible experience once in an airport where she was waiting for me on the first floor and I was waiting for her on the second floor. It took us hours to find each other. And yet with a simple cell phone today all that's solved. We use the cell phone a lot just to synchronize our activities.

BERGMAN: *So there is a strong social motivation for using these technologies?*

NORMAN: Families are having more and more trouble just keeping in touch with one another. There is a fundamental human need for families and close friends to communicate, to do things together, to know where one another is. Some of the newer communication capabilities will be of great social value.

I could imagine the examples I gave earlier where I'm in a strange city and I have some hours to kill. What movies are playing, or where is there a good restaurant, or where are the museums and what are their special shows? And now I have to go hunt up "This Weekend" magazine or some sort of tourist guide, or try to find the local newspaper and see if they have what I want, as opposed to just opening up my device which already knows where I am and therefore can immediately give me answers. Is this breathtaking? Does it change the way the world works? No. But, it is part of the modern revolution that we're in, the information revolution that started in the late 1800s. Those were exciting times: the telegraph, telephone, phonograph, motion picture camera, and radio all were invented in a relatively short interval of time—this was the start of the information revolution.

The information age is now reaching an interesting period of amalgamation. We now have computing devices that are extremely powerful and very small and inexpensively combined with communication servers that allow anybody anyplace in the world to be part of the network. The third component would be the global positioning satellite system that allows you to determine where you are in the world. So these three things together are going to provide all sorts of new powerful tools for everyone, including the lesser developed nations in the world that cannot afford the infrastructure of telephone wires, who can now bypass that entire stage and switch immediately to satellite and wireless telephones. I think that over time, these devices and their simplicity and reliability and low cost, coupled with the ubiquity of communications and positioning information and computation, is going to have dramatic impact.

BERGMAN: *How will designing content for information appliances be different than designing content for the Web?*

NORMAN: Yes. Here we go. Designing in this new world requires a new genre. It's a whole different approach. All of a sudden hey, guess what? It is interactive. All of a sudden we're changing the medium. It does require bringing together different disciplines, but it also requires understanding the special nature of this genre. We don't understand that yet.

Most Web pages are horrible. People think that it's a simple translation from print technology to screen technology, and it isn't. It's interactive. It can change. You can know just who is looking at it, and when, and how much time is spent on each section. This changes everything. In many ways I'm pleased, in other ways it's horrible: it gives the Nielsen Norman Group a lifetime of opportunities, but it also means that people completely miss the point.

Just the other day I was shown a health application to be done on the Internet. Wouldn't it be nice, the health care company said, if we could get all the information we need about patients—their medical and financial history—before they come in.

They have a health questionnaire, 121 questions, given to you one at a time through HTML. HTML has set back the user interface by a decade. HTML is a batch processing mechanism, poorly suited for interaction. It is made for finding Web pages or material of interest and either jumping to the new location or downloading files. It is not for interaction.

In this particular case, I waited and waited and waited and then a question would come, which would say, "Do you feel healthier now than you did last year: Yes or No?" I said, "Yes." Then the question went away and I would have to wait again while it delivered up the next trivial question. I'm supposed to do this for 121 questions? I mean, first of all, it's a clear setback from paper and pencil, which would have been faster and easier and much more convenient. And second of all, the whole point of this medium is interactivity, that you don't have to give me 121 questions. You could design it so that the answers to the first few questions determined what other questions might get asked. This was just a dumb application of a dumb, horrible questionnaire into the worst of all possible delivery mechanisms. What a wasted opportunity: the wrong procedure, with the wrong technology.

BERGMAN: *You just said that HTML has set the user interface back. Can you elaborate on that?*

NORMAN: HTML has a very interesting history. If you look at why it was developed, it was an attempt to allow the sharing of information in a way that was device independent. And as a result, HTML is a very simplified markup language that says, this is the header and this is the emphasis, this is a hyperlink. It does not allow for interaction, it does not allow for control over the typography and layout. These restrictions worked well for the original applications.

The Web should be an interactive medium. HTML is a publishing mechanism. It's a one-way transmission. It allows you to mark up the page to send to others, but others can't respond to it, at least not directly. It's batch-processing mode. I respond and then the whole thing is sent back to the central location, which determines what response it should give.

On top of that, as the Web became more popular with businesses, graphic designers started doing graphic design, and they said, "Oh, this is horrible. We've lost control." And so the graphic designers said, "Look, it's really important for us what fonts we use, what sizes they are, what colors they are, how they're placed on the page." And they're right. I'm not disagreeing, but the fact is they had to distort the whole use of HTML and add structures to it that really were antithetical to the original design goal. All of this was an attempt to give them back some control over what the page looked like, but as they did this, it also became a much more centralized publishing medium, where it was they who decided what it was we were going to see. And once again, it further degraded the interactivity.

This has got to change. It has to change for several different reasons. One will just be natural because we are now starting to move to an extremely wide array of display devices, everything from a very large, high-quality monitor to a cell phone, where the graphics designer no longer will be able to specify the layout because there will be too wide a range of display devices. Something that works on a high-quality monitor isn't going to work on a cell phone display. Also, there is a wide variety of communication lines. The high-quality graphics that look so good over my high-speed line are horrible when you look at them over a very slow telephone connection. So, I think what's going to happen is that XML will become more popular, and then guess what? The power is no longer on the publisher's side. The power is on the receiving side; it's up to my device to figure out what information it wants to extract from the Web and how it wishes to display it. The graphics designer at the publishing side will no longer be in control. Instead, it will be up to the device designer to control the appearance and interaction.

But the other argument is that HTML, even dynamic HTML, is not an interactive language. It is a display language. All the advances in human interface have come from the tight relationship between the user's action and what they see on the screen. All this has been destroyed. It is possible that some day Java can come in and solve this problem. That is not true today. Java applets first of all take a long time to load and, therefore, degrade the initial experience. And second of all, the virtual Java machines on which we run the applets are not effective yet. They're too slow. But I do believe we're going to need some technology, which is either dedicated applications on your system or Java at some future generation that will run more efficiently.

BERGMAN: *So you are a convert to the Java notion of "write once, run anywhere"?*

NORMAN: The "write once, run anywhere" slogan was clearly stated by the software people who thought only of the algorithm, as opposed to the appearance of the screen, because it's fundamentally impossible to do this. Although it is true I could make a satisfactory graphical user interface that could be written in Java and therefore look satisfactory on the Macintosh platform or a Microsoft platform, in fact, either would be probably inferior to what Apple or Microsoft has provided. And second of all, it certainly wouldn't cut across dramatically different platforms such as my cell phone or my Palm device and my high-quality display screen.

It's interesting—the "write once, run anywhere" argument. It is hard to see how that was ever said because for the last decade most of the code has been user interface code. And the concept fails at the user interface as soon as you work on a variety of different platforms with different hardware and different I/O.

BERGMAN: *There is a tension I perceive between making a device for general purposes versus specific purposes. So, for example, taking the Palm as an example, in fact you can load different applications on it and have it be a little planetarium or a chess-playing machine or shopping list and so forth. How is that general-purpose capability to be balanced in a world of information appliances?*

NORMAN: Let me state my design philosophy here. Making specialized devices, making information appliances is not some religion, it is not something where I believe there are true answers and any deviation is wrong. I believe it is a philosophy about trying to simplify our lives, but the whole point is to give a customer-centered, a human-centered approach to the development of tools and devices that we use. So, in many ways we provide whatever it is that people wish.

There is a tension in devices like the Palm that brilliantly focuses upon a few very simple things and does them very well and elegantly and the desire to add more and more features to a device. The Palm has a calculator in it and I find it is occasionally useful, but it isn't a very good calculator. Maybe I need a better calculator in my Palm device. In fact I'd also like a currency converter. And some people put games in their Palm devices. Some people before they travel download into their Palm all sorts of traveling information. When you go to a conference, you can now preload the conference information. I have a friend who before he goes to a meeting, downloads a short biographical sketch of each of the meeting attendees, including their photograph, so when he meets new people, he can quickly look them up and say, oh, that's John, oh, that's Mary.

At what point does this now become overcomplex and lose the power of simplicity? My answer is: I don't know. What I like is that people can tailor it for whatever they like. I think there's a real difference between a device that you have tailored yourself—you put together the things that you like to go together—versus one where the manufacturer has included hundreds of functions, hoping that you will find at least some of them useful. One of the major differences is that I put them all on myself and therefore I'm apt to use them. I know why they're there, and I understand it; as opposed to having it delivered to me with all that extra functionality, most of which I can't understand and most of which I can't figure out—that I'll never use. But you're right. There's tension between keeping it simple and also adding all those extra neat features.

BERGMAN: *Presumably the balancing of which features to include is part of the process by which we develop information appliances. Is the product design and development process different for information appliances than current computer technologies?*

NORMAN: I believe we're entering a new era of devices. The technology we have today is technology for the early adopters, technology for the technologists, technology for the sake of technologists versus for the sake of technology. Most of the technology that we use comes from two different industries, the consumer electronics industry that brings us the audiovisual sets, and the computer industry, neither of which really understands consumers.

Both industries are dominated by engineers, programmers, and technologists. After all, if you look at the consumer electronics industry, that's the industry that brought us the VCR with a flashing 12:00, or the VCRs that people can't program, or the audiovisual equipment in your TV room or living room which consists of a stack of many different devices, each with its own separate remote control, each with lots of buttons and knobs and flashing lights and remote controls that are getting ever more complex.

I think it's time to come to the era of products for the everyday person, products much more like the appliances in the kitchen, or for that matter the furniture in your house, that are meant to fit your lifestyle and meant to give you value and convenience, not to complicate your life. This requires, therefore, a very different approach to the design of our products. It requires an approach in which you observe the way that people live their lives, and you try to make products that fit naturally and seamlessly into people's lives. It requires a human-centered design approach where designers of all sorts—industrial design, graphics design, and interaction design—are working as a team from the very beginning of the concept of the product. First of all, to decide what the product should be in the first place. Second, to decide what its function should be, and third, how it behaves. Fourth, how it looks, how it feels, the aesthetics.

All these are critically important in the consumer sphere, and they're mostly absent in the technology sphere of today. So I think it's time to reconsider the entire way in which we develop products. I'm not convinced the consumer electronics companies or the computer companies are up to it. The "technology first" approach is too deeply ingrained in their culture.

BERGMAN: *If computer technology companies are not up to the challenge of creating information appliances, then what industry will create them?*

NORMAN: I'm fond of saying if you want examples of two companies that seem to understand consumers, it's Procter & Gamble and Disney, neither of which are actually likely to bring us high-technology products. Here are my likely candidates. First are the small start-ups, some of which have already produced some really nice devices. Actually the Palm is a good example. I'm involved with a couple of others that are doing excellent devices for the everyday person, but unfortunately I can't tell you about them . . . yet. Second is some of the consumer electronics companies, and the two that come immediately to mind are Sony and Philips. And last are the computer companies.

BERGMAN: *Clearly some sophisticated technologies will be needed to create successful information appliances and any "back end" infrastructure required to support connectivity for them. Do you see any of the current technology companies having the understanding of consumers that might enable them to make the leap from computers to appliances?*

NORMAN: One of the companies that does understand consumers is America Online. They are consumer oriented. They and maybe Intuit are perhaps the two best examples of computer companies that are not computer companies, that are really trying to offer value to the customers and that understand what the customers need.

It's amazing how the technology companies make fun of them, sneer at them. Let me quote you an excerpt from the March 1999 issue of *Networker Magazine,* on page 6, an article by Dennis Fowler talking about the new relationship between Sun and America Online. [Norman picks up the magazine and begins reading . . .]

> The question remains though, whether AOL can overcome the reputation as a consumer-oriented business. This will determine whether [Steve] Case's hopes for penetrating the e-commerce market will succeed. The Sun [the computer] phase of the deal may be enough to reassure the hardcore techies who are worried about what a consumer outfit like AOL might do to the technically oriented Netscape operation.

I mean, wow, Dennis Fowler has it all backwards. Has he got it wrong! I mean, here he is saying, ooh, these are consumer companies, how are they going to make it in this world? He's got it just backwards. The reason that AOL is successful is because it's a consumer company and offers what people want, and yes, all the technically oriented people sneer at America Online and the colorful graphics and the apparent simplicity. That's what people want. That's what people like. It is time to move away from technology-centered products to human-centered ones. But I fear that the technologists and the technology companies will have great difficulty making the transition.

CHAPTER TWO

Design Considerations for Information Appliances

MICHAEL F. MOHAGEG, PH.D.

User Experience Group
Consumer & Embedded Division
Sun Microsystems, Inc.

ANNETTE WAGNER

User Experience Group
Consumer & Embedded Division
Sun Microsystems, Inc.

2.1   Introduction

Current user interface approaches, developed for the desktop personal computer, are limited in their application to the design of information appliances. While portions of PC design approaches can be leveraged for information appliances, many of the design philosophies do not apply or simply cannot be used. Similarly, only a subset of the considerable knowledge from consumer electronics user interfaces applies to the information appliance domain. Therefore, new design approaches are needed to address the special design needs for these devices.

This chapter describes some of the practical design considerations for developing user interfaces for information appliances. These considerations have been derived from significant experience in designing for the information appliance space. In addition to its traditional server, workstation, and software businesses, Sun Microsystems provides software solutions for consumer devices and information appliances. These solutions have been in the form of a real-time operating system (RTOS), enabling platforms such as Java2 Micro Edition (for phones, televisions, automobiles), and complete applications for television set-top boxes, screen phones, and wireless devices.

The design considerations in this chapter are a sample of the principles yielded from our experiences. They are intended to provide the flavor of our new design approach. They are not design prescriptions, but they do offer a perspective for a user experience that is different from that of PCs. Additionally, the principles discussed in this chapter are supported by a number of design tactics and implementations, which, in the interest of space, are not included in this volume.

Information Appliances Defined

An information appliance is a computer-enhanced consumer device dedicated to a restricted cluster of tasks. A personal digital assistant (PDA), an Internet-enabled screen phone, and a pager are examples of information appliances. The concept of information appliances is borrowed from the traditional notion of an appliance: it is a device that performs only a few tasks, but does them well, efficiently, and with little conscious effort from the user. For instance, refrigerators are bought solely for the purpose of keeping items either cool or frozen; they do little else other than blend aesthetically with the rest of the kitchen. A dishwasher washes dishes. A microwave oven has the task of heating food. Information appliances apply this notion of a dedicated device to computing technology, with the goal of creating small, easy-to-use, low-cost devices that perform only a few tasks. Instead of using a PC that does everything from email to 3D game playing, users can have inexpensive information appliances that perform a restricted collection of tasks. Proponents of these devices claim the user experience of information appliances will be superior to general-purpose PCs because all aspects of the product can be specially designed to meet the needs of the more-restricted device.

Some of the key characteristics of information appliances that differentiate them from PCs are

- Limited purpose and functionality

- Not necessarily extensible or upgradable

- Replacement expectation (the user may have to replace the entire device within a few years)

- Perceived as less expensive (versus PCs)

- Perceived as less complicated to run and maintain (versus PCs)

- Very easy to learn and use

- No expectation of "expert users"

There is another important factor contributing to the viability of information appliances. In comparison to mass market consumer products, PCs have not achieved high penetration and popularity among personal or home users; this is especially true outside North America (Computer Industry Almanac 1998). Many (AllNetDevices 1999) attribute this lack of popularity to the high cost and complexity of using and maintaining PCs. Information appliances offer a compelling alternative due to their low cost and ease of use. For instance, customers may legitimately wonder why they should spend over $1,500 on a PC (with a variety of maintenance complications) when their only interest is in a device to use email and access the World Wide Web.

The Need for a Different User Interface

Information appliances need different user interface solutions for several reasons, but the two most important are

- The consumer audience

- The characteristics of information appliances

Each of these is addressed below.

The Consumer Audience

Information appliances are intended for a very wide base of "consumers"— people who, unlike PC users, may have minimal computer experience. For consumers, user interface metaphors and models that are borrowed from desktop environments may not be appropriate. Pop-up menus, scrollbars, drag and drop, or the computer desktop may be quite unfamiliar. Consumers may feel uncomfortable dealing with anything they consider to be too "high tech" and tend to be unwilling to learn complex interaction models. On the other hand, they are familiar with appliances such as push-button phones, microwave oven control panels, and TV remote controls.

Consumer electronics appliances such as televisions, VCRs, and telephones are common today; however, widespread acceptance of a consumer electronics device can be difficult to achieve. Some products fail because consumers find them too difficult to use. And though some products sell well, consumers actually use only a small fraction of their capabilities. Modern consumers have little patience for learning how to operate new products, and without bothering to consult the user manual, they expect the interfaces to be self-evident. Moreover, our experience has shown that consumers—even those with computer experience—have very different expectations when they interact with a consumer device. There seems to be a low tolerance for learning how to use them.

The Characteristics of Information Appliances

The strength of consumer devices lies in their specialization for particular tasks or groups of tasks. Indeed, what makes certain devices compelling and successful in the marketplace is finding a targeted collection of tasks and supporting them with the right features in the product. Product designers are no longer bound by the generic technology offerings of a PC: CRT and speakers for output, keyboard and mouse for input, and fairly standard, "desktop-oriented" end-user environment to manage and access information. Products can be designed to provide an environment that is well suited to the requirements of the appliance. For instance, small monochrome LCDs with a touch panel may be appropriate for a portable device. A screen phone may not use a physical keyboard at all and instead rely mostly on gesture-based input with a stylus. A PDA user may not need a "desktop" metaphor with files and folders to manage his PDA "objects." Table 2.1 highlights some of the differences between a PC and two popular information appliances— screen phones and TV set-top boxes.

While designers of information appliances are freed from the trappings of the PC, there are still considerable design challenges, due largely to technical limitations of these devices. Compared to PCs, information appliances

TABLE **2.1**

*Some of the key differences among a screen phone,
analog TV set-top box, and a desktop computer*

Characteristic	Screen Phone	TV Set-Top Box	Desktop Computer (personal computer or workstation)
Applications: telephony, voice mail, address book, email, Web browsing		TV, EPG, Web browsing, email	word processing, spreadsheets, presentations, Web browsing, email, productivity applications, vertical applications
Input device: primarily finger, stylus, secondarily keyboard		remote control and remote (IR) keyboard	mouse, keyboard
Mouse support	none	none (some remote controls have trackballs)	yes
Keyboard support	on-screen and/or physical keyboard	on-screen and/or physical keyboard; keyboard usually infrared technology	physical keyboard
Viewing distance	1–1.5 feet	10–15 feet	1–2 feet
Display size (diagonal)	6–8 inches	13 inches to wall size	13–28 inches
Screen resolution: ¼ VGA (320×240) to full VGA (640×480)		broadcast television analog signal (roughly equivalent to 640×444 for NTSC)	640×480 to 1800×1440
Display colors	2-, 4-, or 8-bit color; both black and white and color	broadcast television; color characteristics depend on signal type (e.g., NTSC, PAL, SECAM)	8-, 16-, or 24-bit color
Pixel density	~102 dpi	N/A	~72 to 100 dpi
Multiple screens	no	no	yes
Audio input	telephone handset, microphone	microphone	microphone
Audio output	telephone handset, perhaps speaker	TV speakers up to full surround sound	computer speakers to high-end speakers
Data bandwidth	28.8 Kbps to ISDN	28.8 KBps to cable modem throughput	28.8 Kbps to T1
Printer connection	optional	optional	yes

have less memory (both storage and run-time), smaller displays, potentially less powerful processors, and different input and output devices. Especially in the case of input devices, information appliances tend to use lower-bandwidth mechanisms, which limit the richness of users' inputs. These factors place constraints on the human interface that do not normally exist on a desktop computer. So, ironically, the very factors that are deemed beneficial and essential to the product experience pose hurdles for product designers.

2.2 Design Considerations

The design considerations described in this section are provided as an approach to the design of information appliances enhanced with computing technology. These considerations are not rules or prescriptions for design; rather, they represent a design approach that is quite different from that of traditional PCs and workstations. The five design considerations included here are not an exhaustive list but provide a strong notion of the new approach needed for this design space:

1. Account for the target domain

2. Dedicated devices mean dedicated user interfaces

3. Allocate functions appropriately

4. Simplify

5. Design for responsiveness

Account for the Target Domain

The user interface of an information appliance must suit the application domain for that appliance. A "domain" is characterized by the environment, the applications or tasks, and how the device is likely to be used. The device is intended to be dedicated to a set of very specific and related tasks in a defined setting. Both hardware and software are optimized for this domain.

A basic pager is a clear example of a dedicated information appliance. The pager's tasks are to receive pages and display the number of the caller. The device is used in very short sessions and can be carried to any environment. The user must be able to retrieve necessary information—either a phone number or a short message—quickly and efficiently. Clearly, the domain of use for the pager has considerable design implications for the user interface. There is a wide range of possible domains for consumer devices. The three domains presented below cover the most relevant. Typically, an information appliance may fall into more than one of these domains. These categories are not mutually exclusive. However, the devices will tend to be used "more commonly" in one of these domain types; the user interface should be biased accordingly.

Entertainment

Information appliances used for entertainment, such as a TV-based Web browser or a game-playing device, are characterized by the following:

- Typically, these appliances will be used in a less "directed" setting compared to a PC. That is, the user is approaching the appliance with a more relaxed attitude and is more interested in a pleasant experience than in performing a specific task, such as writing a paper, completing a spreadsheet, or sending email. A game-playing device is an example of an appliance used more for fun and compelling content than for accomplishing a task.

- Use is characterized by long periods of interaction with the device (more than 30 minutes).

- Tasks are generally less structured than those performed on PCs. The user may not know exactly what sort of entertainment is of interest and may take some time to find something of interest.

- Users are likely to have varying levels of concentration and attention during the interaction. The tasks are such that interruptions (from the environment or even the content itself) are possible.

- Generally, interaction occurs in a relaxed, comfortable, and low-stress environment such as the living room. The relaxed nature of the interaction characterizes both the setting and the user's attitude.

These characteristics have several design implications for the user interface:

- Interaction with the content is more important than any other factor. Devote as much input/output bandwidth as possible to viewing, hearing, and interacting with the content.

- The human interface for the device (e.g., browser controls) should interfere as little as possible with the content.

- Task completion time is not a critical factor; the user is not under significant time pressure. Therefore, a pleasant experience is always preferred to an efficient one.

- Note: efficiency is a positive attribute of any system and should be sought after in user interface design as well. However, in the entertainment domain a pleasant and compelling experience is as important as efficiency. Above all, predictability is more important than efficiency.

Information Access and Communication

Consumer devices used for information access and communication, such as an Internet-enabled screen phone or PDA, are quite different from those of the entertainment domain. In particular, users of these devices will concentrate on getting a specific task accomplished quickly, such as creating a calendar appointment or finding a phone number. In fact, usage of these devices may be on a "one task at a time" basis; that is, the user may go to the device (or turn it on) just to perform quick information access or a communication task. Devices in this domain are characterized by the following:

- Users of these devices will be directed and goal oriented. The user is interested in performing a specific task rather than using the device for entertainment. For instance, the user of an Internet screen phone must be able to find the phone number of a restaurant, call, and make reservations.

- Interaction with the device is typically short (less than 10 minutes).

- Users are likely to concentrate on the task while using such devices. Interruptions are still possible, but not as likely as in the entertainment domain. Also, interruptions are more likely to be task relevant, such as receiving a phone call while trying to look up an address book entry.

- Tasks are typically structured and directed. As opposed to interaction with entertainment-oriented devices, users will be motivated to complete a specific task. For instance, the user may need to send an email to his brother to ask about a party. That is the main purpose of the interaction with the device; the user wants the experience to be quick, efficient, and easy.

The design implications for the information access and communication domain include the following:

- Ease of learning and long-term ease of use are more important than any other factor because the user must be able to get tasks done quickly and efficiently.

- Task completion time may be a critical factor. While the users are not concerned about a few extra seconds in performing a task, they are also not interested in spending much time to, say, send a simple email. Tasks should be designed to be accomplished efficiently.

TABLE **2.2**

Characteristics of each target domain and the associated design implications.

Domain	Characteristics	Example Design Implications
Entertainment	1. Long interactions (> 30 minutes) 2. Less structured interaction (versus PC) 3. Not very "directed" tasks 4. More relaxed interaction 5. Various levels of concentration	1. Content is critical so devote significant I/O bandwidth to content. 2. Pleasant experience preferred to efficient one.
Information access and communication	1. Short interactions (< 10 minutes) 2. Structured interaction (versus entertainment) 3. Usually "directed" tasks 4. Various levels of concentration	1. Ease of learning and long-term use are critical. 2. Efficiency can be a key feature of the UI.
Assistant devices	Similar to information access and communication	Similar to information access and communication

Assistant Devices

Assistant devices are appliances dedicated to helping a user perform very specific tasks. Examples include

- A handheld tour guide device for museum patrons

- A device for a waiter to take orders

- A device to help an assembly line supervisor debug a problem

- A device to help delivery personnel collect information on the delivery/pickup schedules, plan the best route from one location to another, and so on

For the most part, the characteristics and design implications of the assistant devices domain are similar to those of the information access and communication domain (see Table 2.2).

Dedicated Devices Mean Dedicated User Interfaces

Consumer products use input and output methods optimized for particular uses. A PDA might use a pen to allow handwriting recognition and touch input. A screen phone may have a keyboard for text input, while a cellular phone may use the number pad. Additionally, the functions available on the

FIGURE **2.1**

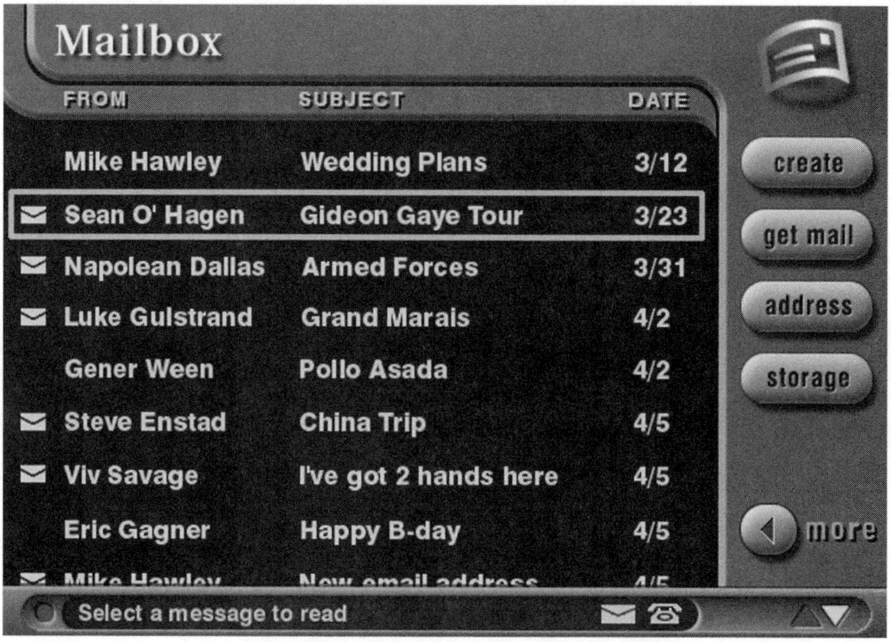

A sample inbox screen from an email application running on a TV set-top box.

devices are tailored to the needs of each device. TVs may have a dedicated electronic program guide (EPG), and a PDA may have an address book and calendar.

The market focus, user tasks, and product requirements for a consumer product should drive the user interface design for the product. This results in a user interface that is cleanly integrated with the applications, I/O, and other characteristics of the system. This tight focus and high level of integration work to the advantage of the user in consumer products because all components have been designed to work well together.

The tight focus also means the user interface may vary from one product to another. This variation can be true even for the same software application deployed on different hardware platforms. For example, consider an email application that must run on a TV set-top box and a PDA. In the case of the set-top box, the application will appear on a color TV screen (at roughly 640 × 444 resolution for an NTSC signal), and the user interacts with the product using a remote control. For the PDA, the application will appear on an integrated 160 × 120 monochrome LCD screen. The user interacts with the product using a touch overlay. Clearly, the display size and color differences, as

FIGURE **2.2**

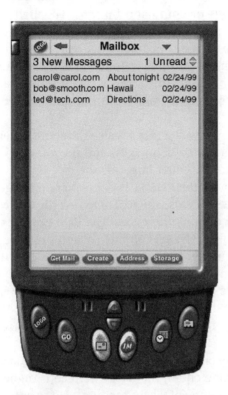

*An inbox screen on a PDA device. This screen is functionally
identical to that shown in Figure 2.1, but the user interface
is altered to meet the requirements of the device.*

well as the differences in input mechanisms, will have significant impact on
the user interfaces for the two products. Figure 2.1 (see also Color Plate)
shows an email inbox screen on a TV set-top box. Figure 2.2 (see also Color
Plate) shows a functionally identical screen on a PDA device. While the two
figures are similar in size for the purposes of presentation, note that in actu-
ality the screen in Figure 2.1 appears on a large color television screen, while
the screen in Figure 2.2 appears on a small handheld device with a much
smaller screen.

A review of the two screens illustrates some of the contrasts in designing
the same screen for these two very different devices. Notice the difference in
layout, in particular the difference in the placement of command buttons
(e.g., Get Mail, Create). For TV usage, buttons must be on the side to allow
easy access with a remote control. With this design users must move the

highlighter (shown in Figure 2.1 on the message from Sean O'Hagen) sequentially from one target to the next; on this screen the targets are basically the email messages or command buttons. Highlighter navigation is done using a remote control that allows the highlighter to be moved on the screen and to select the currently highlighted target. Navigating to a target is a major constraint in this environment. In the PDA device, access to targets is not an issue because the PDA provides a touch screen, allowing touch-based access to any command (random input as opposed to sequential input).

Relative text size for the two screens is also different. Given the poor display quality of TV CRTs (for static images) and the viewing distance for TV usage, the text size must be fairly large for the set-top box version of the screen. On the other hand, the PDA LCD offers a crisp image, and the user will be viewing the screen at close range. Therefore, the text can be smaller.

Note also the visual design differences. The PDA provides a streamlined and "business-like" design. The set-top box version provides more whimsical and decorative elements. These differences are due to the set-top box being an "entertainment" device, while the PDA is more of an "access and communication" device. Textual elements on the PDA can be smaller, but the horizontal space on the screen must be used carefully because there is a limited amount. However, on the TV screen, horizontal space is plentiful by comparison.

While the underlying email application may be the same in both devices (perhaps exactly the same code), the user interface is dedicated and optimized for the requirements of each product. There is a long-standing approach to separating the user interface from the underlying computational side of software products. This approach, known as the model-view approach, contends that the "view" (or UI) can be divorced from the data or "model" component of an application. With this approach different views can be used with the same data set (for further discussion of this approach, see Buschman et al. 1996; Object Arts 1999).

Of course, the notion of a dedicated UI, based on the device, may violate some sensibilities regarding consistency of design. Some designers may be concerned that a dedicated UI, not shared across devices, undermines ease of learning. However, it is not practical to force a consistent user interface across devices with radically different hardware and usage characteristics. Our usability studies have shown that predictability is far more important than consistency or efficiency. The notion here is that the product should just "do the right thing." Imagine using a physical keyboard on a screen phone to create an email. This task is similar to doing the same task on a desktop computer with a keyboard. Now imagine performing the same task on a PDA. Entering text becomes a more tedious process. There are alternate solutions, such as handwriting recognition, that can be used to make the process of entering text easier. But handwriting recognition (gesture-based input) doesn't have much in common with tapping a key on a keyboard. A different user interface approach is required to manage the task on the PDA, which results in a different yet better-suited user interface.

Allocate Functions Appropriately

Being a generic computing platform, the desktop PC must offer standard I/O mechanisms. Therefore, a CRT, a standard QWERTY keyboard with function keys (F1, F2, etc.), and a mouse are the typical I/O devices. Software developers usually design their products to work with these standard PC mechanisms.

However, information appliances offer the opportunity to depart from the standard I/O of a desktop PC. Information appliances provide dedicated user interfaces tuned to the needs of the device and its users (see previous section). This dedicated interface allows product designers to build in the I/O mechanisms that best meet the requirements of the device and to create software that is well matched. Therefore, there is significant freedom as to which features will be supported in hardware, in software, or in both.

This newfound freedom places a special burden on the design. Care must be taken to ensure that features and functions are appropriately assigned (allocated) to hardware versus software. A good example for discussing function allocation is the function of launching applications. Generally, a PC allows users to launch applications using the desktop (typically by double-clicking an icon) or entering the "executable" name. This approach is sensible since the PC is designed to handle all sorts of applications. The PC manufacturer and providers of system software make no specific assumptions about how the device will be used or what applications will be needed.

On the other hand, PDA device designers can make assumptions about the applications used on the device and can support those assumptions in the design. For example, buttons can be included in the hardware to provide one-touch application launching. In this example, launching applications has been allocated to hardware. This decision is justifiable because the number of applications is limited and users need quick access to them.

While the above example is somewhat oversimplified, it is an important approach in designing information appliances. The design freedom exists to allocate functions to best meet the needs of the device and its users. These design decisions have considerable impact on the user interface.

Two of the key factors in determining function allocation are usage frequency and importance.

FIGURE **2.3**

*An example of a remote control with a number of available
functions. These functions are provided either instead of
being on the screen or in addition to what is available on
the screen.*

Frequency of Use

Tasks that users perform frequently should be assigned to very visible and
easily accessible locations in the user interface; this approach applies for
both hardware and software. The "location" may be different depending on
the type of appliance. For example, in designing a TV set-top box user interface, commands with high frequency of use may need to be represented with
physical buttons on the remote control (or IR keyboard). Figure 2.3 provides
an example of a set-top box remote control layout. While many of the functions appear on the TV screen, there are certain functions that must be available on the physical remote control as well. For instance, one-touch access
to a TV picture-in-picture (PIP) window is essential. Users will frequently
access and dismiss the PIP window (for TV viewing) and should be able to

quickly do so at any time. Associated with PIP is switching between full TV viewing and Internet functions. Users will switch between these two modes and should have easy access to this feature.

Importance of Use

Important or critical features must also be made highly available to the user. Importance and frequency of use are somewhat related, but they should be considered separately. There may be functions that are not performed frequently but are quite critical to successful use of the product. A classic example of this distinction is the installation of devices (after first-time purchase). Users of information appliances must be able to install and set up the device easily. For instance, a consumer who returns home with a new Internet-enabled screen phone should have no trouble installing the unit and connecting it to the Internet. Significant design effort must be applied to ensure the process is simple, which often entails making certain features or functions highly visible and available. Typically, users will not perform the installation task frequently (perhaps once or twice total). But successful completion of this task is extremely important for such devices.

Simplify

Simplifying user interfaces has been a prime objective for most designers. However, despite repeated attempts, the industry has been largely unsuccessful in keeping PCs and workstations simple. There are three main reasons for this increasing complexity in products:

1. Business model

2. Continual obsolescence

3. Implementation-driven design

The basic business approach to selling computing equipment and software is to offer more features, better performance, and more quality (stability, user experience, support, etc.) at a lower price than the previous product (or the competition's product). While this is an oversimplification of how the industry sells and markets, it is generally true. The result of this business approach is that products require progressively more complex user interfaces to support the additional features.

Tightly coupled with the business model is the relentless effect of continual obsolescence as a result of Moore's law—every 18 months computing prowess can be doubled. This phenomenon has driven the hardware and software industries to continually "improve" the technology. Improvement means the ability to add features and functionality that the previous technologies were unable to offer. Accordingly, older versions of products quickly become obsolete and ill equipped to handle the new product offerings and features.

Lastly, in the computing industry, there is a tendency toward implementation-driven design. This tendency is derived from a technology-centered prespective, where developers may look for a problem to solve with a collection of technologies. Often this approach leads to an unnecessarily complex product. Of course, a user-centered approach would attack the problem by first defining what users need. At a later stage the proper technologies would be identified to address the product design challenges.

These three biases must be avoided in building consumer devices. Simplification is key. There are two important dimensions to consider when trying to make products simple (or decrease complexity): the functionality versus simplicity trade-off, and the choice versus simplicity trade-off.

Functionality versus Simplicity and the Functionality Threshold

A long-standing truth in the industry is that the more functionality included in a product, the more complex it becomes (Figure 2.4). In designing information appliances, it is critical to reduce functionality to the most essential/needed functions. Consumer devices offer a unique opportunity to justifiably eliminate unneeded functionality because these devices will be targeted for a limited set of tasks and will have dedicated user interfaces. A good way to consider this trade-off in the interface design is to think of the 80/20 rule. For each application or feature set, it's helpful to identify the 20% of functions that will meet 80% of the users' task needs. Those are the functions to support in the product and around which to optimize the design. The remaining 80% of functions are proposed based on other criteria (utility, necessity, competitive edge, price, etc.), and it may be necessary to exclude most of these functions.

A second key part of this approach is to optimize the user interface around the absolutely key features in that 20% of functions in the product. User interface decisions are predicated on making that 20% of functions as accessible as possible. The design should not be driven by providing equal access to all functions. Instead designers should "relegate" some features to a secondary role in order to make the primary functions as accessible and easy to use as possible.

Clearly, gratuitous elimination of functions is not useful either. Removing too much functionality can lead to a product that is either too limited to support users' tasks or simply uncompelling. Therefore, it's important to provide

FIGURE **2.4**

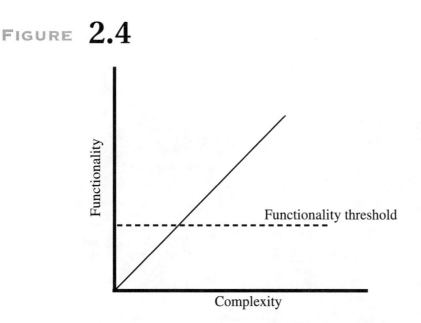

The functionality versus complexity trade-off. As more func-tionality is added to a product, the level of user interface complexity also rises. The "functionality threshold" is the concept that information appliances should limit the func-tionality to the essential few (the threshold) that provide for a compelling product without leading to unmanageable complexity.

enough functionality to have a compelling and useful product without com-plicating the user experience. We refer to that "sweet spot" as the functional-ity threshold: It is just the right collection and number of features to strike the balance between functionality and simplicity.

Choice versus Simplicity

As with functionality, a trade-off exists between simplicity and the number of choices available to a user. A simple example of this concept is the menu at the local restaurant. Say you visit the local restaurant with the intention of ordering a hamburger. In the "old" days you'd have a choice between a Hamburger, a Cheeseburger, and perhaps a SuperBurger, which was basi-cally a larger version of the Hamburger. But in today's choice-filled restau-rant you may be faced with choosing from a Hamburger, Cheeseburger, the SuperBurger, the AvocadoBurger, the Special WesternBurger, the Chef's ExtraBurger, the SlapJack Burger, the Big Daddy Burger, and the "Bring Down

FIGURE **2.5**

An example of a set-top box appliance where the user is browsing the Web and view-
ing television in a PIP window. The user can access or dismiss the PIP window by
pressing a button on the remote control.

the House" Burger! Too much choice and a complicating, perhaps overwhelming, situation.

Choice is not an inherently negative construct. Choice is useful when it is
appropriate, but information appliances can benefit from reduced choice.
This approach is contrary to traditional design practices in the industry,
where it is the norm to provide users with choices on everything from their
desktop color scheme to the "toolbars" they want in the UI. Given the
reduced functionality, targeted user population, and focused nature of these
devices, reasonable defaults can be provided and nonessential options
removed completely. An example of reasonable choice reduction is found in
the TV set-top box picture-in-picture window. Most Internet set-top boxes
allow users to watch TV in a PIP window while performing standard Internet
functions, such as browsing the Web or reading email (see Figure 2.5; see also
Color Plate). However, this PIP window is limited to being accessed and put
away—that's it! Users do not have the "choice" to move the PIP window,
select its size, or change any of its characteristics. Some set-top boxes provide slightly more choice by allowing the user to select a quadrant of the

screen where the PIP window should appear. However, the user is still limited to only one of four quadrants as opposed to positioning the window anywhere on the screen. This approach, while limited, meets the needs of the overwhelming majority of users. Simplification is achieved by removing nonessential choices from the UI. While some users may find the lack of choice limiting, the design bias is toward simplicity and supporting the most common scenarios.

Reducing choice is an approach to yield simple designs. It is more of a strategy than a rule. Clearly, there are functions and features for which users should have choices. However, we believe in limiting choices to only the essential few to reduce the complexity of the design.

Design for Responsiveness

An interesting element of designing for the consumer space is that users expect immediate and reliable responses to their inputs. Certainly, responsiveness is a positive quality of any system and is a goal in the PC domain as well. However, for the consumer audience responsiveness takes on characteristics that are unconventional from a PC perspective. The two most critical aspects of responsiveness that information appliances should support are interruptability and continuous feedback.

Interruptability

In an information appliance, almost all operations should be immediately interruptible. Users have built expectations of behavior through years of using other consumer devices, such as TVs and stereo equipment. Additionally, it's simply good design to allow the user to be in control.

Consider a PC application that has posted a dialog box to the screen asking for confirmation on a command (e.g., delete). Generally, in PCs, the user must deal with the confirmation dialog before doing anything else. This modal approach is definitely true of major system functions like shutting off the PC; the user must deal with the lingering confirmation dialog before the shutdown can proceed. On a set-top box, however, the approach should be different. With few exceptions, designers should not require users to deal with modal dialogs. If the user wants to turn off the set-top box, she should simply press the "Power" button to turn it off. The lingering dialogs or commands must be handled gracefully by the system.

Dialog boxes on a screen phone provide another example (Figure 2.6; see also Color Plate). Most screen phones have a touch screen, allowing users to make inputs with their fingers or a stylus. Consider a situation where a dia-

FIGURE **2.6**

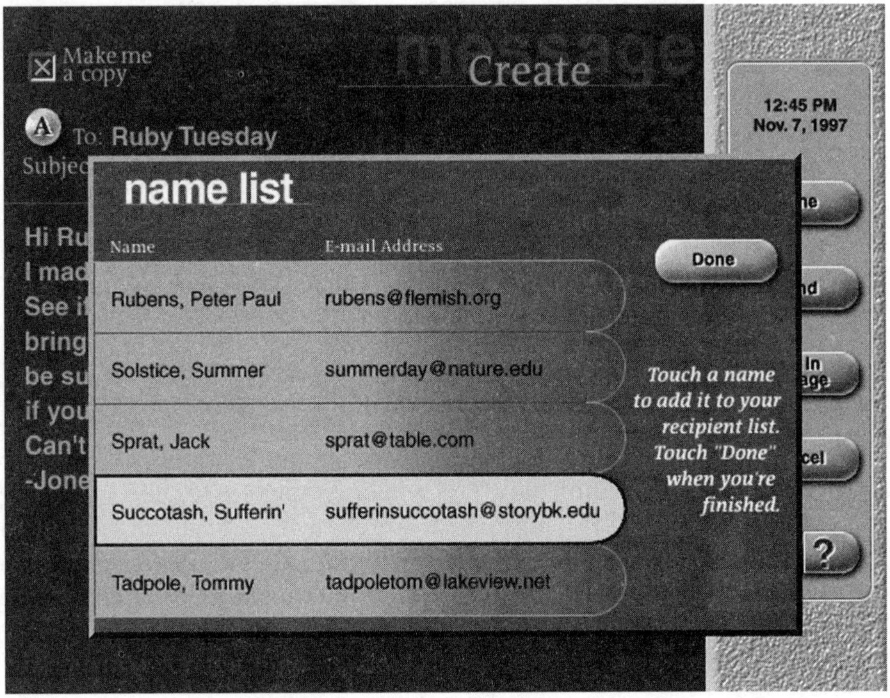

Sample screen from an Internet-enabled screen phone. The screen is an email compo-sition screen, and a dialog box has appeared over the top (based on the user's input). With a touch screen device, it is possible for the user to dismiss this dialog by pressing the "Done" button in the dialog or by simply touching anywhere outside the dialog.

log box has been posted to the screen asking the user for confirmation on an action or simply providing information. A button exists inside the dialog box that the user can touch to dismiss the dialog; this user interface is essentially identical to that of a PC. However, in a touch environment (and with information appliances) it is best to allow for additional mechanisms for interrupting or dismissing the dialog. For instance, touching anywhere outside the dialog can be treated as a dismiss command. This approach provides a solution that presents the product as responsive. Certainly, there may be situations where the user did not intend to dismiss the dialog. However, the product behavior is biased toward the most common cases.

Continuous Feedback

Information appliances should respond continuously so users are confident that their inputs are being processed. However, with these devices, feedback takes on added meaning beyond the typical audiovisual feedback for user inputs and becomes more task related.

Users should have feedback and progress indication even while the product is functioning normally (or as designed). For instance, in usability testing a screen phone, we found that users needed feedback that mail had been sent successfully. Clearly, receiving this type of feedback on a desktop system would be annoying, but computer-novice screen phone users seemed lost without it. Therefore, users of these devices need continuous, unobtrusive feedback about their progress with the device, even when activities are going well!

Of course, many of the feedback principles from the PC domain apply in the information appliance arena as well. For instance, where possible, delays should always be minimized. It is important to provide appropriate feedback in cases where completion of an operation is delayed, for example, when downloading information. Displaying an animated indicator, preferably one that shows how the operation is progressing, is crucial; a static status message is not adequate for such situations. Providing dynamic, live feedback to the user during any operational delays keeps the user engaged and ensures they don't mistakenly perceive the system to be broken. Anecdotal evidence shows that people will perceive a product to be faster if it continues to show activity as opposed to not providing feedback until the operation is done.

Responsiveness starts with feedback but goes further, to "intelligent" responses. For activities that users perform frequently, the product should respond in a way that makes the experience easier for the user. An example of this intelligent responsiveness can be seen in some car navigation systems. When the user starts to enter an address to receive directions, the system turns off the keys on the on-screen keyboard that do not map to real addresses. This helps the user be more accurate in entering addresses and makes the task quicker to complete.

Generally speaking, if products are not perceived to be responsive, users can become annoyed with the product, often repeatedly pressing buttons, and/or assuming the device is broken. When users become frustrated, they stop using a device, or worse, return it to the store.

Summary

The five design considerations discussed above provide a good overview of the design approach we have found successful for information appliances. Some of the considerations are novel, such as the new approach to simplicity. Others are a new twist on a familiar UI design tenet, such as responsiveness. All of the design considerations are extremely helpful in approaching the practical design of information appliances.

2.3 A Proliferation of Wildly Different Interfaces?

If information appliances are successful and ubiquitous, as many predict they will be, then an interesting question arises: Will the proliferation of appliances lead to a proliferation of wildly different user interfaces?

The answer is: probably not. With any new technology/product, new UIs are inevitable. Take a simple example like a wine bottle opener. Initially, there were a variety of tools available for uncorking wine bottles. However, over time users of these devices settled on the one or two interfaces that work best. There is one corkscrew that seems to be the overwhelming choice of waiters and waitresses the world over, despite the variety of available alternatives. One corkscrew mechanism has emerged as the leader because it offers the best usability while meeting all the necessary requirements.

A similar "settling of the dust" will occur with information appliances. Initially, a variety of user interfaces and features will be available on a multitude of devices. However, over time, many of the devices will fail. Of the devices that succeed, only a limited number of user interfaces will remain viable for each device. For any given class of device, a particular approach will be accepted or followed as a de facto standard.

Additionally, there are certain user interface mechanisms that have proven to be successful across different devices and products. For instance, selecting items from lists, pressing buttons, and progress indicators are UI elements that seem to work well universally. There is no logical reason to reinvent mechanisms that users understand and can easily use in different devices. Therefore, these items will likely become standard parts of most cross-device user interfaces.

Note that this process of de facto standardization does not necessarily guarantee a usable or high-quality user interface. In the past, poor interfaces or user interface environments have been accepted as "standard." Hypertext Markup Language (HTML) is a perfect example. HTML became popular and an accepted standard in the early 1990s despite the fact that it did not support many of the rich features available in the user interface technologies of the time. But HTML did offer one very compelling feature: cross-platform access to the same content. Therefore, this one compelling feature drove standardization of content around HTML despite its shortcomings.

Some standardization is already taking place in the information appliance design space. For instance, consider the input mechanisms in TV-based user interfaces, such as those for Internet-enabled set-top boxes. Early versions of set-top boxes provided either a pointer (cursor) or a rectangular highlighter on the screen. The user would then use arrow keys on a remote control or another physical input device to manipulate the on-screen element. The pointer behaved much like a pointer on a PC. The user could move the pointer to any location on the screen (using the input device) and press a button to make a selection (click). Conversely, the rectangular highlighter moved in discrete steps from one "hot spot" (or target) to the next. While the pointer approach provided more flexibility, the highlighter solution has proven easier to learn and use for consumers without much computer experience. This fact is especially true given that arrow keys are used to manipulate the element on the screen. Users found the highlighter to be extremely simple to manipulate (using remote control arrow keys), and its behavior highly predictable—not necessarily efficient, but very predictable. Most TV-based user interfaces now use some version of a discrete, step-by-step input as opposed to a random input (like that of a pointer on a PC). Therefore, while many different TV-based products have been produced recently, their basic approach to navigating a screen is not substantially different.

Clearly, as content accessed and used on TVs becomes richer and more interactive, the input mechanisms may need to be enhanced as well. For instance, the highlighter approach may be too limited for the day when all the neighborhood kids are playing networked interactive games on their television sets. However, with the types of content and bandwidth currently available on set-top boxes (from Internet to satellite boxes), the highlighter approach is practical.

2.4 General versus Specific Trade-off

As mentioned in the section on simplification, designers of information appliances must strike a tenuous balance between offering a product that is simple enough to use, but functional enough to be useful. This balance or "functionality threshold" may be different for various classes of users even with the same device. The benefit of information appliances is in their dedication to a narrow range of tasks. However, picking that range of tasks and providing the appropriate compelling solution is difficult. There are two potential disadvantages in building devices that are too specific:

- The devices may be too limited to be useful or compelling.

- Assuming the devices are useful, users may need to own many such devices for various domains (collection of tasks), which may be unwieldy.

On the other hand, making a device overly general will have the following disadvantages:

- It can lead to a product that is too complex.

- It may yield a product that doesn't appropriately meet the task needs of users.

Consider the example of a personal digital assistant. Generally, PDAs include applications such as an address book, "to do" list, calendar, and notes, among a handful of others. This collection of features/applications is sufficient for many users. But there are users who would benefit from having a telephone integrated into the PDA to allow for real-time voice communication. Additionally, there is a collection of users who would like email.

Now the originally simple PDA has taken on new telephony and email functions. Certainly, each of these in isolation is not a complicated application, but once they are brought together on the same platform a number of complexities are introduced. For instance, the issues associated with managing a wireless connection to collect and send email can have a significant impact on the complexity of the user experience. Also, such a complex product will no longer meet the more practical needs of the users who needed only the original PDA functionality. Of course, in practice, product lines are created to provide different versions of a product to meet the needs of a diverse user base.

Interestingly, this issue of general versus specific can be seen in the "traditional" appliances as well. In some cases appliances become too complex, and in other cases the functionality is inappropriate. For instance, the only purpose of a microwave oven is to heat food. However, there are various models of microwave oven, some of which provide a number of features and functions. These high-end microwave ovens can become so complex that users can't easily determine how to simply heat a dishful of food. Moreover, most users end up drawing on only a limited subset of the myriad functions.

Or consider the case of the combination VCR/TV products. This product was envisioned as a convenient combination of two solid consumer electronics products. However, the VCR/TV has found limited success, largely because, to keep cost and size down, the TVs in the product are not high quality enough to be used regularly and the VCR can't easily be connected to other TVs. Therefore, this more feature-rich product doesn't meet the real needs of users.

Some amount of consolidation of information appliances will occur naturally. As the market for these devices matures, product designers will have a better understanding of the collection of tasks people prefer to perform on, say, a TV as opposed to a screen phone. It will also become more clear as to which types of tasks need to be performed together and which collections of functions and features best support these tasks. However, care should be taken not to create hybrid devices that do too much and are so complex that they are useless to the consumer.

2.5 Conclusions and Implications

There is a third industry that has not been addressed in this chapter: service and content providers. Much of what users want to do with these devices (and therefore their tasks) will be determined by the type of content available on a device. The technology and user interface for information appliances will be driven by the nature of the services and content. It is important to view an information appliance as the work of a triumvirate: manufacturers, technology providers, and content/service providers. In some cases one company may perform the role of two of the parties, but the key components are still the same. To scope these discussions, we have taken a largely device-based view of the user interface challenges. However, content and services will also be factors in this space.

Information appliances provide an opportunity for new, ground-breaking user interface work. The application of computing technology and the traditional notion of appliances to small consumer devices are an exciting challenge for both the computer and consumer electronics industries. Clearly, most of the user-centered design approaches and tools that have matured over the past 20 years of research and practice still apply in this domain. However, information appliances will challenge two very different industries to converge in many areas. User interface and usability will be key components for the products and services resulting from this convergence.

2.6 References

AllNetDevices. 1999. Latest net device news and analysis [online]. Available: *www.allnetdevices.com* (accessed June 7, 1999).

Buschman, F., R. Meunier, H. Rohnert, P. Sommerland, and M. Stal. 1996. *Pattern-Oriented Software Architecture: A System of Patterns*. Boston: John Wiley and Sons.

Computer Industry Almanac, Inc. 1998. Nearly 600 million computers-in-use in year 2000 [online]. Available: *www.c-i-a.com/19981103.htm* (accessed June 7, 1999).

Object Arts, Ltd. 1999. Model view controller [online]. Available: *www.object-arts.com/EducationCentre/Overviews/MVC.htm* (accessed June 8, 1999).

CHAPTER Three

Designing Internet Appliances at Netpliance

SCOTT ISENSEE
BMC Software

KEN KALINOSKI
Netpliance, Inc.

KARL VOCHATZER
Netpliance, Inc.

3.1 Introduction

In early 1999, Netpliance, Inc. formed on the belief that the time is ripe for Internet appliances. The premise of the company is that a huge shift is about to occur in the world of the Internet. The drumbeat of the shift is expected to be more than just new communication speeds (Broadband, Internet2, etc.) and new content feeds (XML). The sound of this drumbeat is coming from the onslaught of a whole new generation of viewers who are lining up to join the digital lifestyle on "The Net." The benefits of a digital lifestyle are attracting new users who do not tolerate technology-centric products that are difficult to master. In order to make the Internet ready for the wave of new users, we believe that a new approach must commence that is focused on human factors and user-centered design. Netpliance is helping to pioneer a new way for "all of us" to get online by building a company from the ground up and focusing on learnability, usability, and affordability. As an Internet appliance service provider, Netpliance is providing the user community with the ability to access their information from anywhere and to have one universal information repository (Prism) that will extend the usefulness of their information appliances.

This chapter provides a case study of the design and development of the Netpliance i-opener—a small, countertop information appliance that supports electronic mail, categorized content (e.g., news, weather, sports, etc.), and Web browsing. We discuss the user-centered design process under which the i-opener was developed.

Market Situation

By mid-1999, the shift of the Internet from public to private sectors had resulted in the number of Web sites doubling every 100 days. Usage of the Internet by government, education, and now industry has redefined public access and introduced entirely new ways to work, live, play, learn, and conduct commerce. We believe that the next Internet wave will be the introduction of new consumer and business services inextricably linked to information appliances. These services will be delivered through new devices with specialized functions that use the Internet to access information and communicate with other devices. Market analysts predict this market will grow to 150 million units, or $15 billion by 2002. The proliferation of Internet appliances is expected to increase the average Internet usage time from less than 30 hours a month to over 70 hours a month in that same time period. Through the specialized tasks, these new devices will differ greatly in their capabilities and processing attributes.

In parallel, access speeds to the Internet are in a state of flux as broadband speeds of up to 7 Mbps through cable modems and xDSL connections begin to displace traditional 28.8 and 56.6 Kbps modem technology. Removal of the "last mile" bottleneck will soon enable much richer types of content that will transform entertainment, communication, education, and other industries beyond imagination. Today's modest deployments of DSL and cable modem access will soon be overcome by the aggressive rollout plans from providers such as Time Warner, TCI, US WEST, SBC, and others. User demand for "always-on, high-speed" service will result in an entirely new set of multimedia services to the home. Finally, wireless access will allow people to always be "connected" and to expect instant and continuous access to their information regardless of proximity. Information and communications will be fully integrated into people's daily routine. The anticipated introduction, adoption, and convergence of these new information and communication services over the Internet create a need for a vehicle designed to support the aggregation and delivery of this "New World."

Total User Experience

Currently in 1999, approximately 50% of the households in the United States don't have a computer. Surveys show the primary inhibitors to computer purchase are ease of use and price. Computer manufacturers are making great strides in reducing price, but to make significant progress simplifying usage requires radical change. However, the need to support legacy standards makes radical change difficult. The industry has evolved to support a model where no one company builds all of a product. Current personal computers are a conglomeration of hardware, software, and services from multiple companies with poor coordination between the partners. To buy a computer and browse the Web, a typical experience might be to go to a CompUSA store, buy a computer branded by Compaq with a Microsoft operating system, install a browser from Netscape, contract an ISP like Mindspring, and visit Web sites designed by a multitude of companies. A problem with any of these components or the interactions between them will cause difficulties for the user. For many consumers, the difficulties exceed the perceived benefits of a computer.

Internet appliance developers have concluded that the best approach is to start over. Rather than trying to increase the usability of general-purpose computers, they are building devices that have more limited functionality and are designed from the ground up for ease of use. They are following the lead of other consumer appliances in which the user just takes it home, plugs it in, and uses it. There is no need for installing software, configuring, taking training classes, reading lengthy user manuals, and so on.

At Netpliance, we are focused on the total user experience. Everything that the user experiences, from the ordering process, to using the device, through connecting to the Internet, is designed to work together seamlessly and to be simple and convenient. Everything is supplied by us or by our business partners working to our specifications. For the user, this means that they call one company, Netpliance, for any need they may have regarding their device, Internet access, and services.

Tailored UI

In order to satisfy the onslaught of new services and devices, information delivered via the Internet should be formatted and presented in many new ways. Device capabilities such as information rendering, processing, and communication should differ according to their target application. These will range from simple beeperlike devices with tiny screens and low-speed wireless connections, to handheld communicators with small screens and asynchronous communication capabilities, on up to high-end home entertainment systems with large screens, high processing power, and broadband communications links. The traditional HTML content that proliferates across the Web today (targeted to conventional PCs with an 800×600 resolution monitor and connected over a slow 28.8–56.6 Kbps modem) will change. The content will have to match the requirements of the new services and the corresponding device and connectivity capabilities. Netpliance reformats content to serve a range of devices, as shown in Figure 3.1.

3.2   Flexibility Begins Early and Continues through Product Ship

The Web is a dynamic, evolving environment, and the product development process must accommodate quick changes in direction.

Rapid, Iterative Development

The Netpliance development formula was built on the Rapid Application Development (RAD) model. The key leverage point that allows Netpliance to develop systems from concept to delivery in seven months was this strong,

IGURE **3.1**

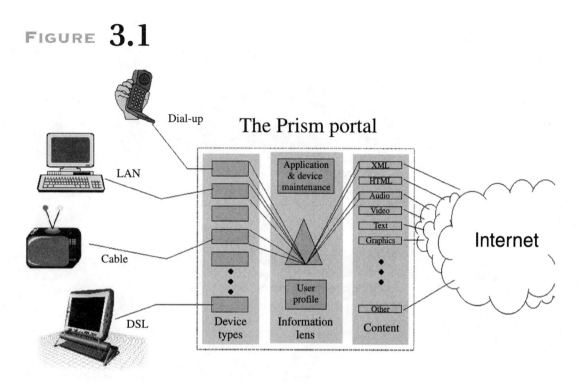

Reformatting Internet data for various devices via Prism.

iterative design and development model. Unlike the traditional waterfall approach, where requirements are well defined, designs are laid out along well-defined architectural system flows, and code and test follow in lock step, a more radical approach was employed along the rapid, yet iterative (spiral) development model (Figure 3.2). In this scenario, senior software engineers crafted the system architecture on the whiteboard, and pieces of the system were broken down against client functions and server functions. For functions that crossed boundaries, a single, seasoned, senior engineer was placed in charge of the entire task. Communication between team members was key, and thus, for pieces of the system that crossed client/server boundaries, those elements were strictly developed by single individuals.

After several days of revising the architecture and designing data and control flows, the development team would regroup to perform a team review of the system design. The actual code development was iterated very rapidly with weekly feedback from internal and external users during the final four months of the development cycle. Typical components were

FIGURE **3.2**

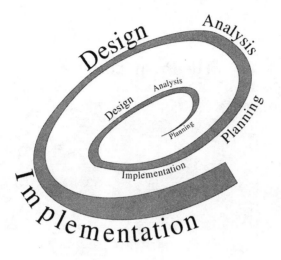

The spiral model of development.

iterated with no less than four revisions, with many iterating upwards to a dozen cycles.

Content "Munging"

Content provided on the i-opener has a simple and consistent user interface style. The information comes from many sources and is "munged."

The verb "munge" refers to the action of processing content information to suit the tastes, requirements, and device limitations of a particular customer with a particular device. Various content providers supply Netpliance with content. This content is formatted and cached by Netpliance. When a client device requests some content (or an external event or time schedule demands that content be provided to the user), the content is pulled from the store, personalized, transcoded, and passed to the device.

Its important that all content is stored in a flexible, consistent, and well-defined format. Since XML (eXtensible Markup Language) meets these requirements, it is used as the format for all content. A large cache is created and content is translated to a standard Netpliance XML format. Each different type of content is stored along with a document type definition, which is a definition to allow real-time processing of the information into a prescribed format and page layout.

Personalization

Personalization is the process of refining the content to best suit a particular user. One user may care about the weather in Austin, Texas, while another user cares about the weather in New York City. Yet another user may be interested in news stories with an international flair, while others prefer local news and headlines.

Content presented to a client may be personalized in three basic ways: content may be included in the presentation based on the preferences of the client, it may be excluded, or it may be sorted. When a request for content is received, the software needs to decide what to include, what to exclude, and in what order the information is presented to the user.

Personalization is performed using a user profile. User profiles are the aggregate of two types of parameters, explicit and implicit. The user states explicit parameters as they fill out forms when they sign up for service or when they fill out subsequent preference forms. Implicit parameters are set by observing the behavior and habits of the user. These are compared to the behavior and patterns of other users.

Transcoding

Transcoding is the process of translating content to adjust it to the characteristics of the target device. It makes no sense, for example, to send an HTML page to a pager unmodified. One device may be able to display JPEG images, while another may not. Some devices have audio capability, while others do not.

Most content can be presented in more than one form. A large picture, for example, may be scaled down to fit the display of a small handheld device. A device that only displays text can't show an image, but it can show the caption that goes with the image. An MP3 player will likely be able to provide pristine audio, yet it will not be able to display the lyrics synchronized to the music.

3.3 Product Design Process

The product design process—from product definition to design implementation—is user centered.

Defining User Requirements

Defining user requirements in a new field is a difficult task. Customers who have owned a particular type of product have many opinions about what they need when buying another. In a new product category, however, it can be difficult for customers to know exactly what they want or whether they would buy anything at all.

Despite the difficulties, this is a critical task. Many new products fail because they have not met user needs. It is common for products to be used in ways the designers never intended. For example, the telephone was predicted to be a device for broadcasting news in the public square. It wasn't designed as a person-to-person communication device, which is where it turned out to be most popular.

A well-defined set of user requirements and market demographics did not exist for the Internet appliance space. There are known market demographics for PC users, as well as information from PC usability studies, that document the breakdown in user satisfaction with their current PCs. This information was our starting point. Netpliance employed focus group studies and surveys to understand customer requirements. These efforts were led by the marketing organization with close involvement by the user interface design team. The developers were invited to witness the focus groups so they could better understand the users for which they were building the product. Most development team members had a background in the computer industry, and it was important that they understand the target audience. It is always tempting for developers to create products they would want to use or similar to what they have done before. However, in the Internet appliance space, it was essential to develop for a new audience that desires a simpler product than the computer industry has previously provided.

Research

We started by researching the market opportunity and also the findings from other related products. The book *The Invisible Computer* (Norman 1998) was instrumental in confirming that computers are too difficult to use and that simple information appliances can address a significant, unmet need in the marketplace.

Our research indicated that people who have not previously purchased computers might be reluctant to purchase an Internet appliance without the help of more knowledgeable associates, referred to as "Recommenders." We defined Recommenders as those who keep up with and use the latest technologies and products. We formed the hypothesis that our targeted "New Users" would rely on these Recommenders in deciding whether or not to buy a Netpliance product. If the hypothesis were true, this meant that our advertising would need to reach and persuade both the New Users and the Recommenders.

Focus Groups

We worked with a market research firm to test our hypotheses and gather user feedback on our plans and prototypes. Forty people participated in the focus groups. Half of them were selected to meet the profile of the New Users, and half were selected to meet the profile of the Recommenders. They were asked questions about what they wanted in an Internet product and what they thought of various product and service offerings that we described.

Participants indicated a preference for a wireless, mobile device, although many also thought they would be interested in a countertop device at a lower price point. They wanted the device to have a small footprint and to be able to store the keyboard under the display. They preferred neutral colors that would fit into any part of any home, but also indicated it would be nice to have a choice of colors or to be able to customize the appearance much like cellular phones are often customized with snap-on covers.

Among the service level options presented, there was a clear preference for unlimited, anytime access even if this were to cost more. Other areas of high importance were unlimited Internet access, electronic mail, ready to go out of the box, extremely easy to use, and affordability.

One of the dangers of focus groups is the potential to be misled by a small number of people who may not be representative of the target market. We addressed this problem by conducting a subsequent telephone survey and through including members of the target audience in the early conceptual design phases. In other words, the focus group provided us with qualitative information for the initial direction, while the subsequent activities provided more quantitative information for making design decisions.

Survey

Two hundred people from throughout the United States who did not currently have a computer in their home were surveyed by telephone. The survey verified that there was a substantial market for Internet appliances and identified the demographic categories most likely to purchase them. The top three functions respondents wanted in an Internet appliance were Web browsing, email, and chat. Their top three requirements were ready to go out of the box, low cost, and ease of use.

Design

Design is the phase where user requirements get translated into a product that meets those requirements.

The 80/20 Rule

There is a well-known rule of thumb that says 20% of the functions of a product are used 80% of the time. Most products get weighted down with infrequently used functions. These extra functions complicate the user interface so that even the frequently used functions are more difficult than they need to be.

Our approach is to simplify. Just provide the fundamentals. Include the key features that the users want and need to accomplish their task, then execute them well.

Multidisciplinary Teamwork

The primary determinant of the success of a project is the quality of the people on the development team (Boehm 1988). A project may seem to fail due to any number of external factors, but these often turn out to be secondary effects. Good people manage the forces outside the team, pick the right tools, and develop good products.

Technology products should be designed by teams because the work involved exceeds the time and talents of a single individual (Collins 1995). Many different skills are needed to design a successful information appliance. Our design team included programmers with varying specialties, hardware engineers, user interface designers, marketing specialists, test specialists, industrial designers, and visual designers. Most important of all, users were involved in the design process. We regularly sought user input to verify our assumptions and help us to make trade-off decisions.

There were no artificial barriers among the disciplines and nothing was thrown over a wall. All parties in the design process sought input from other disciplines when making decisions.

FIGURE **3.3**

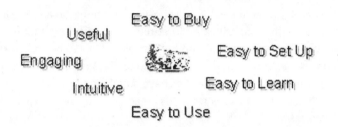

The total user experience.

Designing from the Outside In

It is all too common for technology products to be designed from the inside out. In other words, a technology is chosen or developed and then a user interface is added onto it. This is like putting in plumbing and then designing a house around it.

Even though the design and development cycles were extremely aggressive, we managed to design from the outside in rather than the other way around. The approach was based on user-centric processes rather than a technology-centric approach of wrapping an interface around a new or existing technology. In other words, a user interface was designed to meet the user requirements, and then the hardware and software were developed to fit that user interface. We designed the total user experience (Figure 3.3) for ease of use.

Communicating the Design

Even when a design team works closely together, there should be a way of documenting the design. This ensures that all team members share the same vision and that design decisions are recorded and followed. Most design work took place on whiteboards with small groups being pulled together dynamically to make specific decisions. We wrote a product specification, but in keeping with our fast, lean development process, this was a minimalist document. The text was terse and the illustrations were often hand sketches. The spec evolved into low-fidelity prototypes and then quick-turn development. We did frequent quick iterations of each component of the product.

We also found that usage scenarios helped the team to understand how the system should work from an end-user perspective. Here is an example of a usage scenario:

> Betty is 55 years old and has never used a computer before. She lives in Dallas and wants to communicate more frequently with her children—Bob in Los Angeles and Susan in Pittsburgh. Betty would like to be able to send email to the kids and browse the Web. She has seen the Netpliance i-opener advertisements, and several of her friends have bought it. She calls Bob for advice, and he tells her that the reviews he has read say the i-opener is convenient and easy to use.

> Betty decides to purchase the Netpliance i-opener and calls the 800 sales number. The cheery sales representative tells her about the device and service options. She orders it with a color inkjet printer. She provides credit card and shipping information and then is told the system will be on her doorstep within the next couple of days. They tell her about a Web site where Bob can fill in the address book entries for her.

> The i-opener arrives two days later as indicated. Betty opens the box. There is an instruction sheet on top with six pictures. This looks easy! She pulls the i-opener out of the box and finds it surprisingly lightweight. It lifts out as one unit. She removes the tape that holds the keyboard and cables in place. Betty plugs the power cord and phone cord into their outlets. She presses the power-on button and the unit comes to life in a few seconds.

> The i-opener provides a short navigation tour that explains the basics of using it. After viewing the tour, Betty is prompted to choose a member name and password. She chooses Betty as the member name. The i-opener informs her that Betty is not a unique name and suggests alternatives she may want to choose from: BettySmith or BSmith. She chooses BettySmith and the i-opener informs here that her user name has been registered and that her email address will be "bettysmith@Netpliance.net". This information is automatically entered into her address book.

> Betty now sees the i-opener user interface that was explained to her in the tutorial. She browses through information on health and shopping. By the end of the day, Betty has sent emails and has been off exploring the Web.

Implementation

Implementation is iterative and fast paced.

Achieving the impossible schedule

Getting to market quickly is always important for technology products. We had the additional impetus of needing to get products on the market for the Christmas shopping season and establishing a market presence before a host of competitors started to stake out territory.

We established a very aggressive—some said impossible—development schedule. To meet this schedule, we closely monitored project milestones. Development proceeded in a tight loop of implementation and testing.

We hired very dedicated and motivated staff who worked incredible hours for the opportunity to change the world. We supplemented this in-house staff with contractors and consultants who had specific skills needed at particular times.

Testing

Testing is essential to catch problems early. Large companies can often recover from an initial product failure, but for a startup, failure would probably be fatal.

Alpha and Beta. You learn a tremendous amount when you put your product in the hands of users. It also drives the development team because they have, in effect, many interim product deliveries rather than just one big one at the end of implementation. We scheduled two alpha tests and a beta to get three opportunities to put our product in the hands of ever-larger groups of users. The first alpha tested key parts of our software on someone else's hardware. The second alpha tested the entire set of software components. The beta test married our software and hardware.

Eating Our Own Dog Food (Woof!). Using your own product gives a developer a first-hand view of its flaws. It also provides much motivation for improvements. We provided access to alpha and beta systems to all development personnel and some of their family members as well. It was quite surprising to find how much the developers pushed for improvements in the overall usability of the system—something that doesn't always happen in many companies.

Usability Tests. Alpha and beta tests give much valuable feedback, but don't produce fine-grained measurements. Users often forget about problems they encountered or blame themselves rather than the system. When they have a problem, they often don't have insight into why the problem occurred or how it can be fixed. We conducted rapid usability evaluations to find and fix usability problems in the design and implementation.

Most of the tests were small, one- to five-person evaluations. Occasionally we needed larger samples to answer questions where there was high variability in responses, and we were able to do this quickly by going places where groups of people are available for feedback.

Data Collection from the Product in the Field. Automated data collection is an easy way to collect large amounts of data with great precision. We instrumented our system starting in the beta test so that we could count the number of times a particular functionality was used. That gave us data to prioritize remaining functions and to eliminate those that were infrequently used in order to simplify the interface.

After the product ships we will be able to monitor how our product is used. This data is aggregated across customers to ensure individual privacy. We will be able to prune away content that is infrequently accessed on our content pages and replace that with more popular content to improve the usefulness of the product and make better use of available device memory. We will also use nonintrusive methods of gathering additional feedback from our users to improve our service offering and to provide a higher level of personalization over time.

3.4 Hardware

Hardware is an allover design by Netpliance.

Creating an Appliance

Our user requirements activities showed us that users wanted information appliances that are easy to use and inexpensive. The hardware needed to be much easier to use than a traditional computer, and the design had to convey this to customers.

Some of the important characteristics we identified were

- Instant on

- Small footprint

- Sleek, attractive appearance and differentiated from a PC

- Easy navigation device

- High-quality display

- Expandability

- Portability

- Low cost

To meet the low-cost requirement and to get to market more quickly, we decided to develop a countertop model at a very low price point. Our follow-up product would be a cordless model that was more deluxe.

The hardware design evolved through many iterations as we explored various design trade-offs, feedback from our users, and as new requirements came in from marketing research.

From Sketch to Picture to Model to Product

The design was prototyped in increasingly higher fidelity as the project progressed using techniques described by Isensee and Rudd (1996). The design continually evolved (Figure 3.4), and we explored many alternatives, trying to balance competing requirements. Usability of the product was our primary requirement, but it had to be balanced against cost, resources, manufacturing considerations, and, of course, time to market.

At first, we worked with hand sketches as we brainstormed and went through many design alternatives. The most promising sketches were rendered as color pictures created with a 3D modeling program. These realistic pictures were shown in focus groups and other feedback sessions to get user feedback on them. The winning design was turned into a 3D model where people could see the actual size and color; they could also feel the texture and weight. Later, our manufacturing partner turned out small quantities of sample units that were fully functional (Figure 3.5; see also Color Plate). These were used for usability, beta, system, and quality assurance testing as well as for demonstration purposes by the marketing team.

3.5 Software

The software is designed for ease of use.

FIGURE **3.4**

A sample of variations in design of the device that were explored.

User Interface

We were targeting a market that does not currently own, use, or feel at all comfortable with personal computers. To succeed in this market, we had to abandon the overhead that comes with a PC. To the uninitiated computer user, the PC connotes bulkiness in size; complexity with cables, cards, cords, and sockets; and user interfaces that don't match up well to the real-world tasks they are supposed to assist.

We not only had to eliminate some of the exposed hardware, but we also knew that we had to abandon the traditional desktop metaphor of a

Windows operating system and the sophisticated graphical user interface controls that come with it. Given that our target users are intimidated by personal computers, and since most of them have never used PCs before, we didn't want to overwhelm them with elaborate or sophisticated graphical controls in a myriad of discrepant applications that PC users have learned to take for granted over the years. Of course, it's only fair to point out that Netpliance has the luxury of controlling the scope of our hardware and software, unlike most of the standard hardware and software vendors for current PCs, since we supply both the hardware and the software.

FIGURE **3.5**

A nearly complete industrial design of the i-opener hardware.

Start Simple, Then Make It Simpler

To reach an audience that has not adopted the PC because of its complexity, we needed to develop a very simple and easy-to-learn interface. We did this, in part, by throwing away infrequently used functions from PC applications that performed tasks similar to those we were accommodating. We then iteratively tested and refined the user interface to make it even simpler.

We desired to get rid of the can-do-everything, feature-intensive nature of the PC to give our target users a device that they can master based around a few key needs, tasks, and requirements. This is the true nature of an information appliance—to deliver a quality product that handles a clearly defined, limited set of functionality. With that in mind, the i-opener service provides the following three primary functions:

FIGURE **3.6**

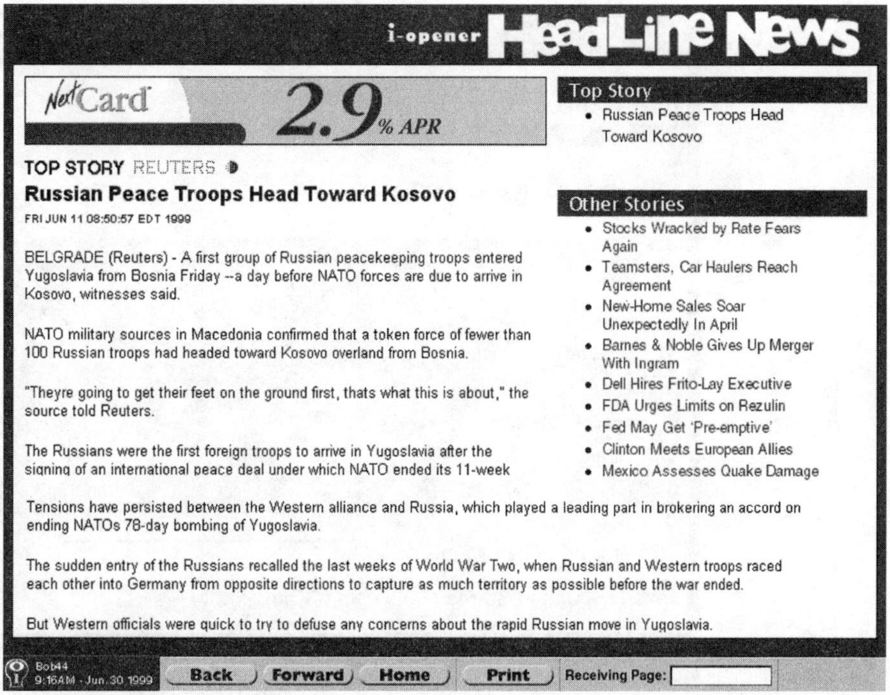

The News Channel as a part of the Categorical Content.

1. Sending and receiving email

2. Categorical content (e.g., news, weather, sports, etc.) shown in Figures 3.6 (see also Color Plate) and 3.7

3. Web accessibility

By limiting our service to just categorical content, access to the Web, and email, we were capturing the top three reasons why many people were purchasing computers in the first place. Likewise, our research in the marketplace of non-PC users validated our assumptions that these were the top three areas of need for them as well. After all, email is becoming the most popular way to communicate with family and friends, and the Web is becoming pervasive in today's society (e.g., URLs are appearing in advertisements and on consumer products).

As mentioned, i-opener is not a personal computer. I-opener is a service that allows users to accomplish these three primary tasks with much greater

FIGURE **3.7**

The Weather Channel as a part of the Information Service.

ease than with a PC. Although a PC incorporates these three functions, it also includes dozens of additional applications and utilities with hundreds of specific functions and features for each application. This very fact complicates the user interface in such a way as to decrease the ease of learning and discovery, ease of use, error recovery or forgiveness, and actual successful completion of the task that the user set out to perform.

Even though we accomplished our goal of a limited set of applications for the i-opener service, we didn't stop there. We felt that it was very important to limit the number of decisions and steps that it takes to perform an individual task in each application. Each and every one of our interfaces, whether it is for email or surfing content, includes only the necessary steps or controls to complete the task. As a comparison, take a look at just about any Windows email program in the marketplace and you will see that there are numerous menus and buttons from which to choose. In fact, this is the very nature of the experience on just about any application for the PC today. For users who grew up on the personal computer or who have been using

FIGURE **3.8**

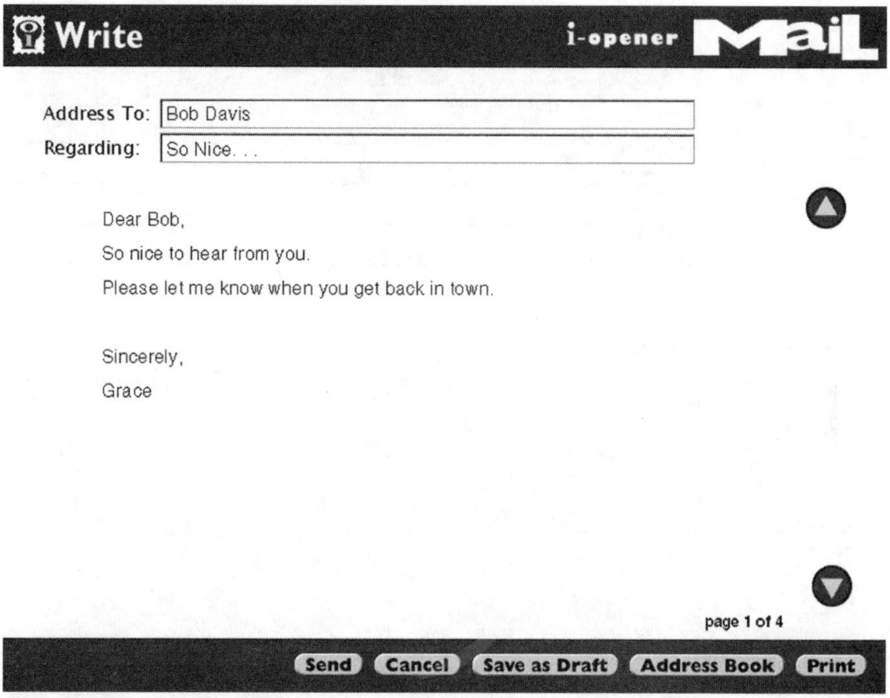

Writing a new email in i-opener Mail.

PCs at work or at home for the last few years, this may not be a big problem. However, for novice users who have never operated personal computers, this is very overwhelming and is a big deterrent to operating a PC. Hence, the strict adherence to the 80/20 rule. Our goal was to provide only the basics and to do those functions very well.

Therefore, not only do we believe that there is a place for the Internet appliance with a limited set of applications, but we also strongly believe in limiting the vast array of functions and features in each of our primary applications. We do not wish to fall into the trap of feature and function bloat like so many other technological devices and applications.

For example, compare the two email programs in Figures 3.8 and 3.9, i-opener Mail and MS Outlook, respectively. I-opener Mail has a handful of functions to support the writing and sending of the email message, while MS Outlook has a row of menu items and two rows of toolbar buttons.

We believe the computer industry has misjudged customer demand to provide interfaces that are feature rich and/or scalable. Simple interfaces are

FIGURE **3.9**

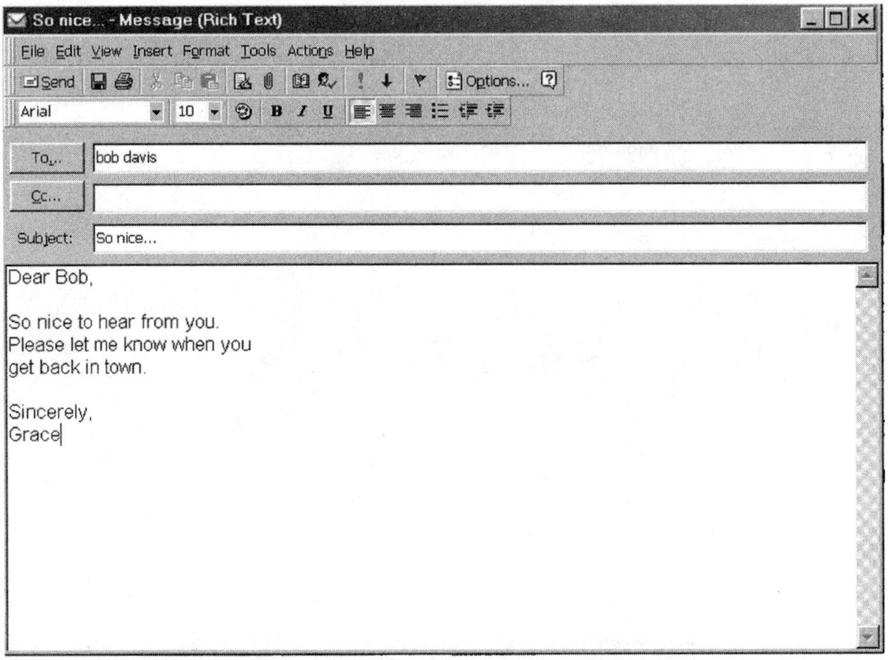

Writing a new email message in Microsoft Outlook.

often sufficient for a broad range of users. A good example is the Palm, which provides far fewer features than the Apple Newton that preceded it, yet has been highly successful because it provides the most commonly used features in a simple fashion.

Real-World Style

We chose to implement real-world metaphors (Figure 3.10; see also Color Plate) with this target user group since they have had most of their experience centered on the actual physical models of the tasks that we would virtually emulate. This helped us to keep the user interface and visuals task-oriented as well. Examples include writing letters, mailing them off, and matching traditional information sources like newspapers, magazines, television, and the evening news on TV through our service.

FIGURE **3.10**

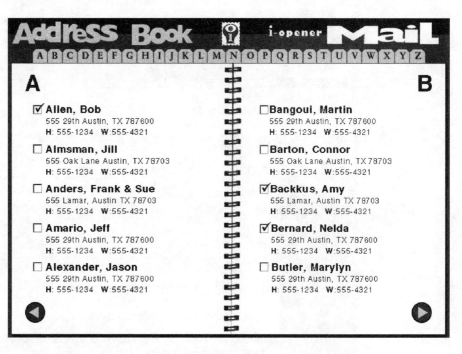

The task-centric, real-world approach of the Address Book for Mail.

Channels

Content areas were organized into channels so that navigating would be similar to the experience of changing channels on a television. The user presses channel up or channel down buttons on the keyboard, which results in the channel being changed. And similar to many cable TV systems, the user can display a list of channels in a channel bar and make a selection from the list (Figure 3.11). The channel bar collapses to a button at the bottom of the screen after use.

The Web Guide and Web Browser (Figure 3.12; see also Color Plate) provide a portal to sites outside the informational content channels, those channels that are stored and updated in the device memory.

A screen saver provides headlines and announcements of new mail when the system isn't in active use (Figure 3.13). This allows the user to see if there is something important at a glance.

FIGURE **3.11**

The Channel Bar menu expanded.

Personalization

Much of the personalization in the i-opener service takes place automatically and without thought from the user. Target marketing and promotions are based on the user's demographics collected at the time of purchase and over time. The i-opener system learns from the user's behavior and interests. As patterns of behavior and interests emerge, i-opener correlates those patterns with other like-minded users. For example, say I like topics A, B, and C; other users that like A, B, and C also like D, therefore I may like D as well. This learning process will be applied toward the direction of informational content, promotions, advertisements, and online communities if the user so chooses.

I-opener has also been programmed to provide information to the end user based on their usage patterns. For example, the i-opener device connects into the i-opener server every several hours by default. As the user's

FIGURE **3.12**

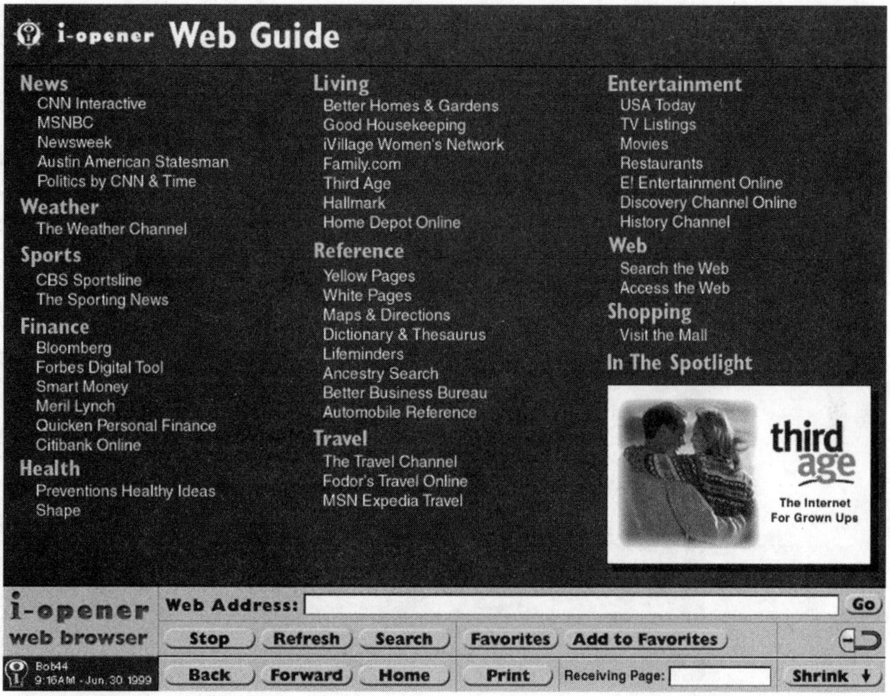

i-opener Web Guide

News
CNN Interactive
MSNBC
Newsweek
Austin American Statesman
Politics by CNN & Time

Weather
The Weather Channel

Sports
CBS Sportsline
The Sporting News

Finance
Bloomberg
Forbes Digital Tool
Smart Money
Meril Lynch
Quicken Personal Finance
Citibank Online

Health
Preventions Healthy Ideas
Shape

Living
Better Homes & Gardens
Good Housekeeping
iVillage Women's Network
Family.com
Third Age
Hallmark
Home Depot Online

Reference
Yellow Pages
White Pages
Maps & Directions
Dictionary & Thesaurus
Lifeminders
Ancestry Search
Better Business Bureau
Automobile Reference

Travel
The Travel Channel
Fodor's Travel Online
MSN Expedia Travel

Entertainment
USA Today
TV Listings
Movies
Restaurants
E! Entertainment Online
Discovery Channel Online
History Channel

Web
Search the Web
Access the Web

Shopping
Visit the Mall

In The Spotlight

third age
The Internet
For Grown Ups

i-opener web browser   Web Address: ⸺ Go
Stop Refresh Search Favorites Add to Favorites
BoM4 9:16AM - Jun. 30 1999   Back Forward Home Print Receiving Page: ⸺ Shrink ↓

The Web Guide page in the i-opener Web Browser.

pattern of connectivity develops around their usage of the service, so will the automatic connectivity for new content.

Likewise, the system downloads a wide range of information to the various channels. The reality is that users may not utilize all of the content that is sent down to the device. As the pattern of usage of that content develops, only the content that is actively accessed is updated. In the event that the user decides to browse the previously neglected content once again, a connection is established to download the latest content at that time.

Although the degree of content personalization is limited in our initial offering, we will be adding personalized settings that add convenience and match lifestyles, interests, and preferred information. In our subsequent releases, users will be able to track stocks and markets, favorite sports and teams, and local topics of interest. Additionally, many of our users may wish to schedule automatic printing of content to read offline in a paper format. Finally, users will be able to completely customize their interface and the content that they wish to receive.

FIGURE **3.13**

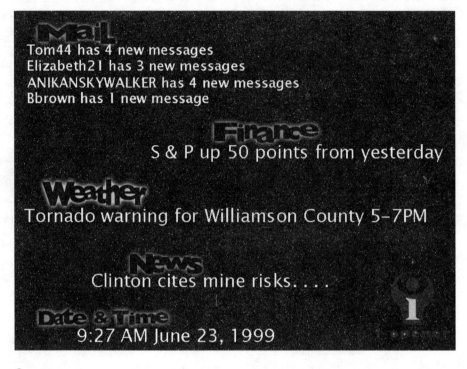

Screen saver.

Technological Advancements versus the Right User Interface

Which will lead to the best user experience on the Internet for users who have never been on the Internet? Even when considering the comparison of dial-up and broadband connectivity, technological advancements don't measure up to meeting the needs of the user as well as the user interface does. If a user still struggles with inconsistent interfaces and fails to accomplish the intended goals, then what good did the technology do for the user?

Likewise, does the latest CPU lead to a greater user experience than one that is a year or two old? How do other improvements factor in, like loading more and more RAM into a PC, or the latest operating system, or a faster hard drive, or one that has more storage capacity? Ever more spectacular technological advancements do not substitute for the right user interface for the task that the device is supposed to facilitate. Technological improvements will help to counter a variety of difficulties that bloated applications have caused for PC hardware and operating systems, but they don't erase the bad experiences of a poorly designed user interface.

Our approach is to drive the user interface by understanding our intended users, their wishes, needs, and desires, and to provide a product and service that exceeds their expectations for what they want to do with them. To that end, we are using technology to aid us in providing the right experience for what we are creating for the end users, rather than looking for technology to save our user interface.

Bulletproof

We've heard many complaints from our target user group (and have many ourselves) about how difficult it is to use software and services for the PC. Take, for example, America Online (AOL) with its multiple pop-up windows, the long connection times, connection failures, AOL's impatience with an online session longer than 45 minutes, and so on. Likewise, services and software require long, belabored installation, setup, updates, and registration processes.

Not only are we providing a simplified hardware device, but also a simplified approach to the software on the device. We wish for our service to be truly seamless to the end user once they plug in the device and sign in for the first time. All of the software is preloaded, and updates are sent down to the device automatically during connection times. We don't even bother the user with accepting the updates because it is invisible to them and there is no advantage to running previous versions of the software.

Additionally, we built the service to be foolproof as well. Say, for example, that one of our customers were to drop the device off a 20-foot balcony, thereby destroying it. That's no problem. Once they connect back into the service for the first time on a new device, all of their information is still available to them from the Netpliance servers. That means all of their email, current content information, and all of their Web favorites (i.e., bookmarks) will be restored as well. Even if a power outage occurs while they are writing email, the device will back up the email in progress in the device memory. The email is treated as a draft message and will be available the next time they go into the mail program.

3.6 Conclusions

Internet appliances are in a market where ease of use is clearly the key to customer acceptance. Computers have provided many capabilities to users that have proven to be very valuable, but they have not made sufficient progress in ease of use, and consequently a substantial portion of the population has not benefited from computers. Internet appliances will bring the key features of the electronic world to a new class of user.

At Netpliance we are developing products to meet the ease-of-use requirement by following a user-centered design process. We don't have the legacy of the PC, and we have the freedom to design from scratch. We are starting with user needs and designing the system from the ground up to meet those needs. Our design and development process is iterative with continual refinement and improvement throughout all cycles.

3.7 Acknowledgments

Many people at Netpliance have contributed to the i-opener product and to the ideas expressed in this article. Key individuals who helped in the preparation of this chapter included, but are not limited to, Munira Fareed, Nick Malkiewicz, Arie Stavchansky, Amy Van Wyngarden, and Marc Willebeek-LeMair.

3.8 References

Boehm, B. 1988. A spiral model of software development and enhancement. *IEEE Computer*, May:61–72.

Collins, D. 1995. *Designing Object-Oriented User Interfaces*. Redwood City, CA: Benjamin/Cummings.

Isensee, S., and J. Rudd. 1996. *The Art of Rapid Prototyping*. Boston: International Thomson Computer Press.

Norman, D. 1998. *The Invisible Computer*. Boston: MIT Press.

CHAPTER Four

Designing the PalmPilot: A Conversation with Rob Haitani

ERIC BERGMAN

Sun Microsystems, Inc.

ROB HAITANI

Handspring, Inc.

FIGURE **4.1**

Rob Haitani

BERGMAN: *You worked on the design of the original Pilot (see Figure 4.2) at Palm Computing. What was your role?*

HAITANI: I was the product manager for the first-generation Pilot. Among other things, I was in charge of designing the user interface of the operating system and the applications. Our president, Donna Dubinsky, one morning asked me if I had ever "done this before." I wondered if she meant whether I had designed an operating system. I hadn't even managed a software project before coming to Palm, actually; so I simply said, "Uh, no."

BERGMAN: *Tell me a little bit about the history of the PalmPilot.*

HAITANI: Before the PalmPilot, we wrote the application software for a product called the Zoomer, which was similar to the Newton. It had a 320 × 240 pixel touch-sensitive display, a pen, and handwriting recognition. It was called "jacket pocket size," which was another way of saying that it was too big to fit in a

FIGURE **4.2**

An early PalmPilot connected organizer.

shirt pocket. We were actually a software company, and our expectation was that these products would become smaller, cheaper, and faster over time, and that we would be the leading software developer for whatever product won out. Trouble was, we didn't anticipate that *none* of the products would win.

What was more discouraging was that the hardware vendors didn't understand the basic problem. They thought the first-generation products failed because they did not provide enough functionality. The second-generation products, much to our dismay, were even bigger, slower, and more expensive. One day at a board meeting, our founder, Jeff Hawkins, was lamenting the fact that the hardware companies didn't know how to build the right product. One of the board members turned around and asked him if Jeff knew what the "right product" was. Jeff answered yes. "Well, then why don't you build it?" he asked. And that's how the Pilot started.

Jeff believed we had to make the product considerably smaller then current PDAs. He carved up a piece of wood in his garage and said this is the size he wanted. He'd walk around with this block in his pocket to feel what it was like. I would print up some screenshots as we were developing UI, and he'd hold it and pretend he was entering things, and people thought he was weird. He'd be in a meeting furiously scribbling on this mockup, and people would say, "Uh, Jeff, that's a piece of wood."

BERGMAN: *How did he decide on* that *size for the piece of wood?*

HAITANI: He believed it had to fit in your pocket, and he did some stack-up analysis to study feasibility. The batteries and the LCD will be this big, so it will be about this thick. That's where we started. Then the question was how to get everything to fit. Making the smallest possible product eliminates much of your flexibility. It's not too much of an exaggeration to say that the buttons are where they are because that's the only place they'd fit. Although that begs the question of why we had buttons rather than on-screen software buttons or buttons printed on the LCD. This approach was counter to the current trends in the industry. The whole point of a computer is that you don't have to have mechanical buttons. You can just turn it on, and then you can put buttons on the screen wherever you want.

But we decided that instant access to your data meant that when you want to see your schedule, you don't want two presses. You don't want to have to pull your pen out. You want one-touch access to your schedule. The only way you can do that is if the application button doubles as a power button.

BERGMAN: *Was there argument about these non-PC design elements during development?*

HAITANI: It was a little controversial, but maybe not as much as you might think, since we were so focused on making it work rather than making a little PC. Another element that would have been more controversial if you took a PC approach was behavior when switching applications. When you press the Date Book button, it only shows today's schedule, and from a PC perspective, that's illogical. On a PC, when you toggle between apps, you want to go back to where you were. It's a no-brainer. In our devices, however, you may be checking a day, then turn the device off. Next time you come back to your calendar it might be hours or days later. You could be trying to take a quick glance at your schedule and not realize you were looking at tomorrow's schedule. Your eye doesn't necessarily go to read the little date at the top of the screen. You're much more likely to want to see your schedule for today than you are to see the last day you happened to have been looking at. Again, from a PC perspective that's not very logical, but that's what you want.

BERGMAN: *Do the right thing?*

HAITANI: Yes, just do the right thing. And the things you do on a PC are different than what you do on a handheld.

BERGMAN: *How did you arrive at the particular display size that's used now?*

HAITANI: It was fairly arbitrary. There were no standard handheld LCD sizes. Jeff was looking for something equivalent to Game Boy screens, so we went for a 160 × 160 resolution. Actually we started at 160 × 128. Jeff came to me one day and asked if I thought we could design an interface that will fit into that screen size. I said with conviction, "Oh absolutely, no problem." Then when he left, I thought, "Oh boy, this is a big problem." When we changed to 160 × 160, I was ecstatic.

BERGMAN: *So you didn't actually know whether you could or couldn't?*

HAITANI: Well, at the time Jeff just said this is the screen size, and everyone was okay with that. But as the person who had to implement it, I was the only person who actually thought, "Is it even feasible?" Everyone else assumed that it was. But I felt it was a great challenge and I wanted to take it on. It reminded me of how Japanese companies have the concept of hardware miniaturization in making a Walkman or a camcorder, and I wanted to apply that same concept to software—in other words, "software miniaturization." Can we take the same amount of information and display it in fewer and fewer pixels?

BERGMAN: *So where did you start?*

HAITANI: Well, I started with the date book. I wanted to display a full day, eight to five, six preferably. And that was our starting point. To fit that in there you very quickly find that every pixel counts and that there's just no room. Any embellishment adds more pixels. Your creativity is very constrained and you can't add a lot of flourishes or fancy graphics. For example, we even eliminated drawing a single line around the main application screen as a border, like you would find on typical PC applications. If you have a border, that means not only do you have to allocate one pixel for the border itself, but you need a margin of three or four pixels between the border and the text. So that's five pixels on four sides. When you only have 160 pixels, that's a huge percentage of your real estate, something like 12%! We realized that because LCDs have a nonactive area, however, there's a natural margin between the LCD pixels and the bezel of the display, so we could gain that space back and draw pixels right to the end of the active area (see Figure 4.3). Another seemingly small example is font size. If the standard average font width is five pixels instead of six, then you fit an additional 16% text on a screen. It doesn't sound like a lot, but these things start to add up—it's like hardware miniaturization. A half-millimeter smaller component is not a big deal, but the cumulative effect makes a big impact.

FIGURE **4.3**

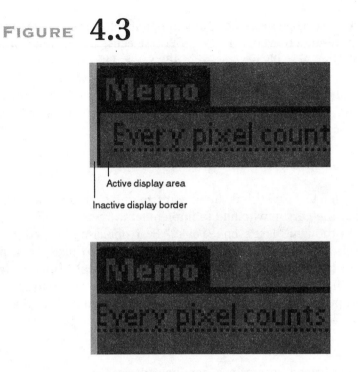

Active display area

Inactive display border

Every pixel counts . . . .

BERGMAN: *So you fought for every pixel . . . .*

HAITANI: Absolutely. For example, we quickly jettisoned any 3D treatment. Any shadow takes up at least one more pixel on each side as compared to a single black line. I spent a lot of time agonizing over font height—we ultimately shaved a pixel off of accented capital letters. They could have looked better, but we felt it was worth getting the extra text (and you know, the French don't use capital accented letters . . .). Most screens get about 11 lines on the page—that extra pixel bought us an extra hour in the day view of the calendar! Or to put it another way, we eliminated some percentage of the times a customer had to scroll to see all the events in their day.

BERGMAN: *Take me back a step to give a sense of designing the product as a whole. How did you decide what was going to be in the Pilot? What wasn't? How did it come to have the set of functions it had and the hardware design it had?*

HAITANI: I think we learned a lot from the Zoomer. On the Zoomer, our philosophy was that we should put as many applications as possible in to make as many people happy as possible. After it shipped, though, we did some user research that made us question that decision. We found that there were a few applications that people used extensively, and usage very quickly dropped off after that. So we said why burden the product with all this extra functionality if people aren't going to use it? We very quickly decided to focus on the basic PIM [personal information management] software: date book, address book, "to do" list, memo pad, and calculator. Then we designed the hardware to support that basic functionality.

BERGMAN: *Were there other functions under consideration that ultimately didn't make it in the final product?*

HAITANI: Yes, actually there were. The conventional wisdom in the handheld market at the time was that the first-generation products didn't succeed because they didn't have enough functionality. If you're going to spend $700 or $800 on a handheld device, then it's really got to do something for you. Specifically at the time the "killer app" was wireless two-way email. That was supposed to be the key. If only PDAs did that, then they would be successful. We held focus groups and went out of Silicon Valley to talk to people. We pitched this email concept, and I remember very clearly one woman who just had a blank look, and she said, "I get three emails a day. I check my mail once every morning. Why do I need access in a handheld device?" When you're in Silicon Valley the tech frenzy starts feeding on itself, and you end up losing context of what real people do with real products.

BERGMAN: *So, when you went out to find out about what people would want, what was your approach or process?*

HAITANI: First, we showed people a mockup of the device, just the little organizer, and asked them what they thought of it. They were mildly positive, and thought it was okay. But unsolicited they said, you know, unless it's hooked up to my PC it's not very interesting, or I really need this linked to my PC. So then we showed them a simulation of synchronization with HotSync and the cradle, which at the time was a revolutionary concept, and they went totally nuts. They went gaga over it. Then we were sitting behind the one-way mirror thinking that when we show them the email, that's going to be a slam dunk. But it died, like a lead balloon. And we thought, maybe we should just focus on the basics. What they were telling us is, "I don't need the bells and whistles. I just want to organize my phone numbers and my schedule. Give me something that does that and then hooks up with a PC very elegantly, and that's great."

BERGMAN: *Was the HotSync part of the product from early on, or was that something suggested by what you found from people?*

HAITANI: No, that was originally a core part of the concept, and was another example of what we learned from the first generation of PDAs. If you remember back to the original vision of PDAs, they were designed to free you from your PC—you wouldn't have to be connected to your desktop. Then they hedged a bit, saying you might want to back up some data once in a while, and provided data backup applications. But since they assumed it was a low priority, those applications were slow and crashed a lot. Then our user research on the Zoomer product told us that 90-odd percent of our customers owned PCs, and we came to the conclusion that you *don't* want to be freed from your computer. You still have important information that's on your PC and you need access to that information. We decided that we needed to design that with that assumption in mind. We had to make the data link to the PC a no-brainer to use. Other people had done it before, but it was always very cumbersome and half the time it didn't work. We said from the beginning we need to make it very simple, so you could press one button and it synchronizes to the PC. It sounds obvious in hindsight, but was another revolutionary aspect of the product.

BERGMAN: *What were the criteria you used to evaluate the success of your designs?*

HAITANI: At the time we viewed the world as consisting of two main types of competitors. On the one hand, there was the electronic organizer market, which was already very well established with players like Sharp and Casio who sold millions of these things. Some of these products were very small, fast, and inexpensive, but had tiny keyboards and were too complicated to figure out how to use. Sometimes for grins Jeff would give someone a product and challenge them to figure out how to set a meeting or enter a phone number within 10 minutes. At the other end of the spectrum, there were PDAs with better interfaces such as the Newton, but they were big, slow, bulky, and expensive. We refused to believe that this was an intractable problem, that there wasn't a better middle ground.

BERGMAN: *Can you elaborate on what ways devices can be too slow or complicated?*

HAITANI   The big problem with our original Zoomer product was that it had a very slow processor, and we found that it was excruciatingly painful to use because it took so long to get simple things done. When I first came on board with Palm, my first job was to spec the second generation of the Zoomer software. It was a software update, so there was nothing we could do about the processor. So we asked, what can we do about performance? I did a little bit of analysis and came to the conclusion that the processor wasn't entirely to blame. Our interface was inefficiently designed and required extra steps to accomplish simple tasks. If you're just setting up an appointment or looking up a phone number, the more steps required compounds the fact that you have a slow processor because every step takes a couple seconds. And at that time, it would take literally 20 or 30 seconds to change the time of an event or enter a phone number. I spent a lot of time stripping that down and asking how could we reduce the number of steps to do common things. Instead of eight taps could we reduce it to five or three or two? We spent a lot of time optimizing navigation, etc. Got into a lot of arguments also.

BERGMAN: *Arguments?*

HAITANI: Well, someone would say, "That's just one more tap," or "That would only take another second." I would respond that it is analogous to the way you organize your desk in your office, your physical desk, in that you have some things on top of your desk and you have some things in drawers or file cabinets. Why is that? Well, if you look at the things on top of your desk, those are the things you use very frequently and they need to be easily within your grasp; whereas things in your drawer you don't use as frequently. So I would say, Imagine taking something you use all the time like your mouse or the phone and put it in a drawer. It's just one extra step to pull it out. It just takes a second. But if you use it that frequently, the cumulative effect of that one extra step is excruciatingly annoying. On the other hand, one more tap does not matter for features you use infrequently. For example, if you have a weekly meeting at four o'clock, which we call a repeating event, you may find out that the regular time has changed. How many times a day do you do that? Maybe once every couple of weeks. Therefore *in that case* it's not a big deal to require the customer to take a couple extra taps to reach that dialog. They don't get annoyed; they don't even notice.

BERGMAN: *I understand one measure you used to evaluate your designs was something called the "phone test." What was the phone test, and how did it come about?*

HAITANI: In the days of early PDAs, you'd be on the phone with someone and they'd ask, "Can we meet next Tuesday?" Then you'd be tapping on your screen and watching wait cursors, and there'd be this dead air you'd have to fill with small talk, which was very embarrassing. So we said that's one thing that we have to fix. It's got to be instantaneous. It's got to be fast. I came up with an informal concept called the "phone test," which was similar to the Turing AI test [can you tell if the writer on the other side of a computer connection is a human or not].

Our challenge was to see if we could design a product fast enough that the person on the other end of the phone doesn't realize you're using an electronic device. The experience we had gained designing apps to minimize the number of steps came in very handy. When these lessons were applied to the Pilot, it was like baseball players warming up with extra bats. When you take the weights away you're really swinging hard. We designed Pilot to be very fast, particularly the things you want to do very frequently and have instant access to.

I actually remember the first day we had the applications running. We fired up the boards and we had a simulated phone test. I said, "Ed, what are you doing next Tuesday? How about 12:00 P.M.? Do you have Ron's phone number? 555-1212." It was kind of a joke, but we literally validated the phone test, which was fun.

BERGMAN: *You spoke earlier about the frequency of tasks and the number of taps. In your design approach, what was the relationship between task frequency and number of taps required for users to perform a task?*

HAITANI: In designing for small screens, we very quickly ran into two conflicting design goals. On one hand, in order to be very fast and have access to features, you want them right on the screen so you can have just one tap to get to everything. On this end of the spectrum the ideal application is to have all the buttons on the screen. On the other hand, since we have a small screen, we don't have a lot of real estate and we want to make it easy to use. You want to make it very simple and you don't want clutter. So the other end of the spectrum is that you want an application that has as few things on the screen as possible. Obviously these goals conflict.

We struggled with this until I came to the conclusion that there's a way out. The key is that most people only use a small percentage of the features in an app. If you drew a chart of features sorted by frequency of use, what you find is there are a few features that people use all the time, and then it very rapidly drops off. Think of your word processor. Cut, copy, paste you use over and over and over again. But things like multiple column layout and drop letters most people use once in a blue moon. This led me to conclude that the features that you use very frequently need to be right up front, but features that you use infrequently, you can bury. That was the breakthrough. That allowed us to design screens that were simple enough to be easy to use, yet providing instant access to 80% of the features you use. [See Figure 4.4 for an example of this approach.]

BERGMAN: *That sounds great in theory, but how did it work in practice?*

HAITANI: From a design perspective, it worked remarkably well, providing you had a good enough understanding of your customer to know what features were really important enough to have on the screen.

FIGURE **4.4**

Datebook dialog before and after. Repeat appointment features were moved into a dialog (not shown) that comes up only if the user chooses repeat appointments.

But that approach tends to generate resistance from engineers. It was difficult conceptually to grasp the concept from an execution perspective because it leads to inconsistent and illogical results. When you design something, you assume things that are equivalent should be placed together. For example "new record" and "delete record" commands, well, those should be next to each other. But I would argue that you're much more likely to add a new phone number than you are to eliminate one. And therefore the New button should be right on the screen, but the Delete button you can safely put behind a menu. We had a lot of heated arguments about that.

Again, I'd point to how your desk is organized. When you think about it, your stapler and your staple remover are "architecturally equivalent" and therefore theoretically should be in the same place. Either both of them are in your drawer, or both of them are on top of your desk. In my case, though, I have my stapler on top of my desk and my staple remover in the drawer. That's because I staple papers much more frequently than I remove staples from papers. If you explain it that way, people tend to get it.

BERGMAN: *So instead of enforcing consistency, would it be fair to say that the design goal was to maximize predictability?*

HAITANI: Yes, exactly. And there's no real scientific method about it. I get great satisfaction out of hearing people say things like, "Gee, the PalmPilot just does what I want to do," and they don't necessarily understand why. They don't care why, but yet it just *works*.

BERGMAN: *Were there any cases where due to testing or feedback you found a particular context where this predictability approach didn't work? Where perhaps you said, we're going to have to bury this function because people hardly ever do it, and then it turned out that finding that function was too difficult? Or cases where you said we really need this function up front, but it turned out to be confusing in that location?*

HAITANI: One thing I think was very important was that I did a great deal of user testing and simulation using HyperCard. It was a very valuable exercise, and we actually did a whole pass at the user interface before any of the code was even written. Many people make the mistake of waiting until alpha to user test, when a functional prototype is available. But by that time it's already architected in a certain way, and to change it introduces a lot of risk, and you end up with buggy products that don't seem to hold together as well. On the other hand, if you decide right up front to spend the time, it's always worth that extra investment.

For example, in the date book we have a very odd design where you can tap right on a line and start to write down a meeting. It introduces a whole host of problems. What if you're in the middle of entering text, and tap somewhere else on the screen? What happens if you tap a command button or pick list when the focus is on the text? It introduced a lot of issues. If your objective is to make a clean design, it's not a really good idea. The more logical PC approach is to have a dialog displayed to edit the settings like alarms. That way you can explicitly confirm or cancel the editing session. I fought against that very hard because I felt that most of the time you're setting up a meeting at, say, one o'clock, and you just want to write it in. When I wasn't able to convince people, I'd say let's defer it and test it. We'd user-test it and I was either right or not—and if I wasn't right, and we built a better product, that's fine!

That approach generated a problem we considered addressing with modality. Since we weren't displaying a dialog, there was not enough space on the screen to put all the buttons we wanted. When you have a record selected, you want cut, copy, paste, etc. And at one point we had an idea that when you tap on a line, it puts you in editing mode and displays a different set of buttons. It made sense since you couldn't edit a record if you hadn't selected it, so those buttons weren't serving any purpose if nothing was selected. As a result, it gave us a lot more flexibility to display more buttons. But when we simulated this design and tested it in HyperCard, people were confused by the buttons that appeared and disappeared.

That painted us into a corner. We can only put four buttons on the screen, so what are we going to do? We could try cramming smaller buttons on the screen, but as I said, we wanted to minimize clutter. We were forced down a path that led ultimately to our design principles. To be honest, it wasn't a case where philosophically we grasped a breakthrough in interaction design. It was more an end result of our pragmatic design approach, starting with the fact that we could only fit four buttons on the screen. Instead of trying to apply a fancy UI model to address the problem, we simply asked the question, "Which four buttons should we put on the screen?" In other words, forget rules and theory, just do the right thing. Over time, however, I started recognizing patterns in our implementation. Our UI seems to be holding together—hmm, I wonder why. Now that you think about it, there's a pattern here. Eventually I was able to articulate what these patterns were, and in future generations we were able to go back and apply those new lessons to iterative improvements and new applications.

BERGMAN: *It is interesting that you were saying you only have four buttons and then everything followed logically from that. One could imagine an alternative model, and some people will argue that this is what Microsoft Windows CE does, in which you provide menus and you can have as many functions as you want. By this line of reasoning, why not just miniaturize those elements people are already familiar with in a PC world?*

HAITANI: Well, this is the issue of complexity. The theory driving that was what they teach you in first-year psychology class in college: your brain can only grasp several objects at once. If you put four dots on a page in random positions and you stare at one point, you can instantly recognize that there are four dots without having to move your eyes. But if you put nine dots in random points and stare at one, you can't tell how many there are. Maybe you can try to look at them peripherally, but that's faking it.

If you have more than the number of objects that your mind can grasp at once, your eyes go into "scanning mode." Your eyes have to travel around the page and you count the dots in a serial fashion. Now, if you have an object like a remote control with 20 buttons, in order to find the right one to press, your eye has to scan through the rows of buttons. But if you had a remote control with just four buttons, you easily memorize the location of the buttons *by feel.* There is no cognitive activity required. This makes it seem fast and easy. It's similar to when you roll dice. You don't toss the dice on the board and then count the dots—at a glance you know the total. So we felt that you simply must have a very few number of items on the screen.

Perhaps a clearer example is the hardware, where we have only four application buttons on the front, and believe me, there were a lot more apps we wanted to assign buttons to. On the original Zoomer, we had a row of about 10 icons on the bottom, and whenever you wanted to launch an app, you'd have to scan through it and find it. You'd have to concentrate. Granted for a split second, but it still required a small amount of effort. With the PalmPilot, with only four buttons, you don't think—you just press the damn button. Again, it sounds trivial, but the cumulative effect of steps and effort adds up.

But let me get back to the concept of fewer objects. If you're trying to make a simple design on a small screen, you're not providing value to the user when you give them a whole slew of buttons. You're being lazy or indecisive, and the result of your inability to make trade-offs is a poor user experience. Let me make an analogy. When you create presentation slides, design people say you should always use big fonts because they are more legible, for example 36-point fonts rather than 8-point. Many people struggle because they want to communicate a point that in prose would take multiple sentences. If you make yourself use 36-point fonts, however, it forces you to be concise and get your point across and be very efficient in communicating. You don't do people any favors by having twice as many words on a presentation slide. The constraint forces you to be concise. It was the same with our interface design. Ten buttons are not acceptable, we must have four. It's similar to the process of editing.

I say if you only read one book to understand handheld user interface, it should be Strunk and White's *The Elements of Style*. It's a classic college reference book that liberal arts majors are more familiar with than engineers are, but it talks about how to edit extraneous words. The gist is that the fewer words you can communicate the same sentence in, the more powerful your writing is. For example, if you clean up a sentence that's in passive voice and it's 14 words, and restate it in 9 words, it's a much stronger sentence. It's very easy to be verbose, as I'm doing now just babbling on. It's easier to write a 20-page paper than it is to write a 5-page paper because it doesn't require any discipline. UI design is like an editing process—you start with a screen and one by one start ripping things out. But the key is you still have to communicate that point—you don't want to throw that out.

BERGMAN: *How do you decide what to keep and what to throw out?*

HAITANI: You have to have an understanding of what your user wants to do. What are their priorities? What's important to them? It's easy to remove buttons, but if you remove the wrong buttons, then you create a poor user experience as well. They end up searching through menus and getting frustrated. On the other hand, if you make the right decisions, then when they launch your app and they're in a hurry, they just seem to find what they need right in front of them. When it comes to advanced features, as I said people use them much less frequently, and are therefore more willing to look around for them. It's not as frustrating an experience.

A lot of people describe our design as "Zen-like." I have a tongue-in-cheek UI design presentation that uses the Zen theme. It concludes that the most important thing is to focus on the "inner tranquility of the customer." That phrase started as a joke, but the more I think of it, the more I think it's an apt analogy. Think about how you feel about PC applications. I swear at my PC all the time and I know a lot of others do as well. It gets very frustrating. You get angry and irritated when you can't do what you want to do. But if you apply the less-is-more approach, your app just does the right thing. For example, if you're in a hurry and you pull out your Palm and you want to know where you're supposed to be. You press one button and it shows you your schedule. No struggle, no effort, no confusion; it just does what you want to do. Your reaction is a contented sigh, and it's very calming. Your blood pressure doesn't rise. That's the key to the whole experience. If you can do that, then the other rules don't even matter. The rules are guidelines, but if you understand the ultimate objective and you can accomplish it by breaking all the rules, then that's great as far as I'm concerned.

BERGMAN: *You're describing the experience on the Palm as being in many ways fundamentally different than the PC experience. What is the philosophical difference between that environment and something like Microsoft Windows CE?*

HAITANI: The Windows CE philosophy is that if you're familiar with the PC it takes less time to learn how to use the product. In other words, what's good for the PC is good for the handheld. Frankly, I have the opposite view because I feel you've got to look at how people use these products. At Palm we analyzed handheld usage versus laptop usage. We asked people how often they access each device, and how long they use it. We found—and this makes sense intuitively—that people access laptops relatively infrequently and for long sessions. You fire up your word processor, your spreadsheet, and you work for 20 minutes or an hour.

Handheld devices, on the other hand, are used in the opposite way. People use handhelds frequently for short bursts to quickly access data, such as to look up Joe's phone number, and then put them away. You have to ask yourself if the usage pattern is diametrically opposite, does it make sense to copy the design paradigm, and our response was no. Forget modeling a UI after something just because it's familiar. I'm familiar with how to use a door, but I wouldn't design a briefcase with a doorknob to open it. What good is familiarity if it doesn't work well?

BERGMAN: *Was that a difficult argument to make? Did you receive much pushback from engineering or management, saying, wait a second, you want to purposely make this different than a PC?*

HAITANI: Not really. I never stated that we should *not* emulate a PC design. In fact, and this may sound contradictory, we tried to emulate PC design concepts as much as possible. For example, we considered more radical approaches to our menu system. It was tempting to take the opportunity to be more creative. But since we concluded our customers were PC users, we decided they would be familiar with PC concepts. But we didn't constrain ourselves to simply copying blindly for the sake of copying. We felt that too literally copying PC user interface objects was doing our customers a disservice. Instead we stripped menus down to an essence that would be recognizable, leveraging the value of familiarity. We optimized the look and behavior to be as easy and fast as possible. I think the proof is in the pudding. If the product works, and the customer achieves "inner tranquility," they don't stop to ask, "Hey, why doesn't it look exactly like my PC?" If we do our job, the question becomes irrelevant.

BERGMAN: *So given this contrast between the Palm philosophy and what Microsoft Windows CE is doing, what's your evaluation of the effectiveness of their product for its intended use?*

HAITANI: I think the evaluation of these products changes over time. When you first see one—if you're looking at a demo or playing with one in a store, you notice the familiar Windows look and feel. You may even think mistakenly that it is Windows compatible. The extra bells and whistles appeal to you. In this environment, a few delays here and there do not discourage you. As you use one over time in real-life situations, however, the sluggish performance begins to bother you.

You could write an equation that says Frequency of Operation × Time per Operation = Frustration. For example, if you boot a word processor three times a day and it takes 30 seconds, that's not a big deal. But if you use the "cut" command 50 times a day and it takes 5 seconds, that would drive you nuts. From that perspective I think people use handheld devices more like the way you use a watch than the way you use the laptop. When you check your watch, you want the time—immediately. You want to grab some information and that's it. Imagine if your watch was designed like a PC. You're late for an appointment, you pull out your watch. You press a button, and for three seconds a splash screen says, "Booting WatchOS." Next, you pull out a stylus and tap to launch the Time app. Wait cursor. Then you see a dialog that asks you to select time zone, which you thought was a neat feature when you bought it. But you almost always seem to be in the same time zone, so now it bothers you that you have to tap this every time. . . . That's obviously a silly example, but imagine one even simpler. What if you had to wait two seconds every time you checked the time on your watch. One . . . two. I guarantee over time it would drive you crazy. Try it!

In other words, we've found that people who use complex handheld devices say their utility diminishes over time. You may initially be impressed with the number of features crammed into a device. But over time, your experience drops off very quickly because (a) you're being frustrated with watching wait cursors, and (b) because you realize that you hardly use any of those features. As a result, many of these products end up in a drawer. Customer experience with Palm products has been the opposite. You pick it up, it just seems to do what you want, and you realize you don't find yourself becoming frustrated. It's just doing the job you want to do and keeping it very simple, and it's hitting that right set of functionality, and people have been very happy with it. That's why word of mouth has been so important for the Palm products.

BERGMAN: *Another way where the Palm differs very strongly from the PC is that nowhere that I can think of do you see a Save button, or nowhere do you lose data because you forgot to save. How did that come about?*

HAITANI: That was in from the beginning. We have no explicit concept of saving files, which is another PC concept that is not necessarily applicable to handheld devices. Think about why you want a Save button on your files. You may be editing a document, then decide that you want to scrap your changes, or go back to an earlier version. There is no such concept on, say, a date book application. You write in "Lunch with Ed" and that's it.

A related concept that we ruled out early on was the ability to have multiple files; for example, if you want to have different address books for personal, business, etc. Again we asked ourselves what a customer really wants to do. Well, I might want to have my business contacts in one file and personal contacts in another. We can solve that with categories, which would not only allow you to switch between lists more quickly, but would also allow you to display all your lists simultaneously. A good engineer could argue that a file system would be more "robust." But then you would need a file menu in each app with Save, Save As, etc. Each decision like this increases complexity and it gets worse and worse. Ironically, the end result of this minimalist thinking is that we have fast performance on a very slow processor. Conventional wisdom in the PC world dictates that the path to faster performance is to use a faster processor. It's the one-way street of constantly upgrading our computers yet always being behind. It doesn't have to be that way if the people writing the OS have some *discipline,* rather than simply adding more code because they assume that people will upgrade their machines. Jeff Hawkins simply said we should make the operating system smaller and more efficient. Another equation: Processing Speed ÷ OS Overhead = Performance. PC thinking is to simply pile on the processing speed to address performance, but we took the opposite approach and addressed the denominator. That's just one example. We assumed we'd reject every feature unless there was a good reason not to. Saving files. Printing. By being merciless, at the end we were left with a very tight core of an operating system.

BERGMAN: *That really goes back to your earlier comment about the Japanese philosophy of hardware miniaturization being applicable to software.*

HAITANI: Yes. There's a parallel between the miniaturization and the Strunk and White approach—it all comes back to "less is more." That's because in handheld devices you have *constraints* that you don't face with a desktop PC. On the desktop, you have all the power you need because you're plugged in the wall. You have the utility company on your side, and you have a huge display, so you have plenty of screen real estate. So there's no penalty. In the PC world, 96 megs of RAM will always be better than 64 megs of RAM. You never say, well, actually I'd rather have 64 megs. You're not penalized for having an extra 50 features, so you might as well have it. Whereas on a handheld device, if you have 50 more features, in order to support them then you find your batteries last half as long, and you need a bigger screen. So you design in larger batteries, and more memory, and they start feeding off each other. And the next thing you know you have this big bloated, sluggish product. We call that the "Death Spiral."

BERGMAN: *How do you think some of the lessons you've learned in the Palm can be applied to make PCs more usable, recognizing they're different devices?*

HAITANI: That's a really good question. I don't see any reason why these lessons couldn't be applied to a PC. If you applied these same constraints to a PC, I think you could develop applications that are very easy to use. As a small example, apps with 20 icons in the tool bar drive me crazy. It's the PC mentality of more-is-better. If I can customize a tool bar, I immediately pare those back to four. Or another example is that I've always thought it would be interesting to take Windows 3.1 and Excel Version 1, load them on a 500 MHz Pentium III, and get you a blistering fast product. But the problem is on the desktop side, perhaps there is a market psychology going on, where people buy into the more-features-is-better approach. I've had people say that to me, "We tried that on the desktop; we tried a 'lite' version, and the competition kicked our ass because people didn't buy into that."

BERGMAN: *Is an alternative to that scenario to have many special-purpose devices that do particular tasks well?*

HAITANI: That's an interesting point, the concept of the "information appliance." To some degree Palm products fit into this definition because of the focused functionality we've been discussing. On the other hand, the fact is that the Palm operating system is open, and there are thousands of applications—from that perspective I wouldn't call that "focused." But the execution of any given application is very focused from the perspective of features and UI design.

But the other difference is that there's a fundamental difference between the types of applications on a handheld and a PC. One approach third-party developers take in the design of handheld applications is to take a PC application and recreate it on a handheld. That's the biggest mistake you can make! That's because, as I said, the PC and handheld are completely different animals. For example, we had an expense report application that let you track lunches and other expenses while on the road. The PC approach is to assume that you want to be able to generate reports and look at your running expense totals and calculate exchange rates on the device because that's what PC expense applications do. But that's not what you need. All you need are those features that are relevant to the mobile nature of the device because you can assume that there's a PC back at your desk. All you really want to do is jot down, say, $5 for the cab, and $12 for lunch. When you get to upload the data to your PC, you can do all the calculating there. You've got plenty of power and speed on the desktop—that's why you bought that Pentium in the first place. Let *it* do the heavy lifting.

Let me make another strained analogy. It's like designing a car. You could do some market research and find that people like to eat in the car. All right, well if we really wanted to provide a robust solution, we'd give them a refrigerator and a microwave and a range and a stove and all that. And you could. You can buy a Winnebago and drive off. But that really detracts from your driving experience. On the other hand, you can ask yourself, how much do you really eat while driving? Most of the time you drink coffee or a soda. If you really think it through and understand your customer's requirements, you decide that maybe you can just provide a cup holder. When you talk about the 80/20 rule, 80% of your customers need a cup holder, and if in order to accommodate the other 20%, you end up with a Winnebago, then forget it. Stick with your 80%, put the cup holder in, you still have your Acura. Customers ask for features like kids ask for candy. In handheld design, you have to make the trade-offs for them. Robust functionality isn't a benefit; it's a cop-out.

By the way, the analogy can be extended to describe why having a PC allows you to unburden the handheld software. You can get away with just a cupholder in the car because, by the way, you happen to live in a house with a refrigerator and a range and a microwave. That's all back in the kitchen, so you don't have to have it everywhere you go. It's very similar to the expense app issue. You don't have to have exchange rate conversion on your expense app because you can do that much more easily on your PC.

BERGMAN: *So who out there "gets" these design concepts besides Palm?*

HAITANI: Well, obviously we do here at Handspring, since we're the ones who developed them! But seriously, I think many of the people who have tried to build handheld devices have difficulty shedding the instincts that make them successful in the desktop world. It's as if the leading supertanker manufacturers tried to design kayaks. The first thing they'd do is assemble world-class welding engineers and experts in dual-hull design. It's not a lack of intelligence— there are plenty of people much brighter than I am at our competitors. It's just a different game. At the beginning of this interview I said that I didn't have previous software experience, and I think that actually helped me. Creativity is simply an absence of assumptions, and I was lucky that I didn't have years of PC software experience to unlearn.

Obviously I'm not naive enough to assume that none of our competitors will ever figure these things out. I would argue, though, that it's easier for people outside of the PC industry who don't have the baggage of desktop preconceptions. I mentioned the Zen design concepts. I've come up with a few riddles to try to "enlighten" people on our design approach. The one people seem to remember most is a simple question: "How do you fit a mountain in a teacup?" If this question stumps you, you're still in the PC mindset.

BERGMAN: *It seems like the question you asked begs a question in return: Why would you want to put a mountain in a teacup in the first place?*

HAITANI: Exactly! If your first reaction is to try to figure out a clever way to shrink the mountain, you're taking the PC approach: *assume* we want to stuff everything in this product. You're not bothering to prioritize or distill, or ask the question about what really matters. The mountain doesn't matter.

The answer to the riddle is, Dig for the diamond and put *that* in the teacup. After all, do you really need all the dirt and rocks?

BERGMAN: *How have you applied these philosophies to your products at your new company, Handspring? Did you do something new, or are these an extension of your existing design philosophy?*

HAITANI: That's a good question. Our first product is called the Visor (see Figure 4.5), and actually we believe it takes handheld design to the next level. Basically the core of our old Palm products was simplicity—eliminating extraneous

FIGURE **4.5**

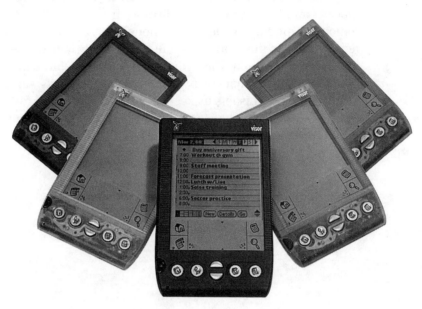

A spread of Visor handheld organizers.

functionality in order to create an optimal user experience. We felt that was a significant accomplishment, but in a sense it was a dead end. The Zen-of-Palm philosophy demonstrated that a simple product that worked well would succeed, and a full-featured product that worked poorly would fail. But what if you *did* want to add a certain feature? We had people all the time come to us and say that they just wanted to have a built-in pager, then they would be happy. Or a voice recorder. Or a cell phone. Individually, these are all great ideas, but if you tried to add all of them, you would end up with a big, klunky, expensive product. The key was to be able to let you customize your handheld to do what you want, when you want. So we developed the Springboard architecture, an open slot on the device that lets you plug in modules.

BERGMAN: *Why a new expansion architecture? What did you see as the limitations of existing technologies?*

HAITANI: Well, as we learned with the PalmPilot, it's not just having a feature, it's all about execution. Backup technology existed when we invented HotSync, but we felt one-touch, no-brainer synchronization was critical if you wanted to synchronize frequently. It's the same with Springboard modules. It's not just configurability per se. You have to make it fast, easy, flexible. Springboard modules are not "installed" or "configured." You just snap in a Springboard module and it launches the software on that module. You can insert or remove a module while applications are running. Any special drivers required to run the module are automatically installed when you insert the module and removed when you pull it out. This eliminates the problem of conflicting drivers that crash your machine. No resets, no crashes, nothing "bad" happens. This lets us keep the base OS lean and mean, but provides the flexibility to add whatever specific functionality you want. That's what we see as the next big step in advancing handheld computer design.

CHAPTER Five

The Interaction Design of Microsoft Windows CE

SARAH ZUBEREC

Productivity Appliance Division, Microsoft Corporation

5.1   Introduction

Interface design for the various Microsoft Windows CE products required the balancing of three variables: level of affinity with PC desktops and applications; degree of focus on user tasks; and range of product-operating environments and form factors. While some may argue that this UI is nothing more than the traditional desktop Microsoft Windows miniaturized to fit a smaller display, UI research has been carried out on each product to better identify and understand the users and the tasks they need to accomplish in the environments in which they work. An interaction design team comprised of designers, user interface program managers, and usability engineers were responsible for guiding the design process. This process led to the development of new form factors and input/output methods to support a range of tasks and environments. Each product was designed to be a desktop companion. To that end, consistency with desktop applications and operating system has played a significant role in defining the user interface for each product. The challenge facing Windows CE designers is to extend the traditional desktop Windows metaphors and designs to the broad spectrum of CE devices, while maintaining focus on task requirements of end users.

5.2   History

Windows CE is an operating system designed to run on computers that are considerably smaller than desktop PCs and laptop PCs. The first version of Windows CE was created to run on the Handheld PC 1.0, which shipped in 1996. While this chapter will describe the Handheld PC (H/PC), Palm-sized PC (P/PC), and Auto PC (A/PC), Windows CE also runs TV-related products, Internet-related products, and products that support vertical applications (such as sausage-making machines and information kiosks). Figure 5.1 is a time line showing the Microsoft portable product effort to date.

FIGURE **5.1**

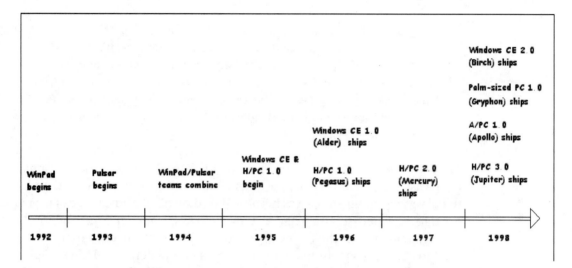

Windows appliance time line (product code names are in parentheses).

The design of Windows CE grew out of early work on two products that did not ship: WinPad and Pulsar. WinPad began in 1992 as a portable device that supported organization and use of personal information. When connected to a PC via a serial cable, WinPad could synchronize appointments, contacts, tasks, email, and other data types. It was a pen-based system that relied on handwriting recognition for data entry. The interface itself contained Windows-like elements (menus, buttons, tabs, file viewer), but elements like "action handles," electronic handwriting, and "dog ears" differentiated it from the desktop. Pulsar focused on viewing information that could be broadcast over a network. The Pulsar project, beginning in 1993, had a "social interface" to target consumer, as opposed to business, use. The Pulsar interface used metaphors like a briefcase for storing daytimer information (appointments and contacts) and a billboard for presenting broadcast information (stock quotes and email). In 1994, the teams were combined to work on a new portable device solution.

In early 1995, work began on interface concepts for the first version of the Handheld PC (code-named Pegasus) running the first version of Windows CE (code-named Alder). The H/PC 1.0 retained the WinPad vision—to create a companion to the desktop PC (O'Hara 1997)—but refocused the interface design to achieve greater affinity with desktop Windows. Of all the product goals for H/PC 1.0 described by O'Hara (1997), the most influential was the following:

> [The goal was to] create a companion to the Windows desktop. The target customer for Windows CE was someone who already used Microsoft Windows 95. It was essential that Windows CE leveraged users' knowledge of and experience with Windows and any Windows-based programs. It was also critical that data could be moved easily between a desktop PC and the Handheld PC. Users should simply place the Handheld PC into its docking cradle to synchronise data on the two machines.

At the time, the design team believed that part of the reason that personal digital assistants had yet to achieve significant market success beyond traditional vertical applications was because they did not take advantage of users' existing PC expertise. Users had already learned UI, applications, and interaction paradigms for their desktop environments. These needed to be leveraged to prevent users from having to learn a completely new UI paradigm. Also, it was thought that current products were difficult to integrate with existing PC systems. Users had invested time to enter their data into the application on their PC and needed a simple way to keep both the device and the PC up to date.

With these characteristics in mind, targeted users of the various Windows CE products were identified as mobile professionals. They were people who spent time away from their desk, had an intermediate understanding of Microsoft Windows, used Microsoft Word or Microsoft Excel on a daily basis, and maintained both an address book and calendar to manage their personal information. In order to achieve the product goal of desktop companion, it was believed that users' current knowledge of Microsoft applications needed to be leveraged. It was also critical to have a straightforward mechanism to exchange data between the device and the PC. As will be seen in subsequent sections of this chapter, these design goals were taken quite literally in the first handheld devices.

The design space for Windows CE user interfaces has grown considerably over the last five years. Today, the design space must take into consideration four-color grayscale to full color; an array of screen sizes and resolutions; interaction styles directed by stylus, mouse, and voice; and platforms for the hand, lap, car, and living room. User tasks that need to be supported across the various devices are sometimes the same and sometimes different. User characteristics, once generally defined, become more specific with each new product. This chapter will provide examples of design decisions and research that influenced decisions over the development of four separate products. The final part of this chapter will discuss consistency challenges when developing a family of products.

5.3 People and Process

The Windows CE product teams take a traditional iterative design approach to product development. As with most product development teams at Microsoft, the Windows CE teams are comprised of a number of different disciplines: Program Management, Product Planning, Product Management, Graphic/Visual/Industrial Design, Usability, Localization, Test, Development, and User Education. Table 5.1 represents the roles and responsibilities of the different disciplines in the software development process at Microsoft. (Most product teams generally follow this process, and the Windows CE product teams are no exception.)

Designers, usability engineers, and user interface program managers (UI PMs) are frequently referred to as the "interaction design team." These disciplines have the most influence on the interface design of Windows CE products. This is not to say that developers, testers, or other team members cannot contribute to feature and/or interface implementation. However, if the issue deals with anything related to the user interface, design, usability, and UI PMs have the greatest impact.

For the most recent version of the Palm-sized PC, an interaction design team formed and met for a minimum of two hours per week during the iterative phase of the design process. In conjunction with these design meetings, an email alias and Web site were created to facilitate additional discussions. During the meetings, design problems were presented. Usability lab testing was a main source of problem identification. Potential solutions were discussed and next steps determined for achieving design solutions. Sometimes more research was needed because the problem was not yet understood. Sometimes a prototype was needed to better visualize and test the various potential solutions. Sometimes a design team member presented a challenging problem and sought guidance on how to approach the solution. Based on the discussions in the meeting, the latest design solutions were posted to the Web site and email was used to debate the various designs.

The process was invaluable for a number of reasons. First, members of the design team learned and shared the most challenging problems. More often than not, a design problem in one area of the product would ultimately affect the design in another part. During these sessions, all team members contributed ideas to solving problems. Second, all members of the design team understood the decisions making the product the way it was. All members agreed upon the design. This is not to say that design was undertaken in a democratic forum. Voting never happened. However, data was presented and pros and cons were weighed. Ultimately the team agreed on the best and most feasible solution. Third, all members of the team could clearly articulate to anyone on the team or across the company the design goals of

TABLE **5.1**

Product team members and process responsibilities.

Organizational Group	Planning	Development	Stabilization
Program Management	create vision statement, schedule, and specification	refine specification and prioritize features	review bugs, research next version, and ship
Product Planning	undertake market research and focus groups	determine pricing, promotions, and packaging	research next version and launch
Usability	undertake site visits (CI) and heuristic evaluations	undertake prototyping and iterative testing	research next version and undertake beta field studies and benchmark tests
Design	prototype concepts	iterate designs and production work	review designs and refine until ship
Development	cost features	write code and fix bugs	refine code until ship
Testing	create test plan and strategy	run automatic test suites	lots more testing
User Education	produce UE strategy	write docs and help	produce and print materials
Localization	create strategy and plan	translate language resources	test, verify, and refine product
Product Support	forecast support calls	determine support issues and strategies	handle customer support and log issues

the product. Because there were no key decisions made during hallway discussions or private emails, all design team members participated in and understood all decisions. Fourth, the Web site became an archive of all designs. When new members joined the team, it was easy for them to learn about the evolution of the product design. Also, other product teams used the Web site to learn about potential solutions to their problems.

A healthy tension emerged between various team members during the interdisciplinary design process. Checks and balances between different disciplines existed throughout the team. PM negotiated with development with respect to what could be implemented. Interaction design negotiated with PM to try to meet users' needs. Marketing and product planning negotiated with PM to determine the optimal feature set. Even usability and design negotiated. What might look the best might not necessarily work the best for users. In one case labels were removed from a find entry field to reduce clutter in the interface. While the result was indeed less cluttered, it was also unusable. In fact, a usability test participant joked that the field was "[the] mystery field, where even the designers didn't know what it was for." This interdisciplinary approach to design, anchored by a highly collaborative usability and design group, is the goal for all Windows CE product teams.

5.4 Evolution of the Design

As previously described, Windows CE target users were identified as mobile professionals. They spent a set amount of time away from their computers, and they were already using Windows desktops and applications. Specifically, they were using Microsoft Word or Microsoft Excel and Microsoft Schedule+ to manage their personal information. Users needed a solution that would enable desktop information to become portable while also being able to create new information while away from their PC. It was also important that the new information be easily transferred back to the PC.

The following is an example of a very early H/PC scenario. While it does not contain all the details to cover all tasks supported by the product, it provides insight to what the designers were thinking about during the initial brainstorming sessions.

> A lawyer spends a lot of time in meetings away from her desk. Although the meetings take place in her office building, she is required to take notes and write up summaries for future reference. She frequently references Microsoft Word documents created on her PC during these meetings. One meeting usually triggers another, so the lawyer needs access to her schedule at all times.

In this scenario it is clear that a keyboard for touch-typing and an application for note taking are necessary. While the lawyer doesn't leave her building, she is still mobile and requires the ability to view and modify her personal information. In this case, she needs to view her upcoming appointments. She also requires the ability to create document outlines and view existing documents. Both the Microsoft Word documents and calendar information need to be transferred back to her PC so that she can have everything, especially her calendar information, up to date in one place.

FIGURE **5.2**

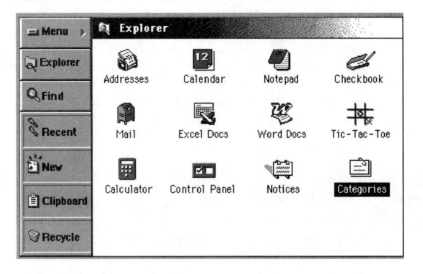

Pegasus initial concept: Explorer view.

During those first few weeks of brainstorming, the team focused on storyboarding concepts that would allow users to create and edit their contacts, appointments, and tasks and allow them to author documents compatible with Microsoft Word and Microsoft Excel. Pegasus, as that first H/PC was known, had a touch screen to navigate the interface and silk-screened buttons that enabled global functionality. Pegasus could share information with the desktop via a serial cable connection.

Figures 5.2 and 5.3 are screenshots of some initial Pegasus concepts. Down the left side of the figures are the silk-screened buttons. In Figure 5.2, users could access their calendar or address book information by activating the appropriate icon in the Explorer view. In Figure 5.3, users were able to flip through their address book entries via the tabs at the bottom of the screen.

This first H/PC prototype contained elements and concepts of its "older brother" desktop counterpart (e.g., file menus, familiar applications, familiar icons), but did not have the affinity necessary to identify itself as a Microsoft Windows product. The interface didn't really "look" like desktop Windows at all. There was no Start button. There was no task bar. However, there were familiar terms like Menu, Find, New, and Clipboard and also familiar applications like Microsoft Word and Microsoft Excel.

The first usability test carried out with these interface concepts was with a paper prototype. Subjects were asked to accomplish a series of basic tasks

FIGURE **5.3**

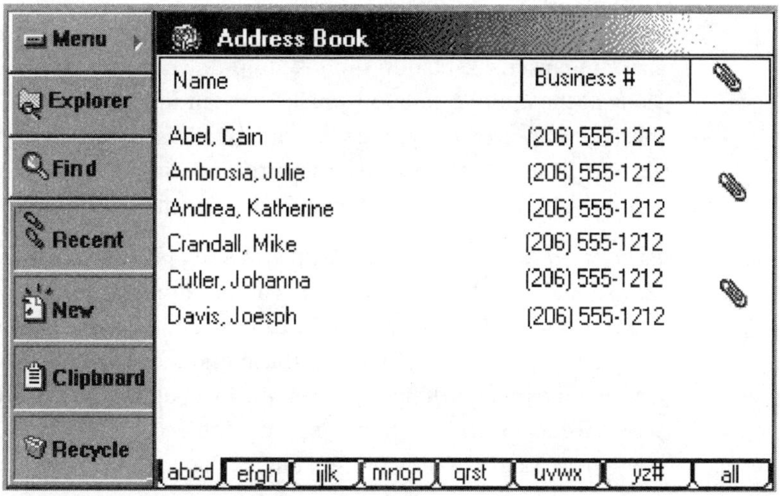

Pegasus initial concept: Address Book view.

that covered general navigation of the device as well as specific tasks within key applications. As an example, starting with the Explorer view (Figure 5.2), subjects were asked to locate the Davis expense report, which was an Excel file. The team wanted to learn if subjects would search for a place to launch the Excel application, or if they would see that they could locate the document directly using the Excel Docs item in the Explorer view. Interestingly enough, half of the subjects thought that the Excel Docs item in the Explorer view should launch the application and then once in the application they could locate the file. The other half of the subjects identified the Excel Docs item as a "container" for all their Excel documents. Another task asked subjects to create an address entry for Mike Crandall. Once again, half of the subjects tapped on the Addresses item in the Explorer view and while viewing the list of default entries tapped the New silk-screened item. The other half initially tapped the New silk-screened item and chose New Address from a list of available New items.

In both of these tasks the subjects were split on whether they viewed Pegasus as a document- or application-centric device. Although the team originally thought that they would implement only a document-centric model of navigation, it was clear from this first study that the alternative application-centric model might also need to be supported. This result was not surprising: subjects were early Windows 95 users and some possessed a document- and others an application-centric understanding of the PC. Although this first test used a low-fidelity paper prototype, it uncovered many other user interaction issues that the team would continuously revisit in future products. Some of these issues are listed below:

1. *People found the size of certain targets too small.* All subjects felt that the target size for items in a list (address book, drop-down menu, arrows on menu bar) and icons in the toolbar were too small. They felt most comfortable with the size of the large icons in the Explorer view and the silk-screened items. These icons were 32 × 32 pixels in size. Pegasus was initially designed to be "finger" accessible. It was thought that the product would not ship with a stylus or pen of any sort.

2. *People were not able to identify active areas on the address card.* Subjects felt that they should be able to touch the area of the address card that required editing. It was not clear to them if specific fields were active, the entire area was active, or the labels on the summary card (Business and Home) were active. Although device interaction is difficult to examine in a paper prototype due to limited on-screen feedback, these comments by the subjects informed the design team that it was necessary to clearly present targets that looked like they could be edited.

3. *People were confused with the selection/activation model.* Pegasus introduced the concept of single-tap activation. All subjects, however, used first-tap selection and second-tap activation to navigate the interface. This is not surprising given their PC experience and the fact that they were interacting with a paper proto-type. As a result of the observations, the design team realized that the selec-tion/activation model would be a difficult problem to address based on people's previous PC interaction experience.

About the time that the design team was planning the next rounds of research, focus group results indicated that the initial interface concepts did not have enough affinity to desktop Windows. While many of the initial con-cepts tested well from a usability standpoint, they did not test well from a product identification standpoint. Based on the results of these focus groups and additional feedback from top-level marketing and executive staff, the design team refocused and began working on a Microsoft Windows 95–like interface for the H/PC.

5.5 A New Direction—Microsoft Windows 95 Affinity

While user characteristics, tasks, and product goals remained the same, the design team was charged with creating an interface that strongly resembled Windows 95. Even with the interface design direction change, some of the fundamental interaction questions still remained. How large would on-

FIGURE **5.4**

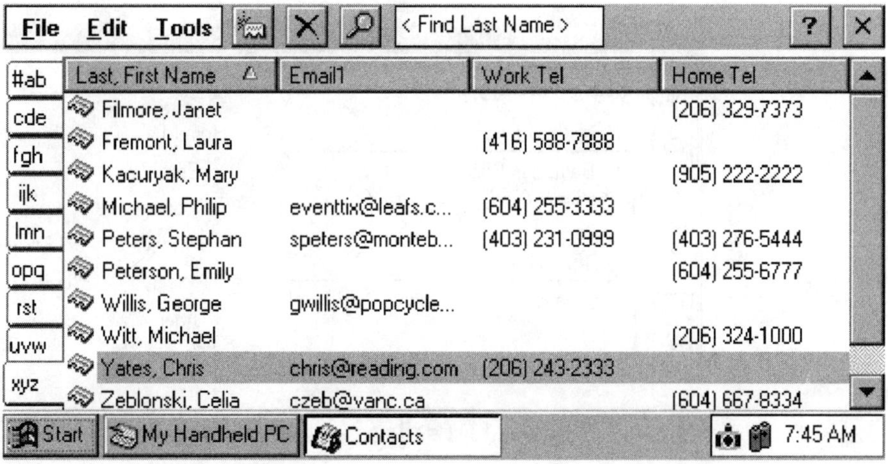

Pegasus: Contacts list view.

screen targets need to be, to be accurately activated with either a finger or a stylus? Could auto-save support and satisfy user's data management needs? Could single-tap activation be a successful method of interaction? Other questions arose dealing with screen real estate. In leveraging the Windows 95 design, it was clear that the team was targeting the familiarity and "walk up and recognize" scenarios. However, it was also clear that the design of Windows 95 was optimized for a large-screen display, not one that was two-bit color (white, black, and two grays) and 480 × 240 pixels in size. The designers needed to determine ways to conserve space and design for black and white. Given the high value of vertical pixel area, was the taskbar necessary? Were users going to need to switch quickly between running applications? Were there other cues that could be implemented, other than color, that could indicate active areas? Suddenly something that was very familiar and used by a lot of people created an immense design challenge.

Figures 5.4–5.6 are some near-to-final screenshots of the Windows 95 version of Pegasus. Both the Contacts list view (Figure 5.4), Contacts card view (Figure 5.5), and the Calendar day view (Figure 5.6) possess a strong visual affinity to the desktop counterpart at the time, Microsoft Schedule+. Also notice the familiar File/Edit/Tools menu structure and the Start button and taskbar. Both the silk-screened version and the taskbar version of the interface usability-tested well. Both proved to be effective when subjects were required to switch between views or documents. Evidence indicated that there was a short time period (perhaps 15–30 seconds) where silk-screen users were unsure what to do to begin the initial task. Taskbar users had no

FIGURE **5.5**

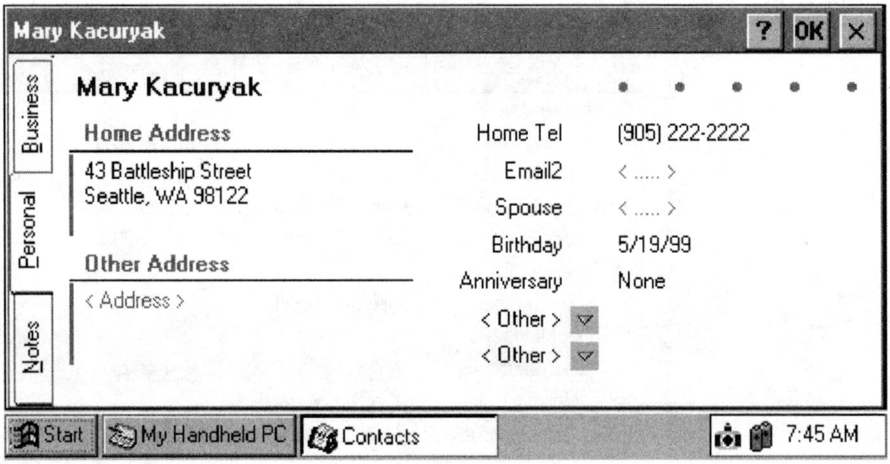

Pegasus: Contacts card view.

hesitations and immediately turned to the Start button to begin tasks. This was not the first nor the last time that the Windows 95 affinity proved to be successful for initial use.

Iterative usability testing addressed additional questions. The single-tap activation and save model was examined over several testing sessions. Conclusions from these tests indicated that while single-tap activation proved to be an efficient and natural style of interaction using a stylus, selection was a feature that was going to be difficult to modify. This feature was too highly ingrained in users to be omitted or redesigned. If the design team were to consider implementing single-tap activation, then other aspects of interaction would have to be revisited. As an example, in the above Contacts list view, if users wanted to delete an item, they would single-tap to select and then tap the delete icon. If single-tap activation were implemented, how could users accomplish this task? These initial touch screen products did not have the luxury of on-screen pointers, so hovering, as in PC Web applications, was not an option to indicate focus. While solutions to this problem do exist (as an example, use a tap and hold action to activate a context menu where the delete command could exist), none resembled any action that could be accomplished on the desktop. In the end, single-tap selection with second-tap activation was implemented.

The auto-save model also failed in initial usability tests. Users heavily relied on the PC save model (save early, save often). Although the design team attempted to make interaction with the device more efficient, users were not comfortable with the changes. The PC save model was too

FIGURE **5.6**

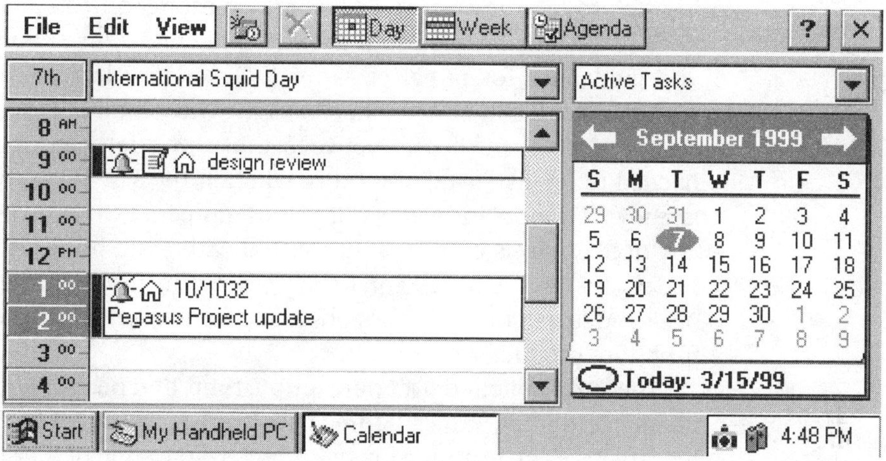

Pegasus: Calendar day view.

ingrained in users. It is interesting to note that while users can work around most usability problems, they were incredibly uncomfortable with a new method of saving their data. When it came to their data, subjects said something like "My data is very precious. I want to be in control of it at all times." It was decided that implementing a new auto-save model was too great a design risk for the first version of this product. As a result of this finding, the standard PC save model was implemented for H/PC 1.0.

Recently, the design team revisited single-tap activation. It has been implemented and is currently undergoing usability evaluation. Preliminary results indicate that single-tap is a successful, automatic, and efficient method of interaction. Additional research has indicated that people delete much less frequently than they create and edit. With this in mind, a tap-and-hold operation is available to activate a context menu where the delete command exists. Granted this is not an immediately discoverable solution, however, preliminary results from extended usage studies indicate that users can learn this operation and use it successfully. This decision trades off initial usability for extended use.

5.6 Touch Target Research

The fundamental question of target size was also addressed with user research. What was the smallest-sized target that a person could accurately tap with their finger or a stylus? With the adoption of the Windows 95–like interface, Pegasus hardware gained a keyboard and stylus. It was clear that in order to take advantage of screen real estate, on-screen elements would need to become smaller. At that time, there was a lot of published research and guidelines for target sizes on CRT screens, but there was very little research that could be referenced dealing with small LCD screens. There was also a constant push/pull between those who felt that more information needed to be displayed and those who felt the screens were dense enough already ("Fit more in!" versus "If you fit more in, I won't be able to see or use any of it!"). Pixels could not be wasted with extra buffer space, but targets had to be large enough for users to see and hit accurately. A study was designed to halt these discussions as well as to establish target size standards for future products.

The study solicited user perception, time, and performance data and was divided into three parts. All three parts were repeated for both finger and stylus targets. As an example for stylus targets: part one of the study showed the range of targets at different sizes one at a time and subjects were asked the question "Do you think you can accurately hit the target?" The design team was interested to learn if people had an idea of how large a target that they could accurately hit. It was felt that if a customer was comparing several competitor product interfaces in a display case, part of their decision as to which one they would first try might be related to whether they thought they could use the interface. If the interface appeared too small, then they might not pick out the product. In part two, subjects interacted with the device and attempted to tap a target when it was displayed on screen. The third part of the study was identical to the first: subjects were presented with the range of targets and asked the question "Do you think you can accurately hit the target?" Here the team was interested to learn if user perception changed after interacting with the interface. The three parts were repeated with both stylus and finger targets. All variables were randomized.

Based on the results of this study the minimum-sized target that could accurately be hit with a stylus was 5.04 mm^2, and with a finger was 9.04mm^2. It was also interesting to note that on average, subjects dragged their stylus approximately 2 mm between tap down and tap up. The perception data showed people generally thought that they could not accurately hit many of the targets. In other words most target sizes presented were perceived as too small to hit. Part three data indicated that people thought they could accurately hit as many of the targets as they actually did. After using the product, the interface wasn't as hard to use as the subjects initially thought. This indicated to the team that it was important to have a hands-on area wherever the products were sold. These were just a few summary results from the study; however, the stylus numbers have set the standard for the size of on-screen elements in all portable Windows CE products to date.

5.7 Post H/PC 1.0

After the first version of the Handheld PC shipped in the fall of 1996, Windows CE was labeled by most consumers and critics as a small version of Windows 95. Future interfaces for the range of Windows CE products were inevitably tied to their desktop counterpart. The Handheld PC was not just an electronic organizer, it was a desktop companion. Essential information stored on the PC could be transferred to the device and accessed. Applications on the handheld product looked and acted like their desktop counterparts. Microsoft Pocket Word looked like Microsoft Word, only without the full range of features. People could sit in meetings or on the bus and create outlines or simple documents that they could then transfer to their PC to complete. Expense report templates could be created on the PC and transferred to the device to be filled out when traveling. Calendar, Contacts, and Tasks began to take on more characteristics of the new PIM standard, Microsoft Outlook. Through the synchronization process, people were able to take their Outlook information with them wherever they went. They could schedule a meeting or look up a phone number while away from their PC. Based on feedback gathered after the release of the first version of the H/PC, it was clear that people required larger devices with larger keyboards to allow touch-typing and smaller devices that were more portable. Based on the release schedule for the Handheld PC 2.0 (1997) and Palm-sized PC 1.0 (1998), the Windows 95–like interface was going to stay. As a result, the design team continued to focus on screen real estate and interaction issues in all products.

5.8 Getting Larger

For the second version of the Handheld PC (code-named Mercury), users and scenarios remained the same as they were in version 1.0. Figure 5.7 is the Contacts card view that appears in both the H/PC 2.0 and H/PC 3.0 products. There are two major differences from the equivalent view on the H/PC 1.0: the default font is larger (9-point Tahoma as opposed to 8-point MS Sans Serif) and the Business, Personal, and Notes tabs have been replaced by view-switching icons in the upper-right portion of the interface. While the view-switching icons were not as discoverable as the tabs (in Western civilizations, people read from left to right and top to bottom), this was an attempt to reduce clutter in the interface. Once again, initial discoverability was sacrificed for long-term use. The larger font also made the card view easier to read.

FIGURE **5.7**

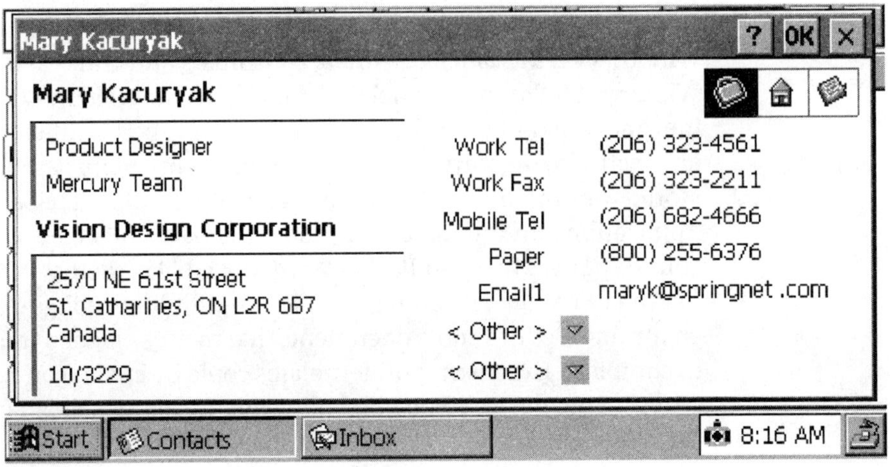

Mercury: Contacts card view.

5.9 Font Study

One of the fundamental design issues that needed to be addressed was system font size. Feedback received from the H/PC 1.0 focused primarily on font legibility. While the target sizes in list views satisfied the hit target data, people complained that the default font size was just too small to read. The design team knew that the larger font sizes were more legible; however, there was a limit to what could be implemented. If the font went over a certain size, it would require an entire redesign of the interface. Dialog boxes and list view headers would no longer fit. While the interface might become more readable, it would drastically reduce the amount of information that could be displayed.

A study was undertaken to determine the size of font that would be most legible on a black-and-white screen. Twenty-five participants, roughly half male and half female, were presented with a paragraph of text on a black-and-white screen. They were asked to locate randomly introduced errors (spelling mistakes or grammatical errors). Up to five errors were introduced in the paragraph of approximately 100 words. Subjects were asked to tap on the error. The conditions that were presented covered three fonts (Microsoft Tahoma, Microsoft Verdana, and Microsoft Sans Serif), two weights (bold and regular), three sizes (8-, 10-, and 12-point) and two backgrounds (white and gray). The 36 conditions were presented twice (randomized), and subjects were asked to locate as many errors as quickly and accurately as possible. Subjects were also asked to rate how easy/hard they thought it was to read the paragraph on a seven-point Likert scale.

While there was no clear winner across all conditions, there were some interesting results. The font implemented should be at least 10 points in size and either MS Tahoma or MS Verdana. Bold or regular fonts on a white background were easy to read. If a gray background was to be used, a bold font was preferred. Although all agreed that the 10-point regular Tahoma font was the best to use as the system default, it could not be implemented without a development hit. Tahoma 10-point was too large to fit in existing dialogs and interface designs. Every dialog and screen would have to be redesigned out to make the new font fit. As usual, a compromise needed to be struck between the design and implementation teams. All team members agreed that any size Tahoma was better than shipping MS Sans. User preference data indicated the same sentiment. As a result, 9-point Tahoma was chosen as the default system font. When rendered, it was not that much smaller than 10-point and it fit into the existing interface designs.

One would think that choosing a system font would be a simple decision: pick something large and easy to read. However, in the end, resource and existing interface constraints ultimately directed the decision. This exercise is a good example to show how all members of the product development team—PM, visual design, usability, development, and test—needed to understand the problem, realize the impact on the user, and ultimately compromised in order to present the best-possible solution.

5.10 Getting Smaller

As the Mercury team focused on shipping the second release of the H/PC, there was another team working concurrently on the first release of the Palm-sized PC. Version 1.0 (code-named Gryphon) was released in the spring of 1998. Based on feedback from the mobile professionals using the H/PC 1.0, one group of users were definitely taking advantage of the Pocket Office applications and wanted a bigger screen to see more data and a larger keyboard to make data entry quicker and easier. Another group wanted a smaller, more portable product that provided quicker methods of data entry and lookup while still providing access to desktop information. This group indicated that they still needed support for managing PIM data and email. However, they also requested alternative methods for entering data into the device. As with the H/PC products, the P/PC relied on synchronization to transfer data between the device and the desktop PC.

FIGURE **5.8**

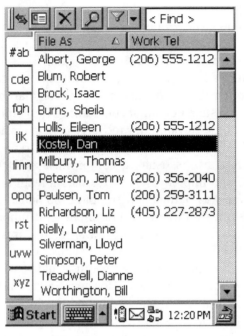

Gryphon: initial Contacts list view.

Figures 5.8–5.10 show three possible versions of the Contacts application list view. In Figure 5.8, while the necessary information appears on screen, the view is quite dense. Essentially it is the H/PC 1.0 design sized to fit the P/PC 1.0 screen size. In order to locate any additional information on the highlighted item, the user is required to open the card view. In the second screenshot (Figure 5.9), the user can scroll through the contact list names using a hardware button or scrollbar. Additional information appears in the preview portion at the top of the screen. Here designers tried to present essential information to users without having them open the item for additional information. The third screenshot (Figure 5.10; see also Color Plate) shows a concept version that deviates most from a traditional Windows CE look. Only the essential pieces of data are presented to the user. Through the flexible second column, the user can customize the piece of information to be displayed. As an example, either a home number or a work number or email could be displayed. Research gathered from the 1.0 product indicated that users wanted to be able to customize the data displayed in the main view. They wanted to be able to quickly locate the pertinent contact infor-

FIGURE **5.9**

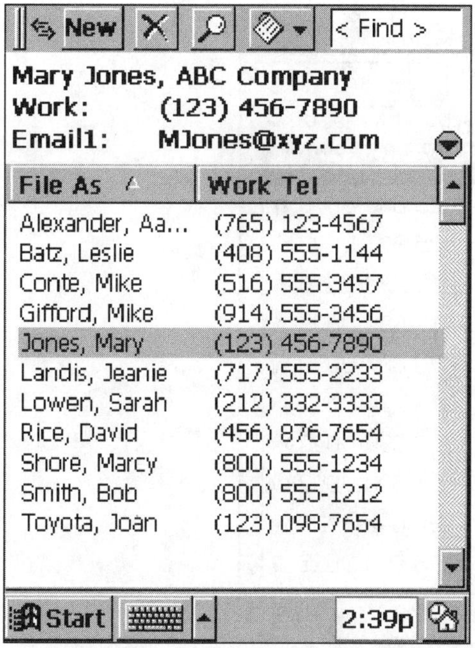

Gryphon: almost-final Contacts list view.

mation without having to open the contact card view. This flexible column was a potential solution for this issue.

The following is an example of a very early P/PC scenario. While it doesn't contain all the details to cover all tasks supported by the product, it gives an idea of what the designers were thinking about during the initial brainstorming sessions. Although this scenario describes a student (who might not normally be considered a mobile professional), it is used to illustrate how a portable solution could possibly satisfy many different user categories.

> Walking from building to building, a university student needs to find out where her next class is located. In class she quickly writes down her homework assignment. A new tutor provides both office hours and contact information that she also records.

In this scenario, the student needs to access her calendar information quickly. The product should be small and easy to carry. She has all of her class locations recorded in her calendar entries, so being able to look up information while walking from class to class is important. Mechanisms are

FIGURE **5.10**

*Palm-sized PC concept: Contacts list view. A list of
contacts showing related telephone number. Single
tap activates the detailed view of the contact.*

necessary to support quick lookup of information, preferably with one hand,
and quick data entry.

During the first few weeks of brainstorming, it was evident that with the
smaller screen size, the Windows 95–style interface began to degrade. The
challenge for the design team was to maintain the Windows 95/Windows CE
affinity and allow quick access to necessary user data. Initial design challenges were obvious. How would an interface originally designed for a 480 ×
240 pixel size screen adapt to a portrait-oriented 320 × 240 pixel screen? Also,
how would a user quickly enter data without a keyboard? Presenting essential information, hardware buttons, voice recording, and a handwriting
application were implemented to address these issues.

One of the hallmark features of Gryphon was input. While the previous
two versions of the Handheld PC relied on a keyboard to enter text, Gryphon
explored new methods of input including handwriting recognition and voice
recording. User research indicated that people wanted to be able to quickly
capture short pieces of information. Research also indicated that people

would not want to author large documents created for 8.5 × 11-inch sheets of paper. Entering data was not difficult, but rather the small-sized screen made it difficult to view the document-like information. The team had the opportunity to choose among several available handwriting recognizers. A user study was used to determine which recognizer would ship with Gryphon.

The study examined the "walk up and use" scenario. It was believed that initial use greatly influenced initial impressions of the product. Twenty subjects were given various text samples to enter into the device using five different types of stylus entry (three potential shipping recognizers, an on-screen QWERTY-style keyboard, and a nonshipping recognizer used for base data). The study was divided into three parts. During part one, subjects were allowed to try out the recognizer for 5 minutes. They could enter anything they wished. Part two allocated them 10 minutes to study documentation on the recognizer. During part three, subjects were required to enter a short sentence, a name and address, and a paragraph of approximately 25 words. All subjects used all input methods and recognizer use order was randomized. Preference data was also collected with subjects rating each method of input on various "ease of use" scales.

During many of the usability studies that were run prior to this test, subjects frequently complained of the tediousness when using a small on-screen keyboard to enter data. So it was surprising to learn that subjects performed fastest and most accurately with the on-screen keyboard. Subjects also rated the keyboard as easiest to use. Based on these results alone, it would appear that a handwriting recognizer would not be necessary. However, it should also be noted that test participants had never before used a handheld product. They had no experience using any method of stylus input. Separate research indicated that experienced handheld users preferred using a handwriting recognizer. So it was necessary to ship both methods of data entry to satisfy both new and experienced users.

5.11 Auto PC: Different, Yet Part of the Family

Auto PC (code-named Apollo) was one of the first products in the Windows CE family to deviate from the pure Windows CE/Windows 95 look. It was not just the look that was different or the fact that the display size had gotten even smaller. There was no stylus. There was no touch screen. It was a product specifically designed to support tasks of a mobile professional while driving. In fact, this leads to the main difference between Auto PC (A/PC) and other Windows CE products. In the car, driving is the primary task. Any interaction with the Auto PC while driving is considered a secondary task, and

FIGURE **5.11**

Apollo: Start Menu. An Auto PC in-car face plate with the Start screen displayed. The left/right control scrolls through the available programs. The green Action button is used to activate the selected application.

input and output methods were designed with this in mind. The following is a simple scenario describing how a person might use an A/PC:

> A real estate agent spends a majority of the day in his car driving from property to property. He uses his cellular phone to set up meeting times and locations with clients. His car becomes his "second office." He listens to the radio to monitor traffic situations.

The agent requires a method to look up the phone number of his next client and to dial his cellular phone to set up the meeting time. Ideally it would be best if he could do this without taking his hands off the wheel and his eyes off the road. He also requires a means to keep track of names and addresses. Since he is in his car driving, directions to his next meeting would also be helpful so that he doesn't need to rely on a printed map. Receiving traffic updates is also important to the agent.

Figure 5.11 (see also Color Plate) shows the Start Menu that displays the available applications. From left to right the applications are Messages (which displays text messages such as traffic information or email), Settings (which contains the configurable system options), Disc Player (which is a standard CD player), Audio (which contains all audio settings), and Directions (which uses GPS technology to provide point-to-point directions between two locations). Not pictured in this view are the Radio and Address Book applications.

Figure 5.12 shows two screenshots from the Address Book application. These pictures show part of the sequence a user goes through to manually

FIGURE **5.12**

Apollo: Address Book screens.

enter text into the Address Book list. Characters can be typed in using the numeric keypad. It should be noted that while many Windows CE products support a Contacts application, the Auto PC adopted the term "Address Book." There were two reasons for this decision: first, Address Book had higher speech recognition rates than the word Contacts, and second, the Auto PC did not support calendar or task applications. Without the complete set of PIM applications, it did not seem appropriate to adopt one application name on its own.

The design of Auto PC was dictated by the car environment and the tasks accomplished by the user. Viewing angle and distance defined the font size. Hardware that fit into the standard-size car stereo slot allowed very few hardware controls. Driving as the primary task required that new forms of input and output control the system. Auto PC used a speaker-independent voice command and control interface to operate portions of the interface. Sound provided feedback about the state of the system and the applications. Voice input and sound output allowed users to interact with the product without using their hands. This satisfied the design team goal to allow users to interact with the Auto PC without taking their eyes off the road or their hands off the wheel.

An Address Book application managed names, addresses, and phone numbers and phone-dialing operations. In cases where users wanted to enter a new name and phone number, they either had to transfer it from an H/PC or P/PC using infrared or they did it manually with the button interface. A Directions application "spoke" point-to-point directions while driving. Auto PC was truly a multimodal product unlike any other Windows CE product.

Even with these radical deviations from the traditional handheld products, A/PC maintained some affinity with its Windows CE counterparts. The Start Button activated the Start Menu that contained the list of applications on the A/PC. Also, each application used the title bar area to provide context to the user about the active application. Also, contact information originating on the desktop could be transferred to the device from a handheld product.

While other Windows CE teams relied on the interaction design team to guide design decisions, a field study technique was used to involve the entire Auto PC team to learn about their product, the environment in which it was used, and its users. It was clear that the A/PC, while still supporting common tasks such as contact lookup, was a very different Windows CE product. Product team members needed first-hand observations to better understand the design space. Research was carried out that had members of the product team accompany users on drives in order to learn about how people interacted with their Auto PC systems. Team members were taught interview and observational techniques during a one-hour orientation meeting. Typically, two members of the product team would collect information about how the Auto PC was used in the field. During the data collection phase, one team member acted as the interviewer while the other member recorded data. Field notes from each visit were recorded, with summaries sent to all team members. The usability engineers analyzed this data. Comments and lessons learned were organized according to questions that were asked going into the study. An ethnographic approach (Beyer and Holtzblatt 1998) was taken to discover and report important questions/issues that emerged during the field study.

The collaborative technique worked well from both a social and product design standpoint. All members of the team who participated gained a richer understanding of the product space. As an example, the field study found that interoperability of in-car productivity equipment with office computer systems was compelling because a lot of business work took place in the car. Before getting into the car, people plan their day and prepare for meetings that will take place. While driving, people need to be kept informed of schedule changes. Waiting at a stoplight is an opportune time to make phone calls or jot down notes that will be dealt with later. Once back at the office, notes and field work are transferred to the business computer system. While the first version of Auto PC does not satisfy all of these needs, the integration of the cell phone with the Address Book was the first step to satisfying needs of car-based mobile professionals.

5.12   Familiarity versus Task-Oriented Design

Unpracticed or inexperienced designers may search for the recipe of good design to ensure product success. What steps can be followed to produce a usable, aesthetically pleasing, successful product? When considering this, it would appear that consistency alone could provide the obvious solutions to the hardest problems. Take something that users understand, use frequently and successfully, and copy it. This was part of the rationale behind making the first version of Windows CE and the applications that ran on it look like Windows 95 and the corresponding desktop applications. Many people use Windows 95 on a daily basis. They have invested time in learning and optimizing their use of the product. They have also invested their data to formats supported by the system. Companies have invested time training people how to use Windows 95. Any new system introduced into the consumer space is another system to learn. A new system introduced into the workplace could increase training costs. It would have been shortsighted to ignore these facts.

It is interesting to note that these points map almost exactly to the advantages of consistency outlined by Nielsen (1989) in *Coordinating User Interfaces for Consistency*. If considered literally, it would appear that all Windows CE products should match Windows desktop counterparts identically. A proven ticket to success would be to map new product designs to the existing system. However, not all Windows CE products support the same functionality because not all devices serve the same purposes. Windows CE designers are now beginning to balance the tasks that a user needs to accomplish, the form factor of the device, and the degree of desktop affinity retained.

When examining the range of Windows CE products and tasks that can be accomplished on each product in relation to their desktop counterpart, various conclusions can be drawn. Form factors are different. Methods of input and output are different. User expectations are different. Tasks that users need to accomplish are also different than their desktop PC counterparts. From a usability standpoint, interface consistency was not enough to ensure success in the first iterations of the Palm-sized PC. Although the product looked like both its handheld and desktop counterparts, the design increased the number of steps it took to accomplish a task. If quick data lookup was a key requirement for the product, then it wasn't being satisfied with the multiple screen taps necessary to acquire information. So while familiarity and functionality were satisfied, usability was not. In this case, ease of learning conflicted with ease of use. While the "walk up and use" scenario was satisfied, long-term use was significantly hampered. Another interesting example of consistency breaking down is the selection/activation model. Although the single-tap activation model was rejected early in the product development cycle due to the lack of a usable selection model, the desktop familiarity approach was also strongly applied. The action of double-tap with a stylus is an unnatural, inefficient, and difficult motor control skill. (Consider that a person skids at least six pixels each time they tap.) There is nothing about a touch screen that indicates a double-tap would be necessary to activate an item. During usability testing, all users new to hand-held devices initially single-tap to activate until they learn that the action is not supported. In this case, consistency worked against learning and use (Grudin 1989). While the initial Windows CE products mapped well to external consistencies (the Windows 95 interface), they didn't map well to internal consistencies (how people thought about and wanted to accomplish the task). Both of the above examples clearly indicate that external consistencies can provide initial usability wins, but satisfying long-term usage scenarios ultimately defines the usability of the product.

5.13 Conclusion

As the family of Windows CE products evolves, the interface takes on new looks and new characteristics. New platforms and environments fuel many of the interface developments. One thing remains clear: to date, Windows CE interfaces have always contained a flavor of desktop Windows. Windows is installed on a great number of PCs, both in the office and home environments. It makes sense to leverage familiar designs in new emerging platforms in both of these environments. As existing Windows CE products have shown, the user tasks and device designs are quite diverse. There is no reason to think the tasks and designs will become any less diverse in the future. Specialized devices will continuously be designed to suit user needs and environments. However, it would be shortsighted to conclude that the same interface would suit all tasks in all potential environments regardless of how recognizable the interface. On the one hand, it would appear that a common interface would satisfy all user needs. On the other hand, it would be impossible to design an interface to satisfy this goal.

Consistency of cross-platform interfaces has become a hot topic. It is one thing to develop a family of products that appear to work in similar environments (like handheld products), but as product lines expand into the realms of TV and cars, interface consistency becomes more difficult. There are no clear rules to follow for when and when not to be consistent. When creating the family of Windows CE products, respect must be given to desktop Windows. To create successful products, the scenarios to be supported cannot ignore Windows, nor can Windows override the design realities and requirements of nonPC environments. Therein lies the design challenge facing Windows CE designers.

5.14 References

Beyer, H., and K. Holtzblatt. 1998. *Contextual Design: Defining Customer-Centered Systems.* San Francisco: Morgan Kaufmann.

Frederiksen, N., and B. Laursen. 1992. *User Interface Consistency: A Case Study Suggesting User Involvement in Consistency Design Issues.* Denmark: Aarhus University, Computer Science Department.

Grudin, J. 1989. The case against user interface consistency. *Communications of the ACM* 32:1164–1173.

O'Hara, R. P. 1997. *Introducing Microsoft Windows CE for the Handheld PC.* Redmond, WA: Microsoft Press.

Nielsen, J. 1993. *Usability Engineering.* Boston: Academic Press Professional.

Nielsen, J. (Ed.). 1989. *Coordinating User Interfaces for Consistency.* San Diego: Academic Press, Inc.

CHAPTER Six

The EPOC User Interface
in the Psion Series 5

NICK HEALEY

Slash Design Ltd.

FIGURE **6.1**

Psion Series 5.

6.1   Introduction

In July 1997 the British company Psion launched the Series 5 palmtop computer (see Figure 6.1; see also Color Plate). With a 640×420 grayscale screen, it included a word processor and spreadsheet, agenda (calendar) and address book, calculator, world time and alarms, voice memo, and programming language, all built in. Its keyboard and hinge mechanisms, for which patents have been applied, produced the first truly typable keyboard on a palmtop and the first "untippable" touchscreen.

The community of Psion users has long displayed the sort of loyalty, occasionally evangelical, that Apple has inspired with its products, and this has continued with the Series 5.

The Series 5 was based on a custom-written software "platform" (operating system plus applications) called EPOC (see Figure 6.2). This is now the product of a separate company, Symbian, which is jointly owned by Nokia,

Symbian, the Symbian logo, EPOC, and the EPOC logo are trademarks of Symbian Ltd. Psion, the Psion logo, Series 3, Series 3a, Series 3mx, Series 5, Series 5mx, and Revo are trademarks of Psion plc. All other trademarks are acknowledged.

FIGURE **6.2**

EPOC logo.

Motorola, Ericsson, Psion, and Matsushita (Panasonic). These companies have agreed to use EPOC in their products, developing its UI further, and to license it to other firms, making it the new global industry standard for new ranges of wireless information devices (WIDs), including smart phones, communicators, palm-sized machines, palmtops, and notebooks.

This rest of this chapter is concerned with the UI of EPOC as it developed in the Psion Series 5 palmtop. (This same UI is to be found in Psion's later machines, the Series 5mx and Revo, launched in 1999 [Figure 6.3; see also Color Plate].) The chapter is arranged as follows:

- A short note on the background to EPOC and the Series 5

- A description of the design procedures used on the project

- A look at some UI design principles and their practical application in EPOC

- A discussion of some of the contentious design issues

- Finally, a brief conclusion on where the industry stands in UI terms

This is not an academic or theoretical paper. I intend to offer suggestions for how to design better UIs and how to let your company be creative, based on our experiences on this project. I also hope to give a little of the flavor of the story/history of the project.

FIGURE **6.3**

Psion Revo.

I led the software specification team on the project and was the chief UI designer. However, in April 1999 I left my position as head of product design at Symbian to start Slash Design; this chapter expresses my personal opinions, not those of Psion or Symbian.

6.2 The Birth of EPOC and the Series 5

The predecessor to the Series 5 was Psion's Series 3a palmtop computer (see Figure 6.4; see also Color Plate). Launched in September 1993, it packed unprecedented functionality and usability into its software, together with innovations in industrial design. While still only a moderate success in the United States, it led the industry in unit sales across the world as a whole.

The Series 3a had a very wide range of uses (and users). The size of a glasses case, and with a 480 × 160 grayscale screen, it included the same range of applications that the Series 5 was to offer, albeit a little simpler and with a keyboard-only UI (no touch screen). It also attracted a huge range of add-on software—including Microsoft Autoroute—expanding its appeal still further.

Understandably, a lot of much larger firms were sitting up and taking notice of this new market. No one could say how long the Series 3a would sell

Figure **6.4**

Psion Series 3mx (latest model in the Series 3a line).

for. It was an uncomfortable time for us at Psion—it was possible that a forthcoming Apple Newton would take over the market, or perhaps the next HP palmtop, or something rumored to be coming from Microsoft.

With the expectation of larger firms trying to move into the area in the near future, and with some knowledge of the likely innovations they might bring and markets they might address, Psion began the project to develop the Series 5. As well as addressing the two seemingly intractable engineering challenges of palmtops—making the keyboard typable without materially increasing size, and stopping touch screen use from tipping the machine over—it would be based on new EPOC software. Designed for more powerful 32-bit processors, EPOC would include more powerful applications than the Series 3a and a new graphical WYSIWYG touch screen UI.

Like the Series 3a, it would be targeted at maximizing the speed of access to the information people wanted while mobile, while minimizing the amount of UI to learn.

However, we also said up front that we were trying to create a new platform to last at least the next 10 years that would be fit for use in an as yet unknown range of devices: online palmtops, probably; industrial laptops, perhaps; on the desktop or in phones, even.

The UI therefore also had the target of being easier to use than existing desktop pointer-based UIs yet also easier to use from the keyboard than any other similar system. It had to provide access to powerful functionality via limited screen sizes, for an enormous range of uses and users.

And the new ranges of devices are coming. Before the launch of the Series 5, Psion had quietly reorganized, starting the process of licensing EPOC outside the Psion Group, a process that led to the formation of Symbian.

6.3 The Design Process for the EPOC UI

The Series 3a's word processor and spreadsheet supported the majority of the everyday features that desktop applications offered; its contacts and agenda applications had been designed from scratch, though, to provide what we thought were an appropriate range of features.

For the Series 5 we wanted to support all the Series 3a's functionality and build on it. The input to our understanding of what to add—the places where the Series 3a was not always satisfying desired usage patterns and key tasks—included feedback from technical support and from marketing, but also a huge amount from personal experience. When you've supplied quite a few machines to family and friends (as most of us in the software team had), you get all the feedback you can handle, from a wide variety of people. Half of the software team had become amateur researchers for the new design.

It was informal, of course, but large-scale field research, covering the myriad of uses people were making of their Series 3as, would have been impractical for a company of our size. It's not unreasonable to consider the Series 3a as providing an enormous prototype for the Series 5 project, producing huge amounts of informal user feedback.

There were no classically trained HCI people on the project, researching a new design. All our ideas about usage patterns, key tasks, users' conceptual models, and so on were informally generated by the company as a whole. They were considered (and reconsidered) throughout the project.

Given the number of design issues, more prototyping and user testing might have helped us with some decisions; but at the time we were too small a company, with too large and too unknown a task in front of us, to do much of either.

One thing we did have on our side, though, was experience. Several of EPOC's senior designers had worked on fast-changing projects, designing small-screen devices, for over a decade. Design uncertainty was for us part of the plan; reacting to changing ideas was something to explain to newer engineers as a positive force.

The uncertainty we felt reminded me of the old Data General project described in *The Soul of a New Machine*, Tracy Kidder's Pulitzer Prize–winning book, which I'd reread at the time (Kidder 1981):

> What a way to design a computer! "There's no grand design . . . . People are just reaching out in the dark, touching hands."

The book struck a chord in many ways. It tells the story of how a team of young engineers worked long hours, to short deadlines, to create a new 32-bit machine that they called "the best small computer in the world."

Major Software Requirements

We began with a huge effort to investigate new software ideas and technologies. Many had come from user feedback and many from technological advances and the extra power of the Series 5 processor.

Some new ideas seemed almost inevitable given the graphical, pen-based nature of this new palmtop. For example, borders and shading seemed obvious for the word processor and spreadsheet; the latter had to support pen-based setting of row heights and column widths. And a drawing application was obviously required.

The major new software components that we investigated and successfully incorporated included WYSIWYG editing and printing; compression of sound recordings; support for rewritable Flash disks; infrared data transfer between machines; a database management system supporting different field types; PC agenda synchronization; and finally, perhaps most significant of all, an object-based architecture that let EPOC embed objects—pictures, documents, spreadsheets, graphs, and sound recordings. Word processor documents may need to include embedded spreadsheets, graphs, or pictures. Address book entries may include a sketched map, say. Agenda entries may use a voice recording as part of the entry, perhaps, or a word-processed note, which itself might include its own objects.

But many software technologies did not, after detailed investigations, make the final cut. These included displaying multiple applications on screen; handwriting recognition; drag and drop and other gestures (like delete, help, select); persistent data stores as alternatives to filing systems; agents; universal password protection; data compression; global search; voice recognition and text-to-speech; switchable portrait orientation; and scalable fonts.

All fell by the wayside because they turned out, in our estimation, not to be quite as beneficial or practical as they might initially sound. Many other companies try to be first out with new technologies, but Psion had always been strongly disinclined to use each new technology or new technique until we felt it was genuinely useful. I think this attitude has a lot to recommend it. Consumer devices have to deliver for consumers.

UI and Application Specifications

In mid-1995—after a false start in 1994, when there were far too many major unknowns to make progress—an HCI design team set about specifying the Series 5's look and feel. In December 1995 it was formally replaced by a wider-ranging Series 5 spec team to guide and review all application and UI specifications. It included the most experienced designers from the software team plus a representative from Psion's product marketing team, and I had the pleasure of leading it.

We then undertook the task, all the way through 1996, of writing and/or reviewing specifications for the UI and functionality of all the applications. The outcome, and some of the difficult decisions made, form most of the rest of this chapter.

Handling Constant Change

A palmtop is like a miniature PC, and the scope of what might go into the specifications for the various applications is huge. We had to accept that there was no way we could write complete, detailed, agreed specs up front, sign them off, and then spend two years developing, with specs under change control. The design work—indeed, all kinds of specification effort—would continue at varying levels throughout the project. Lots of new, improved ideas would inevitably occur; thousands of minor issues would crop up.

And if every idea for improvement had had to go to a meeting of the Series 5 spec team, the project would probably still be going today. Accordingly, in parallel with the spec team, we began using the same fast reaction design technique we'd used on the Series 3a project. Together, three of the most experienced people formed what was referred to (in a semicynical way) as the "Thought Police." If you had an idea for a significant change to the spec of your application, at whatever stage, you had only to get the go-ahead from any two of the Thought Police. It allowed the project to deal with a huge range of new ideas and fixes with minimum overhead and red tape.

We chose not to maintain specs because of the fast pace of design change. In his book, *Dynamics of Software Development*, Jim McCarthy of Microsoft warns against spending your life sticking to and maintaining specs (McCarthy and Gilbert 1995). He felt as we did that doing so restricts you from getting the most out of your people, within your time constraints.

The Effect of Work Culture on Changing Designs

From *Dynamics of Software Development* (McCarthy and Gilbert 1995):

> The creation of a software product is more like a sixties happening than it is a rigorously scheduled and functionally segregated project . . . lurking just beneath the tidy, organised surface is a deep, rich, psychocultural extravaganza, in which creativity, group dynamics, crude instincts, and technological fashion run riot.

In making such a complex consumer device, requiring continual creative design evolution, Psion had a great advantage from its working culture. In June 1996, with the Series 5 project entering its late stages, a group of eight MBA students at London Business School (LBS) conducted a research project to examine the process of software development within Psion. The report they delivered (Boulton et al. 1996) noted the link between culture and design success thus:

> All evidence seems to back up the fact that Psion Software's culture is predisposed to creating the constant hits needed within the industry.

It also explained how they saw this culture, listing aspects such as

- Informal atmosphere

- Trust employees to govern own time and workload

- Encourage plain speaking, directness, and honest expression

- A commitment to visionary products—go beyond the consumer's current demands

Such a culture lets people from all over the company feel like they own the product as much as anyone else, and thus want to contribute, and feel they can contribute—even if it means disagreeing with senior colleagues openly. From the LBS report:

> New product features will always be suggested (often delivered as a fait accompli) by teams, as part of their general enthusiasm for creating the "ultimate software."

If your people don't feel like it's their product, or don't feel they can contribute wherever and whenever they want, or would feel too scared to do so, I can't see how you *can* design a complex, changing consumer device.

User reviews

In March 1997, with alpha release software running, we did our first and only set of user tests. With palmtops having such wide uses, we chose representatives covering new users, nontechnical Series 3a users, and technical Series 3a users.

Despite the limited size of the effort, and the time pressure the project was under, it was a very positive exercise. There were still many things they picked up on that we fixed.

However, we had to remind ourselves that user test feedback at any point is only an input to your design. Even if 100% of user test participants ask for something, you still have to convince yourself that you can really make it work well. Our test participants picked up on drag and drop in a big way, saying in particular that it would be nice if you could drag and drop files into folders. Rightly or wrongly, though, we'd decided that if we had tried to support drag and drop, it might cause more trouble, across the whole spectrum of uses and users, than the benefits it gave. (There's a more detailed discussion of this later in this chapter.)

Every now and then came a clear reminder to weigh comments carefully:

- "Nice weight—I like heavy things." (The Series 5 ended up just a little heavier than the Series 3a.)

- "Nice color—lime green." (Prototypes came in impractical colors. "Fluorescent green" would have been nearer the mark in this case.)

6.4   UI Design Principles in EPOC

Over time, during the design of the EPOC UI in the Psion Series 5, many general design principles began to crystallize. They are collected here, each with one or more examples taken from EPOC's UI; I hope some of them prove interesting and/or useful, and I hope they give a flavor of what EPOC is like to use.

Some of the problems and trade-offs that arose in developing these principles are discussed in a subsequent section.

Hide the Computer

Each time a user encounters something they don't understand, they're one step closer to giving up and throwing the product away.

FIGURE **6.5**

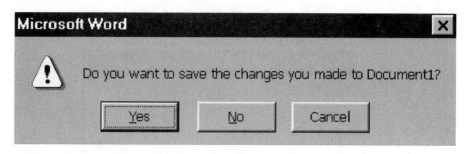

Windows asks the user about "saving changes."

Hide the "System Model"

Here is an example from EPOC's UI:

- In EPOC the difference between files "open in memory" and those "closed on disk" is hidden away. Users just edit their files and do not need to worry about "saving changes" or the like.

  On PC platforms, a user may create a new letter (say), type for a couple of hours, and then, when they close/quit/exit—or turn the machine off, or however they perceive "finishing"—be shown a "save changes" dialog (see Figure 6.5). The user did not ask for this dialog and may well not understand what it's asking, nor even what "Document1" is; they didn't call anything "Document1" themselves. (Have they changed some "thing" called "Document1" by mistake?) They're one wrong choice away from losing hours of work.

  We knew, though, that many people had already learned about saving and closing (sometimes the hard way), on PCs for example. We felt they might be confused; they might want to press "Save" every now and then, for example. Accordingly, EPOC does have Save and Close commands, for people who know them and want to use them. Users don't have to find/understand/use them, though, unless they want to.

Hide Complex or Scary Things

Following is another EPOC UI example:

- Any menu command that is complex, rarely used, or at all intimidating is hidden away on cascaded menus. Result: users can browse the menus seeing only commands they really want and understand. Consider the word processor's "File" menu (see Figure 6.6).

FIGURE **6.6**

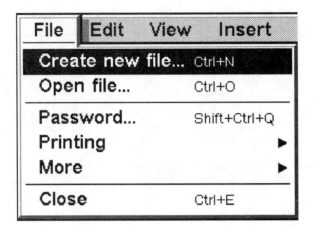

Complex or confusing commands are relegated to cascaded menus.

The more complex file-type commands that we thought might confuse people—like *Save as, Merge in,* and even *Save,* too—live on the "More" menu cascade. If a user understands them and wants them, they're there; if not, they don't see them.

- In EPOC dialogs, too, anything that is complex, rarely used or in any way intimidating is hidden away on secondary dialog pages. For example, the "Tabs" dialog in the word processor presents a simple front page containing only the option for a regular tab position, with all the advanced options like center/right alignment and irregular positioning "hidden" on the second dialog page (see Figure 6.7).

Use Simple, Unambiguous English

A great deal of attention to detail goes into making EPOC's wording and messages jargon-free and as simple and unambiguous as possible:

- EPOC's database/contacts application has "entries" (with "lines" that have "labels"). These are plain English words that people understand. EPOC doesn't use words like "record" or "field." Records are personal bests, or CDs. Fields are where cows live.

- In an apparent hangover from the days when every precious byte of ROM space had to be saved, it's still common to see software compress phrases (especially in "error messages"), omitting verbs, articles, and/or pronouns. The result is that they only make sense if the user already knows what the words are trying to say.

FIGURE **6.7**

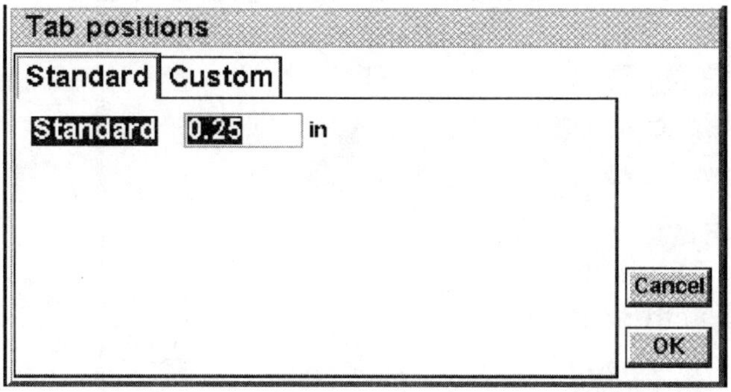

Complex or confusing options are hidden away from a dialog's first page.

For example, to a novice user, "read only file" might be misread as, perhaps, "You are only allowed to read files" or "Only a file was read." So instead, to be unambiguous, EPOC uses proper English sentences such as "This file is read-only."

- EPOC has "Create new file" and "Open file" commands, rather than just "New" and "Open"; it's a small detail, but it's just a little clearer.

Let Users Work Their Way(s)

Each time the user's perfectly reasonable action is rejected because it's not the designer's or programmer's preferred way of doing things, they're one step closer to giving up and throwing the product away.

Don't Force Just One Input Method

On PCs, we'd seen many people who like pointing at things, but many others (often, but not always, more "power users") who prefer keyboard use for as many actions as possible. So EPOC's UI is designed so that practically all tasks and commands can be performed easily both entirely from the screen or entirely from the keyboard:

- Dialogs are entirely keyboard operable if the user so desires, with the single column of dialog lines allowing arrow key–based navigation and setting (see Figure 6.8).
- Practically every menu command has a single hot key, like Ctrl + X, Ctrl + A.

FIGURE **6.8**

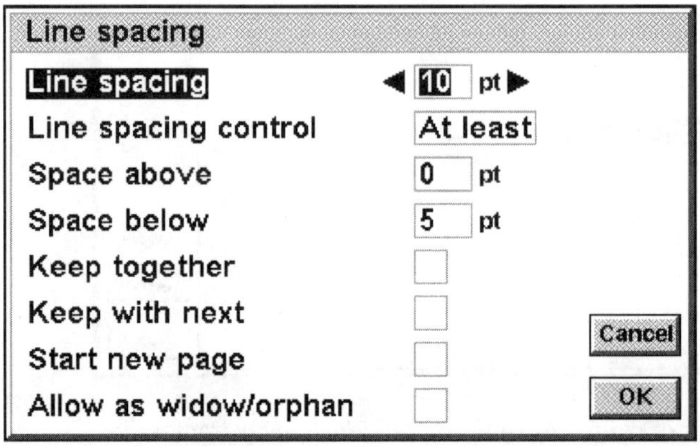

Sample EPOC dialog showing single-column layout for arrow key navigation.

Minimize the Amount to Learn

As with most modern software, EPOC allows the user to rely on consistent menu structures and dialogs across the platform. EPOC borrows common standards where appropriate from other platforms like the PC; many menus, commands and hot keys are immediately familiar. But in addition:

- In EPOC, there's no need to learn double-clicks. One tap selects something, and a second tap opens it. (Users can double-click if they want—it has the same effect as two single-clicks. Though even if they do understand double-clicks, two single-clicks are easier on a touch screen, especially on the move.)

- Toolbar buttons, which every application uses down the right-hand side of the screen, have text as well as icons, so they are easier to understand.

- Also, we avoid cluttering the screen with too many icons, multiple toolbars, hundreds of miniature buttons, and so on, instead focusing on the small number of things we think the user will really want on a frequent basis. For example, the spreadsheet has the standard toolbar of the four commonly used actions down the right of the screen. In common with the word processor, it also has a "toolband" across the top of the screen, containing just everyday useful functions that we felt even casual spreadsheet users would understand (see Figure 6.9).

Even with "accepted" paradigms, though, we still looked for ways to make things easier for the user. As mentioned before, in EPOC there's no need to learn about "saving changes" and the difference between "in memory" and "on disk."

FIGURE **6.9**

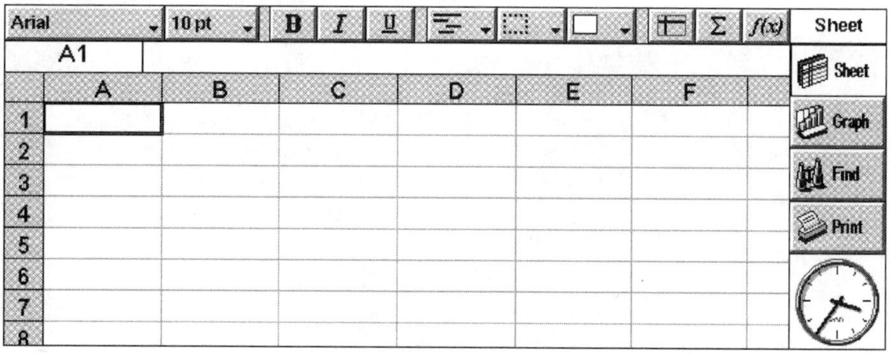

Uncluttered appearance of the EPOC Spreadsheet.

The principle of minimizing the amount to learn applies equally to EPOC's PC connectivity software, "EPOC Connect" (which for Psion machines, like the Series 5, is called "PsiWin"):

- EPOC Connect will automatically find the serial port that is being used and find the speed to communicate at. Users don't need to learn about serial ports to use it.

- The drives of the EPOC machine then just appear in Explorer. If a user has ever used Explorer, they can now manipulate and move files to and from their EPOC machine (see Figure 6.10).

- Once connected to a PC, EPOC Connect also links the two devices' clipboards. To transfer information a user can just Copy on one machine and Paste onto the other. (While linked, a Copy on one machine produces a little beep on the other, as a little clue that this can now be done.)

Finally, it's worth noting that the SDK is accompanied by a style guide for developers, to help ensure that third-party applications are just as usable and consistent.

Ask: "What Else Might They Try Here?"

As well as asking ourselves what a user might want at any point in the UI, we also ask, "What might they *try*?"

- What might they tap on? Tapping anywhere does whatever we feel is most likely to be what the user was hoping for. Consider the Time/Alarms screen (see Figure 6.11).

FIGURE **6.10**

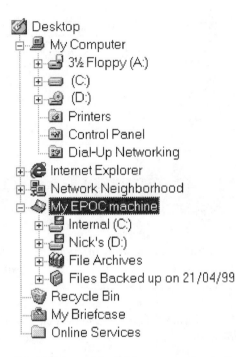

"My EPOC machine" drives appearing in Explorer.

Here, if a user clicks on the time or clock, the time setting dialog appears. If they click on the home city, the "set home city" dialog appears. If they click on the "Next alarm" notification, a dialog listing forthcoming alarms appears (see Figure 6.12).

(This principle was another supporting factor in the decision to make two single-clicks act as a double. If a user clicks somewhere, then they click on it again, chances are they're asking to "go into" the selected thing.)

- There's a metaquestion here though: what is a tap? On touch screen devices, we thought users might try using their finger, sometimes, to save time. So wherever possible—wherever it could be done without compromising anything else in the design—controls are large enough to be pressed by a finger. (For a discussion of target size research, see Section 5.6)

Let the User Customize It Their Way

As far as possible, applications can adapt to the way people work. Users can change a huge range of screen layouts and default entry settings, so that EPOC looks and works the way they want it to, not the way some designer prefers it (see Figure 6.13).

FIGURE **6.11**

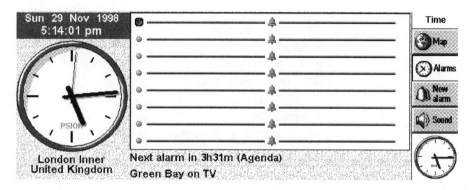

In Time/Alarms, any area—clock, home city or "Next alarm" info—can be clicked.

FIGURE **6.12**

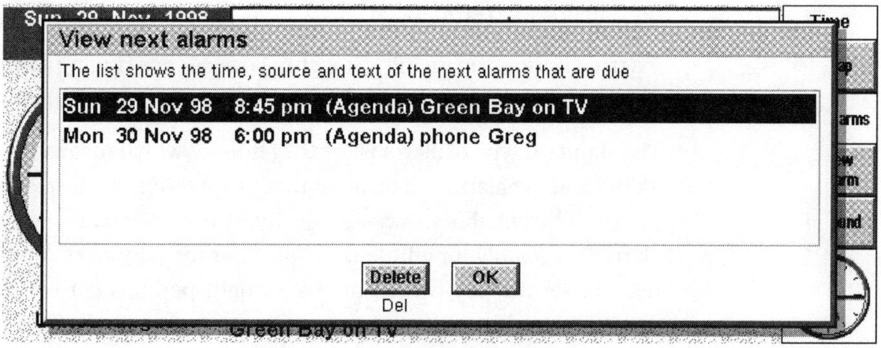

Clicking on "Next alarm" info produces a list of further alarms.

Make the UI as Quick to Use as Possible

Each time it seems to take an unnecessarily long time to achieve something, the user is one step closer to giving up and throwing the product away.

Require as Few User Actions as Possible

- To find an address or phone number, say, the user just presses the button for the contacts/phonebook application, and types the search string. That's all. When they press the application button, the machine will turn on, if necessary, and go

FIGURE **6.13**

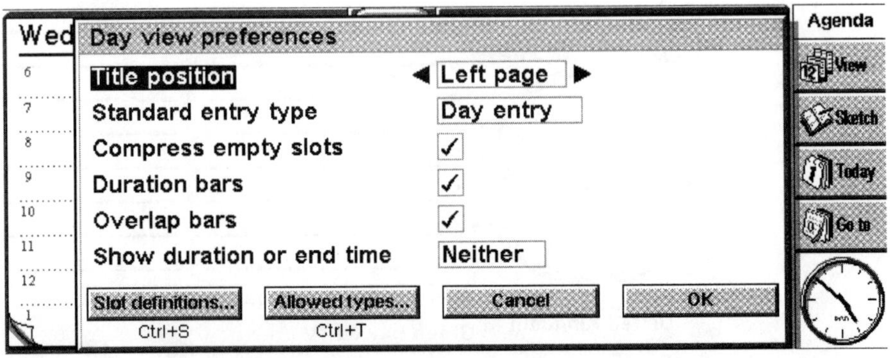

A preferences dialog, showing customizability of an Agenda view.

straight to the application. It will start the application if it's not running, and open the relevant file. And no command or action is required in order to begin entering a new search string.

- External buttons on an EPOC machine can silence ringing alarms without having to interact directly with the software—or even open the machine.

- The standard type of alarm is "next 24 hours," which means the user can just type a time and the alarm will go off at that time within the next 24 hours. We felt people would want this the vast majority of the time when setting an alarm—the alarm is probably for a little later today, or for tomorrow morning. So there's no need to set the day (which the user might perhaps get wrong), say. There's no need even to choose some "new alarm" command, in the Time application, to set the alarm. The user can just start typing the time they want the alarm.

- Alternatively, if the user starts typing letters on the Time screen, instead of numbers, that becomes the text of the alarm instead (see Figure 6.14).

- "Infoprints" show important feedback messages clearly but in a nonintrusive way. They go away after a few seconds without requiring the user to click "OK" like a dialog would (see Figure 6.15).

- Scrollbars' "nudge buttons" are situated together, not one at each end of the scrollbar, so the user can nudge positions up and down, or left and right, without having to move their hand around a screen (see Figure 6.16).

- As mentioned before, shortcut keys for almost every menu command allow an experienced user to do anything quickly (see Figure 6.17).

FIGURE **6.14**

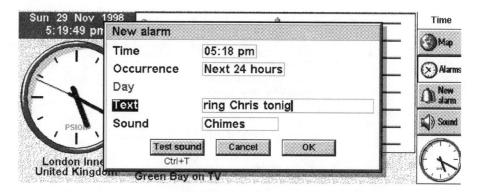

In Time/Alarms, text input goes directly to the appropriate dialog line.

FIGURE **6.15**

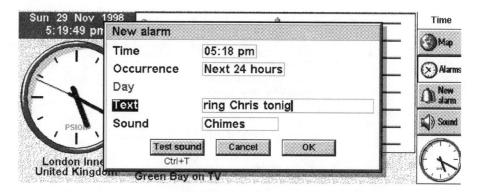

Infoprints provide nonintrusive feedback—here, "Alarm adjusted" appears when a time is changed.

- A user will occasionally use the same menu command repeatedly, for example, when changing the style of a paragraph or phrase, or setting screen display preferences, or looking for something with the "Open file" command, perhaps. So, when the menu is activated, it always appears with the last selected item highlighted, saving time on navigation.

This design decision does mean that the user loses the ability to select a menu command by pressing the menu key followed by a known sequence of right-arrow and down-arrow keypresses. Given that keyboard users almost always have

FIGURE **6.16**

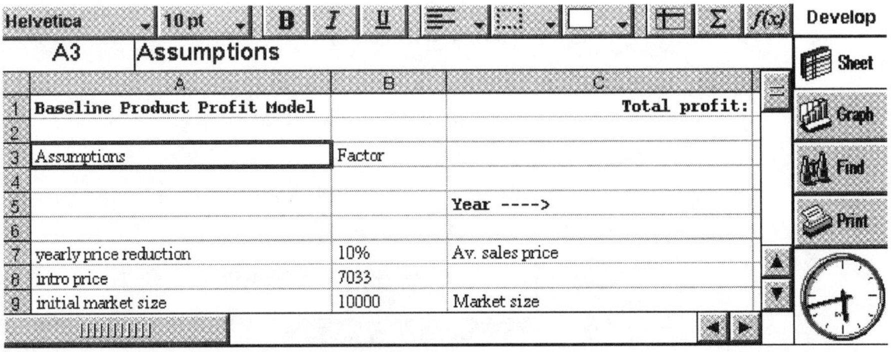

EPOC scrollbars use paired "nudge buttons" for speed.

FIGURE **6.17**

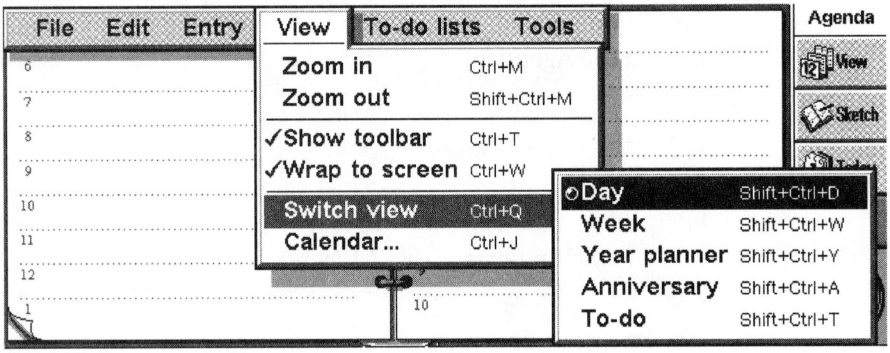

EPOC makes maximum use of shortcut keys.

a single hot key they can use for their favorite commands, we felt this was a sacrifice worth making.

- A user may often want to take a quick look at one view in their agenda, for example, at the Year planner or at ToDos, then go back to where they were. So we allowed the Esc key to toggle between the current and previous view in Agenda.

- A user may often want to take a quick look at today in their agenda, then go back to where they were. So we allowed the Space key to toggle between Today and the day currently being displayed.

FIGURE **6.18**

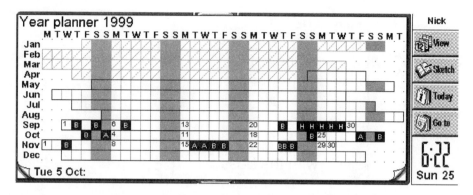

EPOC's Year planner redraws intelligently from the cursor position.

Display the Desired Information as Fast as Possible

This may sound obvious, but we look for every speed advantage we can find. For example, an existing cursor position may offer a clue to what to draw first. In the Agenda:

- The Day view fills out the side the cursor is on first—not just "left side first, then right." We feel a user is slightly more likely to be after that side; they may already have moved the cursor to the evening, say, before changing the day shown.

- The Year planner view buffers a year's worth of information, and so can usually redraw almost instantly. When it does need to recalculate and redraw a whole year, though, this can take a little time, so it draws outwards from the month the cursor is in, rather than just down from the top of the screen. This means that if the user already had the cursor at around the time of year they were interested in, in a different view, the information they're looking for will appear faster. If, for example, I was looking in the Day view for a holiday entry around October, but couldn't find it and so moved to the Year planner, it draws the grid then starts filling it outwards from October (see Figure 6.18).

  And there's my holiday, at the end of September.

Show as Much of the User's Information as Possible

No one wants to spend their time endlessly navigating around. So, to optimize the use of screen space:

- Menus are hidden when not in use.

FIGURE **6.19**

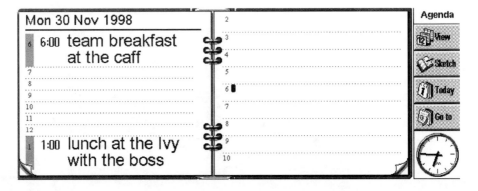

Agenda's Day view squashes empty slots to avoid needing scrollbars.

FIGURE **6.20**

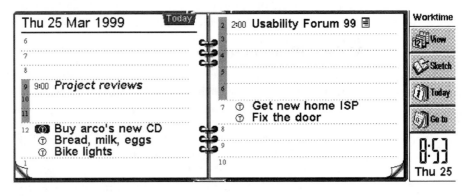

ToDo lists set to appear at suitable positions on the Day view.

- The user can turn off toolbars and scrollbars if they're not wanted.

- A single-keypress Zoom allows the user to show the smallest font appropriate to particular lighting conditions (and thus see the maximum amount of data).

- The Agenda squashes up empty time slots to maximize the amount of data displayed, instead of just displaying scrollbars (see Figure 6.19).

- ToDos can appear on "today" in the Day view, if desired, so the user can see their whole day in one go. Different ToDo lists can appear at different places on the Day view—a user might have their "Shopping" list appear at lunchtime, for example, and a "Home" list appear in the evening (see Figure 6.20).

FIGURE **6.21**

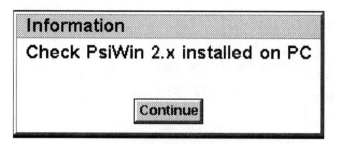

*Use of the less censorious word "Information" in place of
"Error."*

Of course, as time passes the ToDos move forward, always appearing on "today" until the user finally crosses them out or deletes them.

The Agenda can thus show the user all the things they're meant to do at different times of the day, without having to swap between ToDo lists and a Day view.

Make It Pleasant to Use

Each time something unpleasant happens, the user is one step closer to giving up and throwing the product away. Each time something nice happens, though, they're one step closer to joining your company's fan club.

Don't Make the User Feel Stupid

- Words like "error" make it sound like the user has made a mistake. EPOC tries to use friendlier words (see Figure 6.21). Even as simple a change as using "Information" instead of "Error" may make a noticeable difference to the user's experience. (Our vigilance failed us on occasion here, though, as in places "error" crept back in.)

- EPOC avoids blame-implying beeps when "inappropriate" or "invalid" keys are pressed.

Try Never to Annoy the User

- EPOC alarms ring quietly at first, so if the user is around they can acknowledge them without everyone in the vicinity having been annoyed. If there is no

FIGURE **6.22**

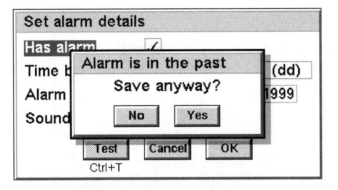

EPOC warns about unlikely input (an alarm set in the past), but does not prohibit it.

acknowledgment, they ring progressively louder, in case the person's some way away, or the machine is in a bag or in a noisy environment. If there is still no acknowledgment, EPOC waits and tries again, and waits and tries again, but with progressively longer waits each time, as it's less and less likely that the user is going to be there to acknowledge. (EPOC machines can flash an LED the whole time this is happening so that even if a user misses an alarm, if they're briefly near their EPOC machine at some later point they can see, without checking the software, that an alarm has rung.)

In hindsight, though, I feel the alarm still rings rather too frequently, despite the above; we weighted the pattern too heavily towards trying to ensure that the user never missed an alarm, and consequently people have been annoyed by unattended machines ringing in their office.

Also, EPOC tries hard not to impose artificial or pedantic constraints. If the user asks to do something that seems odd, EPOC lets them know it may be wrong, in case they're making a mistake, but if they wish to continue they can:

- If an Agenda entry is entered with an alarm set in the past (which therefore would not ring), EPOC warns the user—but then lets them enter it if they wish (see Figure 6.22).

  There may be reasons why someone would want to do this. They might be editing an old entry that they're about to cut and paste forwards, perhaps, or the time on the system screen might be set wrong for some reason. Or—who knows?

6.23

Silencing alarms for a period.

- Agenda entries can be set to go over midnight. When one is entered though it's sometimes an "am/pm" accident on the user's part, so an Infoprint alerts the user to what's happening. It's just an Infoprint, though, and the entry can still be entered.

- EPOC is a proper preemptive multitasking operating system. It does not display an hourglass when it is asked to do anything time-consuming or system critical.

Delight the User

Every now and again you may come up with something that takes your software somewhere new:

- EPOC allows people to make sound or voice recordings and then use them as their alarm sounds. People can wake to the theme from a favorite TV show, or if traveling, to the sound of their spouse, or their children—or someone else.

Protect the User

Each time something bad happens, the user's one step closer to giving up and throwing the product away. Each time something *disastrous* happens, they're probably there.

Don't Let Users Shoot Themselves

- If the user's going into a meeting, they can tell EPOC to set alarm sound off just for the duration of the meeting (see Figure 6.23).

Sounds are turned back on automatically afterward, so (say) next morning's alarm will still wake them.

- EPOC Connect archives old versions of files automatically. If a user accidentally deletes information from a file, but doesn't realize this until after they've backed up—and thus sent this new corrupted version to the PC—they'll still find a good version in the archive.

And, as mentioned before, people don't have to think about "saving changes"; in fact, "Do you want to save changes?" is a strange question to ask them after they've been typing for five hours. They might misread the wording in the dialog and think it was referring to some other file of a similar name. Their finger might slip on a button. Anything might happen. We feel it's a programmer's question. If the underlying "system model" were such that users edited files directly, instead of editing a separate copy in memory, then I don't think UI designers would have invented "saving changes" to ask people, "Do you want to do what you just did?"

Think What Might Go Wrong, at Each Stage

- If a user does turn sounds off, the Time screen shows a clear reminder, in case they then set alarms.

- If battery power is too low to play a certain alarm, a special "low power" alarm sound is played instead.

- When an alarm rings, it shows on the screen that the user can use the spacebar to snooze the alarm, in five-minute increments. So, when an alarm rings in the morning to get them out of bed, they can stretch a hand out from their nice warm bed and have the snooze they want.

    What might go wrong here? Well, they might tap in 20 minutes, say, then have second thoughts ("meeting with the boss?") and decide they should've had 10. Or they might lose count—it's first thing in the morning, after all—or not be sure if that last keypress registered. What should they do? Turn the bedroom light on, so they can see the screen to reset the snooze? Pick the machine up, activate the backlight, read the screen, and start entering new information? It's just going to wake them up. EPOC provides an alternative: they can keep their eyes closed, and just press the spacebar a few more times. After a few more presses it makes a little beep, to inform them that it has "wrapped around" and reset itself to 5 minutes.

    Many people's reaction is that this is taking UI design too far. But it's just one more area where we took the time to ask, "What might go wrong?" and "How could we fix it?" It turned out to be very little work to make EPOC let a user set and even reset

FIGURE **6.24**

Original touch bar layout for the Psion Series 5.

their snooze time while semiconscious, with one arm poking out from under the duvet, in the dark, without really waking up. Because they might want to.

Success is in the details.

6.5 Design Trade-offs in the EPOC UI

This section discusses some of the contentious trade-offs that arose during the development of the EPOC UI, and the reasons behind the eventual choices taken.

Market Position versus Range of Use

You can't just add more and more features without considering their effect on each other. Nobody will buy a car that's also a lawnmower no matter how well it does both jobs.

Application Priority

The first "approved" touch bar used this order of applications (see Figure 6.24). (The Jotter application was later removed from the plans for timescale reasons and has been added to EPOC since the Series 5. It appears in Psion's Series 5mx and Revo machines.)

A little later in the project, with the company deciding to stress the more "professional" applications and markets, the Word and Sheet icons (the "desktop" applications) were "promoted" to the left, by System. They remained there, despite heated debate within the design team, demoting the more commonly used Data (address book/database) and Agenda.

At the time I didn't support this change. Now I think it was the right thing to do because I don't think it was ever going to matter much to users, who quickly learn where their personal favorite application buttons are. And the final order suggests a professional PC companion machine, perhaps, which also does your address book and agenda, rather than just a personal organizer with some sort of word processor and spreadsheet added on.

Professional Feel versus Fun and Games

No games were planned for the Series 5, as Psion felt it might diminish the desired professional feel of the product. This was a trade-off against extra types of use for the machine.

Well into 1997, sitting on a train playing the game built into my Series 3a, I came to the conclusion we were making a mistake—I'd seen so many other people idling away the time like this. So I campaigned to have an existing minesweeper-like game called "Bombs" included in the product. Judging by the number of people still idling away the time playing games on their palmtops—and nowadays even playing "Snake" on their mobile phones—I think this was a good decision.

Usability versus Power

It's always tempting to show the power of your software, but it's often a bad idea.

Vector Drawing versus Bitmap Sketching

In a project as large as the Series 5, entire applications could come and go. Up until mid-1996 the drawing application was a vector-based tool called "Draw," in which vector-drawn or hand-drawn objects could be reselected and manipulated (see Figure 6.25).

We'd chosen vector-based initially as it seemed a more powerful example of what the platform could do graphically. The application was written quickly, as it used only straightforward graphics instead of the more complex UI layers still in development, and was one of the first running on the new platform.

However, in April 1996 at a spec team meeting, we weighed this against the fact that we felt it wasn't quite what most users would want and expect, which would be a simpler pixel-based painting/sketching app. So, despite Draw having been finished, a new bitmap sketching app, Sketch, was born to replace it.

Simple Dialogs versus Complex Dialogs

EPOC dialogs have one-dimensional up-down navigation. But one of the basic principles we stated in the original UI style guide was "Look and work

FIGURE **6.25**

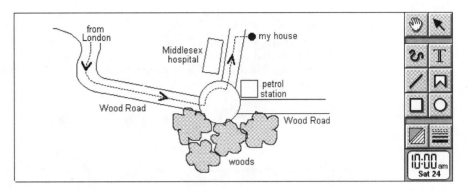

EPOC's original, vector-based drawing application.

like modern OSs except where we have a good reason." The code for displaying dialogs was accordingly written initially to allow dialogs to be laid out freely in two dimensions, as in Windows and many other systems. (This also seemed right for considering future UIs on future machines, which was at the back of our minds.)

In October 1995 I started to think that in doing this we were handicapping keyboard-based users far too much. EPOC dialogs at the time supported the same little-known keyboard controls as Windows: Tab and Shift-Tab to move around the controls, and Space to select the current control.

I proposed that we switch to the current one-dimensional dialog design—a vertical list of controls, navigable with up/down and selectable with left/right. It would mean a small but significant restriction on how we might design our more complex dialogs.

Most of the software team got involved in this one; everyone had an opinion, and it took more than a month to settle. To some it seemed like we were going backward too far for pen users, from the existing all-powerful system to the restricted design of the Series 3a, which was also one-dimensional.

What finally sold the change was that we were planning for the possibility of a non-touchscreen machine, and it would certainly be a far better machine with the new dialog design. We could have done slightly different interfaces for the pen and no-pen machines, but then again, we did also want our pen machine to be easy to use from the keyboard.

Soon afterwards we realized that multipage dialogs would allow us to build better "complex" dialogs than the 2D layout, by allowing us to hide more complex information as well as clearly grouping related controls.

FIGURE **6.26**

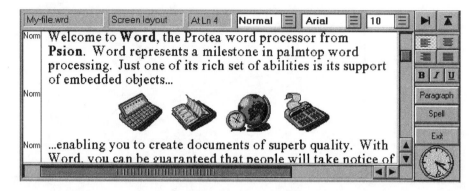

Early toolbar layout of EPOC's word processor.

Toolbar Functions

The initial criteria that toolbar button functions were intended to satisfy were

- Advertise the major functionality of the application

- Be used frequently

- Be wanted/valid for a high proportion of the time

- Be for "instant" operations

- Be expected from other platforms

- Be related to pen activity

We also stressed that we focused on the needs of *non-novices*; toolbars should not include the most basic introductory operations if intermediate users would not want them any more.

At first, all sorts of functions appeared on toolbars (see Figure 6.26). Any number of toolbars were possible at the time, and the word processor featured two toolbars—one across the top of the screen and one down the right-hand side. Several issues were in debate at the time:

- Simplicity versus complexity: Were these toolbars too simple or too complex? We'd all had experience of PC applications displaying endless arrays of tiny icons. (If we'd gone in that direction, note that we also wouldn't have had "tooltips" to help us explain the buttons, as PC applications do, since the Series 5 has no pointer to position over icons.)

- Standardization across applications: Gradually the desire for a "common user experience" across applications made us standardize toolbar use somewhat. We settled on a standard toolbar down the right-hand side for all applications, comprised of four buttons, all with text as well as an icon. (With the toolbar also showing the current application/file name and a clock, there was a little extra width available for text, and the text proved a considerable help—especially with no tooltips available.)

  We decided that the more powerful "desktop" applications—Sheet and Word—could still keep a second "toolband" across the top and include some of the basic functions used in PC applications' toolbars here.

- Conflicting requirements: With just four toolbar buttons for most applications, though, there was inevitable conflict between the principles listed above. For example, "Print" advertised major functionality and was an "instant action" (and was also expected from other platforms) but was not wanted much of the time. Many people would never use it on a device like this, so it would be a wasted button for them. The compromise we settled on was to focus on view changing, plus the major features—Find, Print, Insert Picture, New Entry.

Application Key Actions

Users press an application key to move to the currently running copy of that application. If there is more than one copy running—for example, three word processor applications each with a different file open (file-based applications open one file each)—further presses of the application key go round those running applications.

But if the user presses an application key for a file-based application like the word processor, and the application is not currently running at all, what does the user want, and what should EPOC do? (EPOC's file-based applications do not have a "no open file" state.)

Originally we felt the likeliest thing was that the user wanted a particular file of that type. So we planned that such keypresses should take the user to the System screen (which is a file manager among other things) and move the highlight to the next file of that type (with further presses going to the next, and the next), even if this meant moving to another folder, or even another disk.

But this meant the System screen might move from displaying a folder the user was interested in to some other folder, just because of an application keypress. Also, what if the user just wanted to get into the word processor, for example, to make a new file from there, or even just to be in it for some other reason?

Early in 1997 we tried to allow for both opening relevant files and creating new ones. We changed the design so that in this situation an application keypress caused a dialog to be displayed, asking the user whether they wanted to create a new file, or open an existing file. (If they chose the latter, they could then navigate to the desired file.) It sounded good on paper, as it let the user do whatever it was they were trying to do, but in practice everyone hated it; dialogs should ideally appear at the request of the user.

Finally, we adopted the "keep it simple" approach of just starting the application up and opening the most recently used file. Because if the user just wanted to do a "New" or an "Open" command, this lets them do so in the normal way (we might even have chosen the correct file). The bottom line was that we felt by pressing, say, the Word key, the user was definitely saying, "Get me into the word processor," and this was the best way to do that.

Standards versus Usability

Lots of users use Windows, but that doesn't mean they *know* Windows.

Drag and Drop

The initial UI style guide said that drag and drop needed more investigation, and it certainly got plenty of that. There were conflicting priorities here:

- We felt it would be a nice thing if we could support it well. We already knew we were going to support dragging to select areas in Word and Sheet, including dragging off-screen to extend a selection by scrolling.

- If we did support it, we would have had to support it in many or most applications—wherever the user might then expect to use it. At the very least, this suggested drag and drop from anywhere to the clipboard icon, and moving Sheet cells or Agenda entries, say. It would need a very sizable implementation effort.

- There might be problems designing it to work well in all places. For example, we might need a "drag threshold"—an amount (pixels and/or time) within which pen actions were ignored after a pen-down event. Otherwise users might find themselves accidentally moving things by small amounts.

- There are difficulties in drag and drop with a pen as compared to a mouse. Even with a "drag threshold" a pen is rather more likely to slip on a touch screen than a mouse would—especially in a device used on the move. Also, the object being dragged may be obscured by pen or hand. So accidental drag and drop is more likely.

- Lastly, the Series 5 did not have multiple on-screen windows to drag between, reducing its value.

As you might expect, there was a lot of pressure from marketing to support it. But for the reasons above, it seemed to be too much work for a definite but too little gain, and so we omitted it.

Use of the Word "File"

The original UI style guide included the intention of hiding the filing system as far as we could. Alan Cooper, in his book *About Face,* also advocates this strongly (Cooper 1995). As part of this effort we tried hard to hide the word "file" entirely because despite the word's widespread use in other systems, it is computer jargon.

One of the places we tried to remove it, as we later found Cooper had also recommended, was by replacing the word "File" by "Sheet" or "Document" (as appropriate to each application).

At the end of the day, though, we couldn't quite lose "file" completely; as we worked the design through, some of the general file management functions just had to have a word to describe "any document."

Having reluctantly accepted this, ironically, it meant that using the word "file" *everywhere* then became appropriate—including in the menu titles and in command names ("Create new file" and "Open file")—as it helped users realize more quickly what "file" meant.

This is an example of how it often takes a lot of detailed debate over the minor issues to decide what the correct "big picture" is. A "high-level" meeting declaring grandly that, say, the "File" menu should be called "Word," "Sheet," and so on, would have been a mistake in my opinion.

Templates

Templates for basing new files on (e.g., for the word processor and spreadsheet) are nowadays common on other platforms, and they came and went from the Series 5 spec. Initially, they seemed very desirable, but the more we thought through the details, the bigger the issues became:

- If we included templates, the user would want to create and save their own. This adds lots of new commands.

- If we included templates, they would be required in most applications. Otherwise, the user would not have a common experience in all the applications; in those that didn't have them, they would have to learn to use "Save as" as a workaround.

- Sometimes the user just wants a new file to look like an existing document, not a particular template. "Save as" does actually support this, of course. We considered making a "Look Like" button available on the "Create new file" dialog, which would list templates in the ROM plus all other files of this type. But then the user would soon want to use a "Look Like" function at times other than just when creating a new document.

So, finally, we felt templates did not deliver enough value for the complexity they caused, and we omitted them.

Scientific Calculator

For the calculator application we opted to use UI "standards"; we supplied a simple calculator that worked the way simple desktop calculators do but also a more advanced view that emulated a student's scientific calculator.

The latter might be a standard, but it involves such a difficult-to-use UI that very few people are able to use it properly.

Mnemonics (Underscored Shortcuts)

Following the previously stated basic intention of looking and working like other modern platforms, we planned to support "mnemonics" (where using the Fn key plus underlined letters would allow fast keyboard navigation to a particular place). It's a standard power feature in Windows (based on the PC's Alt key).

Mnemonics in Dialogs. In early dialog designs mnemonics were used, so (say) Fn + B might position the highlight to the "Bold" line (see Figure 6.27). This was later dropped as we felt that it made the dialogs look ugly and more complicated, and that it would rarely actually save any time. It seemed as quick to hit the down arrow two or three times as to look for the underlined character required and then press it with the Fn key.

In addition, by adding this "power user" feature, there would be the slight danger that some nonpower users would discover this less-than-friendly way of navigating the UI, start using it, and not find the friendly version (up/down) for some time.

Mnemonics in Menus. We had tried to combine parts of various common menuing systems:

- We wanted initially to let people use "mnemonics"—underlined shortcuts for choosing a menu tile, then a subsequent command on it.

FIGURE **6.27**

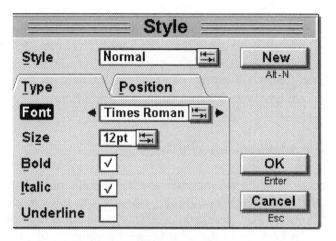

Use of mnemonics in early EPOC dialogs.

- We didn't want to waste screen space by displaying a menu bar all the time, which we'd need to remind people of the menu names and mnemonics.

- For those times when the user selects the same command more than once, we also wanted to allow a single menu keypress, as on the Series 3a, to display the menu and have the previously selected menu command highlighted, ready to be selected again by pressing the Enter key.

To meet these requirements we considered a system where a single Menu key acted both as a Shift key and a "display menu" action key:

- Pressing down the Menu key would display the menu bar across the top of the screen (with no menu tile pulled down).

- Pressing a letter key, while Menu was still held down, would bring down the relevant menu tile (and further mnemonic keypresses would choose the desired item).

- However, if instead the user let go of the Menu key, it would just display and highlight the most recently chosen menu command.

There are some small problems with this. If the user holds down the Menu key, looks at the menu bar displayed, then decides they don't want to be in there, there's an unpleasant moment where they have to let go and have some menu or other displayed before they can cancel. This sort of thing may only take the user a fraction of a second to get out of, but any situation where the user can't avoid something unwanted from happening should be avoided.

Finally, though, we decided that mnemonics in menus were too technical and unpleasant in general for the benefit they brought. We already had single-key hot keys (like Ctrl + X) for almost all commands; that, and the few arrow keypresses required to navigate to anywhere on the entire menu, led us to feel mnemonics should be dropped from menus.

Home, End, PgUp, and PgDn

The Series 3a had a simple rule: the arrow keys moved the cursor in the direction you would expect. Holding the Ctrl key down made the arrow keys move the cursor a greater distance in that same direction. The Psion key (like the PC's Alt key) made for even bigger movements in that direction. And using both Ctrl and Psion keys made for the largest movement possible in that direction.

The Series 3a keyboard designated "Home" as Psion + Left, "End" as Psion + Right, and "PgUp" and "PgDn" as Psion + Up/Down. This was to provide familiarity for PC users, although the key movements do not correspond 100% to what these (separate) keys do on a PC. For example, Ctrl + Home on a PC moves to the top of a document; on a Series 3a it is Ctrl + Psion + Left, which is interpreted as "move the maximum amount to the left." On a PC, Home generally moves upward to the top of a list, while on the Series 3a it would still, being Psion + Left, mean a left movement.

We considered three alternatives for the Series 5:

- Use the same system as the Series 3a.

- Use the same keyboard as the Series 3a, but change the cursor movements to be more PC-like so that, say, Ctrl + Home would go to the top of a document, and Home to the top of most Agenda views.

- Use the same cursor movements as the Series 3a, but change the keyboard so that instead of saying Home, End, etc., it just had double-arrow symbols, to indicate that using the Fn key (the Series 5's version of the Alt or Psion key) would always move even farther in the direction shown.

We chose the second option and became more PC-like. PC power users who know those keypresses can use them. There had also been marketing pressure to keep Home, End, etc. on the keyboard as this let the machine look a little more PC-like, which was felt to be important given the competition it faced from Windows CE machines.

With hindsight, though, I think there's a strong case for the third option because we were following a poor standard, in my view. My prediction would be that for every person who sees a palmtop in a shop and says "Hey, great; it has Home and End," there's another saying "Look at all these little words; what do they mean?" Ironically, with the world becoming more Web-based, "Home" has another important meaning nowadays. But the big PC key marked "Home" doesn't take you there.

Wherever we can make a better system that's easy to understand, we should leave a more confusing system behind, even if it is a standard. It's the better mousetrap that really sells.

6.6 Conclusion—Where Are We?

I do hope there are things to be learned from our experience in developing EPOC for the Psion Series 5, whatever your work culture and your design process. I've certainly learned a lot myself from the project.

While I feel we came up with many good design ideas, the project reminded me that there's a huge amount still to be done before technological products become truly usable. Earlier this year I polled some friends for features they'd like to see in a mobile phone. In more than half the cases they sheepishly admitted that they thought the feature they wanted was actually already in their current phone, but that they couldn't work out either how to enable it or how to use it.

I'm not disparaging phones in particular; informal research suggests to me that this applies to PCs, palmtops, VCRs, answering machines, and I dare say any number of other devices. In software, all the graphics and wizards and good reviews in the world can't hide the fact that too often people fail at all but the simplest of operations. Sure, sometimes it's "because" they haven't read the manual, or they're not very software literate, or they've not been paying close attention, or it's been a while since they last used the software, or they're a bit low on caffeine even, but these are all perfectly reasonable states for a user to be in. So it's not "because" of these at all; it's because our UI designs don't take such reasonable human behavior into account. The people aren't "failing"—the software is failing them.

I hope that in the not-too-distant future *someone* will take the leap and make the much larger investment in UI design and coding that is needed to make products that allow users to approach tasks on their own terms. That someone will be a runaway success.

6.7 Acknowledgments

My thanks to all the people at Symbian and Psion who supplied valuable information and feedback. Special thanks also to Terry Jones and to Eric Bergman, Marilyn Alan, and the team, for sorting out so much for me in a short time.

6.8 References

Boulton, R., J. Christensen, P. Griffith, M. Malmgren, S. Mahony, C. Manchester, M.-L. Neill, A. Pawley. 1996. *Innovation on Time: A Study into Organisational Behaviour, Human Resource Management and Leadership Skills at Psion Software plc.* Internal report. (Reproduced with permission.)

Cooper, A. 1995. *About Face: The Essentials of User Interface Design.* Foster City, CA: IDG Books Worldwide.

Kidder, T. 1981. *The Soul of a New Machine.* New York: Penguin.

McCarthy, J., and D. Gilbert. 1995. *Dynamics of Software Development.* Redmond, WA: Microsoft Press.

CHAPTER Seven

Designing Mobile Phones and Communicators for Consumers' Needs at Nokia

KAISA VÄÄNÄNEN-VAINIO-MATTILA

Nokia

SATU RUUSKA

Nokia

FIGURE **7.1**

*The Mobira Cityman, an NMT phone from the 1980s (left)
and the Nokia 6110, a cellular phone from the late 1990s
(right).*

7.1 Introduction

Mobile phones were initially developed as strategic communication devices
for the military and were then adapted to the needs of mobile businesspeo-
ple. The first mobile phones were bulky and designed more for durability
and less for usability or desirability (see Figure 7.1; see also Color Plate). In
addition to their rather heavy weight, these phones had small displays and
buttons with cryptic character-based command labels that were neither
intuitive nor in direct reference to variable task sequences. Moreover, interaction with early mobile handsets was mode oriented, which in general has
been detected to cause errors and impose a heavy cognitive load on users
(Nielsen 1993; Monk 1986).

Since the early 1980s, other user groups have begun to use mobile
phones as well. In many parts of the world, mobile phones can now be considered to be consumer products, becoming available for everyone as com-
modities, which creates totally new usability requirements for mobile
handsets. In addition, there is an increasing number of associated telephony

Navi™ Roller is a trademark of Nokia Ltd. T9 is a trademark of Tegic Communications.

FIGURE **7.2**

The Nokia 9110 Communicator.

services that are mostly understood as being part of handset functionality by the users. These services must therefore match the usage experience of handsets in their logic and efficiency.

In the past few years (since about the mid-1990s), mobile phones have been joined by personal portable devices like personal digital assistants (see Chapters 4, 5, and 6) and communicators (see Figure 7.2; see also Color Plate). In this chapter, the term "phones" refers to a more basic form of a communication device where the main aims of using the device deal with voice- and text-based communication services. By "communicators" we mean more advanced communication devices—such as the Nokia 9110— where in addition to the multimedia communication capabilities (e.g., fax and Web browsing, including access to visual media), many personal assistant tasks such as appointment making, "to do" lists, and note taking can be carried out with a single mobile terminal. Mobile terminals are therefore starting to combine a wider functionality, which has been the driving force behind the evolution from classic mobile phones to communicators.

On the Structure of This Chapter

This chapter examines special issues in users' experience with mobile hand-held terminals and, in particular, the way in which mobile phones and communicators are developed for the needs of end users at Nokia.

The second section, "Acceptance of Mobile Communication Devices," explores basic sociological and cultural issues related to the spread of mobile communications in different parts of the world. The following section describes the essential concepts behind designing usable and useful mobile communication devices, that is, creating a user experience in mobile usage contexts that has as high a quality as possible. The essential methods behind designing mobile—as with any other type—interactive systems are *context of use, usage scenarios,* and *user tasks.* HCI challenges in mobile handsets are also discussed. The "Design and Evaluation of Mobile Terminals" section discusses the special characteristics in the design process of mobile handsets in the current mobile communication business. It also describes how mobile terminals are designed and evaluated at Nokia. The final section illustrates Nokia's vision of the future for mobile communication terminals and their usage, especially in the so-called third generation of mobile communication.

7.2 Acceptance of Mobile Communication Devices

The early users of mobile phones were mobile business professionals. The ways mobile communication practices are now being adopted by consumers ("the mass market") in different parts of the world heavily depend on the stage at which the area (e.g., country or state) is in "mobile phone usage penetration" development (see Figure 7.3).

Diffusion of Mobile Communication

Partly due to historical reasons—the first wide-area cellular network was the Nordic Mobile Telecommunication (NMT) network—mobile communication has been taken up by the majority of the population of the Scandinavian countries. The popularity of mobile voice communication is also reflected in the usage of other mobile services such as the Short Message Service (SMS), which is a text messaging service defined in the Global System for Mobile Communication (GSM) standard. In Finland, for example, text messaging will soon become as popular as voice calls, since the text messaging service has reached a critical mass of users. All segments of the user base—including teenagers and the elderly—send these messages to each other on a daily basis to the extent that a new communications subculture seems to be developing, which is also facilitated by the operators transmitting messages between subscribers who use competing networks. Further services are also becoming commonly used, such as message-based services where the user

FIGURE **7.3**

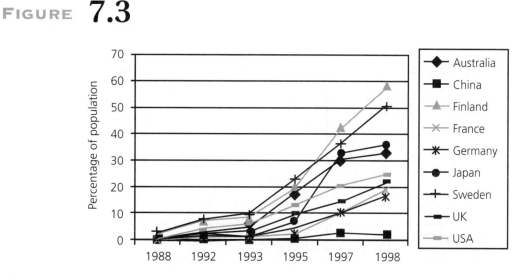

Mobile phone penetration for selected countries, 1988–98 (EMC 1999).

can send a query via a text message to a database about the weather or stock prices, for example.

Mika Pantzar (1996) has presented a model of ways that products can enter the consumer market (see Figure 7.4), and the motives users may have when adopting those products for their everyday use. For a product to become accepted as a genuine and permanent part of a lifestyle in a society, the motives for using it must evolve to be both externally driven (socially accepted—or even required—by that society) and stable (rationally accepted by individuals in their lifestyle).

The wired phone was initially considered useless and even morally suspicious by the general public, but then it spread quickly and became accepted as a rational, useful tool. Cars, to take another example, first started out as products of passion (speed, sports), but later largely turned into prestige objects with a clear connection to their owners' lifestyles, also gaining acceptance as rationally justified necessities.

As was already discussed, the mobile phone was first considered to be a serious tool for certain occupations, especially the military, and then an item for business purposes. After a while—around the early 1990s—it became a consumer product in countries like Finland, Sweden, and the UK. In this adaptation to consumers' lifestyles, the *personalization* of the mobile phone may play an important role: In constant use the mobile handset becomes a very personal object that intensifies the user's feeling of being inseparable from it.

FIGURE 7.4

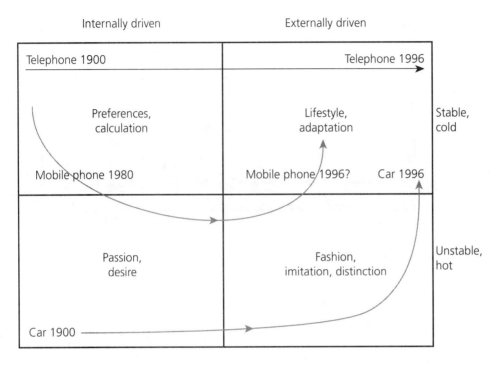

How different consumer products may enter the mass market. Source: Pantzar (1996).

In some areas (for example, in some Eastern European countries where the wireless telecommunication network may offer the first telephone connection to many consumers), there may have been an immediate adaptation to the lifestyle without the transition from a serious tool as a starting point. In other areas (such as China), the mobile phone may be the "hot" possession for showing off one's economic status.

As far as the communicator type of mobile device is concerned, its entry into the market may be a combination of many approaches: High-technology devices are first adopted by people who in general are interested in new gadgets and who usually buy all the latest versions available. It takes some time for a new invention to reach the level of popularity where one really can make full use of it. This seems to be especially true of new communication devices because other people with matching means and possibilities to communicate need to exist in order, for example, to exchange messages. Innovative consumers first form usage patterns that create and/or match their everyday needs. Once the tool has established its cultural position, then mass use starts.

Cultural Issues

The cultural background of a user or a group of users plays a key role in the adoption of new devices. Personal devices, such as communicators and mobile phones, necessarily face challenges in spreading across social strata in different cultures as they strive to support *personal* communication and information management, and therefore have to be personal enough for each individual consumer.

Needless to say, the suitability of a product for any culture starts from the language and metaphors: a personal device has to provide the ability to enter and extract information in the user's own language. For example, there is currently no single input method for portable electronic devices available in Chinese that could be accepted by all Chinese users or that would come close to the speed of handwriting. Aesthetics and a personal style of hand-writing have always been important in many Asian cultures in communicat-ing more about the person on an extra-textual level. None of the currently available input methods in personal mobile devices can achieve this goal that is so characteristic of many Asian cultures (Sacher 1998).

Understanding a novel system is metaphorical in nature: a mental model of system functionality is formed through a metaphorical understanding of the user interface elements and behavior. User interface metaphors are rooted both in experiences common to all humans (e.g., bodily experience), but also in experiences or contexts that are culturally determined (e.g., col-ors are metaphorical and have culturally varied meanings) (Lakoff and Johnsson 1990; Bourges-Waldegg and Scrivener 1998).

Contextual research methods (see "The Contextual Design Approach," page 196) are effective in distinguishing cultural characteristics that would not be noticed in the majority of usability and market research methods. One such difference, voice mail usage, was encountered in the behavior of U.S. communication device users: Compared to voice mail use in Scandinavia or even in the UK, the service was considered more like an equal medium of communication, together with email and fax. Several occa-sions where two parties were settling an issue only through their voice mail without talking to each other personally were observed. An analogy can be seen in SMS in Scandinavia: voice messaging in the United States is used for similar purposes as SMS is, in Finland, for example. Both are answers to the expected availability and presence that mobile devices (or services) create.

Personal safety issues have been observed to vary in importance cultur-ally; in the United States an important reason for purchasing a mobile phone is and has been the need to increase personal safety. Such a strong require-ment cannot avoid affecting the user interface design; therefore, some phone products for the U.S. market have "the red 9" key for accessing the emergency number with the press of a single button.

User Satisfaction Depends on Quality of Use

To achieve sufficient levels of utility and usability in an interactive product, certain quality criteria must be met. Instead of seeing these quality attributes as solely built-in characteristics of the product itself, a user's experience in using a mobile device can be analyzed in terms of "quality of use." Quality of use has been defined as the "extent to which a product can be used by specified users to achieve specified goals with *effectiveness, efficiency,* and *satisfaction* in a specified *context of use*" (ISO 1998):

- *Effectiveness:* the accuracy and completeness with which users achieve specified goals

- *Efficiency:* the resources spent in relation to the accuracy and completeness with which users achieve goals

- *Satisfaction:* freedom from discomfort and a positive attitude to the use of the product

- *Context of use:* characteristics of the users, tasks, and the organizational and physical environments

Obviously, all these quality attributes must also apply to the use of mobile terminals. It is therefore essential to know the detailed contents and the target measures of these attributes for understanding how those products should be designed. The mobile contexts of use and their relation to the user's activity in those contexts are discussed in the following section. Effectiveness, efficiency, and satisfaction are discussed in later sections.

7.3 Phone and Communicator Usage in Mobile Contexts

This section looks into the central concepts in designing mobile handsets—both basic phones and communicators with more complex functions. Since the context of use—together with the specified target user group—should always be the starting point in the design process, we start by describing the kinds of attributes that affect the context in which mobile handsets are used. Together with understanding the usage contexts, the user activity in those contexts must be analyzed. On a higher level we describe these activities by *usage scenarios*; the more detailed activities can be described as user *tasks*. We will give examples of such scenarios and tasks in the mobile domain. All this is the background; at the end of this section we will discuss the challenges and constraints in designing the HCI in mobile terminals.

The Mobile Context of Use

Ideally, in most usage situations, being mobile should remain transparent to the user. This means that the functionality that is available to the user when she or he is not mobile (e.g., at the office) should be available with at least similar quality attributes when "on the move." However, some requirements for usage are fundamentally different. Thus the basic motive in the analysis of the context is to focus on how and when the device should behave differently and offer different interaction/presentation options depending on the context of use (Dix et al. 1998).

Even though the user ideally would not have to understand the underlying technological infrastructure, in some cases it is essential to provide the user with information about the status of the infrastructure. The following characteristics of *mobile infrastructure context* inadvertently cause lower quality of use compared to a nonmobile or fixed usage context:

- *No or bad network coverage:* The user cannot access services or communicate on a continuous basis, or the user has to deal with discontinuities in connections, including understanding and recovering from error situations. Moreover, global mobility is still to come because differences in network systems prevent the user from using the same mobile terminal everywhere in the world.

- *Low communication bandwidth:* Data transfer takes significantly longer than in fixed networks, and therefore one has to be aware of the size of items to transfer. The length of interaction sequences should be minimized, possibly through intelligent adaptation of the device according to the possibilities/constraints of the current infrastructure.

The *physical context* deals with the restrictions on the mobile usage environment that inherently affect the usage of mobile handsets:

- *Wireless use:* Instead of having to stay connected to a network with a physical wire, thus restricting mobility, the user has mobility within the wireless network coverage.

- *Noisy surroundings:* Voice services are difficult to exploit, thus requiring the use of other media.

- *Unstable and varying usage position:* The user needs to hold the terminal in his or her hand or lap; the implication is that there is a need for special ergonomic designs for one- or two-handed use, or even for hands-free use, including speech user interfaces and audio output. This also has to do with the miniaturization of devices: the limited screen space may also suggest adaptive user interface solutions for the ideal exploitation of the display.

- *Moving environment:* There are implications for visual output and manual input. In mobile communication, the user's concentration is divided between the activities related to movement (e.g., walking down the stairs or driving), activities related to communicating (e.g., talking, writing a message), and activities related to using a communication device (e.g., holding the device to an ear, pressing the correct buttons). The first two get the major share of attention; the actual use of the device, however, should require as little concentration as possible.

- *Other environmental factors:* Varying lighting conditions, from direct sunlight to complete darkness, require careful display design and backlighting for both display and keys. Varying climate and weather conditions may require, for example, water resistance to some extent or the ability of the user to wear gloves.

In addition to the contextual attributes described above, the *social context* deals with all aspects where other people—known or unknown—have to be taken into account when using the device. This becomes especially crucial in mobile communication since, by definition, mobility implies variability in the social context of use. Some of the implications are

- The need to collaborate and share information with others

- The need to keep interaction paths, and to some extent communication sequences, relatively short and, in the case of voice communication, quiet

- The need for privacy and discreetness—to use other media (text, for example) rather than audio; the need to hide the display from others or the need to communicate less disruptively

- The need to differentiate oneself from other users of mobile devices and services, which also reflects the highly personal nature of mobile communication and thus the need to tailor the mobile handset itself

An interesting, emerging aspect of the mobile system and application context is *location awareness:* The network and/or mobile terminal knows where the user is located geographically and can thus offer services based on the location (e.g., maps and local yellow pages). The user needs to understand when and how this location information changes the functionality of an application. (Location-aware applications are discussed further

Color Plates

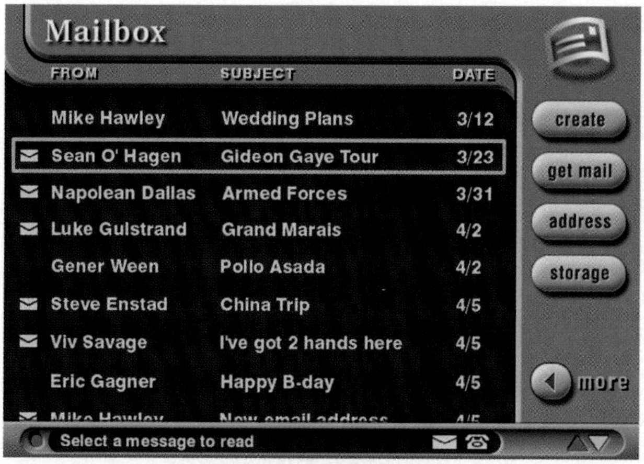

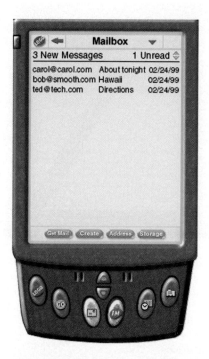

FIGURE 2.1 *(above) A sample inbox screen from an email application running on a TV set-top box.*

FIGURE 2.2 *(right) An inbox screen on a PDA device. This screen is functionally identical to that shown in Figure 2.1, but the user interface is altered to meet the requirements of the device.*

FIGURE 2.5 *An example of a set-top box appliance where the user is browsing the Web and viewing television in a PIP window. The user can access or dismiss the PIP window by pressing a button on the remote control.*

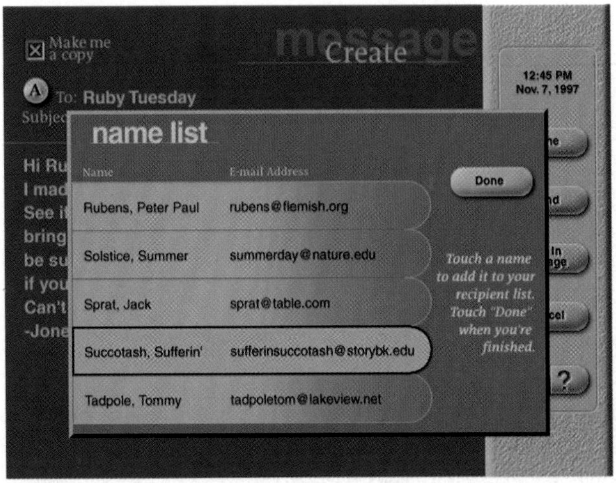

FIGURE 2.6 *Sample screen from an Internet-enabled screen phone. The screen is an email composition screen, and a dialog box has appeared over the top (based on the user's input). With a touch screen device, it is possible for the user to dismiss this dialog by pressing the "Done" button in the dialog or by simply touching anywhere outside the dialog.*

FIGURE 3.5 *A nearly complete industrial design of the i-opener hardware.*

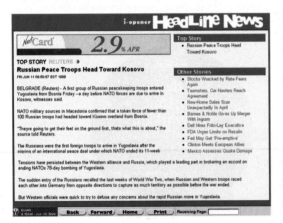

FIGURE 3.6 *The News Channel as a part of the Categorical Content.*

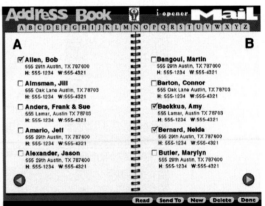

FIGURE 3.10 *The task-centric, real-world approach of the Address Book for Mail.*

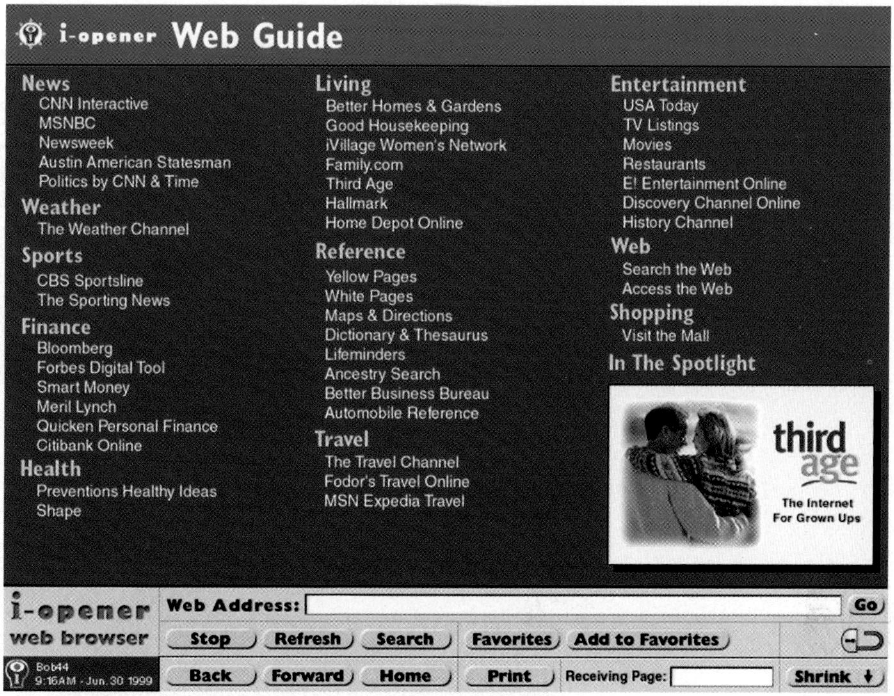

FIGURE 3.12 *The Web Guide page in the i-opener Web Browser.*

FIGURE 5.10 *Palm-sized PC Concept: Contacts list view. A list of contacts showing related telephone number. Single tap activates the detailed view of the contact.*

FIGURE 5.11 *Apollo: Start Menu. An Auto PC in-car face plate with the Start screen displayed. The left/right control scrolls through the available programs. The green Action button is used to activate the selected application.*

FIGURE 6.1 *Psion Series 5.*

FIGURE 6.3 *Psion Revo.*

FIGURE 6.4 *Psion Series 3mx (latest model in the Series 3a line).*

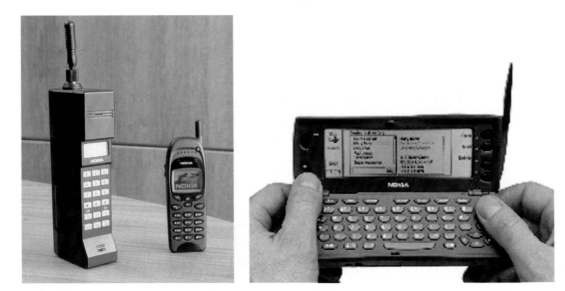

FIGURE 7.1 *The Mobira Cityman, an NMT phone from the 1980s (left) and the Nokia 6110, a cellular phone from the late 1990s (right).*

FIGURE 7.2 *The Nokia 9110 Communicator.*

FIGURE 7.12 *A future communicator concept.*

FIGURE 7.13 *A future smart phone concept.*

FIGURE 8.1 *Screen with expert (left column) and novice (right column) buttons.*

FIGURE 8.5 *Opening screen.*

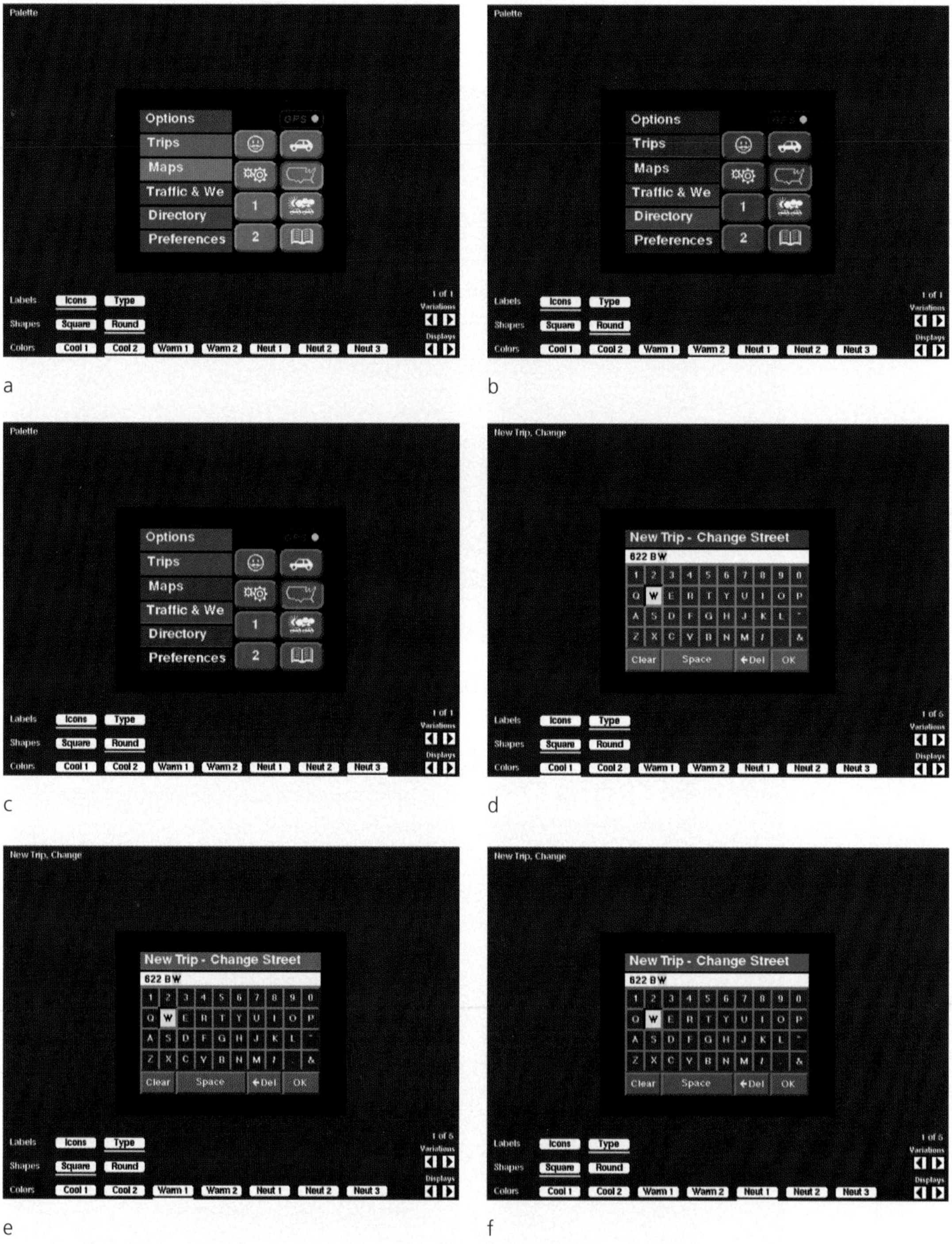

FIGURE 8.51–56 *Options screens with a) cool, b) warm, and c) neutral colors, and New Trip—Change screens with d) cool, e) warm, and f) neutral colors.*

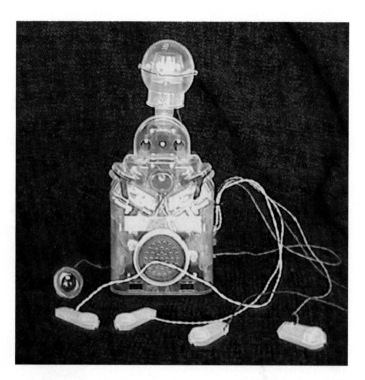

FIGURE 9.1 *Technology without personality. The "chassis" for the Barney interactive character, with hand, foot, and eye sensors attached.*

FIGURE 9.2 *Interactive Barney character, "in the skin." Motors in the shoulders and neck let the character move and gesture while speaking. Children interact with Barney by squeezing sensors in the hands and feet and by covering a light sensor in his eye.*

FIGURE 9.3 *Interactive Teletubbies characters. Children interact with them by squeezing sensors in the hands and feet and pressing the tummy screen.*

FIGURE 9.4 *Interactive Arthur and D. W. characters. Children interact with the characters by squeezing sensors located in the hands, feet, ears, and watch (visible on right arm).*

FIGURE 10.1 *In* Resident Evil, *the player's proxy must defend himself against zombies, here attacking from both sides.*

FIGURE 10.2 *The art direction in* Myst *is exquisite for a game.*

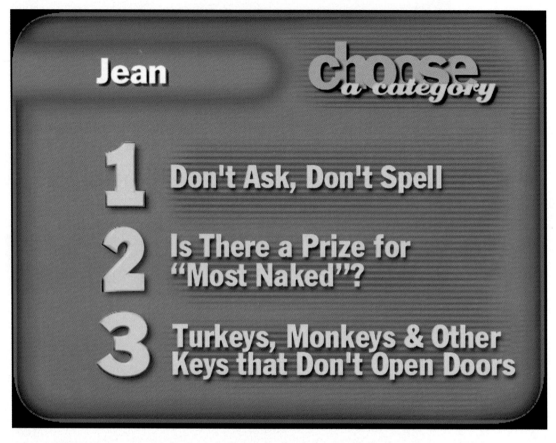

FIGURE 10.3 You Don't Know Jack *is a trivia game with an attitude.* You Don't Know Jack *is a registered trademark of Jellyvision, Inc.*

FIGURE **7.5**

Examples of mobile usage contexts in various physical environments.

in the "Visions of the Future: Toward the Third Generation of Mobile Communication" section).

A further aspect of the mobile usage context is that it may be constantly changing, thus requiring constant adaptation by both the user and the system. Taking this into consideration, we can loosely define two extremes of mobility: semimobile and fully mobile. Semimobile environments include places where not all aspects of the surroundings are constantly changing, such as a train, hotel, or an office building (meeting room), but where the user may still need wireless communication. Fully mobile contexts impose more restrictions on peaceful usage of the device: a street (while walking), a car (while driving), or anywhere outside without peace and physical stability. Figure 7.5 shows examples of mobile usage contexts in various physical invironments.

In summary, many types of contexts and their implications must be taken into account when designing mobile terminals for an optimal usage experience. Compared, for example, to office systems, there are many distinctive challenges in the mobile context that require research on infrastructure, physical, and social contexts alike. (See the "Challenges in the Interaction between the User and a Mobile Terminal" section, page 182.)

In association with an understanding of mobile contexts, the next level of detail is to understand the task flow in the scenarios of use. The next section illustrates the context-dependent challenges by presenting an example of a usage scenario and user tasks in mobile communication.

Scenarios and Tasks

In interactive product development, usage scenarios have several purposes:

- To make work practices more concrete: scenarios and sequences on how users or potential users are carrying out their work currently while mobile

- To identify areas for improvement: scenarios and user tasks as tools for envisioning and concept creation

- To identify critical tasks (frequent or time/context-critical tasks), based on these high-level scenarios

For all these purposes, usage scenarios need to be based on real data and not just pure imagination. How this can be done with the help of contextual research is described in "The Contextual Design Approach," page 196. Scenarios have been used at Nokia in product development to build a broader view of the users' world in order to support transition from one action to another in a smooth task flow. Scenarios have special importance in initial concept creation, whereas tasks especially facilitate later product development, for example, UI (user interface) design and specification.

Tasks with mobile communication and self-organization devices are characteristically ad hoc, time-critical, triggered by other people or events, relatively short in terms of the number of steps and time used, low in the amount of attention dedicated to the task, as well as highly personal in terms of their information content. Moreover, task performance is often interrupted, and the user needs to move between several interrupted tasks—sometimes completion of the task becomes unnecessary. These characteristics seem to be more common in personal mobile devices than in stationary, office-based systems where the physical context does not change, interruptions are less frequent, and concentration and the time dedicated to achieving a goal are greater. Therefore, mobile systems must provide the user with a smooth task flow flexible enough for switches in task and interruptions. Easy task and data flow between contact database, telephone, and the calendar seems to be especially crucial in mobile devices.

The following kinds of usage scenarios and tasks facilitate mobile terminal concept and product creation and should be based on contextual data (for more information, see the "Practicing User-Centered Design for Usable Mobile Phones at Nokia" section).

Example of a Usage Scenario

David works as a legal consultant in an international corporation. He uses a communicator daily for light note taking and communication as well as for his personal organization.

8 A.M. The working day starts with a multiparty conference call to Japan. He uses the communicator as a speakerphone to be able to type notes in it at the same time. At the end of the meeting, he sends everybody a copy of the notes via email directly from the communicator.

1 P.M. At the airport, he downloads all his new email messages to his communicator so that he can start working on them during the flight. On the plane there is always plenty of time to write answers to messages. While downloading, he views the communicator calendar for the day and remembers having promised to send his business card to a potential client. He does this while standing in line for boarding.

At his destination, he switches the communicator phone on, and it automatically starts sending the replies written on the plane. At the same time David can continue reading the rest of the messages.

2:30 P.M. His secretary back in London sends him a calendar reservation for the following week. David checks his calendar in the communicator and accepts the request. His communicator sends the confirmation automatically to the secretary and marks the appointment in David's calendar.

User Tasks

As mobile handsets become an established and accepted means of direct and indirect personal communication, users seem to come up with versatile and creative uses for their personal devices. Although the users' need for flexibility and customizability is given special emphasis, there are common requirements for mobile handset features and telephony services, For example, finding a person in the phone book (handset feature) and making a call (telephony service) must form a coherent user experience and a seamless task flow toward the main goal—contacting a person.

Based on the scenarios, a more detailed *task analysis* can be made. The users' goals and tasks can be divided into subtasks or minor goals that all aim at one common goal. Such classification of user tasks and subtasks serves as a tool for emphasizing the importance of *frequency of use* and *time/context criticality.* The frequency of certain tasks seems to increase with mobile devices because they are ready at hand. Similarly, mobile devices take tasks out of the office when they often have to be carried out under time pressure or with very little attention. These are directly related to the *efficiency* of using the device, which is one of the main usability criteria in mobile communication.

In Figure 7.6, we will present samples of the most important user tasks of basic telephony and personal information products (Hwang and Giusto 1998). (Please note that the task lists are not exhaustive.) Information on the frequency of a feature's use can be acquired through, for example, contextual studies and some market research. Information on which tasks are performed under pressure comes from the nature of the task itself and can also be obtained by observing users in context.

How critical a task is to a user is obviously just one—albeit often the most important one—criterion related to the usability of a mobile handset. The next section explores the principal challenges in designing high-quality user experiences for mobile communication products. The "Design and Evaluation of Mobile Terminals" section then describes the driving forces behind the mobile phone design and the methods used at Nokia to ensure the design of usable mobile terminals.

Challenges in the Interaction between the User and a Mobile Terminal

Human-computer interaction in the PC application base has developed tremendously from the early command-based user interfaces of the late 1970s and early 1980s. The first big step in improving the PC user interfaces was the adoption of the principles of *direct manipulation*—the user acts on visual objects on the screen with a pointing device (Norman 1986). This way the cognitive load of the user—especially the novice—has been reduced; there is no need to learn and memorize cryptic commands, and the user has a feeling of manipulating the visual world presented through the user interface.

Other development trends in PC-based applications and their user interfaces include

- *Multimedia:* combining visual with audio information—and as a further emerging trend, virtual reality (VR) with 3D presentations of objects and respective 3D interaction, including gestures

- *Groupwork support* in various standard applications, such as shared document processing in a remote, real-time meeting

FIGURE **7.6**

> **User Tasks: Classification**
>
> (1)   Done under pressure: very critical
> (2)   Done frequently: critical
> (3)   Medium frequency or medium pressure
> (4)   Not frequent or not done under pressure

Sample 1: User tasks in person-to-person voice communication

Call-making/in-call

(1)   Making a call to an emergency number
(1)   Answering a call
(1)   Rejecting a call
(2)   Making a call to frequently called numbers (usually 4–10 of them)
(2)   Making a call by manually entering each digit
(2)   Redialing a number/person
(2)   Indication of being busy
(3)   Making a call to semifrequently called numbers (e.g., a vet, hairdresser)
(4)   Making a call to occasionally called numbers (i.e., numbers that are often called only once)

Phone book memory

(1/4) Saving a name and number [1 = very critical during a call]
(2/3) Recalling a name and number and dialing [2 = to a frequently called number]
(4)   Editing a name and number
(4)   Erasing a name and number
(4)   Browsing the contents of a phone book, etc.

Sample 2: User tasks in text messaging

Sending

(4)   Sending a text message to a contact in the phone book
(4)   Setting a message center number, etc.

Receiving

(2)   Reading and replying to a message
(2)   Reading and calling back the sender
(3)   Reading and erasing a message
(4)   Reading and storing a message with a new name, etc.

Samples of user tasks.

- *World Wide Web:* the worldwide hypermedia base with easy access to "limitless" information and computing resources

- *Standard UI platforms and programming languages* (Windows, Java, and the Web): wide application base that enables consistency between applications and interaction routines

All these trends, in one form or another, are now also emerging in mobile handsets (see "Visions of the Future" section).

Compared to the user interaction with PC applications, other platforms for interactive applications—including mobile handsets, set-top boxes (interactive TV), game terminals and car terminals—continue to have design constraints (see Chapter 2), such as the following:

- *Indirect manipulation* due to indirect pointing devices and sequential interactions. Interactive TV used with a remote control especially seems to suffer from this indirectness, together with basic mobile phones (see below).

- *Small displays* (especially in car terminals and PDAs), causing continuous trade-off searching in the design of what to put on the screen real estate

- *Miniaturized and monolithic form factor* of the terminal—the terminal is both the input and output device at the same time (PDAs, mobile phones, car terminal). This restricts ergonomic freedom in the design of input methods.

- *Lack of UI standards and conventions* between different manufacturers' products

Mobile phones have to be designed with skillful solutions to many of these design constraints. Communicators, with their larger displays and more direct input methods, escape some of these limitations (discussed below).

HCI Challenges and Solutions in Basic Phones

Challenges in HCI with mobile phones stem especially from the constraints of indirect manipulation in the user interface (Väänänen-Vainio-Mattila and Haataja 1997). The user's part of the user-phone interaction is mainly carried out through sequences of button presses. The user may get feedback from his or her actions by tactile feedback, abstract sounds, and textual as well as animated and/or iconic messages on the phone display. The displays are small due to miniaturization of the physical dimensions of the phones, and the appropriately brief display terminology—customized for each language in the target market—plays a significant role in the phone UI design.

The mapping of the user's keypresses to the device's actions is not always straightforward in an intuitive way that would be based on a clear, innate interaction model. Direct mappings of each button to a single function are not possible. One basic structuring of phone functionality is the use of *hierarchies* (or *menus*) of functions that are related; the user moves in these hierarchies by using the "up," "down," and "back up a level" commands. Still, users must develop a mental model of the phone's states. The idea of such abstract "modes"—which may resemble the functioning of a computer—may be very difficult to understand for people who are not technology-oriented, especially if no clear visual indication of the user's position in the hierarchy is presented.

Example of a Phone Design: Nokia 7110 UI Style

Figure 7.7 shows the Nokia 7110 button layout and semantics. The softkeys—or "selection keys" as they are called in Nokia user manuals—with their context-sensitive functions provide a certain improvement in terms of user friendliness. Softkeys change their semantics according to the user's position in the interaction sequence and thus give more guidance in the limited available screen space. Other phone keys are also used in combination with the softkeys when users perform their mobile communication tasks (see an example interaction sequence in Figure 7.8).

One challenge with softkeys is that if there are only one or two softkeys, then the functions that are not represented in these keys need to be activated from elsewhere. This forces the user to look for the means to execute the next desired action in many places in the UI, thus increasing the cognitive load by "focus transfer." On the other hand, too many softkeys cause similar problems, and thus there remains the challenge of designing a command space so that too many options are not available to the user at the same time.

Figure 7.9 shows a comparison example where the softkeys are shown to improve the user friendliness of a user-phone interaction sequence. In this example, the efficiency in performing a task does not improve in terms of the number of button presses, but most probably improves in performance time and quality in general—it is easier to learn and remember, and also causes fewer errors. These effects escalate—especially for the novice user—because the UI can provide the terminology in the user's native language.

As has been discussed above, in mobile usage contexts the interaction must be as efficient as possible. The time- and pressure-critical interaction sequences especially need to be kept short. This can be achieved by, for example, the following:

- Ordering/prioritizing menus so that the "most likely" or "most critical" functions are available first

- Offering short cuts, for example, by the number of the function in the hierarchy/menu

FIGURE **7.7**

1. Power key. Used for switching the phone on and off. When pressed briefly the user enters the list of profiles (user environments: e.g., *Silent* to turn off all the phone tones).

2. Navi Roller. Used for navigating the Menu and the Phonebook. Navi Roller allows scrolling up and down as well as *selecting*, *saving*, or *sending* the displayed item by clicking the roller.

3. Two Softkeys. The softkeys are assigned actions that enable the user to manipulate the user interface by making selections and *entering*, *editing*, and *deleting* text. The name of the action changes according to the state of the phone. Descriptive labels are shown in the lower corner of the display respective to the key underneath (see Figure 7.8).

4. Send key (green receiver). *Send key* is used for call handling, that is, call creation, and also for bringing up the last-called numbers list.

5. End key (red receiver). *End key* is for call termination. It is also an Exit key that can be used as a panic key since it takes the user from any state of the phone to the idle state without saving changes.

6. Numeric keys, with an alphabet according to the ITU-T.161 standard. Used for number and character input. The 1 key also doubles as the Voice Mailbox speed dial key. The # key is used for changing the character case during editing. Nokia 7110 employs a predictive text input method: only one keypress per letter is required, and the entered text string is continually matched with the words in the built-in dictionary.

- The left softkey is basically used as a yes/positive key. It contains options that execute commands and go deeper into the menu structure. In the idle state the left softkey is *Menu* (the hierarchy of phone functions).

- The right softkey is basically used as a no/negative key. It contains options that cancel commands, delete text, and go higher in the menu structure. In the idle state the right softkey is *Names* (the Phonebook).

Nokia 7110 button layout and semantics.

Figure 7.8

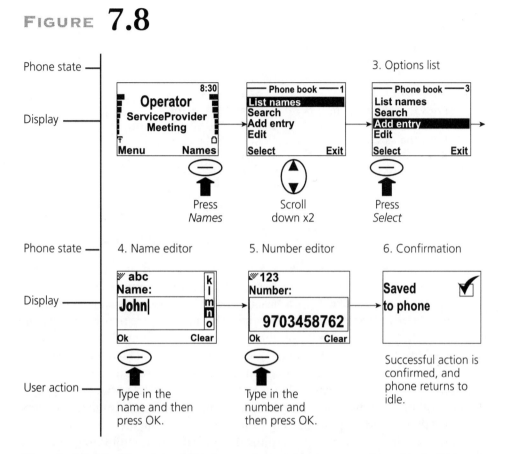

The principle of softkeys in mobile phones when saving a name and number in the memory.

- Designing a limited amount of dedicated (hardware) buttons. However, there is often a trade-off between the visibility/availability of functions and the increasing size of the device. Also, designs from previous products may prevent the introduction of new hardware buttons so that a common UI style between products is maintained.

- Designing the task flow in a flexible enough way so that task switches and interruptions are allowed

As textual communication is increasing in the mobile context, the special problems of alpha input also need to be tackled. The ITU-T standard keypad for alpha input (see Figure 7.7) is widely used, but on average, it requires several button presses per character, thus reducing efficiency. Alternative alpha input methods are being developed. For example, the T9 writing method

FIGURE **7.9**

Entering a name and number to a memory location

Without softkeys:

1. Press the M button.
2. Press the ABC button.
3. Key in the name.
4. Press the ABC button.
5. Key in the phone number
6. Press the M button again.

With softkeys:

1. Press Names (right softkey).
2. Scroll to Add Entry.
3. Press Select (left softkey).
4. Key in the name.
5. Press OK (left softkey)
6. Key in the phone number.
7. Press OK (left softkey).

Saving a name and number into a memory location without softkeys (e.g., Mobira Cityman shown in Figure 7.1) and with softkeys (e.g., Nokia 7110).

allows the faster input of words based on a dictionary approach. The phone proposes the most likely word based on what the user has started to write, thus increasing the efficiency of writing. This approach is now being used in the Nokia 7110, the media phone. Other solutions may depend on pen-based input such as in the Palm.

The personalization of interaction routines is also required, but this only makes sense to some extent. Users should not be forced to become designers of their own devices. One example of such customization is to let users place their favorite application or function (e.g., calling their voice mailbox) in one of the hard buttons. Functions that allow—but do not force—users to change some aspects of their device can significantly increase the subjective satisfaction with the device.

One very basic requirement in the HCI of basic mobile phones is one-handed use. This especially implies that the critical functions/tasks (see "User Tasks," page 181) should be carried out with one hand only—and with as few button presses as possible. This also means that combined button presses, where many buttons are pressed simultaneously, are not ergonomically feasible. The user's grip on the phone suggests that the thumb mostly be used for primary manipulation of the buttons.

Another requirement in some usage contexts (e.g., in the car) is to use the mobile phone hands-free. A partial solution is to use the phone with headsets; while making/receiving a call the user only needs to use his or her hands for starting and ending the call, but the hands are free for other activities during the call. This works well when no other functions (e.g., browsing through the phone book) are required during the call. Another solution for hands-free operation is a speech user interface. The user gives oral commands to operate the phone and thus does not need to perform manual activities to carry out the communication task. Still, both speech UIs and headsets may be inappropriate—or at least awkward—in certain social contexts where other people are around.

Until recently, the users of most models of mobile phones needed high manual dexterity and relatively good eyesight. The situation has improved because of larger phone displays—including limited iconic interaction—in basic phones and improved tactile feedback from physical button presses, and because of the means of interaction described above. Still, the continuing trend for the miniaturization of basic phones requires innovative solutions from user-phone interaction designers.

HCI Challenges and Solutions in Communicators

With the emergence of communicators (see Figure 7.2 for the Nokia 9110 Communicator) we are overcoming some of the disadvantages of "basic phones," but some still persist. In terms of usability, the obvious benefits of communicators over basic phones stem from the following:

- A larger screen area, with graphics to increase visual display quality, manipulatable objects, as well as more descriptive terminology

- Better possibilities for more complete keyboards (even QWERTY) and more softkeys; thus clearer, context-dependent mappings with user actions and device responses in complex tasks are possible

- Two-handed use, although some critical tasks must be possible with one hand only. For example, a Nokia Communicator must also be an efficiently usable phone, and therefore one-handed use of the basic phone functions is a critical design requirement. In the Nokia 9110 (see Figure 7.2) the phone functions are also found on the cover of the device—thus there is no need to use two hands nor to open the device.

Because the tendency especially in communicator design has been to increase the number of features, special attention has been paid to defining the most frequent and critical tasks in each application. A number of usability tests have been carried out with communicator concepts to test and iterate the flow of tasks. Because of inherent time criticality and the interruptive nature of work with personal mobile devices, quick and effortless access to the most important features becomes one of the key design drivers. For example, instant access to create a new document and start entering text, as well as flexible task and application switching, must not require more than one or, at a maximum, two button presses (for more information see Section 7.4, "Design and Evaluation of Mobile Terminals").

FIGURE **7.10**

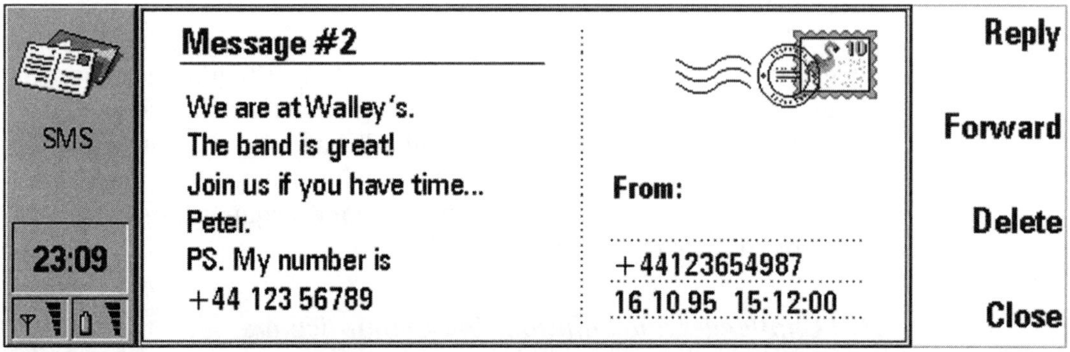

			Reply
Message #2			
We are at Walley's.			**Forward**
The band is great!			
Join us if you have time...	**From:**		**Delete**
Peter.			
PS. My number is	+44123654987		
+44 123 56789	16.10.95 15:12:00		**Close**

The postcard metaphor for the Short Messaging Service (SMS) in a communicator.

Despite all of the advances in communicators in terms of UI and interaction, new challenges have appeared:

- *Media design* requires more versatile design skills than character-based UI or even traditional graphical UI (GUI) design. The new design paradigm must be based on multimedia UI where the media is integrated, not just added "on top."

- *New UI metaphors* [e.g., in Kamba, T., et al. 1996], specially designed for small devices with versatile features will help especially novice users to form a solid mental model of how the system functions (see Figure 7.10).

- *Flexibility* must be offered in terms of how users want to perform their tasks, including switching, undoing, backtracking, and canceling tasks as they wish.

- *Transparency of the underlying technology.* The users should not have to be aware of how their communication happens technically. For example, if the user wants to send a textual message, they should not be forced to decide whether the data is sent as a "short message" or as an email as long as the intended recipient gets the message.

- *Easy personalization of the UI and the device itself.* Personal ringing tones are very popular, as are accessories such as color covers. Good default settings for the UI are also needed for people who are not willing or able to change the settings or "preferences."

- True mobility requires the ability to connect over the air to other remote devices such as office PCs and servers, and message boxes. A prerequisite for connectivity is *compatibility* both on the device and content level.

7.4 Design and Evaluation of Mobile Terminals

The creation of mobile phones and communicators is heavily influenced by the special business environment that currently (at the end of the 1990s) dominates mobile communication. At the turn of the millennium, this business environment can be characterized by

- A constant hurry and need to bring to market new, innovative terminal models (also for specific target markets)

- The speed at which the technology (e.g., networks and I/O) is developing

- The existence and development of various network standards

As a market leader of mobile terminal manufacturers (in February 1999), Nokia is participating in "creating the future" of mobile communication. New technologies are constantly explored for their applicability in new terminal concepts, and the product development life cycles need to be shortened to a minimum in order to maintain the competitive advantage.

The fast-paced and innovative nature of the mobile phone business also implies that, for example, the traditional requirements gathering is not possible for all aspects of terminal design. Target users cannot be "asked" to list their requirements nor can they even be investigated fully by user observations and so on, since the new products being developed—for their part—create new user needs and mobile communication lifestyles. Mobile terminal design also has further requirements due to the very personal nature of the devices—both in terms of the interaction routines and the appearance of the physical device itself.

In the following section, we will first outline the specific issues in the design of mobile communication terminals and then describe in some detail the steps that need to be gone through—or the user-centered methods that are exploited—when developing mobile handsets for high-quality use. After that, the contextual design approach is discussed.

Specific Issues in the Design of Mobile Communication Terminals

This section describes the specific characteristics of the creation of mobile communication terminals. We have divided the issues into six categories: requirements analysis, concept design, interaction design, visual design, industrial design, and iterative evaluation. This structure does not suggest any exact temporal ordering or design process—the whole design process is obviously highly iterative—but rather serves as a means to categorize the needed expertise of people participating in the creation of mobile end-user communication products.

Requirements Analysis

In mobile communication, there are many usage contexts that cannot all be anticipated (as was discussed in "The *Mobile Context of Use*" section). This increases the amount of resources needed to understand user needs and sets extra demands on the skills of the requirements researchers.

The mobile phone business is characterized, on the one hand, by the requirements of first-time buyers and, on the other hand, by the requirements of experienced users. These requirements may differ: experienced users will better be able to state their requirements, but the novice user must be supported as well.

Consumers have a variety of—possibly yet unformed—needs, both in their professional and leisure times, which tend to mix especially in advanced mobile terminal usage. This stems from the partly unforeseeable future, implying the difficulty in gathering requirements. Therefore, more research or investigatory work is needed in the area where the users' work practices and task structures are not clearly goal-oriented (see the "*Scenarios and Tasks*" section for a further discussion).

Concept Design

When designing an initial interaction and functionality concept for a new mobile phone or communicator product, it is important to fulfill specific user needs, but at the same time not to design for a too-limited target market. The variety of offered products must also match the resources of the company to create totally new product concepts.

Some novelty must always be brought into a new concept or updated product version. In new product design, there is a danger of falling into "featurism" rather than striving to create a meaningful functionality sphere that supports a smooth task flow for users. This becomes especially important when the UI has limited input/output mechanisms, (e.g., due to the size of the physical product).

As the requirements elicitation and concept design are closely intertwined, the challenges of the "unknown future" also apply in concept design. It is thus inevitable that risks must be taken in innovative concept design.

Interaction Design

In the detailed HCI design of mobile terminals, the basic usability criteria must obviously apply: it must be consistent, efficient, intuitive, offer shortcuts for experts, minimize the need to look at the display in critical tasks, and so on. Because the interaction possibilities are more limited, it is even more crucial to offer the right forms of interaction—not too many navigation and control alternatives should clutter the "interaction space." Input (and to some extent output) devices are limited. Optimal pointing and input methods must thus be found that match the general design constraints such as one-handed or hands-free use.

As far as subjective user satisfaction is concerned, personalization of interaction possibilities must be offered. The optimum of "some, but not too much" user customization must be found. We must not force the user to become a designer/programmer, so good default values are essential for those who do not want to customize.

Visual Design

In basic phones the main challenge of the visual UI design is to find solutions for increasing visuality even in almost character-based displays. This visuality also informs the novice user of "where am I now," "where can I go next," and "what is available" in the function space of the mobile handset.

In communicators, where screen space is somewhat less limited, there are still visual design constraints to be solved. The visual designer's main task is to find solutions for directing the user's attention to the relevant elements displayed at the time as well as for utilizing efficiently the screen area, which may offer "semidirect manipulation."

Industrial Design

Ergonomics research must offer solutions for the best physical form factors (including button layout for one-handed versus two-handed use, size and form, etc.), taking into account the requirements of miniaturization.

Studies of aesthetics are needed to find out which design attributes fit the target consumers' (real or imagined) lifestyles. The designer's main objective is to make potential target users desire the mobile communication device. The personalization of the physical or other characteristics (e.g., ringing tones and color covers) should support the lifestyle requirements.

Iterative Evaluation throughout the Whole Product Creation Chain

Iterative evaluation—both with users and by expert evaluators from different HCI disciplines—must constantly support the creation and improvement of ideas, concepts, and designs. Principles of participatory design should be exploited to some extent. This is not always easy, however, because target users may not have visions of what is possible in the future, for example.

Special user evaluation challenges in mobile terminal design include

- The difficulty of testing in all possible usage contexts

- The difficulty of testing human communication practices, especially when it concerns still-unestablished practices

- The difficulty of testing services that cannot all be known beforehand

In summary, there are some specific issues in the creation—design and evaluation—of mobile communication terminals. One major objective is to place the emphasis on the usability work toward the early stages of requirements research. The next section describes how these user-centered design methods are exploited at Nokia.

Practicing User-Centered Design for Usable Mobile Phones at Nokia

User-centered design (UCD) as a principle (Preece et al. 1994) has been practiced as part of concept and product creation at Nokia. We are actively searching for, adapting, and modifying the best practices from the HCI community as well as developing methods of our own to better suit the mobile terminal industry, where ever-changing usage contexts play a central role.

In concept and early product development we strive for *interdisciplinarity, iterativeness,* and *context awareness.* Design teams should ideally have people from various disciplines, such as HCI, graphic design, sociology, industrial design, engineering, and psychology, to get a balanced view of the problem. Figure 7.11 shows a top-level model of how UCD has been practiced at Nokia.

1. *Data gathering* includes collecting relevant data from previous projects and usability tests, market research studies, contextual observations (for more information, see "The Contextual Design Approach" section), and so on.

2. Data is then analyzed and *scenarios* are built based on the data. Requirements building also starts at this phase. Design ideas are collected, and first designs are done together with the *task flows.*

3. Then, *usability tests* and/or *contextual interviews* with *paper prototypes* are carried out, emphasizing the most important tasks. Several rounds of design-evaluation iterations are done based on user feedback. At this point it may turn out that more data needs to be collected to support design.

FIGURE **7.11**

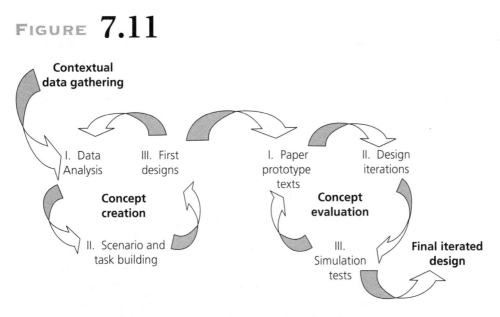

Iterativeness and context awareness in user-centered product development.

- Testing with hi-fi PC simulation starts when the initial design has been developed far enough—usually when the most important task flows have been iterated several times, based on user feedback, to form coherent functionality spheres.

- *Simulation tests* are carried out with end users. Also, *expert evaluations* (using evaluators from different HCI disciplines) are performed in this phase. Simulations are generally used for testing more advanced tasks, interaction between applications, task switches, as well as animations and different indicators such as the availability of services that are out of the scope of paper prototyping.

- In the late concept phase, *testing with functional HW prototypes* (with end users) gives initial feedback about the long-term acceptance, efficiency, and utility of the concept.

4. As the last iteration phase, the final design is evaluated by end users and expert evaluators.

After each test round, the design team goes through the findings and analyzes them. Changes in the prototype are made according to the test results and marketing input. International testing is done with a PC simulation in relevant market areas.

User-centered design practices must be modified to a certain extent based on the requirements of the project in question. The decision criteria include the available resources in the time frame of the project, as well as the level of innovativeness of the product or concept to be developed. In any case, contextual research in the very early stages of the project is a cornerstone to be built on.

The Contextual Design Approach

Involving end users early in the design process has become necessary in current product development. There are several participatory design methodologies that can be exploited in the early design phases of mobile communication devices (Dix et al. 1998). At Nokia, traditional usability evaluations, walkthroughs, contextual interviews, and focus groups involving real users are currently widely used. However, a more recent trend, especially in concept development, is the need to gather more understanding of, and real insight into, users' work practices—that is, to understand users' or potential users' work practices, motives, and the consequences of certain behaviors and trends in varied contexts.

Contextual Inquiry (CI) (Beyer and Holtzblatt 1998) has proved to be one of the most promising methodological approaches in ethnographical and sociological research (Lewis et al. 1996) in exploring the context of use (Väänänen-Vainio-Mattila and Ruuska 1998). CI provides a structured and manageable method—even in mobile situations—for gathering insight into users' or potential users' work context and life in general. This method can also serve as a tool in producing design ideas and background for requirement formation.

The basic idea of CI is to enter the user's world as an "apprentice" to learn, and to make observations and inquiries related to the selected focus areas. CI has proved especially useful as a method in discovering people's personal ways of organizing work and task performance. Since personal ways of working and strategies for performing tasks are often automatic (or semiautomatic), it has turned out to be almost impossible to gather reliable and sufficiently detailed information for concept design purposes on what users really do and why, just by using questionnaires or interviews. CI provides tools for gathering and analyzing data on a level of detail that is useful for producing design solutions (Beyer and Holtzblatt 1998).

Experiences in Contextual Design

We will next describe a contextual design case of a communicator concept that was carried out internationally with mobile users.

At the beginning of the study, the focus was selected to be personal task management and quick note taking, which was communicated thoroughly within the multidisciplinary team to create a shared understanding of what we were supposed to find data on. User observations and inquiries took place with 14 observees in both the United States and Scandinavia. Each observation took 2–3 hours. Some observees were literally on the move all the time, and we "shadowed" them and recorded their every action. Observation in the mobile context is much more challenging than stationary observation, but it can be managed.

After each observation session, the captured data was walked through to share it with other researchers. In the "share," individual observations were captured in electronic format as affinity notes and in different hand-drawn models: cultural, physical, artifact, flow, and sequence models (Beyer and Holtzblatt 1998). After the data capturing in models and affinity notes, each model was then consolidated to one big model, still preserving all the variations from the original models. Also, an affinity wall of observation notes was built. All the consolidations and the affinity wall were put up in one "conceptual room," on view at all times. Based on the affinity wall and the consolidated models, the scenarios and initial designs for the paper prototype were made. The contextual design ended in iterative prototyping rounds and testing the designs with end users.

One of the clear strengths of the methodology is that it makes ethnographic research manageable in a business environment. It provides a structured way of collecting and analyzing vast amounts of qualitative data as well as producing design solutions based on real observations; data on users' work practices and task flows is especially hard to acquire reliably with other methods. Because the details of the findings are not abstracted, but preserved and organized as such in different models, the work can be kept concrete and design solutions can be based on user data.

7.5 Visions of the Future: Toward the Third Generation of Mobile Communication

The first generation of mobile phones consisted of the analog models that emerged in the early 1980s. The second generation of digital mobile phones appeared about 10 years later, along with the first digital mobile networks. During the second generation, the mobile telecommunications industry has experienced exponential growth, both in terms of number of subscribers as well as new types of value-added services. Mobile phones are rapidly becoming the preferred means of personal communication, creating the world's largest consumer electronics industry. More than 100 million mobile phones were sold worldwide in 1997.

In the early years of the new millennium, the third generation (3G) of mobile telecommunications will enhance the use of sophisticated wireless applications. Users will be able to utilize personal wireless services that can be interactive and even location-based. Many companies and corporations are also restructuring their business processes to be able to fully exploit the opportunities provided by the emerging new wireless data services.

Third Generation Services

Many of the services are already available today, and their quality of use will improve with the introduction of the third generation. Future mobile communication will most certainly be a revolution in terms of bandwidth but an evolution of terminals in terms of applications and services. We describe the main service areas that will be enhanced below.

Online Mobile Video Conferencing

The 3G terminals will enable virtual work teams, even when on the move, to work on common tasks and projects. The concept of mobile voice calls will evolve, as multimedia (especially video) capabilities are added to the services and terminals. For example, data and images can simultaneously be shared and acted upon by users who are connected with a voice or video connection, leading to more effective, versatile, and satisfying online visual communications.

Location-Based Information Services

A visitor in a strange city will be able to instantly access local information— video clips of the films being shown at the local cinemas, for example. A tourist will get a map and historical information on a sight or landmark in front of her, directly downloaded to her 3G mobile communication device. A commuter will be able to play a round of bridge with his friends while traveling to work. Alternatively, he will have the opportunity to enjoy his personalized newspaper.

Seamless Connectivity between Devices

The emergence of new 3G terminals is expected to be further enhanced by significant improvements in the interconnectivity between various devices.

The mobile phone will act as a gateway to the outside world for other personal electronic devices, such as PCs, PDAs, and digital cameras. Some of these functions may be integrated into the mobile phone itself, in a way similar to today's Nokia Communicators. A key enabler of this enhanced interconnectivity is Bluetooth technology, a short-range radio link or low-power radio frequency (LPRF), developed by an international consortium in which Nokia is a founding member (for more information on Bluetooth, see *www.bluetooth.com*).

Symbian as a Platform for Usable and Utilizable Mobile Applications

Symbian was founded as a joint venture of Nokia, Ericsson, Motorola, and Psion. The company is developing a common operating system called EPOC (see Chapter 6) for wireless information devices, such as smart phones and communicators. EPOC will be licensed on an equal financial footing to all interested licensees and is expected to become the de facto environment for future multimedia phones and communicators.

Symbian offers an open application platform on which efficient third-party development becomes possible. This openness and free entry of independent solution providers will create competition and added value that will ultimately benefit consumers.

From the end user's point of view, the main benefit of Symbian's platform for mobile communication is that it enables the creation of consistent user-terminal interaction and core functionality across both the licensees' wireless information devices and the available applications. This will further enhance and harmonize the usage of the third generation of mobile communication.

The Evolution of the Usage of Third Generation Mobile Communication

Nokia is heading toward the third millennium with new mobile communication concepts that are based on strong innovativeness, creation of technological solutions, and the adoption of the principles of user-centered design.

Nokia's Future Terminal and Interaction Visions

In this section, we present two still-imaginary multimedia concepts (Figures 7.12 and 7.13; see also Color Plates) with scenarios of mobile interaction and communication practices.

FIGURE **7.12**

A future communicator concept.

6:30 A.M. David wakes up, has breakfast, and reads the morning news selected by the communicator according to his usual topics of interest. Then, he quickly checks the train timetables and sets off to catch the train.

7:15 A.M. He leaves for work. On the train he starts work by reading and answering his email—it is so convenient to stay "online" at all times with the packet connection, General Packet Radio Service (GPRS). The communicator has also found some interesting news on the Web that he decides to read.

For the rest of the journey, he sits back and decides to invite (through a Bluetooth connection) anyone in that train car to a game of chess. Someone seems to be as bored as he is, so they start a game and finish just before he needs to get off.

8:45 A.M. On his way to the office in a taxi, he decides to have a short online video discussion with a client. During the discussion, they exchange documents and work on each other's documents at both ends. Suddenly, he spots an interesting property and shows it to the client over the video. He immediately sends the details of it to the client in case he is interested.

9 A.M. He enters the office. At the same time, he receives an electronic postcard, with an audible anecdote attached to the picture, from his brother, who is on a fishing trip in Canada.

12 A.M. Just before lunch, he gives his communicator an assignment to find information on golf courses in Spain. In the middle of his lunch, the commu-

FIGURE 7.13

A future smart phone concept.

nicator is ready to present the results: 10 Web sites and 5 operator WAP (Wireless Application Protocol) pages about golf courses in southern Spain (for more information on WAP, see www.wapforum.org). He extracts all the addresses and sends a room reservation query to the most interesting one.

3:00 P.M. He sets off to meet his colleague. He is not sure of the exact location of the building and decides to request a map of the area and some instructions on how to get there. With the help of the map and the online guidance, he finds his way to his colleague.

Future User Needs for Mobile Communication

Initially, the end users' needs for third-generation communication may not essentially differ from the second-generation services. After all, many services already exist in a "lighter" form. However, as the services get established in the mass market, they will create new needs, for example, in terms of the quality of service (e.g., video conferencing or the downloading speed of documents). Users' interaction with the services will have to be matched with an equal ease and efficiency of use for mobile communication terminals. New functionality, for example, in the location-based services, may also radically change the way people communicate, plan, and carry out their tasks while mobile.

PC-based (office) systems—multimedia interaction, groupwork support, Web (Internet), and standard UI platforms (see the section on the Symbian platform, page 199)—were discussed in earlier sections. It seems that these will be a reality in the third-generation mobile platforms, and thus users will not have to suffer from a possibly lower quality of use or "stripped down" HCI to the same extent as in the second generation of mobile communication. This will also support the consistent and high-quality user experience between different platforms and thus helps everyone—including computer novices—become effective users of mobile communication.

7.6 Conclusions

Mobility presents new challenges to the HCI community and methods because of the emerging versatile communication and personal organization practices. Users' needs for mobile systems are partly different from office-based practices. In this chapter, we have elaborated the notion of context and the necessity of studying it in connection with mobile communication and work practices. The cultural, social, and physical aspects of context and their relation to the technological infrastructure must be studied in a real environment to reveal nuances and details crucial in personal communication product creation.

We are entering a new communication and work culture where time and place are less critical, and where people are finding new, individually suitable ways of merging or separating their business and personal lives. The overall goals of work and leisure-time activities are not likely to change—users still need to gather and distribute information, remember to be in certain places at certain times, and still win at golf. However, different forms of, and practices in, achieving the goals are likely to change, especially when more personally adaptable systems become available for consumers.

7.7 Acknowledgments

We would like to thank the following people from whom we received comments and valuable hints in the course of writing this chapter: Heikki Huomo, Pekka Isomursu, Timo Jokela, Janne Kari, Turkka Keinonen, Timo Kinnunen, Christian Lindholm, Riitta Nieminen-Sundell, Miika Silfverberg,

Andrej Sonkin, Juha Vaihoja, and Jyrki Yli-Nokari. We thank also Tero Hakala, Jari Ijäs, and Petri Ruutikainen for their valuable help in creating and editing the figures.

Special thanks go to the editor, Eric Bergman, for his patience and good organization, as well as to the excellent and highly professional reviewer for the inspiring comments.

7.8 References

Beyer, H., and K. Holtzblatt. 1998. *Contextual Design: Defining Customer-Centered Systems.* San Francisco: Morgan Kaufmann.

Bourges-Waldegg, P., and S. Scrivener. 1998. Meaning, the central issue in cross-cultural HCI design. *Interacting with Computers* 9(3):287–310.

Dix, A., K. Cheverst, N. Davies, and T. Rodden. 1998. Exploiting context in HCI design for mobile systems. In C. Johnson (Ed.), *Proceedings of First Workshop on HCI for Mobile Devices,* GIST Technical Report G98-1, Department of Computing Science, University of Glasgow, Scotland, 12–17. *www.dcs.ac.uk/~johnson/mobile.html.*

EMC (European Mobile Communications) EMC Cellular Subscribers Penetration on Yearly Database. (1999).

Erickson, T. D. 1990. Working with interface metaphors. In B. Laurel (Ed.), *The Art of Human-Computer Interface Design,* Reading, MA: Addison-Wesley, 65–73.

Hwang, D., and R. Giusto (Eds.). 1998. *Smart Handheld Devices: Boom or Bust? Worldwide Smart Handheld Devices Market Review and Forecast Update, 1997–2001.* International Data Corporation (*www.idc.com*).

ISO. 1998. International Standard Organization/Final Draft International Standard (ISO/FDIS 9241-11): *Ergonomic requirements for office work with visual display terminals (VDTs).* Part 11: Guidance on usability.

Kamba, T., S. A. Elson, H. Harpold, T. Stamper, and P. Sukaviriya. 1996. Using small screen space more efficiently. In M. Tauber (Ed.), *CHI'96 Conference Proceedings: Conference on Human Factors in Computing Systems.* Reading, MA: Addison-Wesley, 383–390.

Lakoff, G., and M. Johnsson. 1990. *Metaphors We Live By.* Chicago: University of Chicago Press.

Lewis, S., M. Mateas, S. Palmiter, and G. Lynch. 1996. Ethnographic data for product development: a collaborative process. *Interactions* 3(6):52–69.

Monk, A. 1986. Mode errors: A user-centered analysis and some preventative measures using keying-contingent sounds. *International Journal of Man-Machine Studies* 24(4):313–327.

Nielsen, J. 1993. *Usability Engineering.* Chestnut Hill, MA: Academic Press.

Norman, D. 1986. Cognitive engineering. In D. Norman and S. Draper (Eds.), *User Centered System Design*. Hillsdale, NJ: Lawrence Erlbaum Associates, 32–61.

Pantzar, M. 1996. *Kuinka Teknologia Kesytetään* (Taming the Everyday Technology). Helsinki: Hanki ja jää.

Preece, J., Y. Rogers, H. Sharp, D. Benyon, S. Holland, and T. Carey. 1994. *Human-Computer Interaction*. Reading, MA: Addison-Wesley.

Sacher, H. 1998. Interactions in Chinese: designing interfaces for Asian cultures interactions. *Interactions* 5(5):28–38.

Shneiderman, B. 1992. *Designing the User Interface*. Reading, MA: Addison-Wesley.

Schuler, D., and A. Namioka (Eds.). 1993. *Participatory Design: Principles and Practises*. Hillsdale, NJ: Lawrence Erlbaum Associates.

Väänänen-Vainio-Mattila, K., and S. Haataja. 1997. Mobile communication user interfaces for everyone. In M.J. Smith, G. Salvendy, and R.J. Koubek (Eds.), *Advances in Human Factors/Ergonomics 21B, Design of Computing Systems: Social and Ergonomic Considerations*. London: Elsevier, 815–919.

Väänänen-Vainio-Mattila, K., and S. Ruuska. 1998. User needs for mobile communication devices: Requirements gathering and analysis through Contextual Inquiry. In C. Johnson (Ed.) *Proceedings of First Workshop on HCI for Mobile Devices*, GIST Technical Report G98-1, Department of Computing Science, University of Glasgow, Scotland, 113–120. *www.dcs.ac.uk/~johnson/mobile.html*.

CHAPTER Eight

User Interface Design for a Vehicle Navigation System

AARON MARCUS

Aaron Marcus and Associates, Inc. (AM+A)

8.1 Introduction

Providing vehicle drivers and passengers access to information about their location, planned trip route, and sites of interest along the way has been a challenge since the early automobile days. For many decades, the American Automobile Association, as well as other organizations and publishers, have produced printed maps, guidebooks, and specialized trip documents. Today, onboard computers, global positioning satellite (GPS) systems, and Internet access now make interactive screen displays a technical reality, but the user interface and information design challenge is more striking than ever because of both the quantity and the quality of information access. Many commercial systems are still in the early stages.

This chapter discusses an early (1989–92) project in user interface and information visualization (UI+IV) design supported by Motorola Corporation. This project attempted to solve a number of constraints for vehicle navigation:

- Legible displays (easily noticed, discernable)

- Readable displays (easily comprehended, appealing)

- Systematic use of visible language (colors, signs, layouts, maps, etc.)

- Variability of key displays to account for users' cognitive preferences

The results continue to have relevance to current systems. The project approaches user interface design from a user and communication perspective, not a technology and code perspective. The chapter will introduce fundamental definitions of user interface design, review the history of the user interface design of a particular kind of product, and explain design issues that are vital to the success of computer-based communication products.

In personalizing technology beyond the desktop, user interfaces of consumer products must provide easy access by users to functions and data in a manner that is also easy for users to comprehend, remember, and use. Successful products consist of partially universal, or general, solutions and partially unique, or local, solutions to the design of user interfaces. The user interface designer can achieve compelling forms that enable the user interface to be more usable and acceptable by managing the user's experience with familiar structures and processes, the user's surprise at novel approaches, as well as the user's preferences and expectations. High-quality user interface design, whose content and visual form are dependent upon visible languages (e.g., typography, color, symbolism, layout, etc.) and effective interaction with them, improves the likelihood that users will be more productive and satisfied with computer-based products in many situations beyond the traditional office desktop.

Demographics, experience, education, and roles in organizations of work or leisure can define users. Individual needs as well as group roles can define a user's tasks. A user-centered, task-oriented design method accounts for these aspects in effective user interface design. User interfaces conceptually consist of metaphors, mental models, navigation, appearance, and interaction. For simplicity, clarity, and consistency with the reader's interpretation, these terms are defined as follows (Marcus 1992, 1995, 1997, 1998b):

- *Metaphors:* essential concepts conveyed through words and images, or through acoustic or tactile means. Metaphors concern both overarching concepts as well as individual items, like the "trashcan" standing for "deletion" within the "desktop" metaphor.

- *Mental models:* organization of data, functions, tasks, roles, and people in groups at work or play. The term (similar to, but distinct from, cognitive models, task models, user models, etc.) is intended to convey the organization observed in the user interface itself, which is presumably learned and understood by users and which reflects the content to be conveyed as well as users' tasks.

- *Navigation:* movement through mental models afforded by windows, menus, dialog areas, control panels, and so on. The term implies process, as opposed to structure; that is, sequences of content potentially accessed by users, as opposed to the static structure of that content.

- *Appearance:* verbal, visual, acoustic, and tactile perceptual characteristics of the displays. The term implies all aspects of visible, acoustic, and haptic languages—for example, typography or color; musical timbre or cultural accent within a spoken language; and surface texture or resistance to force.

- *Interaction:* the means by which users input changes to the system and the feedback supplied by the system. The term implies all aspects of command control devices (e.g., keyboards, mice, joysticks, microphones), as well as sensory feedback (e.g., changes of state of virtual graphical buttons, auditory displays, and tactile surfaces).

For example, an application, its data, the graphical user interface (GUI) environment, and the hardware all contribute to the functional and visual form attributes of the user interface. An advanced English text editor working within the Microsoft Windows 95 GUI environment on a mouse- and keyboard-driven Intel Pentium processor–based PC presents one set of characteristics. The LCD displays and buttons on the front panel of a French paper copier, or the colorful displays and fighter-pilot-like joysticks for a children's video game on a Japanese Sega game machine, present alternative characteristics.

The last decade has witnessed significant worldwide growth of products with small screens and other limited characteristics of appearance and interaction. I have coined the term "baby faces" (Marcus 1998a) for the user interfaces of such products. For these products, the challenge of designing good user interfaces that are accessible immediately by users around the globe becomes an immediate, practical matter, not only a theoretical issue.

This chapter discusses the development of one particular kind of baby face: a user interface for a prototype in-car vehicle navigation system intended for users in many different countries with different cultures, languages, and groups in the context of the emerging information society. The text reviews important design issues in the course of describing attributes of the prototype.

8.2 Project Description

The project described here has a long and interesting history. I briefly review its origins and goals and how the team accomplished our tasks.

Origins and Team Structure

During the late 1980s and into the early 1990s, Allan Kirson, Motorola Intelligent Vehicle-Highway System (IVHS) Product Development Director, Schaumberg, IL, led Motorola's efforts to design a prototype for the Advanced Driver and Vehicle Advisory Navigation Concept (ADVANCE) project, which used GPS technology. The ADVANCE project was a consortium of the U.S. Department of Transportation (USDOT), the Illinois DOT, the Illinois Universities Transportation Research Consortium (the University of Illinois at Chicago and Northwestern University), Motorola, and other corporate sponsors. Numerous auto and IVHS industry publications at the time described the ADVANCE project (see, for example, Tucker 1994).

Among other goals, Motorola's component was intended to give drivers detailed, accurate, timely information about route guidance, traffic congestion, weather, and other information about points of interest along routes that might be trips planned and stored by one or more drivers, or additionally passengers. Motorola's user interface development team consisted of project management and product designers. That team worked with Motorola's in-house industrial designers and with two outside firms, American Institutes of Research (AIR), Concord, MA, which provided human factors consulting, and my firm, Aaron Marcus and Associates, Inc. (AM+A), Emeryville, CA, which provided user interface design. Motorola conducted user focus and usability evaluations prior to, during, and subsequent to the project.

Project Details

By the time that Motorola contracted AM+A to assist in the development process, Motorola team members had completed significant planning and research. Motorola had received and/or prepared extensive documentation about the business objectives, marketing requirements, engineering requirements, and users. These materials included the product's target price-point (under $1,000), the user description (general consumers, in particular U.S. car owners purchasing new cars and/or after-market add-on devices, and car rental customers), use scenarios (e.g., novice versus expert users, daylight and nighttime driving, drivers with gloved hands using a touch-sensitive display, no trip specification while driving, and little or no use of an instruction manual), the required data and functions (e.g., accurate street maps with geographic features, climate conditions, traffic conditions, and political boundaries), and the desired features of the product (e.g., local restaurants and gasoline stations indicated on the maps, address editing, multiple languages, and audio feedback). Motorola had already incorporated technical requirements based on GPS technology and geographic database providers such as Etak.

Equipment located in the car included a CD-ROM device in the trunk used for accessing the database and imagery relevant to sights encountered by the drivers and/or passengers and a GPS device for locating the car with the onboard GPS system.

The display for the Motorola "smart car" navigation system was a Sharp 5-inch liquid crystal display with touch screen surface. At the time, the LCD device was state of the art and exceeded the visual quality of then-current commercial navigation displays. Nevertheless, the display had significant limitations: 16 colors, limited font design, low resolution (one-quarter of SVGA spatial resolution, or 320×240 pixels). In addition, and with significant impact on visual design, the rectangular pixels were not positioned in a right-angled row and column layout. Instead, the pixels were located in a staggered brick pattern. This arrangement meant that a horizontal one-pixel line and a vertical one-pixel differed significantly in apparent width. The display was to be housed in a plastic and metal enclosure of minimal dimensions with 5 to 10 electromechanical buttons.

The trip planning and route navigation functions of the product required maps at 10 levels of magnification, from the scale of the entire United States to a few blocks of city streets. Using GPS technology, the car's location could be pinpointed to a maximum uncertainty of approximately 0.5 meters.

AM+A designed and built prototypes using Macromedia Director. AM+A has found Macromedia to be an effective user interface design prototyping tool, especially during initial and intermediate phases. Designers relatively quickly can render precise, detailed sketches of metaphors, mental models, and navigation, with a preliminary appearance and interaction, that enables the development team to "debug" or eliminate major errors in metaphors, mental models, and navigation. The prototypes also are of high enough quality that the development team can show the prototypes to management, selected key customers, and to prospective users in focus groups, and even in testing sessions, in order to gain buy-in, gather information, or determine specific benefits and failings of the user interface design.

Motorola initially requested that AM+A combine sketches of screen designs representing several disparate design approaches to map navigation, selection of items in lists, and soon into three coordinated prototypes that showed distinctly different explorations of a design space. This task is frequently an early one of user interface design because the design space of possibilities is simply too large to explore exhaustively in a practical time frame. Eventually, AM+A was responsible for designing detailed, interactive prototypes and simulations based on mental model and navigation design documents prepared by AIR with consultation and review by Motorola.

During 1989–92, AM+A, working with AIR and Motorola, developed several partial designs for the user interface and, eventually, approximately 100 detailed screens that were intended to prescribe and describe the metaphors, mental model, navigation, appearance, and interaction. Because it was not feasible to show every screen, we emphasized the importance of showing the top levels of most functions and one navigation path in depth for a primary function, trip navigation. The mental model and navigation structure as a whole were primarily derived from Motorola's and AIR's efforts, which in turn they based on detailed user, task, and functional specifications documented thoroughly in reports published internally at Motorola for the project. Motorola selected AM+A primarily to design high-quality appearance and interaction characteristics, but inevitably the specifics of the screen designs impacted the metaphors, mental model, and navigation.

Motorola's system was intended to give drivers detailed, accurate, timely information about route guidance, traffic congestion, weather, and other information about points of interest. One design challenge was to simplify an earlier design for two initial screens with 18 different functions into one screen with 5 functions so that the consumer would not be intimidated and could easily obtain useful information while driving. AM+A contributed to the development of the touch screen display that enables users to understand the basic functions and the types of data that can be accessed.

From the very beginning of the product's availability in the marketplace, AM+A has used Macromedia Director as a user interface prototyping environment. For this project, too, we used Macromedia Director (Clarke and Swearingen 1994). The application enabled us to mock up quickly demonstrations, animation sequences, and interaction prototypes (not accessing actual databases) that were visually accurate, detailed, and compelling. The rapid prototyping enabled the client immediately to show the product to interested third parties, such as customers, patrons, key internal management, marketers, and others whose opinions influence current and future funding of development.

8.3 User Interface Components

Primary user interface components of the final prototypes included the following:

Metaphors

The essential product references included the following items and their constituent parts:

- Maps, with roads, scales, north arrows, and so on
- Trips, with planners, destinations, route preferences, and so on
- Vehicle dashboard control panel, with buttons, labels, and so on
- Typewriter keyboard and telephone keypad, with buttons, labels, and so on
- Rare: computer-like pop-up control panels, with labels, exit buttons, and so on

The new product provided electronic, interactive access to the equivalent of traditional folded maps and booklets similar to the American Automobile Association's Triptik trip-viewer. Based on user research, Motorola considered it important that the product appear to be an extension of existing vehicle dashboard controls rather than a desktop computer device for which keyboards, windows, mice, and so on, were more typical metaphorical references.

Mental Model

The mental model of the device was quite complex, enabling users to specify trips, edit existing trips, consult map/direction displays while driving, and so on. One significant situation was the initial screen contents upon turning on the device. AM+A believed that the design proposed by other team groups was too complicated; they proposed two screens of 9 items each. We felt the initial screen should have 7 ± 2 items to denote and connote a simple product. After much consideration, the mental model was reconfigured to achieve this level of simplicity.

Navigation

Following upon the developers' desire to emphasize "simple" dashboard controls rather than "complex" and daunting computer navigation, the screen elements changed, with few exceptions, by complete panes, that is, without pop-up dialog boxes or controls. This navigation approach differs from typical desktop personal computer interaction with detailed hypertext-like navigation in which any part of the display may be interactive and show small-scale pop-up controls, or widgets.

Appearance

The product appearance needed to convey a simple, straightforward, appealing product. At the same time, all typography, colors, and layout served very complex functional requirements. These included legibility and readability even of small map symbols under varying light conditions, from bright sunlight in the daytime to nighttime viewing in complete darkness. AM+A was able to use an actual display screen connected to an Apple Macintosh in order to test legibility and readability of fonts, colors, lines, and entire screen layouts.

A relatively simple grid for screen title bars, primary navigation buttons, lists, and other regular screen elements accommodated most displays.

Typographic fonts were initially a problem. AM+A deemed the default fonts provided with the display hardware inadequate, especially for maps. At our recommendation, Motorola decided to incorporate a Helvetica sans serif font.

Colors, limited to 16, were apportioned to semantic references economically but sometimes necessarily repetitively. Four colors in the main title bars acted as visual cues and mnemonics to represent the main functional

FIGURE **8.1**

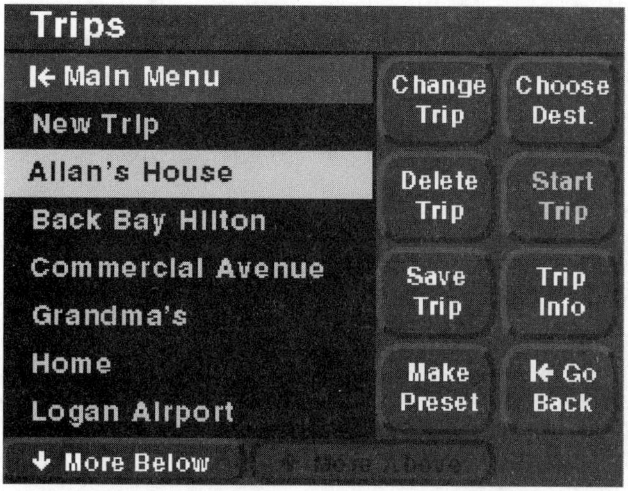

Screen with expert (left column) and novice (right column) buttons.

modules of the product. Other standard colors represented the levels of road capacity, levels of road traffic, levels of warning messages for impending maneuvers, and geographic sites, among other denotations.

Figure 8.1 (see also Color Plate) shows two levels of buttons (novice-intermediate on the right and expert on the left) by which users can choose trip destinations. The prototype featured the optional ability to continually display expert functions. Note the use of light green to highlight text and to indicate the next default button selection.

Interaction

The product was intended for touch interaction for locating and selecting items, generally with a small number of selection points within a display. The user might have long fingernails or be wearing gloves; consequently, most primary selection points (e.g., regular menu buttons) were large in area, often 4% of the display area (essentially elements of a 5×5 matrix).

Interaction techniques included selecting by using single-line scroll-down and scroll-up buttons at the bottom of the screen (to preserve usable screen width), instead of a more typical, and more computer-like, scrollbar at the right side (see Figure 8.2). Experiments with the actual touch screen

FIGURE **8.2**

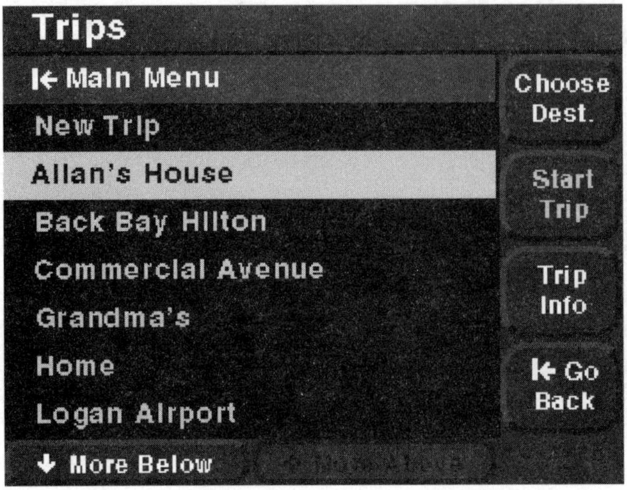

Scrollbar alternative using More Below and More Above buttons.

showed that controlling a scrollbar at arm's length seemed more difficult than taps on screen buttons.

Another typical interaction device was the telephone keyboard, which could be used for future telephony functions. In the current product, this familiar interaction device was not used.

In one exceptional case, a specially laid-out on-screen QWERTY keyboard was used to provide a means to edit short text for names of users, addresses, names of destinations, and so on. Because the keys were substandard in size, the designers added an additional location cursor to assist the user in identifying the appropriate target area: green crosshairs along the entire rows and columns of keys (Figure 8.3).

One other unique cursor control designed to assist location and selection was the "off-center zoom box" cursor (Figure 8.4) used for locating and selecting map targets. This control showed a 100×80-pixel horizontal rectangle outline with a translucent interior and a cross-hair cursor located in the upper left. The off-center cursor enabled the user to place a finger in the lower right of the zoom box in order to move the cursor while maintaining a view of the context and desired target.

Voice output (at the time in English only, but intended for multiple languages) and acoustic cues (bell-like "bongs") complemented visual displays

FIGURE **8.3**

Keyboard with crosshairs.

FIGURE **8.4**

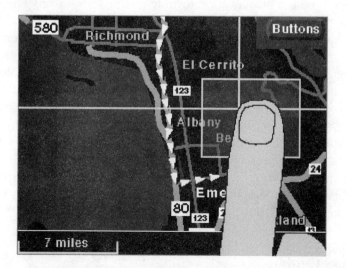

Off-center zoom box cursor.

of warning messages for impending maneuvers. These acoustic messages were optional; the user could turn them off globally in the preference settings.

Note that warning messages of impending maneuvers using graphics, speech output, and musical tones (i.e., two visual and two sound/acoustic means) were timed according to the complexity of the maneuver (single or multiple maneuvers in rapid succession) and the speed of the vehicle (as determined by vehicle sensors).

8.4 Example Screens

The following text and figures show, describe, and explain the user interface design, the development process, and the tools used to facilitate rapid prototyping.

Home Screen

The images show the opening main screen (which depicts the essential functions of the product) with and without expert buttons (the system defaults to novice status throughout), and key trip-planning screens. This screen would be the standard display upon turning on the device, from which users could navigate to other parts of the system.

Figure 8.5 (see also Color Plate) shows an opening screen that enables users to understand the basic functions and data that they can access. The design challenge was to reduce the number of possible choices at the top level of the system so that the user would not be intimidated, but could still obtain useful information quickly and easily. The first screen communicates the essential metaphors and the mental model of the product (e.g., maps, traffic information, etc.). Color codes established on the first screen are used throughout the product as reminders and guides.

Figure 8.6 shows buttons that provide access for expert users to more sophisticated functions of the product. Users access the expert functions by a separate "hard" button on the case of the product.

Route Guidance

Route guidance information is displayed by means of arrow pictogram, map, and text displays. These three techniques account for the three different cognitive abilities/preferences of the user community, as determined from

FIGURE **8.5**

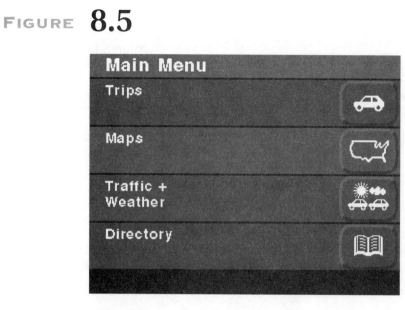

Opening screen.

FIGURE **8.6**

Opening screen with expert buttons on the right.

FIGURE **8.7**

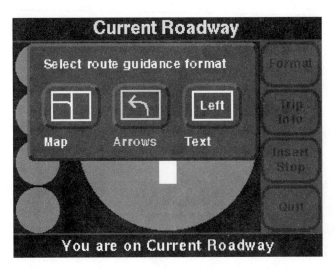

Selector control for type of information visualization.

(nongender-specific) focus group interviews. The selector control for which kind of information visualization is displayed is one of the few computer-like pop-up dialog boxes in the prototype (Figure 8.7).

In each of the three kinds of display, red, yellow, and green colors indicate warning, intermediate, and immediate-decision stages of route navigation actions during maneuvers (Figures 8.8–8.11). In addition to these visual cues, audio cues in the form of five distinct abstract tones and spoken instructions in English, or potentially other languages, provided redundant presentation of information.

User interfaces need to offer various alternatives in presenting content to accommodate groups of users who may have different cognitive styles. This project demonstrates one approach to accomplishing that objective.

Maps, All Zoom Levels

AM+A designed icons (representational, intuitive signs) and symbols (abstract, learned signs) for all maps at 10 levels of magnification, or "zoom" levels. Required route signs changed for different map scales. For example, the smallest levels of road capacity did not need to be shown at the most distant views. Examples of the maps appear in Figures 8.12–8.14.

FIGURE **8.8**

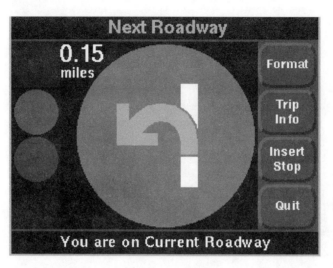

Arrow pictogram display for route guidance information.

FIGURE **8.9**

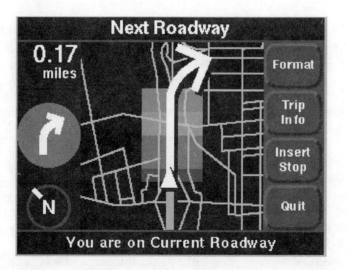

Map display for route guidance information.

FIGURE **8.10**

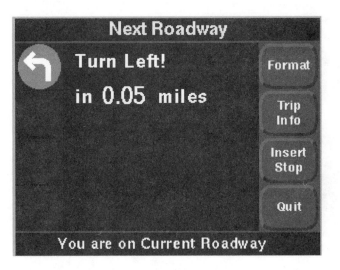

Text display for route guidance information.

FIGURE **8.11**

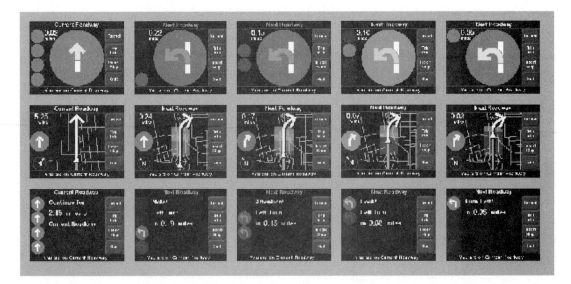

Typical sequences for route guidance information.

FIGURE **8.12**

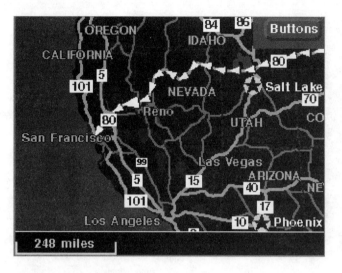

Example map, distant view.

FIGURE **8.13**

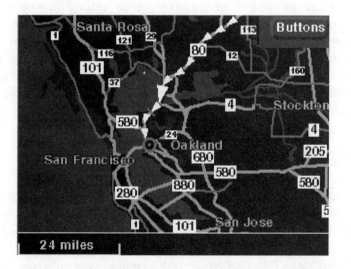

Example map, medium view.

FIGURE **8.14**

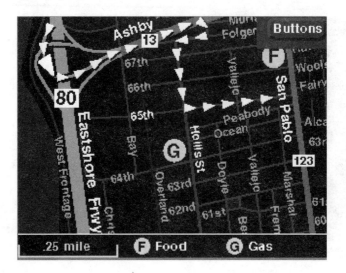

Example map, close view.

Traffic, Weather Legend

Figure 8.15 shows the legend for levels of traffic and weather conditions. These signs are used throughout the displays according to the data displayed (Figure 8.16). On small-scale, detailed local maps where the weather presumably does not vary greatly across the map, the weather symbols are not shown "in the map"; instead, one symbol for the weather condition is displayed prominently in the upper-left corner in order to obscure a minimal amount of other data (Figure 8.17).

Icons

For all of the application functions, especially for maps and route guidance, AM+A designed hundreds of signs, that is, symbols and icons. Many of these, informally called icons, appeared in primary control buttons that occupied approximately 5% of the screen area.

Some signs, often called symbols in maps, were quite small. For example, in detailed maps, sites of interest to travelers, such as gasoline stations, restaurants, and hotels, could not be shown as very small pictograms because of the low resolution of the display. Instead, we chose to present

FIGURE **8.15**

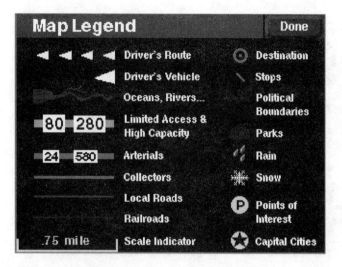

Legend for traffic levels and weather conditions.

FIGURE **8.16**

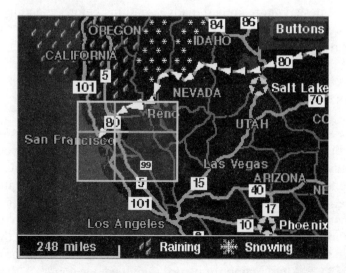

Map with weather symbols.

FIGURE   **8.17**

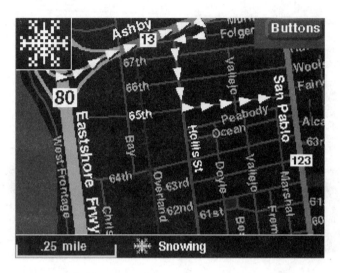

Local map with weather symbol in upper-left corner.

them as initial letters, for example, "G" and "F" for gas and food. This technique presents translation requirements for some languages and may cause problems when two different words begin with the same initial letter.

The design team studied many variations before selecting the final versions. A selection of alternatives for button icons that AM+A and Motorola considered during the design process appears in Figure 8.18.

Interaction

To assist application programmers in evaluating interaction, AM+A designed and built animations of interaction scenarios that depict layout, highlighting, and interaction state sequences precisely for a half-dozen important situations. This kind of information is best displayed as an animation sequence rather than as a textual description because software developers are able to see concrete details of how all the parts relate to each other. In the animation scenarios, AM+A used a human-hand "cursor" to indicate the use of the touch screen and hard buttons located on the casing of the product outside the LCD. The interaction simulations enabled developers to directly observe timing, highlighting, and movement of visual objects rather than forcing them to interpret textual descriptions of interaction techniques and to visualize timing and feedback characteristics. The use of such an animated presentation or, alternatively, of a short interactive prototype that uses basic

FIGURE **8.18**

Alternative icons.

scripting to link several screens and establish limited paths, is essential to user interface development and to the early evaluation of usability.

Figures 8.19 and 8.20 show the user choosing one of the 50 states. By inputting the first 1–3 characters of the desired option with a telephone-style keypad, the user can shorten long lists of options efficiently.

Figures 8.21–8.23 show how the user edits an address using a "soft" on-screen QWERTY keyboard. As mentioned earlier, note the use of green highlighting lines to indicate the location of the selected key even if a user's gloved finger is obscuring one or more key labels.

Figures 8.24–8.26 show how the user scrolls a list using "More Below" and "More Above" buttons. Typical graphical user interface scrollbars do not work well in a touch screen user interface; consequently, the design calls for this unique approach. The display changes by one screenful up or down, or by one line item up or down, depending upon the use of the screen buttons, or of a hard button located at the right of the display area.

Figures 8.27–8.29 show how the user selects a line item from a list. Note the highlighting technique for the item as well as the use of green in the buttons to help the user identify the next probable button choice in a given interaction context.

Figures 8.30–8.32 show how the user pans and scrolls the map using a "zoom box" pointer with cross-hair. Note that the cross-hairs are off-center so that even wearing thick gloves, the user can see accurately the selector on small details of the map. The animation can show precise details about how

FIGURE **8.19**

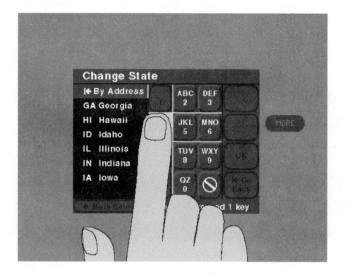

Selecting a state: The user shortens a data list significantly by inputting the first character (the "I" of the GHI button).

FIGURE **8.20**

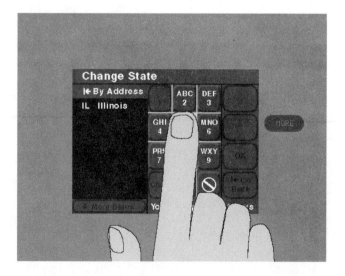

Selecting a state: By inputting a second character (the "L" of the JKL button), the user narrows down the choice to one from an initial set of 50.

FIGURE **8.21**

Editing an address: The user uses a hard button to move the cursor.

FIGURE **8.22**

Editing an address: The user enters the letter G.

FIGURE **8.23**

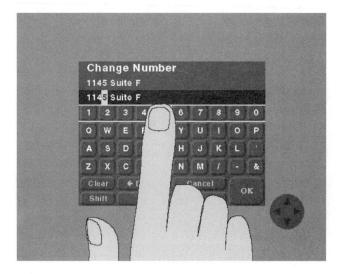

Editing an address: The user enters the number 5.

FIGURE **8.24**

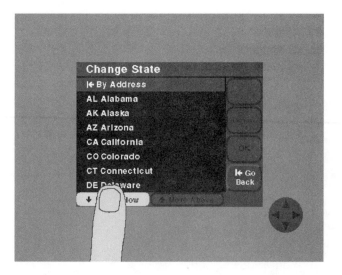

Scrolling a list screen by screen using the More Below button (action).

FIGURE **8.25**

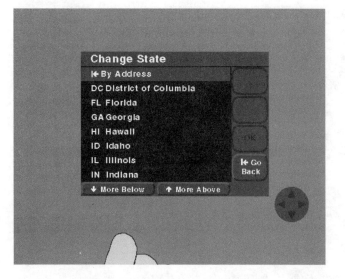

Scrolling a list screen by screen using the More Below button (result).

FIGURE **8.26**

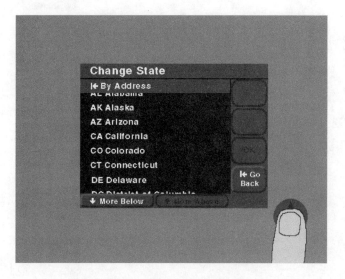

Scrolling a list line by line using the hard button.

8.27

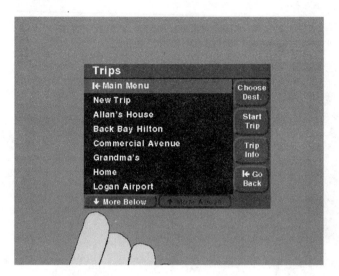

Selecting a line item from a list: Initial screen.

8.28

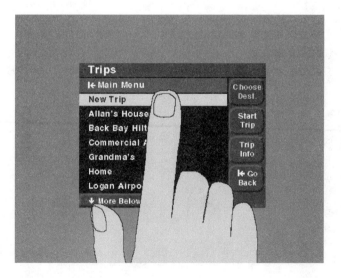

Selecting a line item from a list: The user chooses New Trip.

FIGURE **8.29**

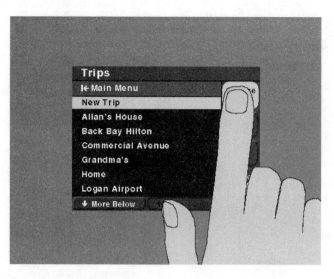

Selecting a line item from a list: The user pushes the Choose Destination button.

FIGURE **8.30**

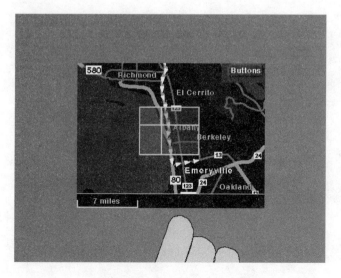

Using the zoom box pointer: Initial view.

FIGURE **8.31**

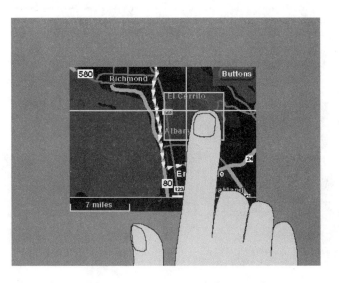

Using the zoom box pointer: Dragging the zoom box.

FIGURE **8.32**

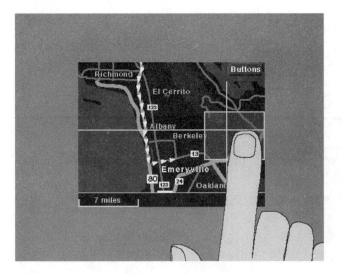

Using the zoom box pointer: At the far edge, the map itself pans to the left.

FIGURE **8.33**

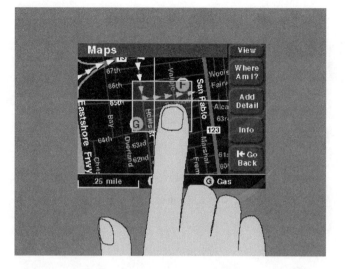

Seeing detailed information: The user selects an item in a map.

different parts of the display change location when the pointer hits the edge of the screen.

Figures 8.33–8.35 show how the user can select an item in a map to see detailed information about the item. Note the use of a pop-up dialog box, which is more typical of standard graphical user interfaces. This is a rare moment in the user interface because most user interface features typical of desktop computers, such as dialog boxes, were intentionally eliminated to ensure that users who are inexperienced with computers would not be intimidated by the product. The use of an overlaid dialog box seemed appropriate so that portions of the current route guidance techniques might appear.

Figures 8.36–8.38 show how the user can zoom map scales from the entire continent to within a few blocks of the car's location in a sequence of 10 changes of scale. Note how the scale changes are indicated at the bottom of the map.

GUI Design Tool by AM+A

To assist the client's project managers and programmers, AM+A designed and built an interactive tool for the client to explore the design space of

8.34

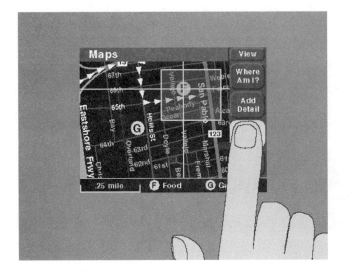

Seeing detailed information: The user pushes the Info button.

8.35

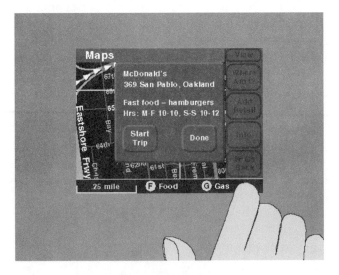

Seeing detailed information: The pop-up dialog box.

FIGURE **8.36**

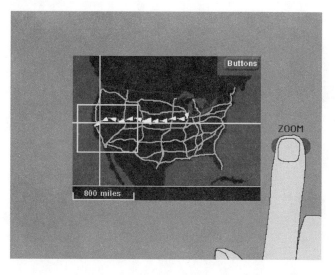

Zooming: Initial view of a large geographical area.

FIGURE **8.37**

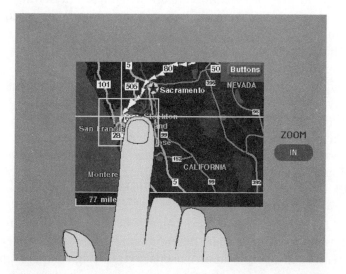

Zooming: Intermediate view of a multistate geographical area.

FIGURE **8.38**

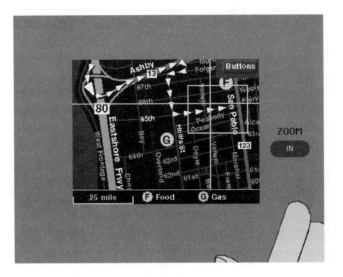

Zooming: Close-up view of a metropolitan area.

appearance, for example, options for showing button outlines, text/icon labels, and color palettes. By considering these options, client representatives could experiment individually with different settings to help them reach conclusions more quickly than large group meetings looking at static or dynamic displays.

The design trade-offs involved in the development of a user interface are often numerous and extremely complex. To assist members of both our design team and the client's team in evaluating symbolism, color, layout, and typography, AM+A developed an interactive "design space exploration tool" (Figures 8.39–8.56).

Viewers are able to select from a wide variety of typical screen content and variations of that content and then to view variations and to change attributes of the display. Once the design team builds a simple template for this kind of design tool, they can easily adapt it to new situations and new design problems.

This kind of interactive tool can enable designers, client representatives, and users to examine many different combinations of visual treatment and content. Such an exploration can enable the design team to rapidly converge on an optimum solution for a design problem with many complex variables.

Figures 8.39–8.56 show different visual treatments for typical display items during interim design stages, for example, buttons with icons versus

FIGURE **8.39**

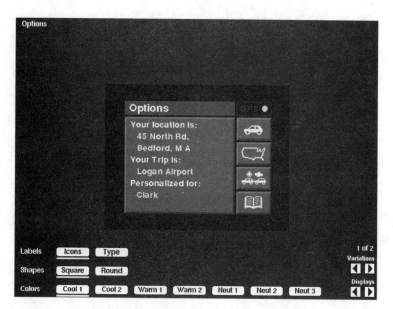

Options screen with icon buttons.

FIGURE **8.40**

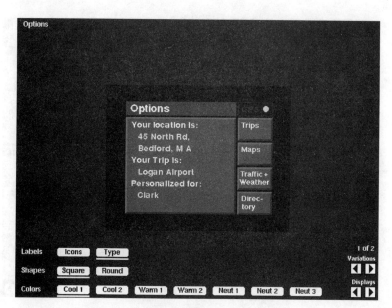

Options screen with text buttons.

FIGURE **8.41**

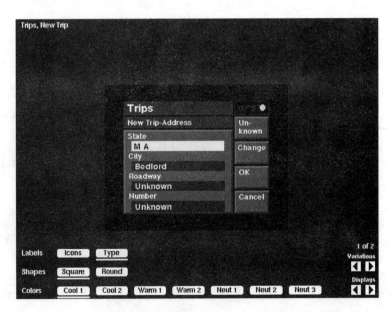

New Trip screen with icon buttons.

FIGURE **8.42**

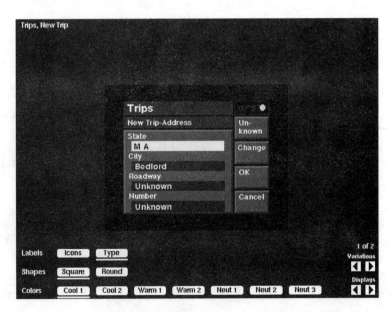

New trip screen with text buttons.

FIGURE **8.43**

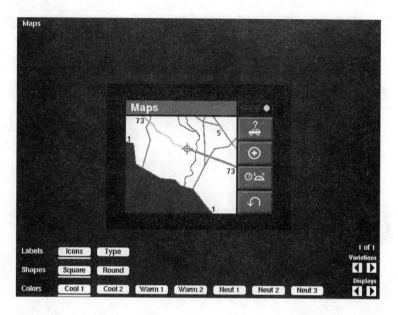

Maps screen with icon buttons.

FIGURE **8.44**

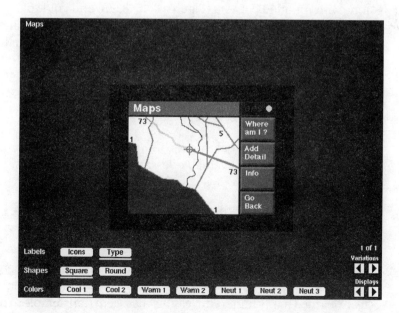

Maps screen with text buttons.

FIGURE **8.45**

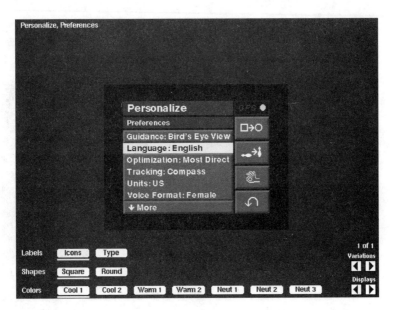

Preferences screen with rectangular buttons.

buttons with text labels (Figures 8.39–8.44); rectangular buttons versus buttons with rounded corners (Figures 8.45–8.50); and color palettes with cool, warm, or neutral colors (Figures 8.51–8.56; see also Color Plates). In the figures, typical screens appear in two or three variations of visual treatment.

8.5   Results of the Project

In addition to its unusual origins, the project came to an unusual conclusion. Besides providing valuable lessons for its participants, it produced a useful project archive.

Lessons Learned

The project did not reach commercial production during the time that my firm was involved in user interface design. Nevertheless, the development team learned many important lessons that seem transferable to other contexts

FIGURE **8.46**

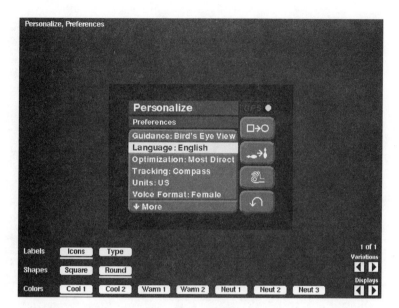

Preferences screen with rounded buttons.

FIGURE **8.47**

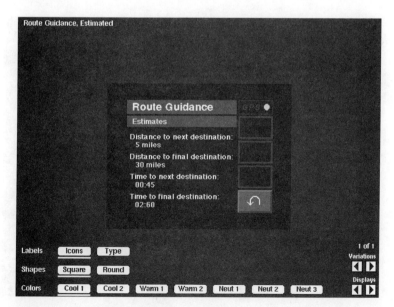

Estimates screen with rectangular buttons.

8.48

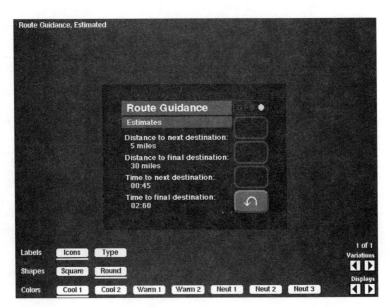

Estimates screen with rounded buttons.

8.49

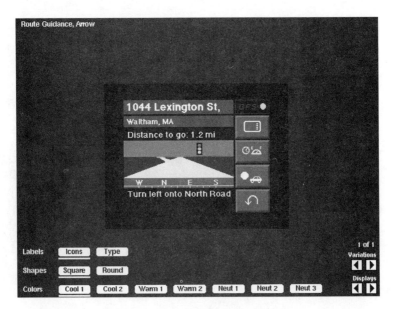

Route Guidance screen with rectangular buttons.

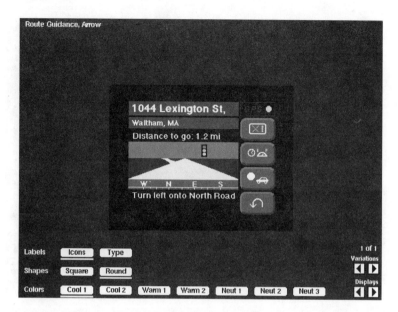

FIGURE **8.50**

Route Guidance screen with rounded buttons.

FIGURE **8.51**

Options screen with cool colors.

FIGURE **8.52**

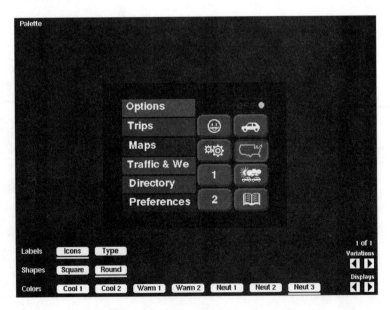

Options screen with warm colors.

FIGURE **8.53**

Options screen with neutral colors.

FIGURE **8.54**

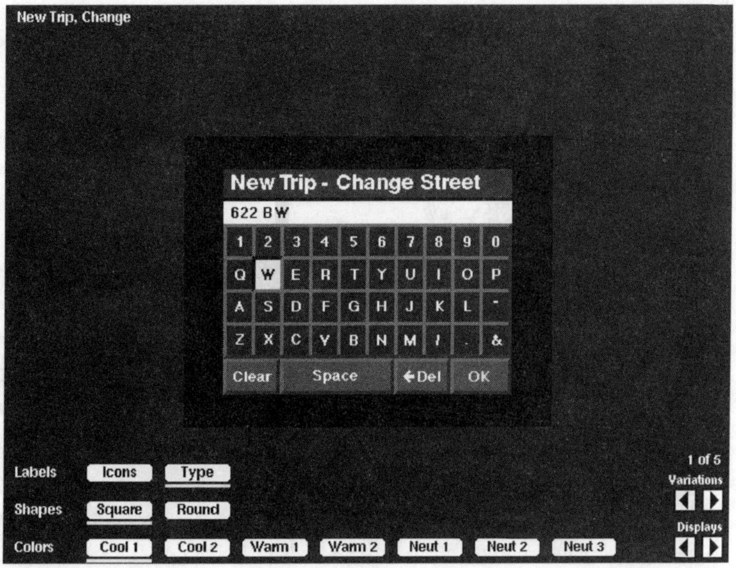

New Trip–Change Street screen with cool colors.

FIGURE **8.55**

New Trip–Change Street screen with warm colors.

FIGURE **8.56**

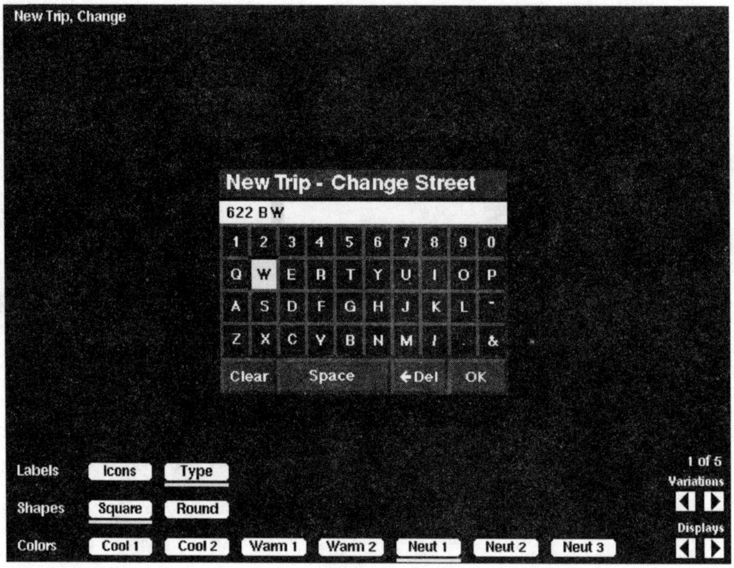

New Trip–Change Street screen with neutral colors.

of user interface and information visualization design, especially for consumer products. Most significant among them were the following:

- The value of multidisciplinary teams (i.e., information-oriented visual designers, industrial designers, marketers, and subject matter experts) in user interface development as well as the need for good communication among team members from different professional disciplines

- In particular, interactive design-space exploration tools were useful to enable clients to understand what variations were possible and to appreciate the professional skill of designers in synthesizing solutions.

- The necessity of setting design goals for both ease of comprehension as well as speed of access. It has been my experience over the last 20 years that technophiles (from either engineering or marketing departments) often seem driven to enable users to navigate the user interface faster and faster whether or not their comprehension keeps pace. Designers must strive continuously to balance these orthogonal forces in the design space.

- The importance of accounting for different cognitive preferences for absorbing information. When designers are targeting "wide-band audiences" with multiple demographic characteristics of age, gender, education level, cultural background, and so on, even if the users are united in their immediate tasks, it seems very important to account for diversity in the fundamental components of the user interface.

- The impact of the cost of user testing on the business model. Motorola was exemplary in its devotion to user testing. Nevertheless, in the end, the unanticipated cost of these efforts may have defeated the product development; Motorola hesitated to bring the product to completion. Again, over the last 20 years, I have noted the hesitation on the part of some clients to undertake appropriate focus group investigation and usability testing during development. The challenge in the design community is to gather valid, precise, accurate, clear statistics of success cases and to make these available to the industry. In almost every one of the design arts, this lack of data hinders designers in arguing the case for good design and what that professional practice requires.

The project earned a design innovation award from *ID Magazine*'s annual competition in 1993. Many of the materials developed for the project have value to the user interface design community beyond historical interest: as examples of professional practice, as possible solutions for visualization of information in small displays with limited screen characteristics, and as teaching materials. Another value arises from special circumstances subsequent to AM+A's involvement, as described in the next section.

Project Document Archive

Although project materials such as the voluminous documents and files developed for this project over several years normally are protected by intellectual property law and have limited reuse, the Motorola project materials can be reused; because of special circumstances, they are now in the public domain.

Subsequent to AM+A's completion of its user interface design project in 1992, Motorola continued to test and revise these prototype designs over a period of several years. As occurs in some development projects because of the absence of funds or because of lack of planning, the original user interface design team was not consulted during implementation. Motorola made many changes in the design, and published images of the later prototypes differed from the earlier prototypes significantly. Unfortunately, I do not have access to explanatory or evaluation documents. Approximately four years after the original project was completed, I learned that Motorola had decided not to bring the prototype into production. A primary reason seems to have been the remaining cost of usability testing, according to verbal statements by a Motorola representative.

One outcome of Motorola's stopping development is that Motorola was required, because initial sponsorship included federal government agencies, to turn over all materials developed by AM+A, as well as many materials developed by Motorola and other third parties, to the government. Consequently, these materials are now in the public domain and are stored in several locations. I do not know the public availability specifically of Motorola usability documents, budgets, and results. To obtain information about what materials are available and where these archives are located, interested parties may contact the following:

Dr. Paul Green, Research Scientist
University of Michigan Transportation Research Institute (UMTRI)
Human Factors Division
2901 Baxter Road
Ann Arbor, MI 48109-2150
Tel: 313-763-3795, Fax: 313-764-1221
Email: Paul Green <pagreen@umich.edu>
Web: *www.umich.edu/~driving*

Recent Systems Compared

A brief *Wall Street Journal* notice of 1993 mentions Pioneer Electronic Corporation's introduction of a GPS/CD-ROM-based car navigation system (Valeriano 1993). By the mid- to late 1990s, several commercial vehicle navigation systems appeared in European, Japanese, and American automobiles. Few of these systems have achieved the level of graphic quality of the Motorola prototype. A comparison of some of these systems appears in Paul (1996). In addition, Web sites now offer traffic and weather information to travelers. Some examples are cited briefly below.

Figures 8.57 and 8.58 show examples of a recent version of the Philips Carin system. While the system as a whole is sophisticated, note the limited graphic quality of the map, text, and other symbolic displays.

The Acura Navigator (see Figure 8.59) is another in-dash system with graphic display quality similar to Philips. Some of the typography of titles is of fair quality, while map symbolism and the user interface controls seem less sophisticated.

The Cadillac OnStar system is a package of services that uses a cellular communication system linked to GPS to provide one-button, one-touch access for travel information, security, and emergency roadside repair service calls. A Cadillac sales representative explained company strategy by noting that in-car systems seemed currently too expensive for their perceived worth,

FIGURE **8.57**

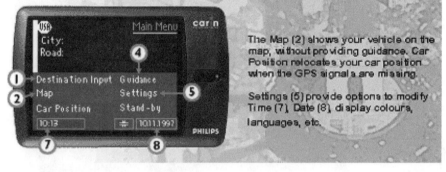

Switching the Carin unit on and pressing Enter on the remote control will bring you to the Main Menu.
Destination Input (1) and Guidance (4) are the basic functions to enter an address and activate navigation.

The Map (2) shows your vehicle on the map, without providing guidance. Car Position relocates your car position when the GPS signals are missing.

Settings (5) provide options to modify Time (7) Date (8) display colours, languages, etc.

Example of the Philips Carin system.

FIGURE **8.58**

Another example of the Philips Carin system.

and drivers did not want to be distracted by visual displays. Instead, verbal driving advice is announced from the vehicle's audio system receiving spoken cues from a human guide at the OnStar call center who knows the vehicle's location to within 500 feet. While the simplicity of the system has merit, note that the Motorola system provided optional speech and sound cue output. The Motorola system was limited to the user-changeable onboard informa- tion CDs, which could cover multistate areas. The OnStar cellular system is limited by cellular communication quality, the lack of visual displays that

FIGURE **8.59**

The Acura Navigator.

may require complex verbal explanation, and the unavailability of displays for drivers with visual information-processing cognitive preferences. I am unaware of OnStar research into drivers' cognitive preferences.

Newspaper advertisements now routinely offer low-cost add-on navigation systems for approximately $500 to $600. However, the visual quality of these systems is far less than the Motorola prototype.

In general, many commercial systems, while solving some functional aspects of information display in a superior manner, seem to have made several sacrifices to achieve their pricing goals and, presumably thereby, commercial success. Revised versions will undoubtedly improve their user interfaces and information visualization design.

The Internet now offers travelers information about traffic and weather. Some Web examples are SmartTrek (*www.SmartTrek.org*), shown in Figure 8.60; Michigan Department of Transportation's Intelligent Transportation Systems (*campus.merit.net/mdot/main.html*), shown in Figure 8.61; and Michigan Department of Transportation's Michigan Travel and Weather information (*campus.merit.net/mdot/mi.html*) shown in Figure 8.62. Another resource of similar information is the TravInfo project in the San Francisco Bay Area, organized by the Metropolitan Transportation Commission in Oakland, CA (see *www.travinfo.org*), which has been building resources for intelligent vehicle-highway communication for approximately four years. Their site links to highway traffic reports, including route maps.

FIGURE **8.60**

SmartTrek.

Although these Internet-based information sites clearly offer detailed, up-to-the-minute information, and they are potentially displayable on monitors mounted in the vehicle or on portable personal communicators, they have the following limitations as driver-oriented displays:

- The displays are sometimes too verbose.

- The graphic images are often not simplified enough for rapid comprehension.

- The organization of contents is not oriented to the driver, but rather a desk-bound information browser at work or at home, or at best a vehicle passenger.

- The colors, fonts, and other appearance characteristics are not necessarily designed for viewing in the typical ambient light or viewing-distance conditions of vehicles, resulting in legibility and readability limitations.

- The interaction paradigms are oriented to detailed target selection more typical of Internet hyperlinks rather than the simplified layout of vehicle dashboard controls.

8.61

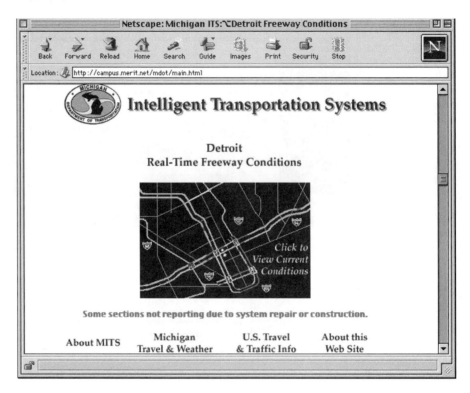

Michigan Department of Transportation's Intelligent Transportation Systems.

Internet-based displays seem still in need of specific design for the specific target market and conditions of the driver en route.

8.6 Conclusions

The project described in this case study is several years and thus several "generations" old, given the rapid pace of technology changes. Nevertheless, the approach to the user interface development process, the specific user interface design results, and the lessons learned have value for designers of current and next-generation traveler information systems. These systems in vehicles, in conjunction with the deployment of advanced traffic management systems (ATMS) (see, for example, Ericson and Fette 1996) make it imperative that good user interface design be an integral part of system development.

FIGURE **8.62**

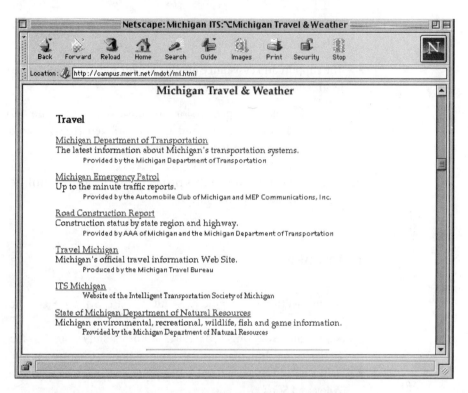

Michigan Department of Transportation's Michigan Travel and Weather.

The project's focus on high-quality information design, metaphor design, allowance for cognitive-preference differences, and appearance characteristics seem valid goals for today's designers of portable products, appliances, and world-wide access to Web content. I hope you will agree. Comments are welcome.

8.7 Acknowledgments and Advisory

I would like to acknowledge the following people:

- The editor of this book, Eric Bergman, Sun Microsystems, for his editorial advice

- Past staff members and associates of AM+A who worked on the project, in particular, N. Greg Galle, Grant Letz, Sandra Ragan, Todd Blank, and Robert Haydock

- Current staff members of AM+A who assisted in the preparation of this chapter, in particular, Jo Ann Pacho and Benjamin Becker

- The assistance of Mike Wiklund, Project Manager, American Institutes of Research, who led his team

- The support and assistance of Allan Kirson and Clark Smith, the two primary project managers at Motorola

- Hayden Books, for permission to reuse and revise the text that originally appeared in Cathy Clarke and Lee Swearingen (1994), "Motorola Smart Car," Chapter 2.3, in *Macromedia Director Design Guide*

Any errors or omissions in this project description are unintentional and are the author's sole responsibility.

8.8 References

American Institute of Graphic Arts (AIGA) 1981. *Symbol Signs*. New York: Hastings House.

Clarke, C., and Swearingen, L. 1994. Motorola smart car. In *Macromedia Director Design Guide*, Indianapolis, IN: Hayden Books, Chapter 2.3.

DelGaldo, E., and Nielsen, J. (ed.). 1996. *International User Interfaces*. New York: John Wiley and Sons.

Dreyfuss, H. 1972. *Symbol Sourcebook*. New York: McGraw-Hill.

Eco, U. 1976. *A Theory of Semiotics*. Bloomington, IN: Indiana University Press.

Ericson, N. and Fette, B. 1996. Setting the pace. *ITS World* 1(2):24–31.

Fernandes, T. 1995. *Global Interface Design: A Guide to Designing International User Interfaces*. Boston: AP Professional.

Gardner, H. (1985). *Frames of Mind: The Theory of Multiple Intelligences*. New York: Basic Books.

Green, P., and Burgess, W. T. 1980. Debugging a symbol set for identifying displays: production and screening studies. Tech. report UM-HSRI-80-64, Highway Safety Research Institute, The University of Michigan, September. U.S. Department of Commerce, National Technical Information Service, No. PB81-113573, Springfield, VA.

Marcus, A. 1992. *Graphic Design for Electronic Documents and User Interfaces*. Reading, MA: Addison-Wesley.

Marcus, A. 1993. Human communication issues in advanced UIs. *Communications of the ACM* 36(4):101–109.

Marcus, A. 1995. Principles of effective visual communication for graphical user interface design. In R.M. Baecker, J. Grudin, W. Buxton, and S. Greenberg (Ed.),

Readings in Human-Computer Interaction, (second edition), San Francisco: Morgan Kaufmann, 425–441.

Marcus, A. 1997. Graphical user interfaces. In M. Helander, T. K. Landauer, and P. Prabhu, (Eds.), *Handbook of Human-Computer Interaction,* The Hague, Netherlands: Elsevier Science, 423–440.

Marcus, A. 1998a. Baby faces: user-interface design for small displays. *Conference Summary, CHI'98,* panel description, 96–97.

Marcus, A. 1998b. Metaphor design in user interfaces. *Journal of Computer Documentation* 22(2):43–57.

Neale, D. C., and Carroll, J. M. 1997. The role of metaphors in user interface design. In M. Helander, T. K. Landauer, and P. Prabhu, (Eds.), *Handbook of Human-Computer Interaction* (second, revised edition), The Hague, Netherlands: Elsevier Science, 441–462.

Olgyay, N. 1995. *Safety Symbols Art.* New York: Van Nostrand Reinhold.

Ota, Y. 1987. *Pictogram Design.* Tokyo: Kashiwashobo.

Paul, R. 1996. Lost? Or found? Finding our way through the high-tech terrain of onboard navigation systems. *Motor Trend* (Dec.).

Pierce, T. 1996. *The International Pictograms Standard.* Cincinnati, OH: ST Publications. For information: Design Pacifica, 725 NW Flanders Street, Portland OR 97209; email: *tpierce@designpacifica.com.*

Tucker, F. 1994. Why run the race for better transportation. *Washington Times* (23 May) p. 17.

Valeriano, L. L. 1993. A movable feast. *Wall Street Journal* (16 Dec.), Technology Updates, column 5, p. A1.

CHAPTER Nine

Interactive Toy Characters as Interfaces for Children

ERIK STROMMEN

Interactive Toy Group
Microsoft Corporation

9.1 Introduction

This chapter describes the theory and practice behind the development of interactive toy interfaces for children. These toys, which resemble familiar characters from children's media, use social mimicry as an interface strategy. Their movement and speech are scripted based on an implicit understanding of the social rules for each interaction—social rules children themselves already obey. These character-based interfaces are designed to build on children's social expectations not just to improve the usability of technology for young users, but also to promote learning and development by applying proven social learning methods to technology interaction. The chapter is organized into three sections. The first section provides an overview of the theory and research behind the development of these physical character interfaces. The second section describes how the theory was applied during the product development process for different character-based interfaces for three specific age groups, and how research with users shaped the interfaces so that they matched the abilities and expectations of the target age groups. Finally, current knowledge and future directions for technology interactions using character-based interfaces is discussed.

Why Make Technology Interactions More Like Human Interactions?

Traditionally, computers and technology have been viewed as powerful, if impersonal, additions to modern life. The assumption has been that technology is simply a tool, similar to a hammer or washing machine, that helps users to either accomplish existing tasks (such as producing spreadsheets or documents) more quickly and easily, or helps them to do new things (such as prototype and test virtual examples of new product designs) that would have been impossible using traditional techniques, such as hand drafting. As interactivity has expanded both in scope and in complexity, integrating computational intelligence with media such as voices and images, a promising new strategy for interface design has emerged in recent years that complements the tool model. This new strategy is to treat human-computer interaction not as if it were a functional interaction between a worker and a tool, but rather as if it were a social interaction between two people instead (Frohlich 1997; Sidner 1997; Terveen 1995; Thorisson 1994). Treating the computer as a partner rather than a tool is thought to be beneficial to users because such collaboration, built on models of collaboration between humans, distributes the burden of remembering, ordering, and executing all the elements of a given task between the computer and the user, rather than requiring the user to always be in control of all aspects of the effort (Maes 1997).

Aside from the advantages of such a collaboration in terms of relieving task-demand burdens from the user, treating the computer as a social partner has another powerful argument in its favor: Users already respond to computers as if they are social agents, endowing them with such properties as personality, politeness, gender, and more (Fogg and Nass 1997; Morkes, Kernal, and Nass 1998; Nass, Steuer, and Tauber 1994). So pervasive is this tendency to endow computers with human attributes that it has given rise to its own interface model, Computers As Social Actors (CASA). The CASA model presumes that such humanlike attributions to technology can actually be deliberately induced in users through specific interface features: "The CASA paradigm maintains that individuals can be induced to behave *as if* computers warranted human considerations, even though users *know* that the machines do not actually warrant this treatment . . . " (Fogg and Nass 1997, p. 552; italics in original). Exploiting the social expectations of users for both collaborative interactions and for other technology interfaces holds great promise as a consumer interface. Social interfaces can make technology interactions simpler and more intuitive because they are built on implicit social understandings that users already have, and hence require no extra learning or accommodation. In conversation, for example, dialog takes the form of simple turn taking between speakers. Structuring audio interactions between users and computers to capitalize on this already-established expectation about interpersonal speech gives the interface a familiar feel to the user and can make the interaction go more smoothly as a result (Sidner 1997; Thorisson 1994).

Using the conventions of social interaction as a model for technology interaction has even more value when the target users are very young. Consider the cognitive and motor limitations young children bring to the interface. Presenting information is a significant challenge. The target user has a short attention span, cannot read, and has a shaky understanding of letters, numbers, shapes, and even colors. In terms of input, young children have immature fine motor skills, cannot write, have limited vocabularies and poorly articulated speech. The typical interface design, conceived as a tool, is a manual point device that presents these users with a variety of serious obstacles. But what young children lack in physical and cognitive competence they make up for in social expertise. By the end of the first year, infants show differential, social responses to humans as compared to other animate stimuli such as mechanical dolls or other objects. They begin engaging in social strategies such as joint attention (following the gaze of another person to see what they are reacting to, for example) and imitation of novel actions with objects previously witnessed only once (Muir and Nadel 1998). By the end of the second year, very young children, even those without language, understand the basic rules or "scripts" for different kinds of social interaction—and change their own behavior accordingly (Furman and Walden 1990; Garner, Jones, and Palmer 1994). Mimicking social behavior in the interface builds on children's social competence to support technology interactions for young users not served by existing point-and-click interfaces.

It is possible to exploit social competence and social expectations in the interface for more ambitious goals than ease of use. Rules of human social interaction can be used not just to define the form of technology interactions, but the content of such interactions as well. Human interaction is charged with emotion, and there is significant data on the role of emotions in behavior. Interaction with the interface character will need emotions as well. One consistent finding in the psychological literature is that positive emotional interactions such as praise, affection, and humor are associated with better learning and a variety of other positive developmental outcomes (Bornstein 1989; Coleman 1992; Jennings and Connors 1992; McGhee 1988). The character's ability to convey emotions provides a unique opportunity to bring these feelings to children as part of toy play. Another consistent finding is that specific kinds of social interactions can promote learning, particularly when the interactions involve other media such as computers or television (Haefner and Wartella 1987; Nastasi and Clements 1992; Collins, Sobol, and Westby 1981; Tudge, Winterhoff, and Hogan 1996). Despite this evidence that social interactions augment learning with electronic media, the fact is that watching television is typically a solitary experience for children, except in formal educational settings like schools (Huston et al. 1992). The social interactions are considered separate from the computer or television content, in a different realm. Social interfaces, with their explicit reliance on human social interaction as a basis for design, present a unique opportunity to integrate beneficial emotional and social-cognitive interactions into learning and interacting with different media. Social interfaces can broaden the range of beneficial experiences children are exposed to in learning situations involving television and computer media by adding social interaction to the media interactions themselves. In this way, the social interface can enrich the media experience in ways not possible with traditional, tool-based interface designs.

Why Use Physical Characters as Interfaces?

It is certainly possible to create social interface characters on the computer screen that behave according to social conventions and interact with users in various social ways. One example of such a technology is the Microsoft

Office Assistant, which appears as a paper clip or other animated form, as part of the graphics of the Office software when the user clicks the Help icon. This character asks questions (in text printed on the screen) and can be queried in the same manner. In addition, Office Assistant also can demonstrate how to execute a given operation, literally modeling the steps to be taken as the user watches. While such graphical characters have obvious benefits, the computer screen itself diminishes the realism and lifelike nature of the interaction. The screen imposes an abstract, arbitrary "wall" between the user and the interaction that limits the appeal of such interfaces—particularly for young children, whose understanding of the world is gained through the senses as much as through mental effort. For young children, a physical character offers several distinct advantages.

What do physical interface characters add to social interfaces? The most obvious factor is size and presence. Unlike the small characters on the PC screen, physical interface characters have a concrete presence. The characters described in this chapter are all 13 to 16 inches tall, or between one-half and one-third the height of the children using them. Their size gives them a salience screen characters lack. In addition, their physical presence contributes to the social interactions they are intended to mimic. When physical interface characters speak to children, their voices come from their body, not a speaker somewhere on the computer's CPU. And when they gesture, their size makes the gesture an attention-drawing event that contributes to the interface. Another advantage is having a tactile presence as well as a seen and heard one. Screen-based characters are physically removed from the user, behind a hard surface. The character interfaces described in this chapter, in contrast, are all soft plush dolls that give pleasant tactile feedback when touched. The softness is motivating to users and encourages them to touch the characters and keep them physically close during interactions. Finally, the character's physical presence with the child means that the character can exploit social strategies, such as shared attention to the computer or television, that are used in human social situations every day. Just as human social actors share a frame of reference when talking about a common object of interest (Clark and Schaefer 1987; Grosz and Sidner 1986), the interface character and the child can share an implicit frame of reference when interacting around other media.

Most importantly, however, the physical presence of the interface character in the form of a plush doll invokes powerful pretend play cues common to early childhood. Young children "animate" dolls and other objects as part of their play behavior. They treat these objects as if they are sentient and responding to them in ways that mimic familiar social interactions (comforting a "crying" doll is a classic example) (Bretherton and Beeghly 1989). Such pretend or "as if" engagement is a sophisticated form of dual representation, in which two levels of understanding operate at the same time. Children interact with the doll as if it is a baby, but still treat it as a toy as well, adjusting its arms, standing it up, and so on (Forys and McCune-Nicolich 1984; Herron and Sutton-Smith 1971). Children are also familiar with puppets and the idea of role-playing with props. By moving and talking in appropriate ways, physical interface characters invite children to participate in pretend role-playing because the characters themselves are obviously not the "real thing"—they are toys. Children respond to these characters as friendly toys that they "play along" with. When the toy is turned off, they use it as a prop for pretend play as they do any other dolls.

The nature of pretend engagement, with its dual levels of representation, is ideally suited to character interface interaction because it allows children to gracefully accommodate the less-than-realistic aspects of the interface in a playful and appropriate manner. In pretend play, children treat playthings as if they are social agents *and* toys. For physical interface characters, this means that children can accommodate the interactive character's nature as a physical interface device while simultaneously engaging it as if it were a social actor. This means they are "forgiving" of the lapses in the illusion of life that the character presents. A good example of this pretend accommodation is the way children actually interact with toy character interfaces. In most social interactions, the medium of interaction is speech. Individuals speak, listen, and respond to the utterances of one another in a shared verbal interaction. Current technology does not permit natural speech communication of this type as an input medium with technology, so a less natural, nonverbal input method must be used. Technical issues aside, there is ample reason to think that a nonverbal interface will always be superior to a verbal one for very young children. While children of this age possess the ability to listen to and understand fairly complex speech from others, they do not produce such language on their own until they are much older (Bloom and Lahey 1978). In addition, shyness or social inhibition can cause even verbally competent children to refuse to speak in social situations. A nonverbal input medium, paired with spoken and/or visual output to the child, makes the interface accessible to a wide range of users who would be excluded by any interface that depended on spoken language input.

What form should such a nonverbal medium take, particularly when the interface is a physical character? The simplest solution is to rely on the physical form of the characters themselves. A basic knowledge of the names and locations of the parts of the body is mastered by age two. This means that even very young children can competently respond to such simple interface prompts as "Squeeze my hand," "Squeeze my foot," or even just "Hand, hand" or "Foot, foot" and engage the interface (McCarthy 1972). By building input devices, such as touch sensors, into easily located parts of the character's body and using those locations as input media, the character's body itself becomes the input device. The dual levels of representation that contribute to pretend play, the pretend fantasy and the physical prop, make such an interface possible. Just as children interact with dolls as if they are babies while manipulating them as dolls, they are able to interact with character interfaces as if they are social actors, but also accommodate the requirements of the toy's interface as well.

Why Use Familiar Media Characters as Interface Agents?

One of the most interesting phenomena involving television and other electronic media is the degree to which it fosters a sort of pseudointimacy and feeling of familiarity in viewers regarding characters they see on the television screen (Reeves and Nass 1996). This "para-social" intimacy has two important effects on the character interfaces. First, the presumed intimacy of para-social relationships creates a friendly and positive disposition to the character in users. Second, the user's knowledge of the character's personality leads them to feel as if they know the personality of the character, and what they can expect from the character in an interaction. This familiarity and the expectations it creates have distinct value for interface character design because it parallels the social expectations that exist between people as well. Personality plays a crucial role in human social interaction because it provides a basis for predicting an individual's behavior. The consistency of an individual's preferences, attitudes, and actions over time creates a consistent set of expectations that makes the behavior of familiar individuals predictable. Even very young children have been shown to make predictions based on knowledge of personality and personal attributes (Dozier 1991; Frye and Moore 1991). Consistency of personality creates consistency in the social interface by making the interface character's behavior predictable as well. Children's para-social familiarity with their favorite media characters creates expectations about the interface character's behavior that are similar to expectations about another person's behavior. Accommodating these expectations is yet another way to capitalize on social processes with character-based interfaces.

A striking way to illustrate the influence of familiarity on character interfaces is to start with a look at the technology itself. Figure 9.1 (see also Color Plate) displays the "chassis" for Microsoft's ActiMates Barney, a physical character interface designed using the social interface model. The durable plastic housing contains a speaker, a circuit board, and a ROM chip that allows the character to speak and interact using an audio interface of prerecorded, digitized speech. Motors in the "shoulders" and "neck" allow the

FIGURE **9.1**

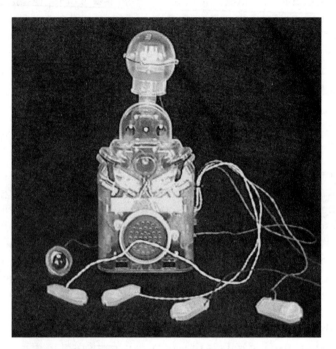

Technology without personality. The "chassis" for the Barney interactive character, with hand, foot, and eye sensors attached.

character to make simple movements and gestures. Sensors (visible on cables in the foreground of the picture) let children make inputs to the character, who responds with speech and motion. Note that the appearance of the chassis offers nothing that would prompt social responses in children or anyone else. Cover the chassis with a plush "skin" however, as shown in Figure 9.2 (see also Color Plate), and the interface becomes instantly recognizable as Barney the dinosaur, a familiar character. The physical similarity of the interface character to the television character shapes children's expectations as to what the interface character will say and do, before the character has actually been played with.

Why So Much Research?

The previous sections have described a theoretical and practical rationale for using physical interface characters as social interfaces for children. While

FIGURE **9.2**

Interactive Barney character, "in the skin." Motors in the shoulders and neck let the character move and gesture while speaking. Children interact with Barney by squeezing sensors in the hands and feet and by covering a light sensor in his eye.

applying social psychological principles to "pretend playmate" character interfaces might appear to be a straightforward process, it is actually confounded by a variety of factors that can only be assessed by seeing children in action. The most significant of these is the impact of the children's developmental status, their social, cognitive, and motor skills, on the interaction. Developmental psychological research studies published in the scientific literature provide helpful insight into children's abilities at different ages, but there is no reliable way to predict children's actual responses to specific interface features. It is one thing to say that children's inputs should be made through hand and foot squeezes, for example, but quite another to decide how those inputs should be organized. Should different activities be associated with individual limbs, right hand doing one thing and the left another? Should repeated squeezes on the same sensor trigger different activities, such that two hand squeezes start one game, three squeezes another, and so on? Another key element that cannot be predicted in advance is children's reactions to and interpretations of the different elements of the interactions that the characters deliver. Consider character movement. Do children expect specific gestures to go with certain speech (moving your head as you count out loud, for example)? What sorts of movements during songs are appropriate? Are there times when movement is inappropriate because it distracts children? Only interaction with children themselves can answer these questions.

The next section presents a summary of the research and development process for three different types of toy character interfaces produced over the past three years by Microsoft's ActiMates group. Each of these toys is based on familiar media characters from popular children's programs broadcast on the Public Broadcasting System (PBS) in the United States, and each is intended for a different age group, although some overlap of ages is inevitable. The ActiMates Teletubbies, from the *Teletubbies* television program, are four different characters sharing a common interface and content design and were designed for children one to four years of age. ActiMates Barney, from the *Barney and Friends* program, is intended for children ages two through five. And ActiMates Arthur and D. W., brother and sister characters who share the same interface and content design, are intended for users ages four through seven years of age. Each product was developed over a 12- to 14-month period, and 12 or more separate research studies, approximately one a month, were conducted on each product type during that period. (Various elements of the Barney and the Arthur/D. W. character interfaces have been described in previous articles; see Strommen 1998, 1999.) The design issues that arose from applying the theoretical framework outlined above, and how the research uncovered additional issues as well as helped resolve them, are described in case studies for each product type. The final section of this chapter considers future applications of toy character interfaces, given advances in technology and in our understanding of social psychological processes.

9.2 Examples of Physical Character Interfaces

Each of the case studies that follows describes the design and development process for a set of physical interface characters intended for users of a specific age. The case studies are presented in age order, starting with interface characters intended for infants and toddlers and ending with interfaces intended for children as old as seven or eight years of age.

Case Study 1: Here Come the Teletubbies

The Teletubbies are four fantasy characters whose television adventures appeal to children ranging in age from less than a year old up to ages three or four. The Teletubbies are playful and childlike technological toddlers, and their behavior is deliberately meant to invoke feelings of identification from children. As characters, the Teletubbies have two specific idiosyncrasies that must be accommodated in any interface mimicking their behavior. First, their use of language is very limited. Their speech is restricted to one- or two-word utterances that sound very much like "baby talk," the immature speech of one- and two-year-old children themselves. What the program lacks in dialog, however, it makes up for with a rich nonverbal aural environment. The Teletubbies program is filled with music and dramatic, larger-than-life sound effects of different kinds. The use of music and vivid sounds in the character's interface along with speech raised troubling questions: Would it confuse children?

The second essential feature of the Teletubbies characters important to the interface is physical: The Teletubbies each have a television screen in their tummies. The tummy screen serves only one simple purpose for the characters on the television program. At least once per program, the Teletubbies periodically receive "broadcasts" on their tummy screens. The screen then displays live action video of children and adults to the eager Teletubbies (and vicariously, to the viewer as well). In a character interface, however, a screen as part of the character's body raises significant issues of how best to integrate the screen into the child's interactions with the character interface itself. On the television program, the Teletubbies do no more than *watch* their own tummy screens. Could that familiar behavior be translated into the interface? Just as the Teletubbies watch their own tummy screens (and children watch with them), would children watch the character interface's tummy screen in the same way?

The presence of the screen, combined with the nonverbal nature of the Teletubbies characters, presented a unique opportunity to combine visual and aural content in a character interface. The interactive character's tummy screen is an actual LED display, measuring 2.5×2 inches, with 5 mm LED lights organized into 8 rows and 10 columns. The lights can be turned on individually and in groups using three different colors (red, green, orange), so simple animations can be displayed in response to sensor inputs. It is known that young children detect and attend to visual and aural synchronies (Kellman and Arterberry 1998). Providing sound effects coordinated with the graphics was presumed to reinforce looking at the screen by adding a visual aspect to character interactions. The interface model was that the child would use the hand and feet sensors to create screen-based visual effects like shapes and patterns that have nonverbal audio elements such as animal noises, musical notes, and other vivid sounds (see Figure 9.3; see also Color Plate). This would present an exclusively nonverbal interaction to children that maintains consistency with the characters themselves as well as avoiding reliance on the language skills of the target users as part of the interface.

FIGURE **9.3**

Interactive Teletubbies characters. Children interact with them by squeezing sensors in the hands and feet and pressing the tummy screen.

Total speech in the entire interface consists of only 22 one- or two-word phrases. Only three of these are directed at the user: "Hand, hand!", "Foot, foot!", and "Again, again!" Yet, because the characters themselves are not particularly articulate, the social nature of the interaction is not diminished by a lack of language in the interface. The emotions in the characters' cooing, giggling, and cheering is obvious. The Teletubbies still cheer in response to child actions, coo in amazement at their efforts, and giggle at surprising or funny events caused by the children as well. As they do in their television program when they watch the events unfolding on their tummy television screens, the interactive Teletubbies characters respond to the effects of the child's actions as they appear in the tummy LED screen.

Our first rounds of testing with a complete functional prototype supported the idea that children would squeeze the hands and feet to control events on the tummy screen. It also produced a dramatic and unexpected result. *Virtually every child, at every age, spontaneously pressed the character's tummy screen as the first action on the doll.* They moved on to hand or foot squeezes after getting no response from the tummy, so these initial tummy attempts didn't interfere with the interface. Why would they go right to the tummy so consistently? Queries of parents were thought provoking because of their consistent theme of transferred expectations. One mother suggested it was because of the Tickle Me Elmo toy, a doll that giggles when the tummy is pressed. Another suggested it was because other Teletubbies dolls talk when their plush tummies are pressed, and children are familiar with them. Transfer of expectations or not, the pervasiveness of the behavior forced a reconsideration of the design. The screen had to become both an output and an input device.

While its inclusion complicated the design from both a hardware and software perspective, the screen's new role as an input device proved to be a boon to the interface in an unexpected way: Pressing the screen proved to be even easier to do than squeezing the hand and foot sensors, an already simple interface. The hand and foot sensors are simple pressure switches embedded in the character's hands and feet. Simple as they are, even these switches require a specific action in order to be triggered. The hand and foot switches require a controlled pincer grasp, a skill that can be attained as early as 9 months, but is usually not achieved until 18 months of age, on average (Bayley 1969, 1993). Yet the tummy screen, also designed as a switch, proved much easier than even the hand and foot sensors. Observations of children's actions with the toy during testing indicated that the screen's surface area not only presented children with a generous, attractive target for pressing, but also was sensitive enough to support a wide variety of presses (from tips of fingers to whole hands, two hands, etc.).

The tummy sensor's popularity with children across the age span had important implications for content design. Accommodating its broad appeal required that it be dedicated to a single, popular activity—an activity simple enough that infants could understand it, but also appealing to older children. The choice was animations set to music. Tummy presses result in brief animations, set to familiar children's tunes played using different instruments (no songs have words, due to the limited language of the Teletubbies themselves). One tune plays with each press of the tummy sensor. Rapid presses cycle through the tunes, so specific selections can be located on demand. In testing with children, this feature proved very popular. Children two and three years old were observed using the repeated presses to "jump" specific tunes they did not like, as well as cycle through in order to find tunes they did like. The tummy thus becomes a digital jukebox, a function that spans the wide age range of intended users.

The screen received the most attention because of its surprise transformation from output device to both input and output medium, but once screen functionality was settled, there was still the question of what to do with the hand and feet sensors. What should the interactions supported by these sensors be? Should they be divided by limb, hands dedicated to one thing, feet to another? Should each hand and foot be dedicated to one of four unique functions, or should they all contribute to one single activity together? The simplest and most consistent solution was to have all four limbs be part of the same function. By using all four limbs in a similar manner within a given game, their integrated nature would be made clear to children during their interactions, encouraging them to see the hands and feet as part of a single activity. In keeping with the nonverbal, visual nature of the content, the hand and feet sensors were used as controls for selecting the color of portions of the screen, or to advance a growing form as it is drawn in, step by step, with each squeeze. Grouping the sensors in this way meant that despite having five distinct sensors, the Teletubbies interface really consists of just two choices: songs (tummy sensor) or games (hands and feet). Movement within and between these two types of content constitutes the entirety of the interface. Such a simple, binary choice is ideally matched to the nascent cognitive skills of the very young children who are the intended users.

The Teletubbies design illustrates how a physical interface character can integrate character attributes with user expectations to create an engaging interactive experience. The reactive and childlike nature of the Teletubbies television characters themselves defined the social role of the characters during interaction. Just as the television characters watch their own tummy screens, the Teletubbies characters react to the effects of the child's actions on their own tummies with coos, cheers, and other responses. The tummy screen itself added new functionality to the character interface. It not only allowed for a graphical, nonverbal output medium appropriate to preverbal users to be added to the design, but observations in early testing of children's responses to the screen helped define the interface itself. Dedicating the tummy to one simple, popular function while using the hands and feet together as part of a different, more complex function creates a contrasting set of options that matches the abilities of both the low end (infants) and high end (preschoolers) of the user population.

Case Study 2: Barney the Dinosaur

The Teletubbies interface emphasizes explicitly graphical elements and nonverbal audio effects like musical notes and animal sounds, while downplaying the use of language. Such a strategy is consistent with both the philosophy of the television program from which the characters originated, as well as with the intellectual skills of the intended users. A different character and different educational emphasis, however, can change the interface dramatically—even if the target age group is largely the same. Change the media character's relationship to the user from that of a toddlerlike peer to one of a parentlike adult, for example, and the nature of the interactions changes as well. This is especially true when the educational goals of the character's television program, in this case *Barney and Friends,* is explicitly concerned with using language as a means of expression. Add the absence of a visual interface like the tummy screen, and it becomes clear that the use of speech, minimized in the Teletubbies interface, becomes the key to the entire interface design.

An emphasis on spoken language is consistent with the educational philosophy of the *Barney and Friends* program. Speech figures prominently not only in the television program, but also in its associated books and CD-ROMs as well. In all these media, Barney is cast in the role of a gentle, encouraging authority figure who does a lot of talking as he leads, guides, explains, and directs the behavior of children on the program. Also unlike the Teletubbies, whose nonverbal nature meant that their musical interactions had to be instrumental only, Barney's musical activities all involve the use of sung lyrics. The deliberate use of language as a medium for promoting learning is drawn from a well-established theoretical and empirical tradition in developmental psychology and pedagogy that emphasizes the power of language to not simply communicate ideas, but actually shape thinking itself. In this model of learning and mental growth, the semantic and syntactic structures of language, and the social processes by which they are imparted to children, are thought to organize children's thinking. The mastery of language is akin to the mastery of reasoning itself (Diaz and Berk 1992; Vygotsky 1978). What would be the most developmentally appropriate way to apply this model of mental growth, and all the speech that goes with it, to a Barney the Dinosaur character interface? The challenge for this interface was to create an appealing set of interactions based primarily in language—interactions that accommodated the same range of cognitive and motor abilities covered by the Teletubbies interface, but that exploited rather than avoided verbal content.

What to Say and When to Say It

Barney's speech was scripted to both preserve Barney's own characteristic verbal style and also to accommodate audio interface design principles. In terms of style, Barney's interface speech is always conversational and familiar. He refers to the child using the pronoun "you" and to their joint activities using the shared pronoun "we." Special attention was paid to Barney's idiosyncratic speech patterns and replicating them in the interface itself. Barney is polite, for example, so in his interface speech he uses the words "please" and "thank you" during interactions. He also has distinctive exclamations, such as "Super-de-duper!" or "Stuuupendous!" and frequently gives praise and expresses affection. These traits were deliberately preserved in the audio interface. Every game and song ends with praise for the child and expressions of pleasure on Barney's part, for example. Random "friendship" phrases such as "I like playing with you!" and "You're my special friend!" play in the interface during idle moments, giving the appearance of spontaneous statements of affection. In user testing with prototype characters, children reacted very positively to these features of the audio interface, often hugging Barney after hearing such phrases or moving the character physically closer to themselves.

In terms of audio interface design principles, several relevant aspects of how such language should be scripted can be found in the research to date, most of it focused primarily on adult users of telephone interfaces (see the review by Resnick and Virzi 1995). A critical issue, for example, is brevity: Speech output should be composed of brief phrases, rather than lengthy sentences. Long speech segments tax the limits of users' sequential memory, causing them to forget part of what they heard. This problem is exacerbated in young children, whose memory capacities are even smaller, relative to adults (Case 1985). In terms of style of speech, research on adults using phone interfaces has found that open queries (for example, "What would you like to do now?") prompt user responses less often than do explicit directives such as "To place a call, press 1 now." These two findings concerning brevity and the value of directive speech have also been reported for preschool children using talking software (Grover 1986; Strommen 1991). Building on these findings, Barney keeps his comments short and does not ask open-ended questions as part of his verbal interface. Instead, he makes simple directive statements such as "Cover my eyes to play peek-a-boo!" or "Squeeze my middle toe to sing a song!"

As another humanoid interactive character, the hardware interface for Barney would obviously share a "family resemblance" to the Teletubbies design, with sensors located in specific parts of the character's body as the mechanism for the child to use to register inputs (see Figure 9.2). Just like the Teletubbies, Barney has five sensors. Four are pressure switches located in his hands and feet, just as in the Teletubbies. The fifth sensor, however, was unique: a light sensor located in the character's eye that registers changes in light level. As would be expected, the same issues raised by the Teletubbies interface, such as how to assign functions to the different sensors and how many functions there should be, had to be addressed for Barney as well.

The strategy finally adopted for the interface was to segregate Barney's different functions by sensor location on his body. In the Teletubbies design, the distinction among sensors was limited to screen (music) versus games (hands and feet). In the Barney interface, functions are associated with each place where a sensor is located on his body: in the feet, hands, or eye. Barney's feet are dedicated to songs. Squeezing the touch sensors in either of Barney's feet causes him to sing one of 16 familiar preschool songs ("The wheels on the bus," "If you're happy and you know it," and so on.). Barney's hands are dedicated to activities and games. Squeezing the sensors in either of Barney's hands causes him to randomly do one of the following: recite nursery rhymes, pose simple queries that require no response ("Is it raining outside? I like rainy days and sunny days!" and so on), or engage the child in an imitation game using animal sounds or simple motor movements. There are a total of 12 different interactions in all. Barney's eyes are dedicated to the game of peek-a-boo. Peek-a-boo was designed as an open-ended series of alternating "It's dark"/"It's light" responses. When Barney detects a loss of light, he responds with an "It's dark" comment such as "Where did everybody go?", "Now I can't see you!", or "It sure is dark!" After playing an "It's dark" comment, when Barney detects an increase in light, he responds with an "It's light" comment: "Peek-a-boo, I see you!", "Oh, there you are!", and so on. The effectiveness of dedicating sensors to functions based on their location on his body was assessed by having children return repeatedly to play with Barney over several months, for different studies. When children returned, they were asked to make Barney sing a song, play a game, or play peek-a-boo. The results were striking: even after just a single session, most children recalled exactly which sensor started a given function, and executed it confidently and reliably.

In the Teletubbies interface, all four hands and feet are used in game play, but each hand and each foot contributes to the games in a unique way. The left hand and right hand, for example, each control a different color or a different portion of the screen. The visual interface supports this diversity of function by letting the child see the effects of different sensor inputs directly on the screen. Children do not have to know left and right to grasp what the sensors do because they receive concrete visual feedback from their actions on the screen. In Barney's interface, in contrast, there are only verbal, not visual, cues to assist in identifying the left and right hands. Given the fact that left and right are not reliably distinguished by children in the target age range (McCarthy 1972), it was decided that the two hands should be redundant with each other, as would the two feet. This redundancy achieved two goals: First, it simplified the audio interface. Barney could say, "Squeeze my hand to play a game" instead of "Squeeze my *left* hand to play a game." Second, it meant the child could grasp either hand and be guaranteed of a game. The chance of confusion over different functions in the different hands was thus eliminated.

The Barney character interface has one additional complexity that the Teletubbies interface did not: movement. In Barney's design, unlike that of the Teletubbies, motors located in the character allowed for simple but expressive head and arm movement. Movement was an important addition to the interface. In his television program, Barney is very physically active, frequently engaging in such activities as dancing, running around, and jumping up and down. Physical movement is thus a key element of Barney's character. More concretely, early testing of Barney's design had revealed that movement by the character had a surprising and powerful effect: It drew and held children's attention in ways that speech alone did not. The movement was particularly effective during singing. In testing with singing interactions, repetitive movements by the character during choruses of songs actually prompted children to mimic the character's actions and dance along themselves. Movement during games and during peek-a-boo enhanced the content of these functions as well, but also created an unexpected complication: In certain games, the movement could actually interfere with the child's performance if it occurred at an inopportune moment. The problem stemmed from the fact that the head and arms were not just part of the output, being the gestural complement to Barney's speech. Because of the sensor locations in the hands and eyes, the hands and arms also served input functions as well. Observations during user testing indicated that during games that required repeated hand squeezes such as counting (where Barney says a number with each squeeze), if the arm moved as he counted, children had trouble "catching" the hand to make their inputs. Similarly, if Barney's head moved while his eyes were being covered by the child, he would inadvertently cause his eyes to be uncovered and disrupt the game. To prevent these difficulties, Barney's head and arm movements for each activity were carefully choreographed so that, for example, he did not move his arms or head at the points in the interactions where they were needed as input devices.

The differences between Barney's interface design and that of the Teletubbies demonstrates the ways that both personality and curriculum can have a significant impact on the nature of the character interface's design and interactions, even when the target age group is basically the same. Both interfaces have five sensors, four of them in the hands and feet. Both interfaces also use sequential, repeated squeezes of the sensors as the means of making inputs when interacting. Yet the Teletubbies interface is simpler, offering but two options (music and games), while Barney's interface offers three (songs, games, and peek-a-boo). More significant from the point of view of character social interface design, however, is Barney's reliance on language and gesture. The speech and motion included in the interface had to address multiple goals. It had to be true to Barney's character in style and content while simultaneously following known interface principles. More importantly, it also had to match the limitations in young children's abilities to understand and respond to language, as well as the limitations of their immature cognitive abilities. Accommodating these limitations led to an interface that, while successful for its users, was restricted in the complexity of interactions it could support. As development progresses and the developmental limitations in children's competence wanes, however, it becomes possible to use the same basic interface to support interactions of much more sophistication.

Case Study 3: Arthur and D. W.

The Teletubbies and Barney the dinosaur are characters who appeal to very young children, typically children under the age of five. The trajectory of child development is such that this brief span of time sees children progress from acquiring basic motor skills and thought processes in infancy through the acquisition and mastery of language, and the orderly thinking that language imposes. Social skills undergo a similar dramatic transition as well. Children progress from the egocentrism of infancy to being able to interact cooperatively with others, both children and adults, and to collaborate on activities like games or shared pretend together. The climax of all of these changes is a new level of basic competence in thinking and doing, and new strengths in interacting with others. These advances mean new opportunities and new challenges for character interface designs. Older children can clearly do more and think in more sophisticated ways than their younger counterparts. What sorts of characters and what sorts of interactions are possible for children older than five years of age?

Meet Arthur and D. W.

Arthur and D. W. are fictional siblings, the literary creations of children's author Marc Brown. They have been familiar to American children for more than 15 years as the central characters in more than 30 children's books, a popular television series, and several educational CD-ROM titles intended for the four- to eight-year-old population. Arthur and D. W. are anthropomorphized aardvarks who live in a suburban neighborhood with other animal families. Their animal-like appearance notwithstanding, Arthur and D. W.'s behavior is completely human. What is more, their abilities and interests, their language use, and their behavior is typical of that of the older children who are their target audience. These personal attributes create new opportunities for more sophisticated interactions than those created for younger children in the Teletubbies and Barney characters.

The new level of sophistication possible with these characters and the older children to whom they appeal is manifested in a very concrete way in

FIGURE **9.4**

Interactive Arthur and D. W. characters. Children interact with the characters by squeezing sensors located in the hands, feet, ears, and watch (visible on right arm).

the hardware interface. While Barney and the Teletubbies have five sensors, Arthur and D. W. have seven: two in the hands, two in the feet, two in the ears, and one in the watch on the character's left arm (see Figure 9.4; see also Color Plate). As Barney and the Teletubbies demonstrated, the number of sensors is not a direct indicator of interface complexity, since both of those interfaces have five sensors but differ in the quantity and type of content they support. The more sensors available in the interface, however, the more opportunities there are to create more and deeper levels of interaction because more sensors provide a broader range of input options. The wider content design possibilities of more sensors notwithstanding, the fact that the interface is a character and that the sensors are still associated with their locations in the characters' bodies places certain constraints on how they can be used in interactions. While the user population is more sophisticated than the preschool population that was the focus of the Barney interface design, certain developmental limitations remain. Left and right identification are still not firmly established in a majority of children at this age, for example, so diversifying the sensors by left and right still has to be avoided (Clark and Klonoff 1990). For reasons such as these, Arthur and D. W.'s interfaces do not represent a dramatic departure from the Barney or Teletubbies designs so much as a new strategy for using such interfaces as a means to control interactions. This strategy maintains a high degree of simplicity, but still capitalizes on the competencies of the older children who are the intended users by using the sensors in both the same and different ways at the same time. The result is an interface that has a strong "family resemblance" to Barney and the Teletubbies, differing from them in degree, rather than kind.

The Arthur and D. W. Interface

As with Barney, the content of the Arthur and D. W. characters is segregated by sensor location. Just as there are three types of function supported by Barney's three sensor locations (eyes, hands, and feet), Arthur and D. W. have three functions as well, associated with the ears, watch, and feet. The interface differs from Barney's in two ways. First, there is an extra set of sensors, located in the hands, that are not associated with any specific function. This is because their role is to be used in conjunction with the other sensors, to allow for more complex interactions in those functions than a single sensor permits. Second, sensors do not remain dedicated to one single purpose during all interactions. This is the key design difference between Arthur and D. W.'s interface and the Barney and Teletubby interface designs. The Barney and Teletubby interfaces rely on no more than sequential inputs on the same sensor as a means of engaging content (repeatedly squeezing the hand to play serial games such as reciting the alphabet, for example, or repeatedly covering and uncovering the eyes to play peek-a-boo). In Arthur and D. W.'s interface, in contrast, games are initiated using one sensor, but once a game is started, a variety of sensors (the hands as well as others) are used in actual game play. How is this multiple-sensor interface—where sensor functions actually change depending on context—laid out? It's done in a way that both resembles and departs from the Barney model.

Ears are to hear what Arthur and D. W. are thinking. Squeezing the ears allows children to "eavesdrop" on Arthur's or D. W.'s thoughts. Each ear squeeze plays one of dozens of unique phrases that ask questions, offer opinions, share jokes, and give compliments. The content of these phrases is scripted to reflect the individual thoughts and feelings of the fictional characters Arthur or D. W., and are consistent with the social and emotional themes central to the Arthur stories and television series on which the characters are based. The comments also reflect the interest and ideas of children in the target age group, as uncovered in our research and in reviews of the existing psychological and educational literature. Such "thoughts" are particularly well suited to a character interface, with its explicitly social nature.

The phrases spoken in response to ear squeezes fall into several categories:

- *Jokes.* Arthur and D. W. share silly ideas or comical events with the child. Arthur, for example, says, "You know what's gross?" and then proceeds to name something silly, such as "sweaty gym socks," that elicits humorous reactions of disgust from the child.

- *Secrets.* Arthur and D. W. say, "Come closer, I want to tell you a secret!" and then confide an embarrassing fact or a private opinion to the child.

- *Playful teasing.* Arthur and D. W. make mock requests or gently tease the child with information they know, such as the child's birthday.

- *Compliments and affection.* Arthur and D. W. both express affection for the child, through such comments as "I'm lucky to have a friend like you!"

- *Speculations about future careers.* Both characters reflect on possible adult career roles, asking, "What should I be when I grow up?" and then answering their own question with a speculation. Arthur, for example, says, "Maybe I'll be an astronaut and discover a new planet!" Reflecting her more ambitious and gregarious nature, D. W.'s speculations are more grandiose, for example, "Maybe I'll be President. You can be my Vice President!"

In the case of ear phrases, the hands function as a reminder and memory aid. If the last input before the hand was squeezed was an ear squeeze, squeezing the hand sensor results in the character's repeating the last ear phrase so it can be heard again on demand.

The watch is for telling time. It is in the four- to eight-year-old age range that most children acquire their first wristwatch or alarm clock, and when an interest in time and calendar knowledge first appears. Arthur and D. W. support this interest by acting as a sort of smart friend, who always knows the time and date. When their watches are squeezed, the characters say the current time, date, and day of the week. If the date is a holiday, the character announces that fact along with the date. The characters can also be programmed to know a specific birthday and will treat that date as a holiday. They can also be programmed as alarms, allowing them to wake the user in the morning or remind them that it is a specific time. The fact that they report the time verbally means that even children who cannot read clocks accurately can know the time when they want to know it, just as if they had asked an older peer or parent. The time and date features thus make Arthur and D. W. seem like friends who are not only intelligent, but supportive and empowering as well. In testing this feature, for example, it was common to observe children comparing their own watches with the time reported by the characters, checking their own accuracy and using the characters to assist them in mastering the skill of reading a clock face. Several children even took the reverse approach, using their own mastery of time skills to check the accuracy of the character, nodding approvingly when the character's time matched the time on their watches or resetting the character's time if it did not.

The hand sensor plays the same complementary role to the watch that it does for the ear. If the last input before the hand was squeezed was the watch, the character repeats the time.

Feet are for games. When a foot is squeezed, the characters play games. Both Arthur and D. W. play the same games. While there are 10 different games the characters can play, several are similar to those of Barney and require only sequential squeezes of the same sensor to play. The games of particular interest to this discussion, however, are those that utilize more than one sensor during play, giving the user more options but also requiring more from the user as a result. There are several of these games:

- *Guess the holiday.* The character gives a date and asks the child to name the holiday that falls on that date. A hand squeeze reports the answer. A second hand squeeze repeats the previous date and holiday. An ear squeeze causes the character to present a new date to be identified. A foot squeeze aborts this game and launches a new game.

- *How long is that?* The character challenges the child to estimate a specific length of time (5, 10, 15, or 20 seconds) and squeeze a hand sensor when the duration is passed. Squeezing a hand again restarts the game again with the same target time. Squeezing an ear restarts the game with a different target time. A foot squeeze aborts this game and launches a new game.

- *The memory game.* In this game, children memorize, then execute, progressively longer lists of sensor squeezes ("Hand, foot, ear"). Each time the list is correctly input using the character sensors, a new element is added to the list on the next round, until an error is made. A foot squeeze aborts this game and launches a new game.

- *Silly sentences.* The character combines randomly selected adjectives, nouns, and verbs to create nonsense sentences such as "The jiggling wombat does the cha-cha with the stinky antelope!" Squeezing the hand repeats the same sentence, squeezing the ear results in a new sentence. A foot squeeze aborts this game and launches a new game.

- *Tongue twisters.* The character challenges the child to say a tongue twister, then waits as the child recites it. A hand squeeze repeats the tongue twister; an ear squeeze results in a new tongue twister. A foot squeeze aborts this game and launches a new game.

The "nested" functions requiring hand and ear inputs within these games have two characteristics intended to make navigation by users easy and understandable. First, the foot sensor keeps its "pick a game" function, even within games. Thus repeated squeezes of the foot always allow the user to select a different game at any time and foot squeezes always end an active game and start a new one. Second, the hand and ear sensors each have a consistent function across games. The ears let users select a new round of a game with new content, while the hands repeat the same round. The use of such consistent rules alleviates much of the risk of confusion that reassigning sensor functions can create, by making sensor actions, even changes in their functions, predictable to children in all contexts. In user testing, it did not take children long to recognize and use these basic conventions to navigate among their choices in the interface, underscoring the advanced competence these older children possess relative to their younger peers, whose abilities required far simpler and more strictly consistent interface rules.

Personality and the Older Child

The deeper and more complicated interface functions intended to match the capabilities of the older children who are the users of the Arthur and D. W. characters are matched by a more varied and subtle design of the social interactions of the character as well. The social interface for the Teletubbies characters is deliberately simple: The characters greet the child and react to the child's inputs using simple, affective responses such as cheering or cooing with admiration. Such responses are not only developmentally appropriate, but are also in keeping with the personalities and social interactions of the Teletubbies themselves on their television program. Barney's social interactions are slightly more complex, owing to both his own personality and his use of simple language in the interface. Barney not only reacts to the child's inputs with pleasure and eagerness ("That was fun!"), but is also encouraging ("Now you try it!") and affectionate ("I like playing with you!").

Arthur and D. W.'s emotional interactions, similar to their game interactions, are more sophisticated than those of Barney and the Teletubbies. Like Barney and the Teletubbies, they respond with pleasure and enthusiasm to the child's input, and like Barney they are explicitly encouraging of the child's efforts. But they also utilize language to engage in more subtle emotional interactions as well. Arthur makes humorous yet self-effacing comments about his appearance, saying for example, "Are my glasses on straight? I don't want to look goofy!" The reaction of children during testing was one of sympathy. They often adjusted his glasses, in effect helping him make sure he looks good to others. D. W. expresses a similar sentiment and elicits a similar reaction. When D. W. says plaintively, "I'm having a bad hair day!" children of both genders responded to her in some manner. Girls in particular frequently began grooming D. W., combing her hair with their fingers. Both characters also speculate about their own adult careers, modeling confidence and curiosity about the future, and both conspire with users, sharing secrets with them. All of these interactions mimic the content of social interactions the child would likely have with a same-aged peer.

Beyond these general emotional interactions, the increased complexity of Arthur and D. W.'s games also requires a more sophisticated use of emotions during game play. How Long Is That (HLIT) and The Memory Game (TMG) are the two most challenging games Arthur and D. W. play. Both games require sustained effort and repeated trials for success, meaning that failures are frequent. In HLIT, for example, children can repeatedly try to estimate the duration of 10 seconds and be wrong again and again as they refine their performance. Even with repeated trials, success is not guaranteed. In TMG, the situation is similar: The list of items to be remembered gets longer and longer with each round, guaranteeing that it will lengthen beyond children's competence as they repeatedly challenge themselves during game play. In the initial designs for both games, failures were not overtly acknowledged by the characters. A failure, such as making the wrong input when recalling the items in TMG, simply led to a new round of the game immediately after the error was confirmed. The character simply said, "Oops, that's not it!" or a similar phrase, and then said, "Let's try again!" Children's reactions to this transition from failure to a new round were striking: They often looked down or looked away from the character, and interacted less frequently with the character for several minutes afterward. Based on this observation, the design of these games was changed such that, after an error was confirmed ("Oops! That's not what comes next!"), Arthur and D. W. praise the child's effort ("That was hard!" or "That was a tough one!") prior to starting the new round. In subsequent testing this sympathy from the character seemed to soften the blow by acknowledging the difficulty of the task. True or not, the decline in positive affect and interaction that had accompanied failures without the comment were not observed during that game in subsequent prototype testing.

9.3 Social Interfaces and Media Convergence

In the previous case studies, the design of three physical character interfaces were described. While they are each distinct products, several common themes cross all their designs. The first is the importance of personality for the interface. This is particularly true with characters from television programs. The intimate nature of television is such that children feel they are familiar with the characters they are viewing, even if they have never interacted with them physically, but simply watched them on the screen. Simply put, they know the character represented in the interface. They have expectations about character behavior, speech, and personal preferences that the interface character must meet in order to hold the user's attention and interest. The second theme in the design of the characters is the importance of understanding the children in the different age groups who are users of the products under discussion. Existing research data on children's social and cognitive competencies in the target user ages, as well as actual tests of child users with the interfaces themselves, were used to inform both the interface design and the role of language in it. Playing to children's strengths in social skills while avoiding the weaknesses in their cognitive and linguistic abilities (such as literacy and attention span) requires careful design and evaluation. When personality and user abilities are combined correctly, the result is a successful social interface design for children.

In the freestanding play described for the above products, the child interacts directly with the character. The social nature of the child's engagement with the character interface was conceived as similar to one-on-one peer play, a two-way exchange or dialog, and the interactions of the characters reflect this one-on-one relationship in specific ways. For example, the character reacts to the child's actions with verbal and nonverbal responses that assume a shared experience: They use personal pronouns such as "you" when referring to the child and "we" when referring to shared play activities. In the case of the Teletubbies, who do not use pronouns, their one- and two-word comments are scripted as reactions and exclamations directed to the child. Not all social interactions are one-on-one interactions, however, and the social rules for different types of social interactions are different, depending on the nature of the interaction. One factor that exerts a significant influence over the rules of social interaction is the presence of different forms of media in the social context. The social rules for sharing such activities as using a computer together or watching television together differ from those deployed in a one-on-one social exchange (Huston et al. 1992). By adopting the appropriate social rules for these interactions around other media, pretend playmate interfaces are able to play a role in children's media interaction beyond the role they play as pretend playmates by themselves. In this section, the nature of pretend playmate interaction with both broadcast and interactive media will be described.

Interaction with the Television

The key element in social interaction with other media is the ability to respond to the new media content in appropriate ways. Interactions around a television or a computer have the media content as their primary focus.

Social exchanges around these media forms are responses to the media content itself, rather than responses to the actions of users. Shared television viewing, for example, is largely a matter of sharing reactions to the events on the screen (Huston et al. 1992). Such interactions are more than idle banter, however. Research on learning from television has established that young children comprehend more program content when their viewing is supplemented by the comments and questions of older peers or adults than when they simply view alone (Collins, Sobol, and Westby 1981; Haefner and Wartella 1987; Huston et al. 1992). These social interactions around the television, described as "co-viewing," are ideal candidates for character interaction because they are almost completely verbal: The children's eyes are on the television screen, but they listen to and respond to the utterances of others watching along. The character's physical presence sitting with the child actually reinforces this social script. Another practical reason why such interactions are ideal is that the presence of the television provides a common focus of attention for both the child and the character. By structuring the interaction as one of sharing reactions to the same experience, the character's verbal comments can be context specific because they are reactions to the content of the program itself.

But how does the interface character know what is on the television? The character must interact with the television in some manner, and the exact nature of the interaction has serious implications for the integrity of the interface's pretend playmate–like nature. The form of interaction with the television itself is subject to social expectations, just as the content of the character's interactions are. If the characters had to be physically plugged into the television, for example, the social repercussions would be significant. Not only is the use of a physical interface like a wire clumsy and artificial, destroying the pretend scenario of lifelike behavior on the part of the character, but it also has the practical effect of restricting the physical location and use of the character itself. The wire imposes a limit on how far the character can be moved around the TV, for example, and the child must accommodate it in order to use the interface. It also creates an artificial transition into and out of the viewing experience, requiring the child to not only plug the character *in* so that viewing can be shared, but also requiring the child to *unplug* the character at the end of the viewing experience.

What would be a more natural (i.e., social) way to engage television content? Human viewers make the transition from not viewing to viewing very easily and transparently, simply by shifting their attention to the television itself and responding to what they see and hear. Socially based character interfaces should do the same if their goal is to mimic social behavior and maintain the social pretense that is the basis for the interface itself. In practical terms, this means that whatever the interface between the character and the television, it should be invisible to the user, and the transition to watching the television should be as simple and easy as it is with a peer: turn on the television and start watching. Clearly, these constraints all dictate a wireless interaction, but a lack of a physical interface like a wire alone is not sufficient, since wireless interactions can also impose their own demands on users. Consider an infrared (IR) interface, like a remote control. It is wireless, but it has an added constraint of requiring a direct line of sight between the character and the IR transceiver. Given the unpredictable positions the character might be placed in (lying down on its back, sitting at an angle, etc.) and the uncertain location of furniture relative to the television, IR interaction is still too limited. The child would be required to position the character in specific ways, another odd and unnatural addition to what is supposed to be a familiar and simple social interaction.

The ideal interface between the character and the television, therefore, is one that is not only wireless but that does not create arbitrary functional restrictions of its own, either. The medium that meets all these criteria is radio frequency (RF) interaction. All of the characters discussed in this chapter interact with other media using RF as a medium. Each character has an internal radio transceiver similar to that of a walkie-talkie that is integrated with the character's other freestanding functions. When a special transmitter is attached to a TV and VCR, new speech and motion for the character on specially encoded tapes and broadcasts of video programming are transmitted to the character in real time while the program is being viewed. When the characters detect the transmitted information, they give a brief comment (Barney says, "Let's watch TV together!" for example, and Arthur says, "Hey, look who's on TV!") and then begin to interact with the program. The real-time interaction with the new content broadcast from the television transmitter allows the characters to respond to the content of the programs in context-sensitive ways, such as singing along with a tune or reacting to onscreen events with context-specific phrases. When the program or tape is over and the signal from the transmitter ceases, the characters make a transition comment indicating they are no longer watching TV (Barney says, for example, "That was fun!"), and freestanding play functionality resumes.

The co-viewing interactions with the television during the broadcast are scripted to match the personality of the character and the developmental status of the child, just as the one-on-one interactions are. The goal of these interactions, like those in one-on-one play, is to engage the user cognitively and emotionally in educational activities. The only difference is that now, instead of interacting with the character interface directly, the child is being directed to the video broadcast content. Each of the different types of characters uses different, character-specific interactions to achieve this goal. For the Teletubbies, interaction with the television is based on the notion that the Teletubbies themselves are children's peers. They participate in the program using language appropriate to the Teletubbies characters, and their participation involves using speech in ways that are consistent with the behavior of the Teletubbies themselves. They either repeat speech on the program after it is said or they say familiar phrases along with the characters on the program at the same time, creating a sort of chorus. If the character on the screen says, "Bye bye!" for example, the Teletubby character watching with the child says, "Bye bye!" in response. If the Teletubbies on TV all say, "Uh-oh!" at the same time, the Teletubby character says, "Uh-oh!" along with them. The Teletubbies react with giggles and cooing to onscreen events in the same manner. The Teletubbies also play music when the Teletubbies on the screen dance to music. The music on the program also plays out of the Teletubby, in synchrony with the music on the television. Testing of these types of interactions confirmed that they engage children in the program content. Children often repeat the phrases said by the characters. For example, they recite familiar lines along with a character on the program more often when an interactive character is present and responding to the program than when viewing without one. Most striking, music played from the character prompted children to dance along, holding the character in their arms, a behavior seen very infrequently without the interactive character. These heightened levels of participation and engagement increase children's understanding of and enjoyment of the program.

Barney, Arthur, and D. W.'s interactions with their television programs are more complex and utilize their more sophisticated language, but they too respond to the program in ways that reflect their co-viewing social role relative to the child user. Like the Teletubbies, their interactions are intended to enhance viewing and the child's participation in program content. Their methods of doing so, however, are different. Unlike the Teletubbies, for example, Barney is not a peer for children but more of a parental figure. While he reacts to events on screen (chuckling at humorous situations, for example), he also anticipates them, saying things like "Oh, look!" to draw children's attention to onscreen action. His comments are also more tutorial in nature, in keeping with his role as guide and authority figure. What he says are phrases shown to stimulate thinking in children. Barney asks questions ("What do you think will happen next?"), he labels onscreen images using appropriate vocabulary ("That's a square!"), he counts along with onscreen characters, and he sings along with songs, reciting the words. He also cheers, laughs, acts surprised, and has other emotional responses to what is onscreen. In testing, these interactions were very effective in prompting responses from children in return. They frequently answered his questions, for example, and often began singing along with a song after hearing Barney sing the chorus once.

What about Arthur and D. W.? Like the Teletubbies, Arthur and D. W.'s social role relative to the child user is that of a peer. The older age of their target users, however, gives their peer exchanges a much different meaning than it does for the Teletubbies. The goal of Arthur and D. W.'s television interactions is to engage the children in thinking about and reflecting on the social and emotional issues that are the central themes of the program itself. The two characters do this by making their own personal comments about what they are watching, comments that state a specific personal reaction to what they see. While watching a segment where Arthur is being teased, for example, the Arthur character interface might say, "I hate this part!" in an embarrassed tone of voice as he watches himself being made fun of. D. W. watching the same segment, however, responds differently. Instead of identifying with the awkward embarrassment her brother feels, she reacts more aggressively, criticizing the teasing comments with a scolding "That's not nice!" The design strategy behind such interactions is to get children to reflect on their own responses to what they are watching. The idea is to get the child to think "D. W. said how she feels. What do I feel?" Arthur and D. W. are modeling engagement with the emotional content of the program. Testing of these segments with children confirmed that they elicit the appropriate reactions. One response to the Arthur character's embarrassment, for example, was that children tended to hug the doll or comfort him after it spoke. This response suggests that the children registered the emotional message Arthur was conveying.

The fact that the goal of television interaction is to engage children in program content, rather than with the interface character, itself raises a critical issue for video interaction: What functions should the character's sensors have during television interaction? The linear nature of video content, and the episode-specific content of each program, mean that the character's normal play functions cannot remain active. If they did, then depending on the character, actuating a sensor would launch a game with its attendant sounds and/or graphics or start a song or tune. These games and music would be unrelated to the program content and would create a distraction, drawing children's attention away from the program rather than keeping them interested in it. But what alternative designs would be better? One possible solution is to simply deactivate the sensors during TV viewing. This would mean that the characters would comment on what was being watched, but would not respond to children's actions if the sensors were squeezed. A test of this scenario showed it was inappropriate. Children acted on the characters' sensors very infrequently, but when the characters failed to respond the children were perplexed. Why was the character talking (commenting on the program), yet not responding to their actions as it had before? The characters' lack of responsiveness actually became a distraction in itself, as children turned their attention to the character and tried to elicit a response, ignoring the content of the program they were viewing.

The design strategy for sensor functions in TV viewing originated in a careful review of how children interacted not only with the interface character but also with their parents during TV viewing. Unlike their interactions with the characters in freestanding mode, children did not give their full attention to the characters when they interacted with them in TV mode. Rather, they tended to reach over and act on the character absently, as a secondary behavior during viewing. Their eyes usually remained on screen. What was striking was that they tended to act in the same manner on another person watching along with them, *often with an identical action.* If during a Barney episode, they patted their parent's arm while viewing, for example, they also patted the Barney character. It was the response of the parents and siblings that provided the design for the characters' response. Their responses to being touched were typically no more than brief recognitory actions (a return pat, a stroke, a verbal comment, etc.). This type of response typically satisfied the child viewer and further interactions ceased. Would children be satisfied with a similar, abbreviated response from pretend playmate characters?

Subsequent testing revealed that this was in fact the case. If the children squeezed Barney's hand or foot, for example, all he had to do was make a friendly comment ("I like watching TV with you"), or give a generic, TV-specific attention directive ("What's happening on the TV?"), and the children were content. No children protested or asked why Barney did not play games or sing while watching TV if his hands or feet were squeezed. This basic design was tested and found to work with the Teletubbies (who giggle in response to sensor inputs) and with Arthur and D. W., who make comments similar to Barney's ("Are you trying to get my attention?" or "This is my favorite show!" etc.).

Interaction with the PC

Television interaction is limited by the fact that while the character interacts with the child through its reactions to the program content, the child's inputs to the character cannot affect the program content. Nor can the child's actions on the character influence the character's behavior in any meaningful way without risking distracting the child from the program. Interaction with computer technologies, however, is a different story. When an RF transmitter is attached to a PC running encoded CD-ROMs or using a Web browser with specially encoded Web sites on the Internet, the characters can both receive new speech and motion content from the computer *and* transmit inputs from their own sensors back to the computer as well. In this way, the characters not only react to children's actions as they use the computer with a keyboard and pointing device, but children's actions on the characters' sensors also affect what happens on the computer as well.

As with television interaction, the critical design issue was choosing what social rules and social role the characters should have at the computer. The Teletubbies characters, designed as they are for very young children, do not have PC-related interactions as this chapter goes to press. However, Barney, Arthur, and D. W. interact with specially encoded CD-ROMs, and Arthur and D. W. interact with the Arthur Web site at *www.pbs.org*. What sorts of interactions are appropriate for pretend playmates during computer interaction, and how does the social role of the character shape the content and style of those interactions? The first step taken in shaping the interactions at the computer was to review the literature on children working together at the computer (Johnson and Johnson 1975; Mevarech, Silber, and Fein 1991; Nastasi and Clements 1992; Slavin 1980). These studies provided insight into the dynamics of situations where social interactions take place around the computer as the common focus of attention. This research also documented the types of verbal interactions used by peers, especially thinking aloud during task execution, praise, and hints, which are most effective in promoting learning and mastery. The literature on computers and learning did not, however, provide insight into how physical character interfaces, as simulacra with their own input sensors, should be integrated with the computer. Was it possible to create computer interactions that combine sensor inputs on the characters with mouse use or keyboard inputs in a single interaction? Or should the two interfaces be kept separate, with complementary but distinct functions?

A test of a mixed interface, using Barney and the mouse together in a simple counting task, provided important guidance. All of the subjects were familiar with Barney from previous tests and all were computer users in their homes, meaning they had extensive experience with both interfaces. When they played with Barney in his freestanding mode at the start of the testing session, they interacted with him directly, attending to him visually, listening to him, and acting on his sensors. When it was time to use him with the computer, however, their performance changed dramatically. They sat Barney next to them by the computer, and then immediately stopped interacting with his sensors and grasped the mouse, gazing expectantly at the computer screen and ignoring Barney. When he spoke to them during computer use, they demonstrated an unexpected ability to listen to him while using the mouse at the same time. When Barney commented on their actions with the mouse or gave instructions for pointing and clicking, for example, children kept their eyes on screen yet responded to him with smiles and comments and, most importantly, by using the mouse as he asked.

When Barney began directing children to use his sensors and the mouse together for software tasks, however, a host of problems emerged. The task was simple in theory: Squeeze Barney's hand to count out a requested number of items (one item for each squeeze) and then use the mouse to click a GO icon when the child judged the set was complete. In practice, however, the children's execution was fraught with problems. As expected, the children reached for Barney's hand with one hand while keeping the other on the mouse, or even let go of the mouse completely to grasp Barney's hand with the same hand they had been using to control the cursor. The result was that they inadvertently moved the cursor as they reached or when they released the mouse to grasp his sensors, forcing them to have to reposition it on the correct icon again before going on with the activity. They were also easily confused by the sequence of events. When, exactly, were they to use the mouse versus Barney's sensors? What were they to do when they made a mistake and counted too many? In an attempt to coordinate the two interfaces together, some children adopted a strategy of keeping one hand on the mouse and one on Barney. This was an awkward posture that degraded their cursor control, especially when they chose to keep their dominant hand on Barney and their other hand on the mouse. But perhaps the most striking result of the study was a strong transfer of expectations about *content*. Children expected that if they squeezed Barney's foot during software use, for example, he would respond as he did in freestanding toy mode: He would sing a song. This expectation persisted even if Barney had explicitly indicated otherwise in his instructions. In other words, not only did young children find it difficult to coordinate the two interfaces together, but they expected Barney's interface to keep the same functionality it had in one-on-one play. He was not expected to change his behavior just because a computer was present. Based on these results, the software and Barney's role in it were deliberately designed to build on children's existing expectations, not only about Barney, but about software use as well.

Barney at the Computer

Reconciling the two interfaces required revisiting Barney's social role in relation to the child user. As an authority figure, children expect him to offer guidance and help in their performance, yet they also expect him to still "be Barney," that is, to still do the things he does in freestanding play. To keep the integrity of Barney's interactions, his social role at the computer was designed to be similar to that at the television. In other words, he acts not as a direct play partner, but in the less dominant role of coach, or sidekick. And to both maintain simplicity and be consistent with user expectations, his own functions are carefully segregated from computer control. To this end, onscreen activities are supervised and directed not by Barney, but by onscreen characters in the software itself. Everything related to computer control is done with the mouse, and the onscreen characters relay all relevant interface information to the child: where to click, the goal of the task, and so on. Barney's focus of attention is the child's actions. His comments are reactions to the child's performance using the software, making his social role a complementary rather than central one. In keeping with his role as an authority figure, he praises correct responses and offers hints when the child makes errors on structured tasks like shape recognition or counting. If a child selected a square when asked for a triangle, for example, Barney might say, "We're looking for a triangle. A triangle has *three* sides. Pick the shape that has three sides!" In addition to this new type of interaction when the child is using the mouse, when his own sensors are actuated Barney remains true to his freestanding performance, but with a new twist. His feet remain an interface for songs, for example, but now the songs are new tunes, written as joint performances shared by Barney and the onscreen characters together. Barney's eyes remain a dedicated peek-a-boo interface, but now the onscreen characters play along, covering and uncovering their eyes along with Barney and reacting appropriately (saying, "Peek-a-boo!" when Barney's eyes are uncovered, for example). Barney's hands remain an interface for games as well, but now the games are on screen. Hand squeezes result in Barney "taking a turn"—coloring a section of the drawing himself, adding his own shape, and so on, and reflecting on his actions. If the child has colored a picture all in red, for example, and his hand is squeezed, he might say "Wow! That's a lot of *red!* I'll color this part red, too!" and a piece of the picture image gets colored red. Just as in his freestanding mode, hand squeezes are the interface that cause him to participate with the child during a game.

Arthur and D. W. at the Computer

Arthur and D. W.'s social role in relation to the older children who are their users is that of a peer, not an authority figure. The dynamics of peer interactions for children of this age, combined with the increased cognitive sophistication of four to seven year olds, mean that Arthur and D. W.'s interactions at the computer will be of a different form than those used by Barney. In terms of peer interaction and older children, the best way to understand Arthur and D. W.'s social role is to contrast it with that of Barney. Barney's role as authority figure or guide means that he is aggressive in his pedagogical role. When a child makes an error he automatically offered a hint, for example. As peers, Arthur and D. W., in contrast, do not rush to the child's assistance if an error is made. Like Barney, they react sympathetically and encouragingly, but they do not offer help at once. They will periodically offer to help, saying, "Squeeze my ear for a hint!" and if the ear is squeezed, they offer a verbal hint. They also offer assistance, saying, "Squeeze my hand and I'll take a turn!" and if the hand is squeezed, they will actually model solving or taking a step toward solving the task the child is working on. But they do not give any assistance until the child acts on one of their sensors, making a conscious choice to seek assistance. Requiring the child to actually choose to get assistance makes Arthur and D. W. more like peers because it makes them appear to respect the child's own efforts. It is as if the child had said, "Don't tell me, I want to get it myself!" and Arthur and D. W. were respecting the child's wishes.

The fact that Arthur and D. W. deliver hints on demand when their ears are squeezed leads to a discussion of the other ways in which Arthur and D. W. differ from Barney in their interactions, based not just on their social roles but on the cognitive sophistication of their target users. Given the younger age of Barney's target users, strict consistency between the functions of his sensors in freestanding play and in PC interaction was necessary for ease of use. Not only were they consistent with freestanding play, but their functions never changed when at the PC. Barney's sensors maintain the same functions throughout PC interaction: Feet always give songs, eyes always result in peek-a-boo, hands are for games. Arthur and D. W., however, do not utilize such strict consistency. Just as their own freestanding interfaces utilize the same sensor for different functions depending on context, their sensor functions at the PC diverge from what they are used for in freestanding play and also change depending on what specific interactions are being engaged in at the PC. The character's interface is still carefully segregated from the PC interface as in Barney's PC interactions. The functions that the sensors do perform, however, are both more context specific to the particular PC interaction being engaged in and less concretely connected to Arthur and D. W.'s freestanding play functions.

In freestanding mode, ear squeezes cause Arthur and D. W. to say phrases that let you hear what they are "thinking." At the PC, ear squeezes result in hints, which can be thought of as a special case of what the characters are "thinking" (in this case what they are thinking while watching the child play a game on the PC). For example, if the child is trying to select the onscreen character who has correctly spelled the word *cat,* Arthur might say, "Cat is spelled C . . . A . . . T. Pick the person who spelled it that way!" The watch sensor, similarly, retains a time function, but one that is augmented by the graphical capabilities of the computer. Squeeze the watch during freestanding play and the characters say the time. Squeeze it when they are interacting with the PC and they not only tell you the time, but an onscreen clock appears that displays the time using both analog and digital clock forms. The hands and feet perform functions very different from their freestanding ones, however. The hands have no specific function in freestanding play, but serve to repeat phrases or augment game play, depending on the interaction the child is engaged in. At the PC, however, hand squeezes cause the characters to "take a turn" and participate in the onscreen activity. The characters not only take a turn, but they "think out loud" about what they are doing in the same way Barney might. For example, if the child is selecting the correct spelling for a given word from among several options presented by onscreen characters and squeezes a hand sensor, Arthur and D. W. say, "Hm. Cat is spelled C . . . A . . . T. I'll pick Muffy!" The computer then executes the next step in the game as if the character had clicked on Muffy. The feet also have a different function during PC interaction. Instead of playing specific games as they do in freestanding play, squeezing the feet sensors at the PC results in social word play in the form of knock-knock jokes. The character asks, "Hey, how about a knock-knock joke!" and the onscreen character responds, saying, "OK! Knock knock!" The character then says, "Who's there?" and the onscreen character delivers the setup line ("Dwayne!", for example). When the character says "Dwayne who?" the onscreen character says "Dwayne the bathtub, I'm dwowning!" and the characters, both onscreen and off, laugh. The effects of the knock-knock jokes were striking. Children laughed along or groaned at the jokes, and then spontaneously began telling their own knock-knock jokes to others in the room with them. The social nature of shared joking modeled by Arthur and D. W. prompted children to initiate that same social behavior with others.

It is possible to use different functions for the character sensors at the PC than are used in freestanding play because Arthur and D. W.'s target users are cognitively more advanced than the young children and infants who are the target audience for Barney and the Teletubbies. Their working memories are larger, allowing them to remember the various functions of the different sensors in the different usage scenarios (Case 1985). Our testing with these older children revealed that they were not confused by changing functions across different usage contexts (freestanding versus PC), and adapted easily to them. The Arthur and D. W. software takes this result one step further by not only changing functions at the PC relative to freestanding play, but by changing functions within the software as well. Each CD-ROM has a special "dance theater" activity in which the child teaches an onscreen version of the interface character to dance by squeezing the character's hands, feet, and ears. Each sensor results in a different dance step, and the steps can be combined to execute unique dances by ordering the steps in different ways. The watch sensor executes the dance. The mouse is used only to select backgrounds and musical themes to dance to. Testing with children found that they easily changed their expectations about the characters' sensors as they moved from the software games to dance theater and back again, confirming that this older age group is able to accommodate diverse interface functions in a way that younger children could not. By building interfaces that match the sophistication of these older users, interface characters capitalize on user competence to deliver a wider variety of interactions to children. By keeping these interactions social (child inputs result in taking turns, offering hints, teaching someone to dance, etc.), they also capitalize on the social expectations that are the basis of the pretend playmate interface itself.

9.4 Whither the Future?

Physical interface characters use rules of social behavior as the basis for the form and content of their playful learning interactions. The nature of the social interactions and the complexity of the functionality required for each character are shaped by both the personalities of the interface characters themselves and by the social and cognitive abilities of the target users for each product. While each character is self-contained with fixed content, a wireless radio link allows the character to receive new speech and new behavior patterns in conjunction with other media, such as the TV or PC. The wireless link makes the character's interaction with these other media invisible and intuitive, just as it is with social actors such as peers or parents. The character's mimicry of social behavior with these other media is appropriate to the medium in question, and extends the social interface in such a way as to augment these other media using social interactions in the same manner that they would be augmented by another person. What are the next steps in the evolution of physical character interfaces? What more can such technologies do? A good way to peer into the future is to examine the limitations of the current design, and to ask what can be added to make the interface characters both more lifelike and better learning partners.

The Social Value of Memory and Change

One limitation of the current design of character interfaces is that they have no memory of their own previous interactions, and their responses to the child are generic in nature. This is not socially appropriate. One of the ways playmates create a feeling of intimacy with one another is through the use of personalized information. Character interfaces would seem much more lifelike and aware of the user, and thus more engaging, if they were able to respond to the user in personalized ways. There are simple and superficial ways to do this, of course. Arthur and D. W., for example, can know the child's birthday and remember when the child wakes up in the morning, using their calendar and clock functions. Another superficial way to create intimacy is through identification. It is possible to enter and save a child's name into the pretend playmate character, for example, so the child can be queried by name during interactions.

A far more subtle and powerful strategy, however, would be to have the character recall not just the child's name or other isolated data, but also recall specific events and activities the child has engaged in with the character. Reminders of such shared experiences can make the pretend playmate seem aware of its own previous experiences and aware of the personal context it shares with the child. The character could spontaneously recall the themes or events from a television program viewed by the child with the character, and ask questions or make comments about them. The shared reference would make the character seem more intelligent. Even more effective would be specific recollections by the character of the child's actions in previous activities. The character might remember a particularly difficult problem the child solved, and say proudly, "Remember that number puzzle you solved yesterday? You are good at that!" Such interactions not only enhance the character's social sophistication, but they also act as important reminders of competence for the child and help build self-esteem.

Another limitation of the current design is the fixed nature of the character's interactions. Human play partners are dynamic. They always bring new and different ideas and activities to their social interactions, and their social play interactions are endlessly variable and spontaneous as a result. Character interfaces would both seem more lifelike and give children richer, more diverse experiences if they could "pick up" new games, phrases, and other content over time. In theory, the character can even track children's usage patterns. This would let the character drop unpopular games and add new ones over time, for example, or even increase the difficulty of problems within games as children demonstrate mastery in their interactions.

A practical question is how such information will be exchanged between the character and the information source. As with the real-time PC and TV interaction of the current characters, a wireless link is clearly superior to any others because it does not impose artificial restrictions on the child's social engagement with the interface character. The social implications of the character storing or sending information go beyond just the concrete question of how the information is physically transferred, however. What does the character do during the information exchange? Current designs, such as Mattel Interactive's My Interactive Pooh, have the character becoming unresponsive and inactive. Such a response is socially inappropriate. If a human peer were to suddenly became inactive and unresponsive, even with a warning, it would be alarming and unnatural. A far better design would be one that let the character continue to interact with the child while exchanging additional information "in the background." Like the wireless connection itself, such a design would make the background data transfer invisible to the user. Such invisibility is key to preserving the character's lifelike pretense, which forms the basis of the pretend playmate interface itself.

9.5 Conclusion

Character interfaces are a form of puppetry. As physical characters who resemble and sound like familiar characters from television, they "stand in" for their television counterparts, evoking the same responses from users that social interaction with the television characters themselves would. The illusion of the interface character's authenticity extends beyond appearances and into the realm of behavior. The character's social interactions with the child must conform to the child's implicit social expectations, not just in terms of the character's personality but in terms of the social rules that govern the social exchanges in any specific social context. Puppeteers, as actors, bring their characters to life in this way, using a form of pretend. They rely on their own social skills, and their ability to mimic different personalities and voices, to cause their puppets to respond and act as if they are the characters they represent. Character interfaces utilize the same pretend strategy to invoke the same sorts of responses from users. The only difference is that they use digital technologies, rather than human actors, to make the interface characters move and speak.

Embodying an interface in a physical character allows users to respond to the interface with the social skills they already possess simply by dint of being human beings. Designing the interface to match these skills, and the expectations they create, makes interaction simple and intuitive for the user. Succeeding with such designs requires balancing the personality of the interface character with the abilities of the target users. As the existing examples demonstrate, this requires careful testing and evaluation—particularly when the users are children, whose competencies and expectations about social interaction are different from those of adults. Using such characters as interfaces makes technology less cold and abstract, and more concrete and emotionally engaging. As technology continues to increase in power and sophistication, the capabilities of social interfaces such as pretend playmate characters will grow as well. While not suitable for all applications, they offer a new and powerful alternative to the standard point-and-click or other impersonal interfaces currently in widespread use. Their simplicity, building on the social skills all users have, makes them a very attractive design for consumer applications, particularly when the users are children or other users who require a human touch in their experience with technology.

9.6 References

Bayley, N. 1969. *Bayley Scales of Infant Development.* San Antonio, TX: Psychological Corporation.

Bayley, N. 1993. *Bayley Scales of Infant Development* (Second edition). San Antonio, TX: Psychological Corporation.

Bloom, L., and M. Lahey. 1978. *Language Development and Language Disorders.* New York: John Wiley and Sons.

Bornstein, M. H. 1989. *Maternal Responsiveness: Characteristics and Consequences.* San Francisco: Jossey-Bass.

Bretherton, I., and M. Beeghly. 1989. Pretence: Acting "as if." In J. J. Lockman and N. L. Hazen (Eds.), *Action in Social Context: Perspectives on Early Development,* New York: Plenum Press, 239–271.

Case, R. 1985. *Intellectual Development: Birth to Adulthood.* New York: Academic Press.

Clark, C. M., and H. Klonoff. 1990. Right and left orientation in children aged 5 to 13 years. *Journal of Clinical and Experimental Neuropsychology* 12(4):459–466.

Clark, H. H., and E. F. Schaefer. 1987. Collaborating on contributions to conversations. *Language and Cognitive Processes* 2(1):19–41.

Coleman, J. 1992. All seriousness aside: The laughing-learning connection. *International Journal of Instructional Media* 19(3):269–276.

Collins, W. A., B. L. Sobol, and S. Westby. 1981. Effects of adult commentary on children's comprehension and inferences about a televised aggressive portrayal. *Child Development* 52:158–163.

Diaz, R. M., and L. E. Berk. (Eds.). 1992. *Private Speech: From Social Interaction to Self-Regulation.* Hillsdale, NJ: Lawrence Erlbaum Associates.

Dozier, M. 1991. Functional measurement assessment of young children's ability to predict future behavior. *Child Development* 62:1091–1099.

Fogg, B. J., and C. Nass. 1997. Silicon sycophants: The effects of computers that flatter. *International Journal of Human-Computer Studies* 46(5):551–561.

Forys, S. K. S., and L. McCune-Nicolich. 1984. Shared pretend: Sociodramatic play at 3 years of age. In I. Bretherton (Ed.), *Symbolic Play: The Development of Social Understanding,* New York: Academic Press, 159–191.

Frohlich, D. 1997. Direct manipulation and other lessons. In M. Helander, T. Landauer, and P. Prabhu (Eds.), *Handbook of Human-Computer Interaction,* New York: North Holland, 463–488.

Frye, D., and C. Moore. (Eds.). 1991. *Children's Theories of Mind: Mental States and Social Understanding.* Hillsdale, NJ: Lawrence Erlbaum Associates.

Furman, L. N., and T. A. Walden. 1990. Effect of script knowledge on preschool children's communicative interactions. *Developmental Psychology* 26(2):227–233.

Garner, P. W., D. C. Jones, and D. J. Palmer. 1994. Social cognitive correlates of preschool children's sibling caregiving behavior. *Developmental Psychology* 30:905–911.

Grosz, B. J., and C. L. Sidner. 1986. Attention, intentions, and the structure of discourse. *Computational Linguistics* 12(3):175–204.

Grover, S. 1986. A field study in the use of cognitive-developmental principles in microcomputer design for young children. *Journal of Educational Research* 79:325–332.

Haefner, M. J., and E. A. Wartella. 1987. Effects of sibling coviewing on children's interpretations of television programs. *Journal of Broadcasting and Electronic Media* 31(2):153–68.

Herron, R. E., and B. Sutton-Smith. (Eds.) 1971. *Child's Play.* Malabar, FL: Robert E. Kreiger Publishing Company.

Huston, A. C., E. Donnerstein, H. Fairchild, P. A. Katz, J. P. Murray, E. A. Rubinstein, B. L. Wilcox, and D. M. Zuckerman. 1992. *Big World, Small Screen: The Role of Television in American Society.* Lincoln, NE: University of Nebraska Press.

Jennings, K., and R. Connors. 1992. Mothers' interactional style and children's competence at 3 years. *International Journal of Behavioral Development* 12:155–175.

Johnson, D. W., and R. Johnson. 1975. *Learning Together and Alone: Cooperation, Competition, and Individualization.* Englewood Cliffs, NJ: Prentice-Hall.

Kellman, P. J., and M. E. Arterberry. 1998. *The Cradle of Knowledge: Development of Perception in Infancy.* Cambridge: MA: MIT Press.

Maes, P. 1997. Intelligent software. In J. Moore, E. Edmonds, and A. Puerta (Eds.), *Proceedings of IUI'97: International Conference on Intelligent User Interfaces,* New York: ACM Press, 41–43.

McCarthy, D. 1972. *Manual for the McCarthy Scales of Children's Abilities.* San Antonio, TX: The Psychological Corporation.

McGhee, P. 1988. The contribution of humor to children's social development. *Journal of Children in Contemporary Society* 20(1–2):119–134.

Mevarech, Z. R., O. Silber, and D. Fein. 1991. Learning with computers in small groups: Cognitive and affective outcomes. *Journal of Educational Computing Research* 7:233–243.

Morkes, J., H. K. Kernal, and C. Nass. 1998. Humor in task-oriented computer-mediated communication and human-computer interaction. In *CHI'98 Summary,* New York: ACM Press, 215–216.

Muir, D. W., and J. Nadel. 1998. Infant social perception. (1998) In A. Slater (Ed.), *Perceptual Development: Visual, Auditory, and Speech Perception in Infancy,* London: Psychology Press (Taylor and Francis), 247–285.

Nass, C., J. Steuer, and E. R. Tauber. 1994. Computers are social actors. In *Proceedings of ACM CHI'94 Conference on Human Factors in Computing Systems,* New York: ACM Press, 72–77.

Nastasi, B. K., and D. H. Clements. 1992. Social-cognitive behaviors and higher-order thinking in educational computing environments. *Learning and Instruction* 2:215–238.

Reeves, B., and C. Nass. 1996. *The Media Equation: How People Treat Computers, Television, and New Media like Real People and Places.* Stanford, CA: CSLI Publications, Cambridge University Press.

Resnick, P., and R. A. Virzi. 1995. Relief from the audio interface blues: expanding the spectrum of menu, list, and form styles. *ACM Transactions on Computer-Human Interaction* 2(2):145–176.

Sidner, C. 1997. Creating interfaces founded on principles of discourse communication and collaboration. In *More than Screen Deep: Toward Every-Citizen Interfaces to the Nation's Information Infrastructure,* National Research Council, Washington, DC: National Academy Press, 315–321.

Slavin, R. E. 1980. Cooperative learning. *Review of Educational Research* 60:315–342.

Strommen, E. F. 1991. "What did he say?": Speech output in preschool software. In *Proceedings of NECC'91,* Eugene, OR: International Society for Technology in Education, 149–151.

Strommen, E. F. 1998. When the interface is a talking dinosaur: Learning across media with ActiMates Barney. In *Proceedings of ACM CHI'98,* New York: ACM Press, 288–295.

Strommen, E. F. 1999, in press. Emotional interfaces for interactive aardvarks: Designing affect into social interfaces for children. Forthcoming in *Proceedings of ACM CHI'99,* New York: ACM Press.

Terveen, L. G. 1995. An overview of human-computer collaboration. *Knowledge-Based Systems* 8(2-3, April-June):67–81.

Thorisson, K. R. 1994. Face to face communication with computer agents. In *AAAI Spring Symposium on Believable Agents,* Palo Alto, CA: Stanford University, 86–90.

Tudge, J. R. H., P. A. Winterhoff, and D. M. Hogan. 1996. The cognitive consequences of collaborative problem solving with and without feedback. *Child Development* 67:2892–2909.

Vygotsky, L. S. 1978. *Mind in Society: The Development of Higher Psychological Processes.* Cambridge, MA: Harvard University Press.

CHAPTER Ten

Lessons from Game Design

CHUCK CLANTON

Aratar, Inc.

10.1 Introduction

The clock hands have slowed to a crawl. Dinner feels like an eternity. The conversation sounds to me like it is echoing through a long pipe. The food is fine, the conversation is not uninteresting, but I am struggling to avoid running back to the TV. No, I am not missing my favorite network TV program. I cannot wait to return to a game on my Sony Playstation where my character has just been captured by terrorists. The terrorists are holding a U.S. nuclear facility in Alaska and are blackmailing the U.S. government. Earlier, they captured my partner and are threatening to kill her. I have been trying to break out of the cell where they are holding me between torture sessions. I have not yet discovered how to escape, but ideas are bouncing around in my head and I can hardly wait to try them.

This is the best combination of cinematic narrative and interactive game play that I have ever experienced, and I am severely entranced. A few million other people are also shelling out their entertainment budget for the month for this game. The market has spoken, and this is a must-have game because it provides an exciting and unique experience. What makes a game great? What magic potion hides within that piece of plastic that causes many millions of people to spend $50 of their discretionary money and 50 hours of their lives with software designed to be difficult to master? It does not make your business more productive. It does not organize your personal information. It does nothing of enduring value. Why? Good question. The answer is game play.

A lot of factors contribute to a great game: a smooth challenge ramp, a well-crafted user interface, fun game mechanics, a compelling fantasy, great production values, but the most important is the game play—what the player is trying to accomplish with the game. Of course, the same is true for an office productivity application or the violin. Ultimately, a problem with the challenge ramp or the user interface or less than terrific production values all matter less than the game play. One of my favorite games illustrates this point. *Resident Evil* is a great game. I played it the first time after work. In this game, you are part of a team that is investigating a house in the country filled with monsters and clues about why they are there. You must shoot well to survive long enough to solve the puzzles leading to the secret of the house. When I came up for air, it was midnight, and I was shaking. The office was dark, my adrenaline level was through the roof, I had cleared a room of zombies, and I did not want to explore any further for fear of what I might find. What a great game! It took a few days before I was ready to continue the

All game titles in this chapter may be trademarks or registered trademarks. For a list of the games' publishers and/or developers, see page 334.

game. *Resident Evil* has also been purchased by millions of people. Although it has a serious user interface flaw, a laughable introductory cinematic, and some of the worst dialog and voice acting I have ever survived, it is a fun game that is a best seller.

Here, I first describe what is so special about game design, then deconstruct some of the elements of games, and finally review specific games for principles of what makes a great game.

10.2 About Game Design

The game industry has a substantial design community with a great deal of knowledge and folklore. Is their knowledge of interest to the wider software design community? Think about games for a moment. A great game for a console sells several million units. Once mastered, it is discarded. The experience of mastering the game is its sole value. Why? Because games are fun to play. A great game hooks the player in the first 10 minutes of play into accepting an interesting challenge, keeps luring the player into learning more and more skills to achieve greater accomplishments, and creates a well-paced experience of defeats and victories that is the substance of a satisfying experience. These flavors are useful for any designed experience. Many will tell you why it cannot be added to their design area. A few just add them anyway. What you do not understand as a designer, you cannot use in your craft.

Two Isolated Design Communities

Few software application designers attend game design conferences, and few game designers know much about the human-computer interface (HCI) design community. Almost every game I play has one or more flaws that HCI designers know how to remedy. Yet, I suspect that few HCI designers could design a great game. Likewise, few software applications show any awareness of techniques of game design that could make them easier and more fun to learn and use. These two design communities have complementary skills but rarely mingle and have little awareness of one another.

For example, game designers know that frustration is not an enemy but a friend to be carefully sought and pampered and massaged into shape. There can be no sense of accomplishment without it. The pleasure of mastery only occurs by overcoming obstacles whose level of frustration has been carefully paced and tuned to not be excessive or annoying yet be sufficient to give a sense of accomplishment. Nothing is more boring than being told something in exquisite detail, and nothing is more interesting than solving a problem that is not too easy or too hard. This is true whether it is discovering how to accomplish a complex task with an office automation application or sneaking past watchful guards in a nuclear power plant held by terrorists (in a game!).

The HCI design community has gathered empirical evidence for the value of user testing and iterative design, yet these techniques often still meet with resistance in serious software companies. Ironically, play-testing of games (as distinct from quality assurance testing) is a well-accepted technique during game development, and most game designers expect the fun of a game to improve as the design evolves during development. It is play-testing not HCI expertise that eliminates the most crippling user interface mistakes from games, though it is not unusual for a game to emerge from development unplayable by anyone other than hard-core gamers when, as often happens, it is play-tested only on them.

Game Platforms

Retailers sell games for general-purpose PCs and for specialized computer systems for games called *game consoles*, like the Sony Playstation, the Nintendo 64, or Sega's Dreamcast. Stores also sell games for small handheld devices like the Nintendo Gameboy. At this writing in 1999, a good game for the PC sells a few hundred thousand copies, and a great game sells up to a few million copies. Console games can expect to sell about twice as many copies. However, the type of game and the audience differ for the PC and consoles.

The home PC is often used by the gamer's parents. Mom and dad are unlikely to allow games to be installed once one of them has caused an operational problem. Once a child's game stops the parent's home office computer from working, it is easy to imagine the appeal of console games. Console games do not need to be "installed"—just plug them in and start playing. Because a console is dedicated to one game at a time, games cannot interfere with one another nor with any software that parents care about. Its sole purpose is playing games, and games cannot alter any of its operating system software. So, younger gamers often have a console, and their parents may play on the PC. Computer owners may forego the added cost of a console, but their game preferences may affect that decision.

PC games are controlled with a mouse and keyboard and sometimes a joystick or even more rarely a steering wheel. In some, the entire keyboard may be used, with concomitant difficulty of learning. (Admittedly, this richness of user interface is usually only seen in "gear-head sims," highly detailed simulations that may use a joystick and every key on the keyboard. An example would be a flying game that comes with a user manual copied from the plane's original manual, along with a card mapping the controls of the plane to the keyboard and joystick. These games appeal to a highly enthusiastic niche audience.) A mouse does not work on the carpeted family room floor, so console games have a control pad, relatively simple two-handed devices with a limited number of buttons in a relatively distinct layout. Control pads are easily held and used, but do not have any pointing device as natural as the mouse, so, for example, console games almost never have a cursor. As a consequence, complicated games, such as complex strategy games, are played primarily on PCs. More mass-market games for less hard-core gamers are better suited to a console.

The PC can be upgraded with new and more hardware, like memory, and better display adapters, such as powerful 3D accelerators. Consoles cannot be significantly upgraded. Because consoles have a single dedicated purpose, when a new one is introduced, it is likely to be far more powerful for games than existing PCs. However, by the end of the console's life, evolving PC technology has surpassed it. So games whose appeal is performance and graphic quality appear on consoles when they are new but are released on PCs as the console platforms age.

Consoles have the reputation as the platform of choice for action gamers, while more cerebral games for an older audience appear on the PC. One of the most successful interactive movie games, *The Beast Within: A Gabriel Knight Mystery,* was created for the PC, and it has a deep story with a subtle and quite thoughtful theme. On the other hand, "twitch" action games demand very quick reactions of both the human and the game engine. At the time of the writing of this chapter, hot 3D display adapters have pushed PC technology beyond the aging Playstation and N64. So the hottest action games like *Quake* and *Half-Life* are played on the PC. This may have changed by the time you are reading this with a new generation of consoles expected soon.

The Audience

The total audience for games is quite broad because of the deep penetration of computers and consoles into our society and the enduring appeal of computer games. Computer games have been created and played since the early days of computers. For those raised with computers, computers fill many needs for community, for information, and for fun. As the population ages, the role of the computer as a source of entertainment is likely to increase as more of the population have been using computers most of their lives.

Though the audience for computer entertainment is very broad, it is highly segmented. The audience for a game is always a limited segment of the total audience. Boys are the primary audience for most games. Though the Barbie franchise has spawned a series of games that are arguably the first computer entertainment blockbusters for girls, whether this anticipates many more games for the "other half" of the market is not yet clear. Just like the application designer, the game designer needs to have a very clear vision of the audience for the game. The sense in which the designer represents the player is much deeper in games than in application software because making something fun is much more intractable to analysis than making something productive. So the designer must have a very clear and appealing fantasy of the game, and the designer's sense of fun must match that of the audience. Of course, focus group evaluation of game concepts, play-testing of prototypes, and other user-oriented design methods help, but what makes a game fun cannot be synthesized from them. I once asked Frank Thomas and Ollie Johnson, the Disney animators, how they did such a great job of making films for kids. They replied, "We did not make them for kids. We made them for ourselves."

All but megahit games depend on game magazine and webzine reviews to reach their market. Game magazine reviewers are hard-core gamers, and it is part of the attitude of the gamer culture to ridicule games that are easy. So, marketing a game to light gamers is tricky, though sometimes spectacularly successful. *Myst* is the classic example of a game that was not well reviewed and took a long time for word of mouth to make it popular. It is one of the largest selling games of all time. Because of much greater competition in stores, today no game stays on the shelves long enough to duplicate that kind of marketing ramp over time. *Deerhunter* has been a huge hit because it appeals to an easily targeted audience of hunters, is easily learned, and captures some of the fun of the hunting experience. The embarrassment of *Deerhunter*'s success is that it is so poorly made. *Deerhunter 2* is much better and illustrates a common pattern: a flawed but successful game secures money for the developers to do in the sequel what they had wanted to do in the original game.

Computer Games

Few personal computer users have missed the experience of a hand of solitaire on their computer. The number of computer users who have played a game they purchased at retail is much smaller, and many of these replicate various board games, crossword puzzles, sports simulations, and other recreations that are not native to interactive computing. In the rest of this chapter, I only discuss interactive games unique to the computer.

1 O.3 Elements of Games

Just as novels are divided into paragraphs and films are divided into scenes, games are divided into levels expressing a single coherent challenge to the player. During the game, the player progresses through the levels in an order that may be predetermined or may depend on the player's action. The player's choices, within and sometimes between levels, constitute the game experience.

Challenge Ramp and Level Design

The first 10 minutes or so of game play, like the first 10 minutes of a film, should hook the player. The first hour should convince the player to buy the game. To keep a player committed to playing the game, levels need variety and pacing. After the player is well into the game, some levels should be quite challenging. Those levels are often best followed by a quick easy level as a reward. Then levels should increase in difficulty to the next peak. Levels should also vary in the type of challenge. Through the course of the entire game, the player should have a sense of direction and progress toward some final goal. Ideally, each level feels like a definite step in the direction of that goal.

The designer of a game insures that the game mechanics are fun and that the game play creates a sense of purpose and pacing throughout the game. The levels of a game present a sequence of encounters or problems that occur within the context of the game design. Each level exists within a structure and a progression that is dictated by the game design. Levels are created by level designers, who focus on the presentation of fun situations within the game and how they contribute to the arc of the game. The game designer defines how the game world works and the nature and progression of the player's objectives. The level designer creates the details of each episode in the game within the structure set by the game designer.

Level design is a speciality. Its practitioners are responsible for insuring that the player is introduced to the complexity of the game in measured steps and that the game remains engaging from beginning to end. The progression of player skill and game challenge through the game is called the "challenge ramp" and it must be carefully crafted. If either outpaces the other, the game becomes either frustrating or boring.

Level designers work under the direction of the game designer and respond to play-test feedback. Their skill determines how players perceive the game. Few serious software projects have as much specialized attention placed on the challenge ramp, but in games a very large proportion of the entire design effort is focused here because it is vital for insuring that the player enjoys the entire arc of the game.

Stories versus Histories

Games can be divided into those that recount a story and those where the interaction of player and game composes a history—the history of the player's experience of the game.[1] Designing these two types of games is a very different endeavor.

Most games are like football. They provide an environment, a set of game mechanics, and game objectives. They are designed (authored) to engross the player in a make-believe world. Imagine playing *Age of Empires*. You choose to control the Assyrian civilization because of their powerful cavalry. Your opponent chooses Egyptians, with their seafaring capabilities. You build your empire, feverishly preparing for war. You attack, testing your preparation and skills, and then comes victory . . . or defeat. The game is a history of your tragic setbacks and great triumphs. What the designer authored was this game environment for a fantasy of controlling great empires, the nature of winning and the means for achieving it, and the mechanics for controlling the game. Games like this are "open." There is no mandated path to victory. The premise of the game, like the premise of a story, should convey the environment and the core of the fantasy with economy of words. On the box of *Age of Empires*, "An Epic Game of Empire-Building and Conquest," the game is described this way: "How will you rule the world? Conquer enemy civilizations? Discover the world's secrets? Accumulate wealth?"[2]

Story games are fundamentally different. In a story game, the player must solve game problems to get more of the story. In some games, these problems are puzzles that relate only vaguely to the underlying story. In other games, these problems are tightly integrated into the story as obstacles in the plot. At best, this is a compelling journey of discovery of a deeper, more compelling story than the player could experience in a history. At worst, the player feels trapped, always trying to figure out the solution mandated by the designer. In the adventure game *Phantasmagoria*, the player controls a woman married to a photographer. The couple has just moved into a huge old house in the country. Of course, it is haunted by an ancient demon. As the player explores and solves problems (how to find hidden passages and open locked rooms), the story is told in short "cut scenes," noninteractive in-

---

1. I first heard this distinction in a talk by Hal Barwood at the Computer Game Developers Conference in 1994 or so.

2. *Age of Empires,* © 1997 Microsoft Corporation, from the back of the box.

game movies of conversations and events. Great storytellers have always taught and amazed us with plots and insights we could never have invented. These games share that potential with films, plays, and books. Because game media is expensive to produce, player choices must be quickly pruned. Players recognize and dislike inconsequential choices, where either decision leads to the same result. So, wrong choices often cause the protagonist to get killed and the game to resume prior to the choice. This "game tree of death" makes story games into closed experiences.

In the mid-1990s, Hollywood attempted to enter the game business. After losing a lot of money, the great film storytellers retreated. All games, even those with a rich and deep story, are very different from linear media. Game play and story can be mixed, but not without a deep understanding that the fun of games comes from the player's participation.

Even as Hollywood has retreated, some games have become more cinematic. Why are films so close in structure to games? Plays are mostly about dialog, what the actors say to each other, and the revelation expressed by those words. Novels are mostly about the interior landscape of the characters and how that shapes what they do. Films are mostly about actions. Because games focus on action, film is the closest linear narrative form to games, much more similar than either plays or novels. In fact, whether a game contains a story or not, much of the craft of filmmaking applies to computer games as well.

Game Design Dissected

The player interacts with a game at the following levels:

- *Game interface:* the details of how the controller or keyboard map to functions, and the output displays on the screen that provide game information

- *Game mechanics:* the "physics" of the world of the game; for example, the simulated and simplified flight mechanics of a fighter pilot game

- *Game play:* the mission of the player in terms of goals and subgoals, including both official scoring and secondary rewards (e.g., more backstory about the hero, a secret room with a view)

Game Interface

Contrary to the common wisdom of the HCI design community, game user interfaces are designed with little standardization. This results in a fascinating diversity of innovation far beyond that of application software. Look at games if you want to see a large number of user interface ideas, elegant and hideous.

This does not mean that game players enjoy learning user interfaces. Game designers motivate their users to learn a new interface by matching the interface to the task as closely as possible. A game may even have a unique user interface for just one obstacle that the player must overcome. Game designers know that those accustomed to computers often prefer learning an appropriate user interface—if it is anticipated, well presented, and significantly better—rather than struggling with an awkward control method. Mastering a new game mechanic or "physics" of the game world is much harder—one reason why new game genres are difficult to introduce.

The game interface itself is fun in some games. In fighting games (e.g., *Soul Blade*), the player controls a protagonist in a fight that resembles a boxing match, or perhaps more aptly the theatrics of U.S. "professional" wrestling, though the style usually resembles some form of martial arts. In some fighting games just hitting the buttons on the controller rapidly without stopping will assure a visually exciting fight and frequent victories at the beginning. With experience, the player begins to learn the meaning of the controls, simple blocks, attacks, dodges, and ducks are on single keys. Both simultaneous and sequential key combinations result in more complicated and daring moves that are dramatic and effective when used well. The same key combination does not cause the same action twice in a row but a selection from a repertoire of related actions depending on the context, the situation, and the opponent's position and actions. The player's intentionality is preserved, so players can exercise increasing mastery of timing and moves while continuing to enjoy the visual feast of rare moves and unexpected combinations. The user interface in fighting games shares the physical pleasure of a sport.

The user interfaces of other game genres contribute less to the fun but are still important. Console games are particularly dependent upon the feel of the controls. In some cases, what makes a game better is extremely difficult to articulate because it has to do with the shape of the sensitivity curves for a specific control. A game idea may depend entirely upon the designer's fantasy of what the controller for the game would feel like.

Game Mechanics

The mechanics of a game consist of the nature of the game environment and how the player can interact with it. Running, flying, driving, shooting, picking up keys, and adding ingredients to soup are all examples of possible mechanics. Mastering the game mechanics, the physics of the simulated world of the game, can be a great source of pleasure. Learning to race a motorcycle in *Road Rash* is great fun even before managing to win a race. Game mechanics are often what make a game special. The game *Populous* was invented when its designer Peter Molyneux saw a game mechanic devised by the programmer, Glenn Corpes, having to do with raising and lowering land.[3] In this "god game," the player has no direct control over the people, but must shape their destinies by reshaping the land and casting spells upon its people. This is one of the greatest games of all time because of this incredibly fun game mechanic.

Game Play

Successful games present a clear mission early so that the player understands what they are trying to achieve. Game play is structured by the player's goals and consists of the tactics and strategies to achieve them. The levels in a game should provide a progression of challenges and a sense of pacing. In an adventure game, the final puzzle in a level may open a door to new territory to explore and is often a major problem to be solved. In an action game, the final challenge is often a "level boss," the big villain at the end of the level. Often, the game play up to the end of the level anticipates and subtly teaches the player how to approach the final obstacle of the level.

Games often contain fun side quests and activities that add optional game play (riding a horse around in a field in *The Legend of Zelda: Ocarina of Time*) and occasional "Easter eggs," small delightful surprises that are irrelevant but fun in most games.

Conflict and Challenge

Conflict and opposed positions, expressed through antagonistic attitudes, is the strongest tool for hooking interest in games and most narrative media. Even if the game play is cooperative, the players are working to overcome some challenge that brings them into conflict with some other force or person.

A game needs great villains more than it needs a great hero. Consider the classic Disney films. The villains are always far more interesting visually and dramatically than the protagonists. The hero and heroine are measured by the scale of the villain they defeat. So, it is important to have a great villain to define the measure of the victory.

This is a variant on the realization that the satisfaction of solving a problem is proportional to its difficulty and the amount of frustration that was tolerated prior to solving it. Overcoming a hard problem or a bad villain is very satisfying.

3. Glenn Corpes, personal communication, 1998.

Point of View

In the early game *Rogue*, the player looks down on the game world represented as letters, moving his character (the "X") to escape the vampire ("V"). The player has a third-person perspective on the game. By contrast, on starting the early text adventure *Zork*, the player sees "Welcome to Zork. West of House. You are in an open field west of a big white house with a boarded front door. There is a small mailbox there." If the player then types "Go north," the game responds, "You are facing the north side of a white house. There is no door here, and all the windows are barred." This is a first-person game. In a third-person game, the player portrays and identifies with a character on the screen who may have a quite independent identity, like a medieval thief or an alien who has landed on earth. In a first-person game, the player has no visual proxy, and may or may not have an identified role. In the first-person game *Half-Life*, the player is given the role of a new employee at a research facility. In another first-person game, *Myst*, the player continues in the role of just being who they are. Although first-person games tend to have the impact of greater immediacy, seeing the emotions of the character the player has identified with on screen can create a wider range of emotions. Emotions of fear, excitement, and triumph are evoked in first-person games. The poignancy of leaving behind one's girlfriend for a great adventure in the big world, early in *The Legend of Zelda, the Ocarina of Time* can only be expressed in a third-person game where you identify with a character showing those feelings.

Fun

Above all else, a game must be fun. This is a dimension lacking in most software applications and is not a property solely of the user interface, game mechanics, or game play. Fun comes from both the fantasy of the game and the way these three combine to shape the player's experience of the game. The fantasy itself must be compelling to the audience. However, to make a great game from a great fantasy requires a deep intuitive knowledge of what is fun.

Games are carefully crafted to take advantage of the pleasure of figuring things out, of acquiring mastery. Stated in the most provocative way possible, frustration is necessary to achievement. Game designers are sensitive to the vitality of difficult choices, uncertainty, and challenge because these are the wellspring of our sense of achievement, mastery, and triumph. Too easy is as wearisome as too hard. Great games do not focus on the beginner or on the expert but on the path from one to the other and how to create challenges without exceeding the player's threshold for tolerable frustration, how to reward success while engaging the player in the next challenge.

The whole of a game is much more than the sum of its parts. A game may have obvious flaws in its interface or game mechanics, or some problems in the game play, but all is forgiven if it is fun.

A Taxonomy of Gaming

Computer games were once easily categorized into genres. Action games were hand-eye coordination and constant decision making about where to jump or who to shoot. Adventure games had puzzles to solve to travel through a world on your quest, meeting and talking to a variety of characters. Strategy games were dedicated to the logistics and strategy of war. Driving games were races. Fighting games required well-timed moves to defeat your opponent. In role-playing games, the player chose to be a knight or a sorcerer, more strength or more wisdom, and explored a world filled with dungeons and dragons. The deep structure was even simpler. Motor skills and reaction time dominated action, fighting, and racing games. Problem solving dominated adventure and strategy games, the former tactical and immediate, the latter strategic and long term.

Games have become more complicated. One of the largest action subgenres, the shooter, marched forward with technology to first-person navigation in a 3D world, beginning with *Wolfenstein 3D* and continuing through *Doom* and *Quake*. At the time of this writing, *Half-Life* has become a major hit by adding a story to the first-person shooter subgenre.

Since *Dune II*, the strategy genre has been dominated by real-time strategy games as exemplified by the recent series of hit games starting with *Command and Conquer. Populous* added "god sims," where the player controls the environment rather than the characters; that is also seen in *SimCity*, *Theme Park,* and other simulation games whose deep structure of game play remains strategy but with very different player control.

In the last few years, *Resident Evil, Tomb Raider, Metal Gear: Solid,* and *The Legend of Zelda: Ocarina of Time* have sold millions of copies each. These games have the game interface and mechanics of an action game, yet game play that resembles an adventure game. Sid Meier's *Pirates* adds role-playing and strategy to the action-adventure mix. *Diablo* combines role-playing and action. *Phantasmagoria* is an adventure game with a powerful action game ending. *Dune II* mixes action and strategy. These crossover games have a deep structure that combines more types of challenges for the player.

Acknowledging that many games require multiple skills, let's consider game genres based on the skills.

Games of Reasoning

Some computer games such as *7th Guest* have classic puzzles in the context of an adventure game. The player explores the house of a dead man. The puzzles have no relationship to the rest of the game, so the environment feels like decoration for the game play.

Graphic adventure games are the best example of games where the principal dynamic is problem solving integrated into the game world. In an adventure game, the player wanders around in an environment looking for items to pick up (e.g., a steak) and locked "doors" (e.g., a hungry dog guarding the entrance to a cave). Give the steak to the dog and then walk past it while it is eating to enter a new and unexplored portion of the world. Adventure games depend on the human desire to explore. When graphics were added to the old text adventure games, they became "graphic adventures." Solving puzzles may open locked doors to more of the world and reveal more story.

Because adventure games are about reasoning the solution to a problem, there is rarely any time pressure. Players often report arriving at a solution (Eureka!) while away from the game.

Because adventure games focus on reasoning, the user interface is typically designed to allow the player to signal intention as easily as possible. In an action game the player controls the direction and speed of his proxy, but in an adventure game the player need only click on the intended destination for his proxy to go there.

Challenges for the player in adventure games are either key-lock or combination-lock problems. Key-lock problems are easier to design. The player must find, pick up, and place a key into "inventory." Then, that key must be used on the lock where it fits. The key can be any item—a tomato to bribe a wizard to open a refrigerator. Adventure games usually have an inventory window that contains icons for the items picked up from the game world. To use an item, the player summons the inventory window, drags the icon of the object onto the window of the game world, then drops it on the target. Then the proxy character takes an action that makes sense given the nature of the key and the target.

The combination in a combination-lock problem is knowledge. Experienced adventure game players become quite sensitive to possible combination locks. If a young girl is playing hopscotch, write down the numbers she lands on. There are seven numbers? Look for a phone to dial.

In these kinds of puzzles, it makes a difference in feel whether the solution or the lock is found first. If the solution has been found, then it can be tried on likely locks as the player explores the world. When a lock is found, the player can try the solution out immediately, creating little suspense. On the other hand, if the lock is found first and then the solution is found, the player must run back to try it out. This delay increases anticipation and the sense of reward if the player is right.

Adventure games are often preferred by older players, often have an involved story in the traditional sense of authored narrative elements, and make few demands on motor skills. The player usually has a mission with subgoals that sounds like the plot points of a story (find the sorcerer's castle, kill the dragon, defeat the sorcerer, and rescue the maiden). *Grim Fandango* is a recent example of a popular adventure game.

Games of Hand-Eye Skill and a Bit of Luck

Action games require that the player learn hand-eye skills to control their proxy's actions. This category includes driving games, flying games, first- and third-person shooters, and other related action games. The player must "drive" their proxy both to move around and to act (e.g., manipulate controls to turn 90 degrees left, move forward across the room, stop, turn 160 degrees around, raise gun to level, fire).

As the player masters these skills, the game usually demands increasingly sophisticated tactics and strategy to win, so action games tend to be quite deep. In some sense, action games subsume adventure games. As the player masters the physical skills of an action game, they must then solve the problem of outwitting enemies with clever tactics and strategies. However, the problems are not solved by thoughtful contemplation as in an adventure game.

In single-player action games, the player competes against nonplayer characters (NPCs). Typically, NPCs are not as intelligent as the player, but they play their tactics without pause so they are faster. It feels like cheating if the NPCs have access to knowledge or abilities that the player does not have. In a game, defeat must always feel fair and, if the player were only a bit more skilled, avoidable. Chance can influence the outcome, but skill must dominate over time.

The game player learns how the NPCs behave to defeat them. After the NPCs are easily defeated, the gamer seeks a better opponent, another human player. Multiplayer action games satisfy this desire and are very popular among hard-core gamers, who form teams to cooperate in battling one another.

Many driving games involve racing, where the simulation of the physics of the car provides much of the enjoyment of the game. The same is true for flight simulations that can focus more on the fantasy of flying or on more realistic flight dynamics. Fantasy driving and flying are often the backdrop for action shooting games as well.

Games of Attention and Strategic Thinking

Strategy games require the player to make choices whose impact is felt over a long period of time. Often, the player chooses what resources to obtain, what units to research and build, where to place men and equipment, when to attack, and how to defend. The player's units act autonomously when unattended so that the player can choose where to intervene and what new orders to give. When battle is joined, the decisions made up to that point determine the strength of the player's forces and make a big difference to the outcome of the game. Strategy games can be turn-based, like board games, or real-time, where decisions are made continuously by all players. Different strategy games vary in how much emphasis they place on building and battling.

Strategy games usually combine menus and direct manipulation control over units and often are quite complicated to learn and play. Designing the challenge ramp for the first hour of play is quite demanding. The designer must also balance different units to have approximately equal costs and benefits, but different advantages. This gives the player a reason to select a variety of units. To simplify the design, enemy units are often identical to player units, though sporting a different color scheme or signage.

Most strategy games today are real-time rather than turn-based, though turn-based games are still popular. Imagine a game of chess where both players can move at any time without regard to the other player. Real-time strategy games require constant attention to everything that is happening while enacting a winning strategy.

Strategy games usually have a single-player mode in a series of levels where the player can learn tactics and strategies by watching how the NPCs play. Multiplayer strategy games either pit cooperative players against NPCs, or competitive players against one another.

Meta-Gaming

Game play can occur outside the make-believe world of the game as well. For example, in action shooters, enemies are often located in a series of rooms connected by corridors. Save your game before entering a room. If you are killed in the room, instantly reload the saved game and try again. You may want to reload even if you survive to leave with more ammo or health. This meta-game play detracts from immersion but is commonly accepted in action games today. Adventure games may also have meta-game play. Inventory puzzles often require that two inventory objects be combined to a more useful form (e.g., picking up a battery in inventory and dropping it on a radio in inventory to make the radio functional).

10.4 Lessons from Games

Now let's talk about specific games and the lessons that they teach. Unless noted otherwise, these are all games applauded by their audience with extremely good sales.

Resident Evil and Resident Evil 2

In *Resident Evil* and *Resident Evil 2 (RE)*, quite similar Sony Playstation action-adventure games, the player portrays a character in an environment reminiscent of the film *Night of the Living Dead*. The player must explore while killing or avoiding zombies and other monsters to uncover the mystery of how and why these menacing creatures came into existence. Figure 10.1 (see also Color Plate) shows the player's proxy trapped between two attacking zombies.

Combining Action and Adventure Successfully

RE combines elements of console action game mechanics with those of an adventure game. The player steers his proxy and shoots enemies, but also endeavors to traverse the world and uncover the story, solving puzzles to unlock doors to more territory. The action is occasionally fast and furious, for example, when poisonous snakes fall from the trees and attack.

Action and puzzle-solving adventure do not always combine gracefully. Players may prefer to choose whether to stress their brains or their adrenal glands in a particular evening by picking which game to play. *RE* fundamentally provides an action experience with periods of menacing calm that keep the tension up.

Puzzle Motifs Enhance Pacing

Adventure games often have game play with very complex puzzles that are not quickly solved. These kinds of puzzles are not well suited to action game play, where the pace is much faster and there is little time to think. In essence, the player's ability to succeed depends upon a combination of time and complexity. With less time, the complexity must be lower to maintain the same likelihood of success. Puzzle motifs are a way of decreasing complexity through a game.

In one puzzle in *RE*, the player comes across a shotgun on a wall rack. If the player takes the shotgun, it triggers events that kill the proxy. To avoid the trap, find a shotgun with a bent barrel that does not work. Take the working shotgun from the rack and immediately replace it with the bent shotgun.

FIGURE **10.1**

In Resident Evil, *the player's proxy must defend himself against zombies, here attacking from both sides.*

This object replacement puzzle recurs in *RE* as a motif. Puzzle motifs serve two functions: they improve pacing, and they create a sense of cohesiveness through setups and payoffs. Once the player recognizes the motif, they solve a puzzle of similar difficulty more quickly, heightening the pace and making the player feel smart. The initial puzzle also provides the setup for which the second puzzle is the satisfying payoff.

How Characters Intensify the Game

Everyone who plays games has spent many hours watching Hollywood films. Everyone is programmed by these films to understand a visual and aural language that engages our empathy with the characters, and through the characters to the story. As a result, third-person games where our character appears on the screen have a powerful emotional tool for sucking the player emotionally into the game. *RE* matches the film *Night of the Living Dead* almost exactly. The characters and story are not very deep, but the horror of the situation strikes a deep enough chord that the audience is deeply affected. The first time I played this game, I ended up sitting in an empty office at midnight, shaking, unwilling to continue the game, listening intently to the little sounds all around, and unhappy about the prospect of walking across the dark parking lot to my car. The character and story had created almost as powerful an emotional impact on me as the film.

The role of character is not confined to enhancing the sense of threat from horrible monsters. In the Playstation action-adventure *Metal Gear: Solid* (*MGS*, discussed below), the player portrays a modern antiterrorist operative, skilled but weary and isolated from life and love. Through the course of the game, he finds kinship with a woman desperately trying to prove herself to her military father. In this game, at a certain point, the player chooses whether to let the enemy kill the woman he loves or not. After finishing the game, the player gets a special enhancement to use in playing through the game again. If the player has chosen not to save the woman, the enhancement is a very cool invisibility suit. If the woman lives (with satisfyingly romantic ending), the enhancement is unlimited ammo which is much less enticing. Despite the much better result for replay, I could not let the woman die. I was much too hooked into the story. So the story not only enriches the emotional impact of the game, it also guides game play.

The high adrenaline state of a terrific first-person action game with a strong story, like *Half-Life*, has a similar intensity but nowhere near the breadth of emotions. Because it is a first-person game, complicated interpersonal emotions like those between the man and the woman in *MGS* are nearly impossible to elicit. Showing the player the emotional response of the proxy character in a third-person game using the language universalized by Hollywood causes the player to feel them.

Sound Tells the Player What to Feel

Sound is a secret weapon for controlling emotions. The score of the original *Star Wars* film creates more of its epic quality than its visuals and acting. To prove this, watch it with the sound turned off. If you listen very carefully, the sound track of a film tells the story, almost always in advance of the visuals, preparing the audience to feel what the story is about to say. In the opening scene of *Star Wars*, the sound track tells the audience that the big warship is an evil bully attacking the good underdog. The sound track underscores the unfairness of the conflict and anticipates the story of a huge evil empire attacking a small band of heroic rebels. The story has been told by the sound design before any characters appear on screen. Oddly enough, without the sound track raising the audience's anxiety by musically stating that the character on the screen is in danger, the sudden appearance of the monster is less frightening, not more. Sound is one modality for anticipation, a general principle that the audience must always be prepared to see what is about to happen or they miss it.

RE has excellent sound design. It telegraphs impending danger. When the attacking dogs crashed through the window unexpectedly, the sound had already raised my anxiety level, so that I jumped out of my seat at the sudden sharp crashing of the glass followed by the growling dogs.[4]

Camera Conveys Affect

RE has a third-person perspective so the player sees his proxy on the screen. In the highly successful *Tomb Raider* games, the camera flies around to keep the heroine Lara Croft on screen at all times and tries to look over her shoulder so the player sees what she sees.

RE takes a different, more cinematic approach. Instead of devotedly following the proxy's every move, each room has one or more positions for the camera. As the proxy moves, the camera switches positions as needed to cover the action. In films, the camera position establishes emotional tone and conveys information, sometimes even contradicting the action of the scene.[5] In *RE*, camera positions are carefully chosen to dramatize the scene.

In the attack-dog episode described above where I jumped out of my chair in fright, the camera was responsible for much of its impact. The player enters a long hall with windows on the right and a blank wall on the left. The camera is positioned near the entry door and points down the hall. After the proxy walks most of the way down the hall away from the camera, the pack of vicious dogs crash through the windows on the right of the hall and attack the proxy. Sudden entry from the right edge of the screen is cinematic language for an attack by a dangerous antagonist. Because the dogs are closer to the camera, they loom large and threaten the more distant proxy, who is smaller, and surrounded visually on the screen. The cinematic staging of the action in front of the camera in *Resident Evil* is unmatched among games. Cinematic staging, camera position, and sound design combine to create a Hollywood-quality game experience.

The camera in *RE* is a mixed blessing. The proxy sometimes gets in a location not well covered by the camera, making it difficult to fight well. This is a common result of a camera controlled by the game. Giving the player con-

---

4. *Phantasmagoria* even has the old horror cliché of a cat screeching unexpectedly while exploring a spooky area. I was playing at home with earphones and let out a startled yelp then had to explain with some embarrassment to someone nearby that nothing was wrong—I just got surprised.

5. In *The Graduate*, just as Mrs. Robinson (Anne Bancroft) is denying her seductive intentions, the camera switches to a shot where Benjamin (Dustin Hoffman) is framed by her leg. The camera says that he is sexually entrapped, and we believe the camera rather than her words.

trol of the camera makes this a game play problem. This can be fun, or the added burden can detract from the overall experience. Even if it is fun, it is likely to change the audience for the game significantly since the game will require more skill to control.

Grabbing the Camera, Drama at a Cost

In *RE,* the game "grabs" the camera at times to heighten the drama. The first time the proxy walks into a room, there is a figure hunched over a body on the floor. We hear a crunching sound and see blood spread from the body. Then, the camera suddenly cuts to a close-up of the hunched figure, and we see our first frightening close-up of a zombie as it slowly turns to look at us. The camera cuts back and we regain control over the game. The camera grab added drama at a time when there was no cost. Grabbing the camera to give the player more information works well if it is done carefully, but it can be a significant nuisance done at a time when the player is active.

In another situation, the player confronts a number of zombies in an enclosed courtyard. The action in the courtyard is covered by two camera positions. As the proxy moves around, the screen switches automatically between the two cameras. The designer has to make a choice about aiming: Is it relative to the screen (press LEFT to face an enemy on the left of the screen) or relative to the character (press LEFT to face an enemy on the proxy's left, which could be screen right)? A change in camera position does not interrupt the player's control actions if it is character relative. It does interrupt if it is screen relative, because the screen positions have all changed. Unfortunately, character-relative controls require the user to calculate all directional commands by looking at both the current orientation of the proxy and the location of the goal, which is difficult and takes more play time to learn well.

The decision to enhance the game with a cinematic camera adds a significant flaw to the usability of the game mechanics. *RE* sold very well, but many complain about the difficulty of mastering the controls.

Myst

One of the largest selling retail games of all time, *Myst* is a first-person adventure game introduced on the Macintosh. For an adventure game, *Myst* has a very simple user interface because it has no inventory.[6] The images and sound design in *Myst* are exquisite (Figure 10.2; see also Color Plate). The

---

6. This statement is not strictly true. It has a single inventory item that is "held" in the cursor and can be accidentally dropped rather easily. This is a source of confusion for many players.

FIGURE **10.2**

The art direction in Myst *is exquisite for a game.*

visual and auditory production values certainly contributed to its success. The player does not die in *Myst* and is not subjected to any time pressure. Adults, younger game players, and women buy and play it. The puzzles are mechanically plausible and interesting.

An Intriguing On-Ramp

Myst begins with an intriguing cinematic introduction about a person and a book of unexplained significance. Then, the player lands on an island, uncertain what to do. Because the user interface is simple, the player is soon exploring the island and discovers clues to a dangerous intrigue between a father and his sons. One son appears to be trapped in a red book and asks you to bring back red pages. The other is in a blue book and asks for blue pages. Both accuse the other of deceit and warn of the danger of helping their sibling.

So, in initial game play, the player masters navigation and the user interface quickly but without any pressure. The art direction is superb, so it is fun to explore, and that exploration leads to a mission with a story question at its heart: which brother to help.

Leaving and Returning as Pacing

To fulfill the quest in *Myst*, the player solves a series of puzzles to travel from the island to another world, explores that world, finds the living quarters for each of the brothers, takes a red or blue page from one of them, and solves a series of puzzles to return. This pattern is repeated for four different worlds. This classic story template of departure and return (for example, the labors of Hercules) creates a rhythmic pacing, going out into the unknown and then returning to the increasingly familiar. Puzzles on each world have a motif that unify each world's game play and improve the pacing on that world.

Simple UI for the Mass Market

Myst's user interface is extremely simple and easy to learn. The cursor changes shape when over an active area on the screen to anticipate the results of clicking. Over a door, the cursor turns into an arrow pointing through the door. On the left and right sides of the screen, it turns into a left or right arrow to indicate a turn of the camera. These movements are accomplished in cinematic "cuts," almost instantaneous changes in the camera view to the new location. Typically, four images comprise a complete turn around in one place. When the cursor is over something that can be manipulated, a lever, button, or object to be picked up, the cursor changes to indicate the action.

Console games tend to have simple user interfaces because they have a more mass-market audience than most PC games. In *Quake*, the player can control the direction of the camera with the mouse and the direction of movement with the cursor keys. If this is not too sensitive, it can be quite intuitive and is used by *Deerhunter 2*, definitely a mass-market game. However, experienced *Quake* players turn the sensitivity way up. MGS and many console action and action adventures use a high-angle camera looking down on the scene so the player does not need to control the camera.

The Structure of a Quest

The quest in *Myst* is clear: free one of the brothers. The choice is uncertain and becomes more so as the living quarters of the brothers on different worlds evidence the disreputable life of both. The choice is uncertain, but the quest itself is not. This is important. The player's quest is the spine of the game. It must be clear to prevent the player from feeling lost and confused about the nature of the game. The solution is the problem of the game.

Film Craft and Production Values

Myst was carefully designed to fit comfortably within the capabilities of computers of the time. Its story justifies small windows of poor-quality video of the main characters. *Myst* substitutes sound for movement. The image of the ocean is static, but the sound of waves makes it almost appear to move. The player hears doors close after passing through them. This sound replaces an animation. The forest comes alive because of the sound.

Some scenes have a bit of movement, a bird in the sky or a butterfly fluttering across the path. Movement helps keep an image from flattening, "posterizing." With the spread of more powerful computers, the sequel *Riven* puts motion into almost every shot to make the environment feel more alive.

Cuts to Eliminate Traversal of Space

Myst is a first-person game. The player can look left or right, in a full circle of four views. The camera cuts instantly between the views so that each can be carefully framed. Forward motion is also done with cuts, which works well. One of the problems of many first-person games is that they have refused to cut the bonds of time and space. The proxy always walks, runs, or drives at game-world speeds. Movement between two locations takes as long as it takes to cover all the territory in between. Films were freed from this terrible restriction a long time ago, when the cut was invented. Films cut ahead to eliminate tedious traversal of space and time. Walking across some of the worlds in *Myst* requires quite a few clicks—not much fun—though many action games with their gruesomely continuous first-person perspective are far worse.

Violation of Consistency

Almost everywhere, *Myst* represents the player's view of the world by turning around through four images. However, in a few places, only two or three images are used. This confuses players because it violates the uniform mechanics established earlier in the game. In *Riven*, the sequel to *Myst*, the number of images when looking around varies all the time. The result is that players are not confused because there is no violation of their expectations. Uniformity is less important than maintaining consistency with the user's expectations.

Puzzles Distributed across Time and Space

Myst attracts light game players, yet its puzzles tend to be quite hard for many of them. The elements needed to solve the puzzle are widely distributed across the locations within the game. If all the elements were nearby, these puzzles would be much easier to solve. This is not the most fun way to make puzzles hard.

Populous, the Beginning

Populous, the Beginning (*PopTB*) is a real-time strategy game where your proxy is a Shaman, and the player controls her and her tribe.[7] The game consists of many levels. In each level, the player's goal is to build a village, train warriors and preachers and spies (your units), win spells, then defeat one or more enemies in battle using units and spells.

Progression and Level Design

In some games, levels are problems or challenges that are buried seamlessly within the flow of the game, like the obstacles in a story. In *PopTB*, levels are completely distinct, separated by a meta-game screen that allows the player to choose to go on to the next level or replay a prior level.

Players need a sense of progression through a game. This feeling is conveyed not only by having greater skills and more challenging obstacles, but also by having more and better "tools" for playing (better weapons, more vehicles, greater strength). *PopTB* creates a sense of progression as the player acquires more spells and more types of buildings and units. In each level, the enemy has something the player does not, and the player acquires it by defeating the enemy. Unfortunately, the sense of progression in this game is blunted by the repetitive structure of the levels that do not build on each other.

Design the Game, Then Design How It Is Learned

Most gamers do not play the tutorial unless they are confused, so the tutorial signals an unhappy first game experience. Our goal in *PopTB* was that the first level could be successfully completed in 15 minutes, and the first three levels in an hour—all without playing the tutorial. We also wanted to make it easy for the player to win all of the first three levels, so that the first experience of the game would be positive.

The design team decided explicitly what lessons should be taught by each of the first five levels to best introduce the game. For example, the first level was intended to teach basic building and training, acquiring new powers, using a few simple spells, and defeating an enemy. The second and third

---

7. I was involved in the design of this game.

levels extended the player's knowledge about the units, how they are trained, and how they can best be used against an enemy. The NPCs were scripted to use strategies that the player could see and use.

Once these beginning levels were designed and implemented, I play-tested them. As is often the case, the initial design for the levels was far too hard (the first level took an hour or more), and the user interface took hours to master. By watching naive players, the game and level designers were able to clarify the levels, fix the user interface, and create a smooth challenge ramp for the game.

Anticipate the Cool Game Elements

Early in a game, the player has little knowledge and few abilities. By the time they are experienced and can do a lot, the game may be provocative of a great and fun fantasy. How can we anticipate these later abilities early in the game without interfering with the challenge ramp? In *PopTB*, a game device was created where a player could win a few "shots" of a spell and another device for gaining the spell permanently. Early in the game, powerful spells are given temporarily so the player can try them out. The user interface suggests that they will later acquire them permanently, so this whets their appetite. Even though the best spells have to be saved for last as permanent acquisitions, this mechanism reassured players of even more fun ahead.

In-Game Help . . . Keeping Players from Killing Their Own Joy

PopTB also has extensive help features. The game delivers messages that include level goals, hints, explanations, and ZoomTos that take a player to interesting events and back again. These messages are kept in an on-screen stack until dismissed or no longer relevant. "Tool tips" pop up over most user interface elements when the cursor hovers over them. Most of these help features make the game itself easier to learn. Only occasional messages were written as "advice" on game play.

Curiously, if a game provides too much help on game play, players use it at the first hint of frustration and ruin their own play experience. It is not fun to be told how to solve a problem. The longer a game keeps the player working on a problem, the greater their ultimate sense of accomplishment in solving it. It is vital to provide just enough assistance to avoid untenable frustration. In the adventure game *Phantasmagoria*, the environment was very large. It was tedious looking around for the next thing to do. So, it had an in-game "hint keeper" who would only tell you where to go. ("Danger awaits you in the house.") That worked well because it did not give away too much yet eliminated frustration.

Interpret Testing Results Carefully

The game community learned long ago that it is important to play-test games. However, such testing in the game community is sometimes unsophisticated and poorly done.

During play-testing of *PopTB*, a serious user interface flaw was discovered. Players did not report it directly because they were unaware of the cause, though painfully aware of the result. This flaw was introduced because of an earlier focus test that recommended the user interface be changed for compatibility with a recent hit game. Unfortunately, a difference in the two games turned that suggestion into a disaster. Watching subjects play, not listening to their comments, revealed this flaw.

Test subjects should be treated like the valued patrons of a restaurant. Listen carefully to what they say. They are experts on what they like. But let the chef adjust the recipe. Subjects are not designers. Their suggestions are valuable, but designers need to think about the results carefully.

Testing the Fun

I play-test a game for design insight. I want to know what prevents players from enjoying the experience that I am imagining or that I am actually having once the game is well along in its implementation. Much of what is learned during play testing is unexpected, and it often takes awhile to discover where a problem resides . . . in the interface, the mechanics, or the game play. Market testing is no substitute. Marketing has different questions and different methodologies. Feedback of astute marketing analysis is very valuable, but a successful game remains the realization of a vision of its designers rather than of its audience.

While most of the above is obvious to those who user-test software applications, game play-testing has an added dimension. During a play-test, it is important to assess how much fun the subject is having. It is vital to figure out what elements of the game are creating the fun, and what elements are detracting from it. There are many markers for fun during testing. A think-aloud protocol does not work when someone is having fun. They are too busy to talk. When subjects get so involved in the game that they do not hear your questions or begin to react emotionally to what is happening, you know. I often tell subjects they can continue to play after the test is over. When the subject asks to call home to delay their pickup time, you know. As others in the company try the game, watch how long and hard they play it. Once a game is in the QA department, watch whether the testers stay past their shift to continue playing your game.

These are all gross measures. It is not possible to assess the fun of an individual element of a game because fun resides in the whole experience, not its component parts. If the fantasy rings true and clear in the designer's head, testing can discover problems and ways that the details interfere with communicating that fantasy. However, not everyone has the qualities of imagination to create a fantasy that others will want to share and enjoy. As the obstacles are removed, the universality of this particular fantasy becomes apparent, for better or worse.

Silent Steel

This game was not a major hit, but it is a very interesting failure. When I first played this game, I got so excited that I ended up screaming in frustration at its flaws. How did this game get me so engaged? What were those flaws that frustrated me so badly?

In *Silent Steel (SS)*, the player portrays the commander of a U.S. nuclear submarine in a naval exercise that is interrupted by several subs belonging to unfriendly nations. This game is constructed out of video segments where the player's only input is to choose statements or questions by the commander at the end of each video segment. Depending upon the selection, a different video plays. This game is an interactive movie, where the web of choices is intended to create a strategy game of submarine warfare.

Conversation Mechanics Done Right

A number of games have included conversations as a game mechanic, but *SS* has one of the best user interfaces. In a variety of games, conversations have been implemented by asking players to choose from a list of items such as the following:

- The emotion of the response represented as a word (e.g., angry, happy, sad)

- The emotion of the response represented as an icon (e.g., a facial expression)

- The "temperature" of the emotional response (from blue to red on a slider)

- A short written phrase summarizing what will be said, not voiced on rollover

- A short written phrase summarizing what will be said, with the actual statement voiced on rollover before selection

- The complete written sentence of what will be said, not voiced on rollover

- The complete written sentence of what will be said, voiced on rollover

The ambiguities of all but the last two make them annoying when your proxy surprises you by saying something unexpected.[8] Even a complete sentence can occasionally be misleading because of the importance of inflection to meaning. *SS* uses a complete written sentence voiced on rollover. When selected, it is not repeated.[9] The voicing is slightly delayed to avoid spurious choices, and it is interruptible to avoid having to wait when you do not want to. This works very well.

The worst design combination would be a highly ambiguous selection like the color slider and no voicing by your proxy of your selection. *Midnight Stranger* uses this. It is an interesting title, but its one-sided interactive conversations are difficult to follow.

The conversational mechanics in games are also handled in two different ways. Some games just provide a list of topics for the player to pick, occasionally adding or deleting a topic. Other games try to structure a more naturalistic conversation, where each choice changes the choices that follow. Because the choice in the former lacks consequence, it is not fun. In *SS*, conversations are consequential. What you say determines what can happen next. Say the wrong thing, and it can cost you the game. This makes conversations into an interactive puzzle, and that can be quite fun.

For games designed for replay, repeating interactive conversation puzzles is boring. A good compromise is to bury useful information (the combination to the safe) in an interactive conversation whose other purpose is to reveal interesting story points. If the designer is thoughtful, the conversation need not be repeated on replay since the player knows the combination to the safe and can use it directly.

Fairness in Game Play 1: Consequences Match Actions

SS tells a complex story through video segments selected by your conversational choices (your orders as captain of the submarine). When it came out, it was common knowledge that interactive movies had failed in games. However, the acting and situations in *SS* were well done and emotionally powerful. When the player erred and his sub was destroyed, faces of the crew members would fade up over the background of the sub disintegrating in the depths of the ocean, sometimes accusing you of their deaths. In playing this game, the video was not the problem; *SS* was hurt by two serious problems with its game play.

8. For an incomplete and unvoiced selection to work, the response has to convey what the proxy said. Bob Newhart performs comedy routines of phone conversations where the conversation is understandable despite hearing only his side. This quality of writing has yet to be seen in a game.

9. In a small informal study, it was usually perceived as annoying to have to listen to the sentence that you just heard on rollover voiced again on selection. Players did not even seem to notice when it was not repeated.

Playing a game is fun once the player understands the rules and the game responds fairly, within those rules, to the player's actions. In *SS*, the player is the captain of the submarine and is able to give orders to his crew. This means that the game must provide the player with an opportunity to make a decision whenever it would be reasonable for the captain to do so. Early in *SS*, the player is likely to come across a painfully spectacular violation of this rule. A subordinate volunteers to explain an idea about how to smoke out the enemy. If the player assents, the subordinate does not explain the action, he does it. The captain would undoubtedly tell him to stop, but the player does not have the opportunity to do so. The scheme works far too well, and the unfriendly sub attacks. Again, a captain would at this point be shouting orders to evade, dive, fire back, or take some other appropriate action. Those are the choices at other points in the game in a similar situation, but here there are no choices. A full minute passes in cinematic mode, with a torpedo approaching, tension mounting, and no opportunity for interaction. The torpedo hits, the submarine is destroyed, and everyone is killed. The full power of cinematic narrative is dropped squarely upon the head of the player, who at this point feels horribly mistreated by the unfairness of the game. This outcome was not a fair consequence of the player's choice.

Fairness in Gameplay 2: Immediacy of Consequence

The branching tree in *SS* is very complex. As long as outcomes follow consequences closely and in an intuitive way, complexity is fine. However, in *SS*, the result of actions made late in the game depended on choices early in the game. Unfortunately, the game world lacks any clear representation of the change in state. With a clear representation, this would be bad game design because it means the player must replay a very large segment of the game to try a different path through the game. Without any such representation, it is an insult to the player because it gives them no opportunity to win the game.

This problem results from the core idea of *SS*, that it is a strategy game of submarine warfare. In strategy games, players make choices with long-term impacts. They might choose whether to build defensive or offensive capabilities, and that structures the entire game experience. Strategy games are open, and so no single choice determines the outcome. Story games are closed, so choices may end up in assured defeat. When that is the case, the defeat should be near the choice. Otherwise the player feels cheated by the game because there was no chance of victory. It is also hard to learn and improve because the cause of the defeat is likely to be unclear. (The *SS* help line is unable to help unless the player can recount much earlier choices that determine the current state in ways that are not visible.)

FIGURE **10.3**

You Don't Know Jack *is a trivia game with an attitude.* You Don't Know Jack *is a registered trademark of Jellyvision, Inc.*

You Don't Know Jack

All user interface designers should play this game and study it closely. *You Don't Know Jack (YDKJ)* is a very funny trivia contest for one, two, or three players. The attitude and humor of the master of ceremonies (MC) makes the game appealing to a very broad range of ages. My Stanford students fight for the chance to demo this game to my class on game design. Figure 10.3 (see also Color Plate) is a screen from one of its many versions.

YDKJ uses very simple but dynamic graphics, TV game show sound design, and a large selection of phrases pasted together seamlessly to create the variety of expression of a human MC. Players choose a 7- or 21-question game (about 8 to 30 minutes). The game is best played with others.

A typical 7-round two-person game begins with a number of trivia questions. The first player to "buzz in" (by hitting a particular key) gets a crack at answering. After some number of trivia questions, the game changes pace to a "Gibberish Question," a nonsense phrase that is an anagram of a proverb or famous phrase. This has a 30-second time-out and is very tense but slower than the trivia questions. Then, perhaps some more trivia questions before the final Jack Attack. In the Jack Attack, words and phrases fly across the screen and the two players must notice that they are related in a certain way. This is very fast paced, lasts another minute, and is very intense. At the end of the Jack Attack, the MC tells the score and makes sarcastic comments about the player's scores.

Feedback

In the two-player game, if a player excitedly hits the answer without hitting the key that identifies him, the MC shouts, "Buzz in, buzz in." When one player selects an answer, it is highlighted first, so the other player can tell what was selected; then the MC responds.

Because two people play the game at the same keyboard and it is not easy to see what key the other player has hit, the game has to comment on what has happened. During the Jack Attack, both players compete to hit their key. Whichever player hits the key either wins or loses money, but both players could hit their keys quite closely in time so the game has to show who won. All this is accomplished through careful sound and graphic design.

Awareness of the Player

Game designers know how exciting it is for a player when a game is aware of them. *YDKJ* is very careful to do this often enough that it successfully makes the player feel part of a quiz show with a live host. Although the quiz show itself is an artifice during the introduction that is quickly ignored, suspension of disbelief is maintained by a superb degree of awareness.

For example, a character in the game asks the player to type their name. Unlike computers that have no sense of time, *YDKJ* acts like an impatient human. It begins to hassle the player if they do not respond quickly. If they delay until the hassling has started, then type their name, the MC responds in relief the instant the player hits the first key, just like a human would. It does not wait for the player to hit Enter before noticing that they have acted.

In a two-player game, if one player does nothing for awhile, the MC comments on it sarcastically. The MC heckles or praises the players for their scores in the Jack Attack and while displaying the final scores at the end of the round. If one player makes several mistakes in a row, they can expect to be heckled. If a player buzzes in before the question and answers have all appeared, the MC gets very sarcastic, clears the screen completely, and asks for the player's answer—which is always wrong—prompting the MC to tell the player to wait until he is ready next time.

In fact, the game has a lot of devices for displaying awareness of the player and what they have done—some rare. Given a believable context, an occasional remark or action demonstrating awareness is all it takes for the player to feel that the game MC is an actual person.

Awareness of the World

Awareness of the world outside the player is difficult. If it is late on a Friday night in a single-player *YDKJ* game, the MC might point out that you must be a loser to have nothing better to do on a date night.

In *Metal Gear: Solid*, the game reads the console's removable memory card used to save games. (Consoles have no persistent internal memory.) If the player has saved the game frequently, a character in the game remarks that the player is a very cautious person. If it detects the saved image of a prior game by the same company, it remarks upon it.

Pacing

YDKJ is a very insistently paced game. Its simple graphics bounce and stretch and roll, all in time to sound effects and music. There is never any break in the media. Sentences are stitched together seamlessly. There are many variants so it doesn't seem repetitive.

In the example mentioned above, if you do not type in your name when asked, it gives up fairly quickly, chooses a name for you (e.g, "Okay, player one, I'll call you 'toilet seat'"), and goes on. In fact, if you now do nothing, it will play a complete game, commenting throughout about your inattention.

The pacing never stops. There is never any break in the media to interfere with suspension of disbelief. Each game has a rhythm as well; from simple questions and answers, through the Jack Attack, the tension builds and the pacing accelerates.

Attitude

A neutral character is not interesting. A colorful character is defined largely by their statements and their actions, which flow from their attitude. *YDKJ* has a lot of attitude. It harasses and belittles the player (and everything else) in a very humorous way. This limits the age and nature of the audience, but is very fun for a wide audience.

Metal Gear: Solid

This hit console action-adventure game sets a new standard for quality of story combined with quality of action game play. It has many interesting innovations worthy of study. You play Solid Snake, a secret agent of the U.S. government assigned to break into a nuclear disposal plant in Alaska that has been taken over by terrorists. The story is deep, complicated by quite a few plot twists, including a romance, and quite compelling.

In-Game Retry on Failure

In most games, characters including your proxy have a certain amount of health, and they have weapons that cause a certain amount of damage. Your proxy usually can survive some number of handgun bullets and a smaller number of rifle bullets because they are more powerful. *Tom Clancy's Rainbow Six* has a more realistic single-shot death, but the probability of hitting the target depends on the situation. Games usually have ways to restore health (first-aid kits, medicinal plants, potions).

In most games, the proxy dies often as you replay and practice until you can get through a scenario. How this retry is designed has a significant impact on the experience. In some games, the player is responsible for interrupting game play with a special key to get a meta-game screen to save the game. The player reloads the saved game after losing or dying. Even if the player wins a battle but at too great a cost in ammunition or health, the player may want to try again to decrease the cost. This style of play emphasizes the meta-game over the game.

MGS relieves the player of any need for a meta-game save strategy. Instead, the game automatically restarts at the most recent continuation point. In *MGS*, Solid Snake dies many times before the player masters the game. New game players sometimes complain about their proxy dying. In *Full Throttle*, your proxy rides a motorcycle down Old Mine Road fighting with other motorcycle riders who drive by. On losing, the proxy falls and rolls down the side of the road. Then, he gets back on the motorcycle, and starts over. This is failure without the metaphor of death. In either case, in-game retry after failure eliminates the need for a meta-game and keeps the player better engaged with the problem at hand.

Levels Need Not Be Won

In Hollywood films, the middle of the film is filled with obstacles that increasingly limit the protagonist's choices, making the final confrontation inevitable. In confronting these obstacles, the protagonist often fails to reach objectives. This failure sharpens the tension as it narrows the field of confrontation.

In games, the player expects a series of obstacles but also expects to retry the level until victory. Players expect to defeat a level boss at the end of each level in an action game, leading up to the big bad villain at the end. How is it possible to reconcile these game mechanics with story mechanics?

In *MGS,* our proxy Solid Snake defeats a villain in an M1 tank, then leaves the scene. This triggers a noninteractive video. The camera cuts back to the M1 tank, and the villain re-emerges unexpectedly. We thought he was dead! He calls someone to report that Solid Snake is on the way and a very dangerous warrior indeed. This speech makes it clear that the enemy staged the victory. Since that knowledge does not have any impact on later play, it works fine within the game, as it adds tension to the story.

So, while the player needs the sense of accomplishment at each level, the content of the game can make it clear that the level was completed successfully even though the story of the level does not match the success of the game play.

Breaking the Frame

Most games assiduously avoid mentioning any element of the game user interface within the game, just as feature film characters rarely address the audience directly (Woody Allen excepted). *MGS* breaks the frame of the game often. The player's commander explains how to play: "While being tortured, press the circle key repeatedly and rapidly to stay alive. Press the square key to surrender." Before the villain tortures Solid Snake, he first threatens, "This is for keeps. If you die, you lose. There will be no continues." That is a direct reference to the meta-structure of the game. Indeed, if the player does not mash the circle key repeatedly with incredible speed, Solid Snake dies and the player is thrown out to the load game screen rather than to a recent continue point. (Thankfully, just before Solid Snake is captured and taken to the torture room, one of the characters warns him, "I have a bad feeling about this. You had better save your game." It is the foolish player who ignores such hints from the game designer.)

Few games break the frame in this way because breaking the frame usually also breaks the suspension of disbelief that underlies the fantasy. Done well, it can work.

10.5   Across the Great Divide

In software application design, if the designer has carefully studied users and what they need, translated that into a functional design, and created a reasonable user interface architecture, the product will probably be well received. In fact, if the user interface is demonstrably bad, but the functionality is valuable, the product may well succeed, as many current major software applications attest.

Game design is more brutal. A game that looks like other successful games and repeats what was fun about them will certainly fail. No entertainment industry has found a way to measure the likelihood of success of its products prior to marketing them. The design center for all games is the experience of fun, an elusive quality that is a by-product of the imagination and cannot be managed by a good process. Ultimately, as in all entertainment, the game designer must express a vision in the finished product that a substantial number of people respond to. Despite the fact that a great game can survive some flaws, flaws have caused many great game ideas to fail. It is not uncommon to see rudimentary design mistakes in games. Playtesting can help avoid that pitfall, but so can knowledge about design.

Most game designers know little about the science of design that the application design community has built and do not care because they believe that it would add little to their art. Likewise, most application designers know little about the art of design that the game design community has built and do not care because they believe that it would add little to their science. After working in both areas, I question the attitudes of both. Poor design methods and flaws in design hurt games. Failure to spark our imaginations and to take advantage of our curiosity and emotional responses hurts applications. Most games could use a lot more attention to simplifying their user interface. Most applications could use a lot more attention to their challenge ramp and level design.

These two communities share a common core truth: the vision of what a product offers its user is its heart, and every facet of the design must be fashioned to clothe and strengthen and give visibility to that heart. Features and distractions that obscure the designer's vision of the product lead to mediocrity. When the user can see and appreciate the core value in a product, the designer has realized his vision with integrity and can do no more to ensure its success.

Games referenced in this chapter are cited here in alphabetical order, followed by publisher (p) and/or developer (d): *Age of Empires* (p: Microsoft Corporation); *The Beast Within: A Gabriel Knight Mystery* (Sierra); *Command and Conquer* (p: Virgin Interactive Entertainment/d: Westwood Studios); *Deerhunter* and *Deerhunter 2* (p: GT Interactive Software Corp. [WizardWorks label]/d: Sun Storm); *Diablo* (p: Blizzard Entertainment/d: Blizzard North); *Doom* (d: id Software, Inc.); *Dune II* (p/d: Westwood Studios); *Full Throttle* (LucasArts Entertainment Company LLC); *Grim Fandango* (LucasArts Entertainment Company LLC); *Half-Life* (p: Sierra On-Line/d: Valve Software); *The Legend of Zelda: Ocarina of Time* (Nintendo); *Metal Gear: Solid* (Metal Gear™ is a trademark of Konami Co., Ltd.); *Pirates* (p/d: Micropose [now owned by Hasbro Interactive, Inc.]); *Midnight Stranger* (p: Gazelle Technologies of San Diego/d: Animatics Multimedia Corporation of Ottawa); *Myst* (Myst is a registered trademark of Cyan, Inc.); *Phantasmagoria* (p/d: Sierra); *Pirates* (p/d: Micropose [now owned by Hasbro Interactive, Inc.]); *Populous* and *Populous, the Beginning* (p: Electronic Arts/d: Bullfrog Productions, LTD.); *Quake* (Quake is a registered trademark of Id Software, Inc.); *Resident Evil* (p/d: Capcom Entertainment); *Resident Evil 2* (p: Capcom Entertainment/d: Angel Studios); *Riven* (p: Broderbund Software, Inc./d: Cyan, Inc.); *Road Rash* (p/d: Electronic Arts); *Rogue* (none); *7th Guest* (p: Virgin Interactive Entertainment/d: Trilobyte, Inc.); *Silent Steel* (p/d: Tsunami Media, Inc.); *SimCity* (Maxis, an EA Company); *Theme Park* (p: EA/d: Bullfrog Productions, LTD.); *Tomb Raider* (p/d: Eidos Interactive); *Tom Clancy's Rainbow Six* (Red Storm Entertainment), *Wolfenstein 3D* (p: Apogee Software/d: id Software, Inc.); *You Don't Know Jack* (You Don't Know Jack is a registered trademark of Jellyvision, Inc.; p: Berkeley Systems/d: Jellyvision, Inc.); *Zork* (Infocom).

Eleven

Persuasive Technologies and Netsmart Devices

B. J. FOGG

Stanford Persuasive Technology Lab
Casio U.S. Research and Development

11.1 Introduction

One soggy day in January, 15 students stood on the edge of a bridge that spans Highway 101 in Palo Alto, California. Each student held a poster painted with a bold orange letter. Lined up in order, the letters spelled a simple but provocative message for the Silicon Valley drivers below: "W-H-Y N-O-T C-A-R-P-O-O-L-?" The automobiles were moving at a snail's pace, bumper to bumper. However, one lane was nearly empty: the carpool lane.

As I read about this event in the *San Jose Mercury News,* I admired those students. Not only did they take action to improve the environment and quality of life in Silicon Valley, they also found a potentially powerful way to reach and influence people. It's hard to imagine a driver trapped in the rush hour crawl who didn't—at least for a moment—reconsider his or her commute strategy. "Yeah, why not carpool? I could be home by now."

When I finished reading the article, I gazed at the picture and sensed something familiar, something symbolic. After a while, I recognized that this event matched my view on what many interactive technologies will do in the future. I identified five resonant elements from what the students did that January day:

1. They targeted a specific problem.

2. They attempted to persuade—to change attitudes and behaviors.

3. They advocated prosocial behavior.

4. They acted at an opportune time and place.

5. They intervened on a collective level, not an individual level.

As odd as it may seem, the "why not carpool?" event holds implications for ways we think about, design, and distribute new interactive technologies. Of course, it's unlikely that computers will line up on a bridge during rush hour, but I propose that technologies of the future will have many—or all—of the five attributes listed above. This chapter won't directly address all five points, but in order to launch this discussion with a common understanding, I'll begin with item #2: attempting to persuade.

11.2 What Are "Persuasive Technologies"?

Although most people think of computers in terms of productivity or entertainment applications, it is becoming clear that computers and related interactive technologies are, can be, and will be designed to influence people's attitudes and behavior. I call this "persuasive computing," or more broadly "persuasive technologies" (the study of this area is called "captology").

First, some definitions and examples: A persuasive technology is any type of interactive system, device, or application that was designed to change a person's attitudes or behaviors in a predetermined way. A modest number of such technologies currently exist in today's market. I expect many more to follow, until the concept of persuasive technologies will be as ordinary as the idea of computers in the kitchen.

One good example of a persuasive technology is a device called "Baby Think It Over." A U.S. company (*www.btio.com*) designed this interactive doll to persuade young people to avoid becoming teen parents. Used as part of many school programs, the Baby Think It Over infant simulator looks, weighs, and cries something like a real baby. However, unlike a real baby the doll has a small computer embedded inside it. This computer triggers a crying sound at random intervals; in order to stop the crying sound, the teen caregiver must pay immediate attention to the doll. If not, the embedded computer system records the neglect and shows it on a tiny display locked inside. Using a key to open the computer, the teacher who administers the Baby Think It Over program can view the display. The teacher can also change the settings to make the baby cranky or good natured.

Another example of a persuasive technology is an exercise bicycle manufactured by Tectrix (*www.tectrix.com*). This device looks much like any ordinary exercise bike at the gym, except this one has a computer monitor attached. As people pedal the bike, they can navigate their way through a virtual world (they can choose a tropical island or a snowy mountain). The faster they pedal, the faster they go. In this world, exercisers encounter people to race or follow along the various paths. Other versions of this device let two exercisers compete against each other in an ancient Aztec game that is something like field hockey. The purpose of the bike is not just entertainment. According to Tectrix, the device is designed to influence people to have a more positive attitude about fitness and to motivate people to exercise more often.

Persuasive technologies can also be part of desktop applications, though the constraints posed by a keyboard and screen can be limiting. A good desktop-based example is a CD-ROM named "5 A Day Adventures" (*www.dole5aday.com*). This computer application was created to persuade kids to eat more fruits and vegetables, ideally five servings a day. The CD-ROM presents a virtual world with characters like "Bobby Banana" and "Pamela Pineapple" who help kids go through the various activities, praising them for making good choices and completing the various elements of the application, such as practice in reading food labels or making a virtual salad.

So what is *not* a persuasive technology? Most computing technologies are not persuasive. Productivity software, such as a word processor, is not persuasive; it simply allows a person to manipulate text. A pocket calculator is not persuasive; it simply allows people to crunch numbers.

Even when the use of a computing technology results in changed attitudes or behaviors, the distinction between what is and is not a persuasive technology hinges on the role of intentionality. In my view, an interactive device qualifies as a persuasive technology when people who create the product do so with an intent to change attitudes or behaviors in a predetermined way. This is true for Baby Think It Over, the Tectrix VR Bike, and for 5 A Day Adventures. My point about intentionality may seem subtle, but it is not trivial. Intentionality determines whether behavior or attitude change is a *side effect* or a *planned effect* of a technology.

While some side effects of technology are benign, others are not. Consider for example, the possible effects of violent video arcade games. Those who play these games injure and kill dozens of virtual entities during a single game. Violence is a key feature, and inflicting harm leads to rewards—extra lives, extended play, applause, or high point scores. One could reasonably conclude that playing these types of video games changes the players' attitudes—and possibly their behaviors. Players likely view violence more favorably, they may be more likely to view violence as a viable strategy to resolve conflicts, and they may be more likely to use violence in their own lives. However, these outcomes are side effects of playing violent video games, not planned effects. As such, violent video games—at least the ones I'm aware of—are not intentionally designed to promote violence in the users' everyday lives. So, according to the definition I propose here, these games are not "persuasive technologies." Instead, they are entertainment technologies with undesirable side effects. (To be clear: understanding the side effects of technology use is an important endeavor; however, this chapter focuses on planned persuasive effects.)

With this foundation—a definition, some examples, and some rough boundaries—I now turn to the question of applications. In other words, "What good are persuasive technologies?"

Like the human persuaders in our lives, persuasive technologies can bring about constructive changes in many domains, including health, safety, and education. In the process, interactive devices can help us improve ourselves, our communities, and our society. However, persuasive technologies can also be used for destructive purposes; the dark side of changing attitudes and behaviors leads toward manipulation and coercion. Even if a technology doesn't use manipulation or coercion, it could still use legitimate persuasion toward undesirable ends, such as wasting the earth's resources, smoking cigarettes, or adopting prejudice toward particular groups. Of course, most

TABLE **11.1**

Candidate domains for persuasive technologies.

Domain for Persuasive Technologies	*An Example Target Behavior or Attitude*
Retail—buying and branding	To buy a certain product or think favorably about a brand
Education, learning, and training	To engage in activities that promote learning
Safety	To drive more safely
Environmental conservation	To reuse shopping bags
Occupational productivity	To set and achieve goals at work
Preventative health care	To quit smoking
Fitness	To exercise with optimal intensity and frequency
Disease management	To manage diabetes better
Personal finance	To create and adhere to a personal budget
Community involvement/activism	To volunteer time at a community center
Personal relationships	To keep in touch with aging parents
Personal management and improvement	To avoid procrastination

people don't want technologies to operate in these realms (and, fortunately, few technologies have to this point). But the possibility certainly exists. Similar to other powerful forces, such as electricity or nuclear energy, the application of persuasive technologies depends largely on what we, as creators, adopters, or distributors of these technologies, choose to do. It's my hope that we choose wisely.

In Table 11.1 I specify 12 domains that are candidates for persuasive technologies. While some of these domains—such as retail—are obvious, others are less obvious. The point of the table is to show that technologies can be used to persuade in many areas, from selling products to motivating closer relationships within families. In virtually all the areas listed (with the possible exception of education), the most effective persuasive technologies will be those that don't look or feel like computers at all. Consider the following three fictional scenarios as examples of interactive technologies that motivate or persuade, noting how the devices don't look or feel anything like traditional computers of today.

Scenario 1: The Study Buddy

Someday in the near future, a first-year student named Pamela will be sitting in a college library with a technology designed to influence her study habits. This device will look like an ordinary pen—in fact, it will write with normal ink—but this pen will have other capabilities that we would consider remarkable (see Figure 11.1). To Pamela, this type of pen is relatively new, but it's not particularly surprising. This device is called "Study Buddy" and here's what it might do:

As Pamela begins her evening study session, she simply clicks Study Buddy, much like an ordinary pen. The device comes to life. Study Buddy congratulates her for studying for the third time that day, meeting the goal she set at the beginning of the quarter. The device suggests that Pamela start with a five-minute review of her biology vocabulary words and then read the two chapters for tomorrow's sociology lecture. Pamela agrees.

In the past, Study Buddy has almost always given Pamela good advice—keeping her on track with her classes and suggesting the periodic review she needs to master new concepts from her survey courses. Pamela views Study Buddy like a coach, one that keeps her motivated through thick and thin. Of course, she doesn't always follow Study Buddy's suggestions, but usually she does. Like tonight. Pamela starts in with the suggested vocabulary review: *mitochondria, nucleolus, . . .*

When Pamela finishes the biology review, Study Buddy displays a cluster of shapes that pulse slowly, like breathing. These shapes represent her classmates who are currently studying; she can view a set of shapes for each course she is taking. Pamela likes knowing that other people are studying too. Not everyone is out playing tonight. This makes her feel in good company as she starts reading her sociology chapters.

Later that evening, as Pamela wraps up her work, she's curious about her mentor, Jean, so she consults Study Buddy. She learns that Jean is currently in one of the campus libraries.

As part of the university program, Jean has previously volunteered to be a study mentor for Pamela. Jean is a senior who was recently admitted to a top

FIGURE **11.1**

*Netsmart pens could motivate students to study more
effectively.*

graduate school. Being a study mentor means that Jean has agreed to let
Pamela remotely sense Jean's studying habits. For example, Pamela's Study
Buddy vibrates each time Jean enters a campus library or study area.
Sometimes this prompts Pamela to start studying too.

Scenario 2: Traffic Tattler

When a reckless driver cuts Mark off, endangering his life, Mark no longer gets
mad; he gets even. Well, not exactly. But that's how Mark thinks about Traffic
Tattler, a highway monitoring system that allows him to report bad driving
when and where it happens (see Figure 11.2). Using Traffic Tattler soothes
Mark's nerves after a driving incident; he calms down. And he knows his tat-
tling may result in increased revenues to improve roads in his area. Here's how
it might work:

"Traffic Tattler, I have a report," Mark says while driving.

"Please continue," the in-car system replies.

"A red car just made a dangerous lane change; it nearly hit me."

"Can you identify the car?"

"It was a four-door. American made. Fairly new."

FIGURE **11.2**

Netsmart driving systems could allow people to report dangerous driving behaviors.

"The system has identified the offending car and filed your complaint. Thank you and drive safely."

With the report filed, Mark feels satisfied. He knows that if two other drivers file a report against the same car within a five-minute period, the owner of the car will receive a citation. He hopes that others saw the infraction and that they will report it. Despite the vigilante nature of the system, Mark thinks this process is fair because it puts power in the hands of the people best suited to judge the situation.

Scenario 3: HydroTech

Phil has been having horrible headaches for a few years now, probably since about 2002. His doctor can't say exactly what's wrong, but she thinks Phil's headaches are caused by inadequate hydration. In other words, Phil's body needs more water. Phil admits he is terrible about drinking water. He gets busy and he forgets. Then he gulps down water until he feels bloated. This isn't what the doctor ordered.

Because his doctor can't rule out dehydration as the cause of the headaches until Phil maintains adequate hydration, Phil and his doctor agree to use the HydroTech system for a couple of months (see Figure 11.3). Then they'll go from there. It hurts only momentarily as the doctor implants the HydroTech

FIGURE **11.3**

A Netsmart drinking glass could remind people about health needs.

sensor/transmitter under Phil's skin. About the size of two aspirin tablets, this device measures hydration levels and broadcasts the data.

The hydration data is sent to Phil's new water glass, which looks like pretty much any other drinking glass, except that it has the outline of a human body etched into it. The body image changes colors according to Phil's level of hydration. Deep blue is good—adequate hydration. Bright green means Phil should drink more water. Phil sets the water glass on his office desk, viewing it as a surrogate for his sense of thirst. He sort of likes it.

Phil also knows his hydration data gets sent to his doctor's office in real time. This is the part he doesn't like so much. Privacy is not his concern; he understands the network is secure. Instead, Phil knows that someone else is tracking his hydration levels, and he doesn't want to disappoint his doctor. Talk about motivation. If things go as Phil plans, HydroTech will help him maintain adequate hydration in the short term. Whether or not dehydration is the cause of his headaches, Phil hopes drinking adequate water will become a lifelong habit.

The three scenarios above describe hypothetical examples of persuasive technologies that differ in important ways. They show different locations for technology, different domains of intervention, and different persuasion strategies. But the above scenarios share three characteristics that I find important. Each technology in the scenarios is

- Specialized

- Embedded

- Networked

Taken together, these three characteristics define a category of technology I call "netsmart devices." As I see it, many technologies of the future will share these three characteristics (the purpose of the technology doesn't need to be to influence or persuade; netsmart devices will have many uses). In the next few paragraphs I'll describe each characteristic in more detail. Then I'll show how these three characteristics have special application in persuasive technologies.

First of all, I propose the netsmart devices need to be specialized, meaning that they are created for a limited purpose. Examples of specialized devices include the Tamagotchi, the computers used by FedEx delivery personnel, handheld language translators, and GPS devices.

Desktop and laptop computers are not specialized devices, even if they are running specialized applications. In fact, any device that allows Web browsing is not a specialized device. And small size doesn't define a device as specialized. For example, the Palm organizer may seem like a specialized device, but it's really a computing platform with a small form factor.

The next characteristic of netsmart devices is that they are embedded. An embedded computer is part of an ordinary object, an environment, or a body. When embedded computing systems are most successful, people will rarely think of them as computers. They will seem more like devices or environments that have special capabilities.

Finally, netsmart devices, as the name implies, must also be networked in some way. This includes computer systems that use the Internet or other network infrastructure. The precise networking technology doesn't matter; what counts is that a device can exchange data with remote people and devices.

Although the word "netsmart" is a new term to describe future computing technology, the overall idea of specialized, embedded, and networked technologies is not new. Some have suggested terms such as "ubiquitous computing" or "deep computing" to describe similar visions of technology (Weiser 1993).

One common phrase to describe similar—though not identical—technologies is "information appliance." At first, "information appliance" might seem an appropriate moniker; computers are information devices after all. But I find this view of technology far too narrow because it implies that computing is all about gathering, storing, and presenting information. From a user perspective, computers do more than provide information. Computers can entertain, persuade, or offer us aesthetic pleasures. They can be tools that facilitate creation, media that give us experiences, or social actors that provide us with companionship. Because "information appliance" is too narrow a phrase to capture this rich range of possibilities, I prefer to shift gears in wording (and meaning) and talk about "netsmart devices."

Semantic quibbles aside, I now pose the question, "Do we have netsmart devices today?" My answer: "Yes, but not very many." And the examples of netsmart devices that currently exist are sometimes hard to identify. Perhaps this is how it should be. When netsmart devices are designed well, we don't think of them as computing devices. Consider an in-car navigation system. If the system can exchange data, say, through a cell phone network, then it would qualify as a netsmart technology. The best in-car navigation systems don't seem like computers; they seem like very smart road maps.

With time, more and more netsmart technologies will emerge, some without much fanfare. But we probably shouldn't look to the prominent software or hardware companies for these technologies. Instead, netsmart devices are the domain of companies who are experts in the target activity, be it education, health, automotive safety, or whatever. Although these domain-expert companies may seek help or collaboration from the high-tech world, the domain experts are in the best position to design and market netsmart devices. They understand their domain; they know their customers, and the customers know them.

As I said before, netsmart devices aren't necessarily persuasive technologies. Netsmart devices can do many things, from offering efficiency to entertainment. But the most effective persuasive technologies will have netsmart characteristics: they will be specialized, embedded, and networked. This seems inevitable because these netsmart characteristics create additional opportunities to change attitudes and behaviors. To make this connection between netsmart devices and persuasive technologies clear, I will now discuss how each netsmart characteristic leads to greater potential to persuade.

Let's start with specialization.

Specialized Technologies and Persuasion

When interactive technologies are specialized (created for a single purpose), they have more potential to persuade than a general device. Below I offer three arguments to support this assertion.

First, consider the designers and developers who have the opportunity to create a specialized device. Compared with people creating a general device, those who design specialized devices have a better opportunity to achieve excellence because they don't need to compromise to make the new device compatible with a wide variety of applications or existing operating systems. They can focus exclusively on the purpose of the persuasive technology, tailoring every aspect of the design to persuade: the form factor, the interaction, the interface. In short, specialization enhances the design process.

Not only do specialized technologies gain the upper hand during the design process, they also gain a psychological advantage with people who use them. Research has shown that people assume a specialized technology is better than a general technology (Nass, Reeves, and Leshner 1996). In this study, a technology was labeled either as a specialist or a general device. In reality, the content and functionality of the two devices were identical; only the labels changed. But the labels made a difference. The study showed the technology labeled as a specialized device was perceived to be better in various ways, including being more credible—an important aspect of persuasive technologies. This research suggests that a specialized interactive technology will automatically seem more credible in users' minds than a general technology (such as a desktop computer), even when the functionality and content are identical (Reeves and Nass 1996).

See if your intuition matches the research results described above: Suppose you are driving in unfamiliar territory and need directions. Would you rather receive directions from an in-car navigation system—a specialized device—or from a CD-ROM in your laptop? With all other factors being equal (including the trouble of getting the information and the recency of information), most people would likely opt to consult the specialized navigation system.

Now let's change the situation some: Suppose you consulted both sources—the navigation system and the laptop—and they gave you different information. Which would you trust more? This is the moment of truth. I suspect that most people would believe the information from the in-car navigation system.

There's no surprise here. In the world of human-human interactions, it's a common dynamic: Individuals reported to be experts are perceived to have more expertise, even if people know the title is nothing but a label (Zimbardo and Leippe 1991). Apparently, the same is true for the way we view technologies.

There's one more advantage that specialized devices offer in terms of persuasion: group influence. Specifically, a set of specialized devices that work together for a persuasive purpose will likely generate more influence than a single device working alone—even if both options offer the same information and functionality. In other words, if three devices say the temperature outside is 107 degrees, I'm going to believe that more than I would a single device that reports the same measurement three times. There is strength in numbers.

You can get a feel for this classic persuasion effect by making the following comparisons in your mind. Try this thought experiment. Consider two cases of getting information from people about biking to work:

- *Case A:* one friend offers three different reasons you should ride your bike to work.

- *Case B:* three friends each offer a different reason you should ride your bike to work.

Let's suppose that in both cases, the information you get (the three reasons given) is identical. Which case is likely to be more persuasive? A or B? One source or three sources? From a rational, "just the facts," information-based standpoint, there should be no difference between Case A and B because the information is the same in both cases. However, if you're like the participants in the psychology studies, you'll find that Case B is more influential (Harkins and Petty 1981). The sheer number of advocates for an idea makes a difference.

Although we like to think of ourselves as rational beings, persuasion doesn't hinge on the logical; it hinges on the *psycho*logical. And human psychological hardwiring suggests that a variety of specialized devices all working toward one behavioral outcome will generate more influence than a single device or system. Let's suppose the persuasive goal is to motivate family members to eat more fruits and vegetables. A series of devices—such as the fridge, the shopping cart, and the compost bin—could motivate this behavior more effectively than could a single system alone.

Some might worry that having so many specialized devices will lead to a deluge of high-tech gadgets, placed in every nook and cranny, or strewn about our house, office, and car. It might seem like we'll be drowning in the clutter of technology. I don't think so.

Specialized devices should be embedded in ordinary objects and environments. So we won't necessarily add more objects to our lives; instead, we'll replace the old objects with new ones that are a lot smarter, just like we can replace the clutter of paper maps in our car with a single onboard navigation system. Specialized computing goes hand in hand with embedded computing. This is the topic I address next.

Embedded Computing and Persuasion

Working in tandem with specialization, embedded computing opens additional avenues for persuasion. As I see it, embedded computing systems offer three promising paths: placing computing functionality into everyday objects, common environments, or human bodies.

Look around your house or office and notice all the objects: books, tables, lamps, and more. Look inside your bag or briefcase—still more objects. And what about the objects you carry or wear? As humans, we're surrounded (and outnumbered) by objects of our own creation. Now think about all those objects being smart—able to calculate, regulate, communicate, and store. Of course, not every last paper clip will have computing functionality, but many ordinary objects will. And as objects become smarter, some will play a role in changing our attitudes and behaviors.

Computer technology can also be embedded in environments such as houses, cars, parks, and restaurants. This doesn't mean adding a traditional kiosk at every street corner or park bench; that's simply traditional computing in a new location. The design challenge for embedded computing environments is to make the technology disappear. As some might say, it's "calm" technology (Weiser 1997). We can access the computing system when we need it, but it disappears when we don't. The inputs may be sensors; the outputs may be audio or tactile changes that we may not notice or even think about.

In reality, most of us encounter embedded computing systems everyday, the majority of which are not under our control—and we wouldn't want them to be. These systems regulate heating, lighting, and airflow in the spaces we inhabit. Traffic control systems can sense when we are approaching an intersection and change the light colors to give us passage (now that's one embedded system I *would* like to control). Subway trains and airport shuttles automatically announce the next stop. These are all embedded systems.

While the idea of embedding computing functionality in objects and environments is common, it's less common to think about embedding computing devices into human bodies. In some sense, this approach is not new: doctors have implanted pacemakers for years, and new types of assistive technologies, such as hearing devices, are now implanted inside the body. These technologies are not controversial, largely because the embedded computing devices regulate or restore common human functionality. Also, in these cases the interactivity is not under user control.

But how we will—or *should* we—respond when implantable interactive technologies are created to extend human capability far beyond the norm? Are we ready to discuss the ethics of the Bionic Human, especially when this is an elective procedure? ("Hey, I got my memory upgraded this weekend!")

And how should we react when implantable devices are created not just to restore or enhance human ability but to *change human behavior*? Although the HydroTech scenario from the early part of this chapter seems harmless—and even beneficial—technologies with similar functionality may not be so benign. Who decides when it is good to use these technologies? Who should have access to the information produced? And who should control the functionality of the embedded devices? Important questions. Unfortunately, our current understanding of what I call "behavioronics" is small, so we don't have solid answers to these questions. Especially as we combine computing technology with pharmacological interventions, behavioronics is a frontier that we need to explore before we begin to settle the territory.

The overall point in these last few paragraphs is that embedded computing systems increase the power of technology to influence attitudes and behaviors. The big advantage for persuasion is that embedded computers can seek to persuade during a person's normal routine; the technology becomes a seamless part of going through life. With embedded technology, people interact with ordinary objects and inhabit ordinary spaces. And people who seek help from persuasive technologies are freed from the desktop. Specifically, persuasive technologies can then influence people at any of four pivotal times:

- *Point of attitude formation:* this is the moment when someone is ready to form or change an attitude.

    Example: Scout Troop 101 finishes their first day of hiking in the High Sierra. The camp table technology shows them a map of where the bears currently are and how to pack up the scout troop food to avoid unwanted night visitors.

- *Point of decision:* this is the moment when someone decides on a course of action.

    Example: Cheryl has finished her iced tea and is debating whether to discard the empty bottle or make the extra effort to recycle it. The bottle's embedded technology advocates recycling.

- *Point of behavior:* this is the moment when someone takes action.

    Example: the Fife family just arrived at La Selva Beach. As the parents put sunscreen on their kids, the smart sunscreen bottle plays a happy tune with lyrics, which reinforce the idea that wearing sunscreen is a good thing to do.

- *Point of consequences:* this is the moment just after taking action.

    Example: Mike just finished his afternoon at the shooting range. As he packs up, the technology embedded in his hearing protectors points out that his ears would be ringing for the next three hours had he not worn his hearing safety equipment.

Computing technology embedded in objects, environments, and bodies can address the critical moments of persuasion I've outlined above. Those who design persuasive technologies do well to identify those moments and find the optimal avenue for influencing users.

Networked Computing and Persuasion

The final criterion for a netsmart device is that the device be networked. This means the device should have the capability to exchange data with remote devices and people via the Internet or another communication infrastructure. Networked devices have two clear persuasive advantages over nonnetworked technology: they can provide better information and they can leverage social influence dynamics.

First, consider information quality. Networked technologies can provide higher quality information to users in three ways: through currency, contingency, and coordination.

Current information

With the ability to receive new data, networked devices can provide the most current information. Consider a modified version of the boy scouts and bears example above. If the boy scouts arrived at camp and found a printed sign (or even a stand-alone information technology) that warned about the presence of bears, attitudes could range from apathy to paranoia. And these attitudes would not be enduring because the boy scouts would have little assurance the information was current. In situations of information uncertainty, people tend to watch for cues from other people before they form an opinion or take action (Latane and Darley 1970). This can lead to what's called the "bystander effect," where people do nothing, or to contagion, where people panic. Either response is usually inappropriate.

In contrast, if the boy scouts could obtain information from a system that tracks the movement of the bears in real time, the boy scouts would form more homogenous and more appropriate attitudes toward any potential threat. Their precautionary behaviors would also be more appropriate. In most cases, current information is quality information; it has powerful effects on forming or changing attitudes and in motivating appropriate behavior.

We humans value current information. Think about the amount of energy and money invested on news—TV, radio, newspapers, and so on. For most of us, finding out about current events has little real impact on our day-to-day activities, yet we still seek news. Some evolutionary psychologists believe the need for news—for current information—is hardwired into us (Shoemaker 1996). They say the appetite for current information provided an evolutionary advantage over those who lacked this drive. With better information, our ancestors were more likely to survive and reproduce, passing this appetite along to us. If the need for news is indeed a fundamental human drive, then any technology that fills this need will get more of our attention, ultimately giving the technology more power to persuade. Even the *perception* of receiving current information should lead to more persuasion.

Contingent information

Next, networked technology can provide better information by providing contingent information. By "contingent information" I mean information that has been targeted to address emerging needs or situations (of course, a nonnetworked technology can provide contingent information, but not as well). Just as a good trainer or salesperson will modify the information they provide according to people's previous responses, networked technologies can do the same. Not only can networked technologies draw on a large database of information organized around contingencies, but they can also make human experts the source of the contingent information. For example, after receiving data from a persuasive health technology, a person's family doctor may then modify the treatment protocol. The expert-in-the-loop factor makes this type of information highly credible.

Coordinated information

Finally, networking technology allows information to be coordinated among various people and devices. Let's suppose a persuasive technology exchanges data with various medical specialists. The specialists can then coordinate their efforts. That's one example. However, it seems that in most cases, it will be devices coordinating among themselves, using the network to do so. Consider a 55-year-old man who has set a goal to exercise 30 minutes each day. When he suddenly decides to take a rigorous lunchtime walk through the city, the personal activity monitor embedded in his watch could inform the stairstepping machine at the gym. When he arrives at the gym that evening, he may then get a different type of workout, perhaps focusing on strength or flexibility. This adaptability not only makes the intervention more effective, but it would likely increase a person's confidence in the persuasive technology: it senses, it knows, it coordinates.

Not only do networked devices provide better information, as described above, they can also leverage social influence dynamics to persuade. This is a large domain, one that I want to describe in terms of netsmart devices, not just networked devices. So in the next few pages I shift from discussing the persuasive power of networked technologies to the more general idea of netsmart devices and social influence.

11.3 Netsmart Devices and Social Influence

Thanks to their networking capability, netsmart devices can tap into one of the most powerful persuasive forces available—social influence. Think about it: Why do people join support groups, aerobics classes, or study groups? Because groups play a key role in motivation and persuasion. In many situations, people can achieve more attitude and behavior change working together than working alone. Netsmart devices can provide grouplike experiences over distances and over time.

Social influence is a general term that includes a range of persuasion theories from social psychology. Each theory has been the subject of books and sometimes the focus of entire careers. Although this chapter will briefly describe a handful of these theories, I hope the main points remain clear: (1) Other people have a huge influence on our attitudes and behaviors, even more than we might think, and (2) netsmart devices can connect people to other people, creating many opportunities for social influence from both peers and experts. Let's look at four theories that describe how people influence each other.

Social Facilitation and Netsmart Devices

Long-distance runners train best by running in packs. Artists work together in studios. People dance comfortably with other dancers around them but feel awkward on the floor alone. Why? One possible answer is social facilitation. The principle of social facilitation suggests that people perform better—more, longer, harder—when other people are present, participating, or observing (Zajonc 1965). But it's not just people who are influenced by social facilitation dynamics; social facilitation occurs in other species as well. Chickens have been shown to eat more when other chickens are present. A bee performs more work when working with other bees. And so on.

Netsmart devices create provocative opportunities to generate social facilitation effects. Because netsmart devices can allow other people to be virtually present, we can create situations through computer technology that will enhance performance. For example, if a person is performing a well-learned activity—such as running on a treadmill—they will likely perform better if a netsmart device shows that other people are virtually present, performing the same activity. Consider a virtual fitness facility: You work out at home but through netsmart technology you can see others doing the same thing, and you know they can see you. This should produce some of the same beneficial social facilitation effects of working out at a regular gym.

The representation of others doesn't have to be a videoconference link to generate the social facilitation effects. In fact, the virtual representation of others may not need to be realistic at all. Avatars could represent other people. Or moving shapes would probably work in some cases, as I described earlier in the Study Buddy scenario. Even bar graphs might effectively represent the presence and performance of people in a group. Although computer scientists and game designers have created various ways to represent other people's presence and performance (Ackerman and Starr 1995), I have yet to find a controlled study that investigates if virtual representations of other people lead to social facilitation effects. It likely would. And the implications for using such principles to improve performance are important.

But I must also share the bad news: for activities that are not well learned, the presence of others will *decrease* performance. In other words, people will do worse learning a new skill or performing a complicated behavior if they know others are observing. So if you are just learning to perform an Irish jig, you would do better practicing in relative privacy. However, once you've mastered the dance, you will perform it better when others are present and observing.

In summary, for simple, well-learned tasks, netsmart devices that allow onlookers and co-participants will likely enhance performance. For complex, unmastered skills, netsmart devices should avoid allowing onlookers—or even the perception that others can observe—in order to avoid impaired performance.

Social Comparison and Netsmart Devices

Netsmart devices also can change behaviors and attitudes through a phenomenon called "social comparison." This theory holds that people seek to know the attitudes and behaviors of others to help form their own attitudes and behaviors. This is *not* a peer-pressure effect (I'll discuss that later). According to social comparison theory, first articulated by Leon Festinger (Festinger 1954), people seek information about others to figure out how they compare and what they should be thinking or doing.

To attract and involve readers, certain magazines know how to engage our natural drive for social comparison. The magazines offer surveys on health, safety, relationships, and so on, each with a title like "How do you measure up?" or "What's your safety IQ?" These quizzes allow people to compare their knowledge, attitudes, or behavior against what the editors say is normal or desirable. Social comparison is all about benchmarking your performance, reactions, attitudes, or behaviors against that of others.

Social comparison has many practical applications, including pain management. One study demonstrates that people experiencing pain benefited from social comparison (Craig and Prkachin 1978). When patients could compare their pain reaction to others who were coping well with pain, the perception of their own pain decreased. Information about another's pain response not only caused patients to report feeling less pain, but physiological measures indicated that the patients *actually* experienced less pain. Amazing. Social comparison is so powerful it can change physiological responses.

Let's apply this finding to netsmart devices. Consider a scenario where a cancer patient is going through painful treatment. In this case, the fewer narcotics the patient takes for pain management, the better. The netsmart device could then link this patient to other patients who are coping well with pain. In theory, this would reduce the perception of pain and reduce the need for narcotics.

One way to strengthen the social comparison effect is by allowing people to compare themselves with *similar* others. This seems to be true for all types of social comparisons—not just reactions to pain. Similarity matters. People change their attitudes and behaviors more when they can compare themselves to others who are similar in age, ability, ethnicity, and so on. In the case of a cancer patient's pain management, the netsmart device would be more persuasive and effective if it allowed a patient to observe responses from a similar patient—same type of cancer, same treatment, same age, and so on.

In sum, social comparison is natural and powerful. Netsmart devices can use social comparison principles to change attitudes and behaviors in many areas, including personal hygiene, financial management, or recreational safety.

Conformity—and Resistance—through Netsmart Devices

Social comparison, discussed in the preceding paragraphs, leverages what's called "informational influence." Another type of influence, called "normative influence," works through a different process, leveraging what some call "peer pressure" or what psychologists call "pressures to conform." In essence, research on conformity shows that we tend to change our attitudes and behaviors in order to match the expectations, attitudes, and behaviors of our "in-groups"; this could be our classmates, a team to which we belong, a family, a work group, and so on.

The conformity dynamic is common and powerful; we've all experienced it. Sometimes the pressure to conform is explicit: people badger or belittle those who don't fit in with the rest of the group. But the pressure to conform isn't always so blatant. Even when not consciously aware of the pressure to conform, people tend to change their attitudes and behaviors in order to match the expectations of their in-group (Turner 1991). To be sure, normative influence can be subtle yet still very effective.

Networked technologies can create situations that leverage normative influence to change people's attitudes and behavior. In other words, technology can increase the reach and effectiveness of peer pressure. On the face of it, this application of technology sounds quite negative, and it certainly can be. But in some situations conformity technology can be used for prosocial ends, such as in helping members of an athletic team or a study group to achieve their personal goals. In such cases, normative influence can be a good and useful persuasion strategy.

The opportunity to use technology to induce conformity seems fairly obvious. But more interesting and less obvious is using technology to unleash a dynamic that runs counter to conformity: minority influence. While studies have shown the power of group conformity, other studies have shown that people are more likely to resist group conformity influence when at least one person defies the group. In other words, one "deviant" (the term used in this research) will make it easier for others to resist the pressure to conform. The deviant doesn't even need to be physically present—just the knowledge that someone else is not following the group provides sufficient support for other people to dissent.

What does this mean for netsmart technologies? Suppose a teen is facing pressure to conform with her group norm of smoking cigarettes. That's pretty powerful pressure. If a technology could convincingly show her that at least one other person in her in-group has successfully resisted the pressure to start smoking—maybe it's someone she doesn't even know personally—she will be much less likely to give in to group pressure. The CD-ROM "Alcohol 101" uses this type of persuasion strategy (this isn't a netsmart technology, but it's still a good example of the principle). The application seeks to change teen attitudes toward drinking alcoholic beverages by "positive norming." It points out that drinking in high school isn't as common or as excessive as most teens perceive it to be.

In sum, while netsmart technologies can leverage conformity dynamics, they can also weaken or undermine the pressure to conform by providing potential deviators with an awareness of others who have resisted this pressure.

Social Learning Theory and Netsmart Devices

The fourth theory I discuss is one of the most popular and effective theories about attitudes and behavior change: social learning theory (also called "social cognitive theory"). Developed by Stanford psychologist Albert Bandura (Bandura 1986), this theory has a broad scope, but one part is especially relevant to netsmart technologies: the power of role models (although Bandura doesn't use that exact term). Research on social learning theory has shown that people learn new attitudes and behaviors by observing others' actions and the consequences of their actions. The theory calls this "observational learning" and shows how this is pervasive throughout our lives.

People tend to observe and learn most from those who are similar to themselves but somewhat older or ahead on the path of life: older siblings, a colleague with a few more years' experience, and so on (Bandura 1997). Also, models who are warm and supportive tend to be more influential (Grusec 1971).

Turn your mind back (or flip the pages back) to the earlier part of this chapter where Pamela used a netsmart device to observe the study behavior of Jean, her mentor. In this situation, Jean is modeling study behavior. The netsmart technology has allowed Pamela to observe Jean over the course of the year. And, according to social learning theory, Pamela should be able to see how Jean's diligent study behavior has led to a positive outcome: Jean got accepted to a top graduate school.

As shown briefly in the Study Buddy scenario, netsmart devices can leverage social learning principles in ways that are potentially powerful. The persuasive technology can focus attention on desirable models: people with warm personalities who perform the target behaviors successfully. The basic strategy is not new. Parents naturally seek to expose their children to positive role models. And as adults, we seek our own models—people who are doing what we wish to do and are doing it well (Bandura 1997). Netsmart devices can facilitate this process.

11.4 What Motivates Groups Naturally

In addition to social influence principles, we can also examine intrinsic motivation principles for clues on how netsmart devices might operate in the future. Intrinsic motivation is a type of energizing force that arises directly from the activity or situation itself. (In contrast, *extrinsic* motivators are not an inherent part of an activity or experience. For example, receiving a bonus at work or the threat of being fired are extrinsic motivators.) MIT's Tom Malone and Stanford's Mark Lepper have outlined seven types of intrinsic motivators (Malone and Lepper 1987); three of these apply to situations where people interact with each other.

First, there's competition. We've all seen how people are motivated by competition, some more than others, but in general this principle is powerful. When you set up a competition, people perk up; there's just something about it that energizes people.

Next, there's cooperation. Again, some people are more motivated by this than others, but the notion of cooperation will motivate most everyone to some degree.

Finally, people are intrinsically motivated by recognition; this means making the process, product, or result visible to others. Many organizations use recognition effectively: companies create "employee of the month" awards, blood drive programs give out stickers to donors so peers recognize they've done a good thing, and top students get listed on the honor roll. All of this is about recognition. But recognition can also take on a negative flair, such as Hester Prynne's scarlet letter. Public shame is the dark side of the recognition coin.

Because netsmart devices can connect people over distance and time, they can also create group situations that leverage these interpersonal intrinsic motivations. To show how these intrinsic motivators might work in netsmart devices, I briefly describe three versions of an "eco-copy" system below.

Eco-Copy: A Conceptual Example

The average copy machine is a stand-alone device that makes photocopies and performs a host of other useful services. Whether we recognize it or not, most copy machines are specialized computing devices. And a few copy machines are even networked: they can send and receive print jobs over a network. In essence, today's cutting-edge copy machines are netsmart devices. But copy machines are not persuasive—at least not yet.

The "eco-copy machine" is a concept for a netsmart device that performs all the functions of a normal copy machine, but it is also a persuasive technology. Eco-copy is designed to motivate people to conserve paper, specifically by persuading them to make double-sided copies instead of single-sided copies. We all know that conserving paper is a good thing to do; it saves both money and trees. Eco-copy would be designed with this goal in mind.

In all three scenarios below, the eco-copy machine would be networked with other eco-copy machines. Each device could send and receive information. And they could leverage one of three intrinsic motivators to persuade people to conserve paper.

First, there's the competition scenario. Let's pretend that five big companies in Silicon Valley decide to make their copy machines netsmart in order to motivate their employees to conserve. So Sun, Intel, HP, Oracle, and IBM all join the initiative to conserve paper (unfortunately, this is unlikely; remember, this is a hypothetical scenario). The conservation program includes a competition to see which company will make the fewest single-sided copies, or the highest percentage of double-sided copies.

When people in these five companies use the eco-copy machines, the machines remind them about the competition and prompt the users to make double-sided copies. The eco-copy machine could also display which company is currently leading the competition. In this scenario there doesn't need to be a prize; there doesn't need to be any external incentive. Simply having a competition may be sufficiently motivating for many people.

The next scenario uses cooperation, not competition, as the motivating force. In the cooperation scenario, let's suppose a single company decides to make all their copy machines netsmart in order to conserve paper throughout the company. The machine's appeal to the user is different from the competition appeal. Instead of challenging users to outperform other groups, the eco-copy machine would advocate cooperating for a common cause: saving money and saving trees. The device would make clear that by making double-sided copies the user would be cooperating with others in their group.

The third scenario leverages the power of recognition. Again, let's suppose that five Silicon Valley companies join a eco-copy machine program. Instead of competing against each other, each compliant company would be recognized as an "Eco-Star," a designation that would appear on every copy machine that belongs to the program. To become an Eco-Star a company would have to reach a certain benchmark, such as making 80% of its copies on two sides of a sheet of paper.

Of course, the above scenarios for the eco-copy system have not been implemented or tested. No one knows for sure if these designs would work as described. But it does seem clear that there's significant potential in using the principles of intrinsic motivation in netsmart devices to change attitudes and behaviors.

11.5 Conclusion

When it comes to creating technologies that motivate and persuade, netsmart devices (interactive technologies that are specialized, embedded, and networked) represent a promising and provocative use of the Internet. Although netsmart devices are not very common today, they will be. Most key technologies are now in place, and many forward-thinking companies and designers have caught the vision.

But what most people have not yet seen is how these types of devices can influence people—causing them to change attitudes and behaviors. As this chapter shows, not only will netsmart devices be highly credible and highly integrated in people's daily routines, netsmart technologies will also have the potential to leverage social influence principles. In the future, these types of technologies will have a significant impact on what we think and what we do. It's our responsibility, I believe, to help see that these new technologies benefit individuals, families, communities, and society.

11.6 References

Ackerman, M., and B. Starr. 1995. *Proceedings of the ACM Symposium on User Interface Software and Technology. www.ics.uci.edu/~ackerman/docs/uist95/uist95.*

Bandura, A. 1986. *Social Foundations of Thought and Action: A Social Cognitive Theory.* Englewoods Cliffs, NJ: Prentice Hall.

Bandura, A. 1997. *Self-Efficacy: The Exercise of Self-Control.* New York: W. H. Freeman.

Craig, K., and K. Prkachin. 1978. Social modeling influences on sensory decision theory and psychophysiological indexes of pain. *Journal of Personality and Social Psychology* 36:805–815.

Festinger, L. 1954. A theory of social comparison process. *Human Relations,* 7:117–140.

Grusec, J. 1971. Power and the internalization of self-denial. *Child Development* 42:93–105.

Harkins, S., and R. Petty. 1981. Effects of source magnification of cognitive effort on attitudes: An information processing view. *Journal of Personality and Social Psychology* 40:401–413.

Latane, B., and J. Darley. 1970. *The Unresponsive Bystander: Why Doesn't He Help?* New York: Appleton-Century-Crofts.

Malone, T., and M. Lepper. 1987. Making learning fun: A taxonomy of intrinsic motivation for learning. In R. E. Snow and M. J. Farr (Eds.), *Aptitude, Learning, and Instruction,* Hillsdale, NJ: Lawrence Erlbaum Associates.

Nass, C., B. Reeves, and G. Leshner. 1996. Technology and roles: A tale of two TVs. *Journal of Communication* 46(2), 121–128.

Reeves, B., and C. Nass. 1996. *The Media Equation: How People Treat Computers, Television, and New Media like Real People and Places.* New York: Cambridge University.

Shoemaker, P. 1996. Hardwired for news: Using biological and cultural evolution to explain the surveillance function. *Journal of Communication* 46(3):32–47.

Turner, J. 1991. *Social Influence.* Pacific Grove, CA: Brooks/Cole.

Weiser, M. 1993. Some computer science issues in ubiquitous computing. *Communications of the ACM* 36(7):74–84.

Weiser, M. 1997. The coming age of calm technology. In P. Denning and R. Metcalfe (Eds.), *Beyond Calculation: The Next Fifty Years of Computing,* New York: Springer-Verlag.

Zajonc, R. 1965. Social facilitation. *Science* 149:269–274.

Zimbardo, P. G., and M. R. Leippe. 1991. *The Psychology of Attitude Change and Social Influence.* New York: McGraw-Hill.

Index

About the Authors

Eric Bergman is a senior interaction designer in the User Experience Group within the Consumer and Embedded organization at Sun Microsystems. His recent work includes leading the interaction design team responsible for the user experience of an internet-enabled telephone and leading the interaction design activities for a television set-top box. He is currently working on user experience issues for wireless devices. He has a long-standing interest in design for a broad range of users, including providing accessibility for users who have disabilities (through his work with Sun's accessibility group) and by serving as editor of an HFES-sponsored accessibility standards effort. He has been active in HCI professional organizations as a presenter and organizer, including co-chairing technical tracks for two CHI conferences. He holds a Ph.D. in cognitive psychology from Emory University.

Chuck Clanton has consulted on human-computer interface design for almost two decades. When he started working on graphical user interfaces, he began having flashbacks from his brief stint in film school. In a fit of workload insanity, he created a tutorial on Film Craft in User Interface Design with Emilie Young for SIGCHI and SIGGRAPH. That started the red ball rolling downhill. He joined the team that was creating Java to build interactive multimedia applications, and his early Java prototypes resembled adventure games. He is not casual about advocating more "fun" in increasingly ubiquitous and casual software applications. That explains why he followed the hastening red ball downhill and across the chasm to games, a separate design community with expertise in fun. To keep his facade as a chap serious about fun, he teaches a course "Lessons from Game Design" for the Computer Science Department at Stanford University. When you mention that he has been designing games for six years, with occasional relapses into "serious" and not-so-serious (Web) design, he tosses the red ball into the air, smiles, and comments that time flies when you are having fun.

B. J. Fogg (Ph.D., Stanford University) directs research and design at Stanford's Persuasive Technology Lab. An experimental psychologist, he teaches courses in persuasive computing for the Computer Science Department. In addition to his Stanford work, he is the director of research & innovation at Casio's U.S. R & D Center, where he leads Casio's efforts to create next-generation consumer electronic devices. He holds several patents, and his work has been featured in the *New York Times*, the *Washington Post*, and *I.D. Magazine*.

Rob Haitani is director of product marketing at Handspring, Inc. Previously at Palm Computing, he designed the user interface of the OS and the device applications for the first three generations of the PalmPilot. He has had four patents granted for his work on the PalmPilot.

Nick Healey designs innovative UIs at Slash Design, a company he founded. Before Slash Design he worked at Symbian, which is jointly owned by Motorola, Nokia, Psion, Ericsson, and Matsushita (Panasonic). As Symbian's head of product design he managed the team responsible for the software specification and UI design of smartphones and online PDAs. He previously spent many years as the lead UI/functionality designer for Psion's multiple award-winning Series 3 and Series 5 ranges of palmtops.

He holds a B.Sc. (honors) in computer engineering from Essex University in the U.K. He occasionally lectures on interface design at conferences and universities.

Scott Isensee is a user interface designer with BMC Software in Austin, Texas. He was the user interface team leader for Netpliance, Inc. during development of the i-opener product and prior to that spent 16 years with IBM in a variety of usability positions. He has served on ISO, ANSI, and W3C committees writing software user interface and usability standards. He has authored 20 patents and over 50 publications on user interface topics including the books *Designing for the User with OVID* and *The Art of Rapid Prototyping*.

Ken Kalinoski is a founder and vice president of development at Netpliance, Inc. Prior to working at Netpliance, Inc., he was the program director of PC Systems Solutions and Product Licensing for the IBM Personal Systems Group. He managed a broad range of multinational projects, including IBM's broadcast and video streaming programs, AIX/UNIX development, and the VM mainframe operating system.

He has six U.S. patents and two external and six internal IBM publications. He received his bachelor's degree in computer science from Wilkes College and his master's degree in computer engineering from the State University of New York.

Aaron Marcus is the founder and president of Aaron Marcus and Associates, Inc. (AM+A). A graduate in physics from Princeton University and in graphic design from Yale University, in 1967 he became the world's first graphic designer to be involved full time in computer graphics. In the 1970s he programmed a prototype desktop publishing page layout application for the Picturephone at AT&T Bell Labs, programmed virtual reality spaces while a faculty member at Princeton University, and directed an international team of visual communicators as a Research Fellow at the East-West Center in Honolulu. In the early 1980s he was a staff scientist at Lawrence Berkeley Laboratory in Berkeley, founded AM+A, and began research as a co-principal investigator of a project funded by the U.S. Department of Defense's Advanced Research Projects Agency (DARPA). In 1992, he received the National Computer Graphics Association's annual award for contributions to industry. Mr. Marcus has written over 100 articles and written/cowritten five books, including (with Ron Baecker) *Human Factors and Typography for More Readable Programs* (1990), *Graphic Design for Electronic Documents and User Interfaces* (1992), and *The Cross-GUI Handbook for Multiplatform User Interface Design* (1994), all published by Addison-Wesley. For the last five years, Mr. Marcus has turned his attention to the Web, helping the industry to learn about good user-interface and information-visualization design, providing guidelines for globalization/localization, and focusing on challenges of "baby faces" (small displays for consumer information appliances), ubiquitous devices, and cross-cultural communication. Mr. Marcus has published, lectured, tutored, and consulted internationally for more than 20 years and has been an invited keynote/plenary speaker at conferences of ACM/SIGCHI, ACM/SIGGRAPH, and the Human Factors and Ergonomic Society. He is a visionary thinker, designer, and writer, well-respected in international professional communities, with connections throughout the Web, user interface, human factors, graphic design, and publishing industries.

Mike Mohageg is manager of the User Experience Group within the Consumer and Embedded organization at Sun Microsystems. He has designed a variety of information appliances including screen phones and television set-top boxes. Prior to working at Sun, he was UI architect at Diba, Inc.—a Silicon Valley startup company focused on creating information appliances. He has also held interaction design positions at NYNEX and Silicon Graphics, where he worked on the first commercially available Virtual Reality Markup Language (VRML) browser. He holds a Ph.D. in industrial and systems engineering from Virginia Tech.

Don Norman calls himself a "user advocate." *Business Week* calls him a "cantankerous visionary"—cantankerous in his quest for excellence. Dr. Norman is president of Learning Systems, a division of UNext.com, a distance education company located just north of Chicago. He is also cofounder of the

Nielsen Norman Group, an executive consulting firm that helps companies produce human-centered products and services. In this role, he serves on the advisory boards of numerous companies.

Dr. Norman is Professor Emeritus at the University of California, San Diego (cognitive science), former vice president of the advanced technology group, Apple Computer, and an executive at Hewlett-Packard. Dr. Norman is the author of *The Psychology of Everyday Things* (also published as *The Design of Everyday Things), Things That Make Us Smart,* and most recently, *The Invisible Computer,* a book that *Business Week* has called "the bible of the 'post PC' thinking."

Satu Ruuska is currently working as a researcher at Nokia Mobile Phones Usability and User Interfaces Research Group. She acquired her master's degree from Oulu University in 1999 in linguistics. She also has background in psychology, sociology, and educational science. Since joining Nokia in 1995 she has worked in the fields of product internationalization and localization as well as in various fields of HCI, especially mobile HCI.

Erik Strommen, Ph.D. is a developmental psychologist and researcher who has been program manager for research and design in Microsoft's Interactive Toy Group since 1996. Prior to working at Microsoft, he spent seven years at Children's Television Workshop as research director for the Interactive Technologies Division where he designed and studied interactive learning products for children of various ages on almost every interactive platform available. He has published research and theoretical papers on a wide range of children's interface issues, covering everything from speech recognition to electronic drawing pads; in 1994 he presented one of the first papers at ACM SIGCHI ever to feature child users. His primary interests in interactive design are (1) distinguishing between designing for adults and designing for children, who represent a very different user population; and (2) developing interactions for novel interfaces, such as talking character toys, where conventional interface rules do not apply.

Kaisa Väänänen-Vainio-Mattila heads a research group for usability and user interfaces at Nokia Mobile Phones. Her group conducts research on user needs of mobile terminals of the future. Before joining Nokia in 1995, she worked as a research scientist for Computer Graphics Center in Darmstadt, Germany. She earned a Ph.D. (Dr.-Ing.) degree from Technical University of Darmstadt in information technology in 1995, focusing on user interface metaphors and their use in multimedia information systems. She also has M.Sc.s in HCI and information technology from University of London and Technical University of Helsinki in 1990 and 1991, respectively.

Since January 2000, she has also held a part-time professorship at Tampere University of Technology, where her aim is to develop interdisciplinary education and research in the area of usability.

Karl G. Vochatzer serves as the lead user interface designer at Netpliance, Inc.—a startup company based in Austin, TX, developing information appliances and services to support them. Prior to his UI design work at Netpliance, Inc., he designed and evaluated a variety of user interfaces for Web sites and business applications during his tenures at c2o Interactive Architects (EDS), Sabre/American Airlines, and IBM. In addition to his usability and user interface design roles at Sabre, he co-invented a process for corporate travel management and cofounded the Sabre Business Travel Solutions division. He holds a master of science degree in experimental psychology from Iowa State University of Science and Technology.

Annette Wagner is a senior member of the User Experience Group in the Consumer Embedded organization of Sun Microsystems, Inc. She helps design technologies, which include the Java 2 MicroEdition, to be usable on devices like cell phones, screen phones, and TVs. Ms. Wagner is currently working on developing Java technologies for the wireless marketplace.

She began her career at Apple Computer working on the Lisa personal computer. In the last 18 years she has focused on how to be successful designing human interfaces for products and what human interface designers need to do to become respected members of a product team. Her goal is to design and build products that have a positive impact on people's lives. Ms. Wagner has written several papers and has given talks at CHI and other conferences over the years.

Sarah Zuberec is the user research group manager for Microsoft Windows CE mobile electronics products. With over five years of experience working on mobile electronic products, she leads a team of usability and field research specialists bringing usability and user interaction data analysis into the product design process. Her group works with product and graphic designers, and together they form the Windows CE Interaction Design Team. In addition to the practical aspects of moving user research into product design cycles, Ms. Zuberec has an interest in interdisciplinary design processes and has contributed to various HCI professional organizations including International HCI, HFES, and International Symposium on Wearable Computers. She holds a B.Sc. and an M.Sc. in industrial engineering from the University of Toronto.